A PHILOSOPHY
OF THE
UNSAYABLE

A PHILOSOPHY OF THE UNSAYABLE

WILLIAM FRANKE

University of Notre Dame Press
Notre Dame, Indiana

University of Notre Dame Press
Notre Dame, Indiana 46556
undpress.nd.edu
All Rights Reserved

Copyright © 2014 by University of Notre Dame
Published in the United States of America

Library of Congress Cataloging-in-Publication Data

Franke, William.
A philosophy of the unsayable / William Franke.
pages   cm
Includes bibliographical references and index.
ISBN 978-0-268-02894-7 (pbk. : alk. paper) — ISBN 0-268-02894-X (pbk. : alk. paper)
1. Silence (Philosophy) 2. Negativity (Philosophy) I. Title.
BD360.F73   2014
120—dc23

                    2013044534

∞ *The paper in this book meets the guidelines for permanence and durability
of the Committee on Production Guidelines for Book Longevity of the
Council on Library Resources.*

For Maddalena Cerqui

"Oltre la spera che più larga gira . . ."

CONTENTS

PRE-FACE

The present volume sketches a distinctive philosophical outlook that emerges irrepressibly from the predicament of philosophy today. It interprets what are widespread intimations of thinking in the current milieu of critical reflection across disciplines in the arts and sciences and beyond into technical and professional fields and culture generally. We are in an age in which discourse becomes acutely conscious of its intrinsic limits and is dominated by what it cannot say. Especially the last two and a half centuries have abounded in new and radical currents of thinking about the limits of language and what may or may not lie beyond them. The pace of such thinking seems to have greatly accelerated in the initial decades of the twenty-first century. This thinking is rooted, however, in millenary discourses of mysticism and negative theology that can be traced back to the origins of the Western intellectual tradition. A kind of perennial counter-philosophy to the philosophy of Logos has resisted its claims throughout the history of Western thought.

There is, in fact, an amorphous but immense sea of discourse concerned with the ways that discourse has of doubting and denying itself. This type of reflection arises when language runs up against the limits of what it is able to say. Certain discourses concentrate on these limits and on how language necessarily speaks from and out of them. This generates counter-discourses to every powerful explanatory paradigm that makes positive claims to comprehend reality, to say what really is. The counter-discourses typically emphasize that what is not and even *cannot* be said is actually the basis for all that *is* said. They shift attention away from what discourse is saying to what it is not saying and cannot say—even though this involves, paradoxically, an even more intense focus precisely on language, on its limited capabilities, its borders, its "beyond."

These counter-discourses can even take a more aggressive stance. They can position themselves not only at the limits and margins of normative discourse but as infiltrating it through and through. All discourse in this perspective, which I call "apophatic," shows up as necessarily preceded by and predicated on what cannot be said. This entails a claim to a yet more powerful comprehensiveness, though one at first purely negative in nature, evoking a power beyond discourse, a potential that words release but cannot master. Metaphysics, monotheisms, and mysticisms, as well as philosophies of existence and poetics of revelation, can be understood in their deeper, driving motivations only from this perspective, which nevertheless all too easily slips from view because it eludes logical articulation and defies discursive expression.

Ineffability was once a leading theme of the Neoplatonists (particularly Plotinus, Porphyry, Proclus, Iamblichus, and Damascius) and of their heirs in the monotheistic traditions of Christian mysticism (Dionysius the Areopagite, John Scotus Eriugena), of the Kabbalah, of Sufism, and again of certain post-Scholastics (Meister Eckhart, Nicholas Cusanus). Baroque mystics such as John of the Cross, Jakob Böhme, and Silesius Angelus share this same obsession with Romantic thinkers like Kierkegaard and the late Schelling, as well as with imaginative writers such as Hölderlin, Emily Dickinson, Rilke, and Kafka. The expressiveness of silence, the void, nothingness has been explored equally in modern music (Schoenberg, Cage), in painting (Malevich, Kandinsky), and in architecture (Le Corbusier, Mies van der Rohe, Daniel Libeskind) in tandem with the apophatic philosophical reflections of Wittgenstein, Heidegger, and Franz Rosenzweig. These major monuments of modern apophatic culture were announced by apocalyptic prophecies of the collapse of language and civilization altogether, emblematically around the fin de siècle in the Vienna of Hugo von Hofmannsthal, Gustav Klimt, Karl Kraus, and Freud.

Similar accents and thematics were hauntingly echoed, furthermore, in assimilating the Holocaust and its aftermath, by philosophical critics such as Walter Benjamin and Theodor Adorno, as well as by poets like Paul Celan and Edmond Jabès. And the unsayable has again become the keynote of innumerable expressions of contemporary culture. These range from the widely diffused use of deconstructive critique—inspired especially by Jacques Derrida, Emmanuel Levinas, and Maurice Blanchot—in all sorts of theoretical discourses to the clamor of silence heard so frequently in fiction and poetry, influentially in the writings of Louis-René Des Forêts or Samuel Beckett or Yukio Mishima.

These references are obviously far-flung and move across widely disparate spheres of culture. Still, in every case, they flag an attitude toward words that is at once skeptical and fideistic—unconvinced by the pretended adequacy of words, yet acutely attuned to what they must miss grasping and passionately open to what they cannot say. The unsayable is what repels language, yet it requires language of some kind in order to be descried, so as to register at all. Such discourse or counter-discourse, moreover, traverses a whole spectrum of different disciplines and can be surprised in the most diverse sorts of guises. However, these various manifestations of unsayability all pivot on the fact that discourse has a self-reflexive, self-critical ability to call itself into question and to withdraw, leaving what it cannot say in its wake. This trajectory, which is produced by the movement of thought and speech vis-à-vis what it cannot comprehend and therefore recoils from, constitutes the trace of the unsayable. The unsayable cannot be made manifest at all, except in terms of this trace that it leaves in the speech that fails to say it.

As is inevitably the case with whatever philosophy, the significance and force of what it says depends to a high degree on how it refracts other philosophies—on how it funnels currents familiar from elsewhere, whether historical or contemporaneous ways of thinking, into forms of presentation that are efficacious and revealing. Hence these widespread allusions to what can be conceived of as a loosely coherent tradition of discourse about (or from or out of) what cannot be said. This perennial philosophy of the unsayable, moreover, has close affinities with literature—indeed, it is a philosophy in which philosophical and literary thinking coalesce inextricably.

Accordingly, this philosophical vision hinging on unsayability can be illuminated—and is best complemented—by literary-critical and theoretical reflection. Such reflection is proposed here in the form of an interpretive essay (chapter 3) that places in parallel two provocative contemporary poets as writers of the unsayable. Together they display how what can be learned especially from ancient and medieval rhetorics of silence translates into the currency of a contemporary language or anti-language of unsaying. The other main literary-critical excursus (chapter 1) is offered by way of introduction or "invitation" to the leading philosophical meditation on unsayability in my second essay (chapter 2).

While I refer to my chapters as "essays," this book is not a congeries of separate compositions. The "essays" interlock and fit together in an architectonic that adumbrates (were it only possible) a critique of apophatic reason. More exactly, philosophical critique, as the rational examination of first principles, is overtaken and transforms itself into a literary hermeneutics or poetics and into religious reflection. The first I understand as elucidation of certain rhetorical conditions, such as figuration and narration, that make meaningful discourse possible, while the second—the "tying-back" reflections of "re-ligion"—I understand as cultivated awareness of relation to an infinite, never exhaustively specifiable context of relations. Poetic and religious theory are thus deployed critically to illuminate the conditions of possibility of meaning—and therewith also of being—in the unsayable.

Beyond describing the general logic of the unsayable—or rather its subversion of logical generalities—this book aspires to illustrate its workings and finds them perhaps most powerfully operative in literary texts. Hence, crucial to my approach is the conviction that any verbal expression of the unsayable cannot but share in the gratuitous, creative nature of literary expression, or, in other words, that philosophy at this point necessarily becomes literary. A fourth essay then situates the question of the unsayable, as it arises in philosophy and literature today, historically with reference especially to Neoplatonic negative theology. This negative turn in philosophy is traced all the way forward to postmodern negations of theology. Therewith, another of the book's overarching aims is declared: namely, to show how literary exploration of language as infinitely open points language—eminently, the language of philosophy—in a direction which is best understood as theological.

However, an endeavor to (un)define and (de)situate the theological also lies at the heart of this philosophy of the unsayable. It maintains that a religious moment in language and thought is found simply in the irreducibility of our experience and being to words and thoughts. This does not directly warrant positing transcendent realities or Being or God, but it does illuminate the necessity from which such conceptions spring. Pursuant to deconstructive and other types of critique (such as Richard Rorty's pragmatic anti-foundationalism), we may have to forego any directly realist language in religion. But the very same arguments have undermined realist language as an authoritative disclosure of truth in any domain whatsoever. Indeed, theology, particularly negative theology, has long tended to question and to relativize the capabilities of human language to truly convey the real. And yet realist language is not necessarily shown thereby to be simply erroneous, or even outmoded. Language remains, after all, expressive of an orientation to a real world within which it effectively works and articulates and objectifies all things, including itself. But the sense of that reality is affected: it becomes a relation to something else beyond itself that language cannot encompass.

Viewed from the perspective opened by these reflections on the unsayable, theological language suddenly begins to make another kind of sense than it did when it was judged as merely another object-oriented language. Yet neither am I claiming that theological language is essentially different from any other language, including ordinary language. Rather, language as such shows up as estranged in light of the theological adumbrations that hover over and glance across all our language: this shadowy half-light makes what is enigmatic about language in general show up in relief.

From this theological perspective, which is worked out in relation to competing contemporary philosophies of religion in my fifth and sixth essays, the book proposes a general philosophy, indeed, an original philosophy of the unsayable. A word of explanation, however, is in order concerning this claim: it is a claim above all to be an original enactment of what is discerned as a perennial type of trans-philosophical thinking.[1] This is not exactly a matter of saying something new, some new *thing*. It cannot be reduced to a thesis. It is the saying itself that is original, that strives to draw directly from the origin of apophatic thinking—and therewith of all thinking—in the bottomless abyss of the unsayable that is marked only by the never exhausted streams of discourse that issue out of it. In that depth absconds the namelessness of whatever or whoever speaks in the silent night of luminous darkness.

A certain dimension of literary performance is as crucial for this act of ventriloquism (of lending voice to the unspeakable) as are its conceptual contents. Its method is less that of scholarly research and documentation of exactly what has been written on the myriad aspects of this topic, with minute discrimination of what belongs to this author or to that one, than of reaching out toward the intention of apophatic discourse broadly considered. It sets out, by means of the word loosened from its usual moorings, in search of what exceeds all academic definitions. It does not eschew painstaking scholarly work—there is that here, too—but such honest labor is not sufficient for addressing what refuses to yield itself fully to scientific research and demands rather something of the order of personal witness.

With regard to the performative language demanded by this project, I beg the reader's indulgence for a certain poetic license exercised from the very first word of the book by my breaking its integrity as a word and writing "Pre-face." A book on the unsayable necessarily begins at a preverbal point before words and prefaces and before any face or figure that can be given to or conferred by discourse. This admittedly, but designedly, awkward inscription corresponds to another at the other end of the "Contents," with the eliding of a space by running two words together in "Inconclusion." Both anomalies are animations of the unruly energy of the unsayable and embody the central message of the book, which concerns the space between and within words: I argue that understanding cannot be just a matter of taking ready-made significances of words and combining them. The words themselves break open or flow together in the creation and de-creation of sense in ways that may prove unfathomable or even vertiginous. Discerning such action in and behind words opens vision into the unlimited relatedness of all with all, which words tend, by their artificial segmentation and separation, as well as by their fictive unity, to mask. In this manner, the vision inspiring the work spills out over and breaks its frame: it reformulates the very frame of the book, which cannot contain or tame its contents. This gesture calls for rethinking some of the elementary automatisms of our reading, which is continually at risk of degenerating into mere consumption of standardized intellectual commodities.

In this spirit, then, the vast traditions of learning on this subject are worked with and played upon and troped in order to produce a philosophy of the unsayable that is original in the specified sense. The aim is more to experience the essential motivations for this distinctive style of thought and language than to announce some particular new point to be made about it, something that seems a little different and thus "original" with respect to what X, Y, and Z have written. The question is not so much one of what *I* say and its specific difference from what other authors have said as one of *where* any of these discourses come from. Can we reach somehow to their generative sources and touch their originating motives? This I conceive as a matter not so much of choosing precisely the right philosophy to which to adhere as of realizing more translucently than ever before the common possibility from which they all spring. This arguably universal aspiration of philosophical reflection can be realized in an unrestricted openness of thinking such as can be enacted most intensively of all—at least in my experience—through a philosophy of the unsayable.

ACKNOWLEDGMENTS

A preliminary version of chapter 1 was published as "Varieties and Valences of Unsayability in Literature," *Philosophy and Literature* 29, no. 2 (2005): 489–97.

A fragment of section i of chapter 2 appeared as "A Philosophy of the Unsayable: Apophasis and the Experience of Truth and Totality," *Analecta Husserliana: Imaginatio Creatrix* 83 (2004): 65–83. Section iii was presented at the University of Bochum in the Faculty for Evangelical Theology at the invitation of Günter Thomas and Markus Höfner and is forthcoming in their edited volume *Ende oder Umbau einer Erlösungsreligion?* (Tübingen: Mohr Siebeck, 2014).

Material from section i of chapter 3 was delivered extemporaneously at the International Phenomenological Symposium "Singularity—Subjectivity—The Other" in Perugia, Italy, on July 17, 2001, for which I thank particularly Uwe Bernhardt. The article "The Singular and the Other at the Limits of Language in the Post-Holocaust Poetry of Edmond Jabès and Paul Celan" was subsequently published in *New Literary History* 36, no. 4 (2005): 621–38. A version of section ii appears in French as "Le nom de Dieu comme vanité du langage au fond de tout mot selon Edmond Jabès," in *Edmond Jabès: L'éclosion des énigmes,* edited by Daniel Lançon and Catherine Mayaux (Vincennes: Presses Universitaires de

Vincennes, 2008), and a related piece in English as "Edmond Jabès, or the Endless Self-Emptying of Language in the Name of God," *Literature and Theology* (2007): 1–16. I am grateful to Daniel Lançon and to Catherine Mayaux for the opportunity to participate in the colloquium on Jabès at CERISY, Centre Culturel International, in August 2003. My text on Jabès profited especially from discussions with Geoffrey Obin. The Celan section (iii) informed my presentation at the International Advanced Research Seminar on Trauma at the University of Macao in August 2012 and is scheduled to appear in a special issue of *The Journal of Literature and Trauma Studies*.

Some material drawn from chapter 4 was presented to the Society for the Contemporary Assessment of Platonism in San Francisco in March 2003 under the title "Negative Theology in the Neoplatonic Parmenides-Commentary Tradition and as Revived in Contemporary Apophatic Forms of Thinking." I thank John Rose for this invitation. Some of the ground covered by the first section of chapter 4 was broached in an article on "Apophasis and the Turn of Philosophy to Religion: From Neoplatonic Negative Theology to Postmodern Negation of Theology," which appeared in *Self and Other: Essays in Continental Philosophy of Religion,* edited by Eugene Long, special issue of *International Journal for Philosophy of Religion* 60, nos. 1–3 (2006): 61–76. Further elaborations of this work were presented in French at the CERISY colloquium "Philosophie et mystique: Autour de Stanislas Breton" in August 2011, organized by Jean Greisch, Jérôme de Gramont, and Marie-Odile Métral.

The concluding movement (section vi) of chapter 5 subsumes the last section of my article "Praising the Unsayable: An Apophatic Defense of Metaphysics Based on the Neoplatonic *Parmenides* Commentaries," *Epoché: A Journal for the History of Philosophy* 11, no. 1 (2006): 143–73.

Chapter 6 owes thanks to Heinrich Bedford-Strohm for the invitation to a conference on "Public Theology" at the University of Bamberg in June 2011. The resulting article "The Paramount Importance of What Cannot Be Said in Public Theological Discourse" will be part of *Contextuality and Intercontextuality in Public Theology,* edited by Heinrich Bedford-Strohm, Florian Höhne, and Tobias Reitmeier (Berlin: LIT-Verlag, 2014). This chapter also draws from my "Apophasis as the Common Root of Radically Secular and Radically Orthodox Theology," *International Journal for Philosophy of Religion* 73, no. 1 (2013): 57–76.

I thank all the publishers concerned for permission to adapt and reprint. Throughout the book, where no English editions are cited, I have provided translations myself, juxtaposing them with the originals, although the originals, where judged unnecessary or cumbersome by current publishing standards, have sometimes been suppressed.

Part I
_____

PHILOSOPHY AND LITERATURE

Chapter One

INVITATORY

Varieties and Valences of Unsayability in Literature

> *Ce qui n'est pas ineffable n'a aucune importance.*
> *(That which is not ineffable has no importance.)*
> —Paul Valéry, *Mon Faust*

Paul Valéry's famous statement concerning the paramount, indeed the unique importance of the ineffable receives an unlikely and unwitting confirmation from the character of Bottom the Weaver in Shakespeare's *A Midsummer Night's Dream.*

> "I have had a most rare vision. I have had a dream—past the wit of man to say what dream it was.—Man is but an ass if he go about to expound this dream. Methought I was—there is no man can tell what. Methought I was, and methought I had,—But man is but a patched fool, if he will offer to say what methought I had. The eye of man hath not heard, the ear of man hath not seen; man's hand is not able to taste, his tongue to conceive, nor his heart to report what my dream was." (*Midsummer Night's Dream*, Act IV, scene i)

As is typical of those who speak about what cannot be said, Bottom cannot keep it short. He stammers on. He says over and over again . . . what he cannot say. Since he cannot really say what he feels compelled to try and say, he keeps on trying. In so doing, he reflects indirectly on what fascinates him by reflecting directly on his own incapacities and foolishness, as brought out by the experience of being checked in his attempt to express what he cannot. There is endlessly much to say about this experience of inadequacy vis-à-vis the unsayable and miraculous, and precisely this verbiage constitutes perhaps its only possible expression. Bottom speaks from the bottom end of what can also be the most elevated of all discursive modes—as Longinus appreciated and as can be illustrated by contrasting Bottom's comic voice and its ludicrous malapropisms with Valéry's rather superb, perhaps even supercilious, tone. Nevertheless, Bottom's words are indicative of an important direction in the drift across the centuries of discourse on what cannot be said. This drifting is precisely what severe moralists, such as Augustine and Wittgenstein, have wished to put a stop to by enjoining silence. While in principle the Unsayable would seem to demand silence as the only appropriate response, in practice endless discourses are engendered by this ostensibly most forbidding and unapproachable of topics.

This predicament of prolix speechlessness is found over and over again in literature of all kinds, especially at its dramatic climaxes of revelatory disclosure or "epiphany." Another especially poignant instance in familiar literature of how precisely the issue of the unsayable, the nameless, emerges eloquently as the secret key to all meaning and mystery is Ishmael's consternation vis-à-vis the whiteness of the White Whale in *Moby Dick*. This color, or rather "visible absence of color," speaks by its very unspeakability: it is "a dumb blankness, full of meaning," says Ishmael, "and yet so mystical and well-nigh ineffable was it, that I almost despair of putting it in a comprehensible form. It was the whiteness of the whale that above all things appalled me. But how can I hope to explain myself here; and yet, in some dim, random way, explain myself I must, else all these chapters might be naught."[1]

The terror of the Unnameable expressed in these lines suggests another register, besides those of Bottom and Valéry, of the limitless range of tones resorted to by speakers face to face with what cannot be said. It is a register familiar also from Kurtz's last words—the exclamation "The horror! The horror!"—as narrated by Marlow in *Heart of Darkness*. Conrad's novel is a further example of a fiction hovering obsessively around something unsayable as its generating source, something that the narrator despairs of being able to retell:

> "It seems to me I am trying to tell you a dream—making a vain attempt, because no relation of a dream can convey the dream-sensation, that commingling of absurdity, surprise, and bewilderment in a tremor of struggling revolt, that notion of being captured by the incredible which is of the very essence of dreams. . . ."
>
> He was silent for a while.
>
> ". . . No, it is impossible; it is impossible to convey the life-sensation of any given epoch of one's existence—that which makes its truth, its meaning—its subtle and penetrating essence. It is impossible. We live, as we dream, alone. . . ."[2]

Although such experience is so unique as to be ineffable, it is nevertheless rather prevalent, presumably in life as well as in literature, as these brief examples already suffice to suggest. These samples indeed serve to adumbrate an unlimited field. It is, after all, hard to expressly exclude any discourse whatever, where the criterion for inclusion is nothing . . . that can be said. But then the question arises: What, if anything, do all these different discourses, which we can bring together as discourses on what cannot be said, share in common? Of course, the unsayable and indefinable, in every instance, can only be incomparable. And any answer that can be said is, by that very fact, not an answer.

To get around this difficulty, we can begin by asking: What are the narrative structures and strategies that enable this type of discourse about what is in principle intractable to narration and discourse? Bruce Kawain develops an interesting theory about how "secondary first-person" narrators—in telling about someone else's experience of the absolute—provide more intellectual and verbal energy, less purely physical and heroic force, that serves to follow and record the paths of the primary protagonists into the ineffable core of experience of essential mystery, the "heart of darkness." Marlow serves precisely this function for Kurtz. And Marlow's narration is itself framed by that of the narrator of *Heart of Darkness,* so that from Kurtz (whose name pronounced in German means, not just incidentally, "short"—*kurz*), to Marlow, to the narrator of the story, there is a scale of increasing verbal skill or readiness to speak correlated with decreasing intensity of attunement to the inexpressible or transcendent power of the unsayable. As Kawain cogently explains, "If this were not so, and if it were possible to communicate the heart of darkness itself, directly, in words, then both Marlow and the narrator would be as shaken as Kurtz. Indeed, each successive relation dilutes the primary experience. In this way the unrelatable material is reduced to relatable terms." Something similar can be said again for the *nearly* negligible narrator "Sam," who transcribes the incredible monologue of Watt in Samuel Beckett's novel *Watt*. Or again, "Carlos," the narrator of Carlos Castaneda's initiatory novels, performs a similar function with respect to "don Juan," the mysterious Yaqui Indian sorcerer.[3]

Thanks, then, to these diluting devices, that which ultimately defeats all efforts of articulation remains nevertheless the object-elect, the darling, of copious discourses. In Marlow's narration, it is the privacy of the individual's own experience or unique "life-sensation" that turns out to be incommunicable. This constitutes, in effect, a Neo-Romantic interpretation of the mystery that apophatic, literally "negative," discourse intimates and yet leaves undefined. What this private, individual core of experience might be cannot be said, and such a private meaning is perhaps not even a coherent concept (as Wittgenstein argues in *Philosophical Investigations* I, 243–314). So we are left with only the self-denying, self-subverting linguistic form for . . . what cannot be said. And then all verbal interpretations are only guesses—"conjectures," in the vocabulary that Nicholas Cusanus (1401–1464) developed for apophatic or self-*un*saying discourse. Such a postulation of the self as a secret, inexpressible core of mystery is questioned and yields to a variety of other interpretations of the sources of unsayability in modern authors such as Virginia Woolf.[4] Louis-René Des Forêts's *bavard* sustains his compulsive talking precisely on the basis of having nothing to say.[5] Another paradoxically telling example can be found in Henry James's later fictions, which witness to the author's increasing doubts about and distancing of himself from language.[6]

In James, the space of the unspeakable oftentimes may be interpreted interchangeably in terms of metaphysical sublimities, sexual secrets, or social banalities. Such a layered interpretation of the Inexpressible is elaborated by James in his novel *The Sacred Fount* (1901). Here it may be some special insight, a "nameless idea," or the narrator's theory about his companions, that remains beyond the threshold of speech and communication in a realm that is "unspoken and untouched, unspeakable and untouchable."[7] Or it may be quite common experiences that are transfigured by the rhetoric of unsayability, which permeates the novel, so as to take on mysterious, quasi-mystical connotations. This may happen, for instance, in the collective experience of a piano recital:

> The whole scene was as composed as if there were scarce one of us but had a secret thirst for the infinite to be quenched. And it was the infinite that, for the hour the distinguished foreigner poured out to us, causing it to roll in wonderful waves of sound, almost of colour, over our receptive attitudes and faces. Each of us, I think, now wore the expression—or confessed at least to the suggestion—of some indescribable thought; which might well, it was true, have been nothing more unmentionable than the simple sense of how the posture of deference to this noble art has always a certain personal grace to contribute. (*Sacred Fount*, p. 166)

James titillates us with the possibility that this extraordinary transport, which cannot be described, may be about nothing extraordinary after all, since, in any case, there is no *telling* what it is that subjectively excites such rapture in correspondence with the infinite, inexpressible desire of each listener. Nevertheless, in all these cases—in the sacred fount as also in the white whale and the heart of darkness—something mythic and transcendent is hinted at precisely by a declared shortcoming of language, something which, however, provokes a scarcely containable abundance of discourse. It is difficult, even impossible, to contain discourse when we do not and indeed *cannot* know or say what it is about.

The case study from James collapses the distance between ordinary experience and extreme experiences at the outer limits, where no language can suffice. Indeed, the most provocative hypothesis concerning this apophatic dimension of the unsayable is that it is necessarily present everywhere in language. The extreme or liminal experiences, in that case, would only make more starkly evident something that is perhaps always indiscernibly there, even in the most mediocre transactions involving language. And that includes, in some sense, all human experience. All our expressions harbor and are punctuated by silences. Even very banal forms of silence may, after all, be akin to absolute silence and participate in the pregnant pauses characteristic of apophasis—and thereby point to an ultimate impotence of the word.

If this is true, then the investigation of the topos of unsayability in some of its more dramatic and spectacular forms might be expected to illuminate a pervasive dimension of all experience and consciousness in language. What is awesomely manifest in the heroes of metaphysical quests and in protagonists responding to supernatural vocations or divine visions is perhaps, albeit to a lesser degree, true for all of us and true even at the level of our collective endeavors. The impossible quest to articulate the ineffable may be found as always already there implicitly, in some form, in any articulation whatever that breaks the silence.

There are, of course, innumerable different motives for inexpressibility. Many of these motives seem to fight shy of the intrinsic unsayability commonly attributed to the mystical and transcendent. But there are also strong tendencies and temptations to blur these boundaries wherever we really do not and, for whatever reasons, *cannot* know or say exactly what we are talking about. The scatological, the morally indecent, the religiously blasphemous, and the ritually abject are all either socially unavowable or, in various ways, subjectively or psychologically inadmissible and so liable to shrink back from express verbalization.[8] All can become avenues leading to rupture with any and all systems of communication establishing normative sense. They can thus lead to experience that is beyond the net of language and, as such, removed to a transgressive or, indistinguishably, so far as words are concerned, a transcendent zone.

Such apparently circumstantial motives for silence dominate even in the case of Cassandra, the prophetess who foretells Troy's doom but is effectively silenced because no one will believe what she says. In Christa Wolf's rewriting of the myth, building on Aeschylus's character, who is isolated and condemned to silence by her inexpressible visions, this fall from grace is due to the curse of Apollo, who was not sexually gratified as promised in exchange for granting her the power of prophecy. Cassandra says: "Now I understood what the god had devised: You speak the truth but no one will believe you."[9] Confronted with disbelief, Cassandra feels herself trapped within "a ring of silence" ("ein Ring des Schweigens"). Being right isolates her, and she feels herself "grow dumb" ("verstummen") in a society bent on wrong and having ears only for what is false. Nevertheless, she discovers a unique, incomparable kind of power in this very impotence of enforced silence. It becomes her essential form of expression. In time, she learns to wield silence itself as a weapon: "I learned in that I observed the ways of being silent. Only much later did I myself learn to be silent—and what a useful weapon it is."[10] This suggests how even external, circumstantial silence can be revealed as a sign of deeper, more intrinsic silence, where alone all true being and power are gathered in secret and hiding. It is only at this level of what cannot be said that some fugitive sort of unity of comprehension and a semblance of apprehension of the absolutely true is possible, if at all.

The most banal reasons for silence communicate in myriad ways with its most deeply metaphysical grounds in a great range of literature. The strong transcendental drive of literature in German, from Meister Eckhart through Friedrich Hölderlin and Rainer Maria Rilke, and continuing in novels, notably Hermann Broch's *Der Tod des Vergil* and Thomas Mann's *Doktor Faustus,* with their attempts to exceed (and even to destroy) language, must be ranged alongside the oftentimes deflationary approaches characteristic of Louis-René Des Forêts's *Le bavard* or Samuel Beckett's *The Unnamable,* as well as of contemporary theatre by playwrights such as Harold Pinter and Nathalie Sarraute.[11] The ambiguities, however, can be traced all the way back in literary tradition. In ancient Greek tragedy, emblematic cases are plentiful. Aeschylus's Niobe (in his *Niobe Fragment*) famously introduces the principle of *patheis-matheis*—learning by suffering silently what cannot possibly be said (see, further, *Prometheus Bound,* 105–6). In a similar vein, Sophocles's Electra recalls Niobe's eternal mourning that can never be expressed (*Electra,* lines 150ff.). And the "dangerous silence" of Creon's queen, Eurydice, signifies her own imminent extinction by anticipating an absolute cessation of all expression through suicide (*Antigone,* lines 1251–55).

In more modern tragedy, the drama of silence is played out loquaciously in Spanish Baroque theatre, particularly that of Calderón, with its speculative penchant for the explicitly transcendental. Shakespeare, on the other hand, makes even everyday language, when it touches upon silence, tremble with metaphysical resonances. Cordelia's motto "Love, and be silent," her saying "nothing" in response to her father's demand for words of love, is a poignant instance. "Unhappy that I am," she says, "I cannot heave / My heart into my mouth," and yet she is not so miserable as one who does not love, for, "I am sure my love's / More ponderous than my tongue" (*King Lear*, I, i, 93–94, 79–80). It is impossible for her to say anything sincere after her sisters, vying in lies, have so debased the currency of the word. The king himself, reduced in the course of the tragedy from his pompous self-importance, becomes beggar enough by the end to follow her example: "No, I will be the pattern of all patience, I will say nothing" (III, ii, 38).[12]

These select illustrations must suffice to suggest the uncircumscribable diversity of motives for unsayability. The question is whether they all have anything in common. When something cannot be said because of politeness or obscenity or deceit or strategy, does this have anything to do with the metaphysical motives for unsayability? The former things are not per se unsayable but only conditionally so—or in certain circumstances. However, the problem is that any way of *distinguishing* accidental from essential unsayability is itself circumstantial. An essential unsayability must necessarily remain, precisely, unsayable because any supposedly essential distinction that might be proposed to qualify it could only be itself unsayable. This does not mean that there is no distinction—it suggests rather the opposite. But still, the distinction cannot be made explicit without becoming arbitrary with respect to what is really unsayable and, therefore, strictly indefinable.

The compelling interest of this problem lies in what it reveals, for example, about the very logic of essence and accident, to take just one instance of a classical philosophical dichotomy. The idea of essence has come to be treated as plainly erroneous and illusory in much critical discourse since postmodernism. The locution "essentialist" is currently used as a term of abuse and for disqualification and automatic dismissal of what is so designated. But to condemn all attributions of essence as illusory and false is just another way of rigidifying an important insight concerning the inherent instability and contingency of every *definable* essence into a general, formulaic skepticism that can apply its own principle with presumed assurance and authority. What needs to be acknowledged, rather, is that any purported essences can be adequately *stated* only in the accidental terms of some contingent, arbitrary language. What is unsayable on intrinsic grounds cannot be separated by any fully explicit criterion from what is unsayable for only extrinsic reasons. Any definition of the unsayable introduces linguistic factors and their contingencies that do not and cannot belong to unsayability per se. If an essential definition were possible, its object would not be unsayable, much less unsayability itself.

Of course, the idea that there is anything such as unsayability *per se* may itself be a verbal mirage, but it is a necessary illusion because language cannot exhaustively account for itself: *that* there is language at all cannot be explained in language, any more than language can explain, among all the facts it can state about the world, the fact *that* there is a world. What language *shows* by its logical form, enabling it to represent the world, is unsayable in language (Wittgenstein, *Tractatus* 4.12). What lends power of purchase to our language about the world remains itself unsayable. This is the unsayable or "inexpressible" ("das Unaussprechliche") that Wittgenstein calls "the mystical" ("das Mystische," 6.522).[13]

The apophatic, as expressed in literature, gestures beyond all casual motives for unsayability to what cannot under any circumstances be said and yet holds our attention rapt to its specific, indefinable mystery. There will always be some element in the mystery of the unsayable that escapes exhaustive definition in every supposedly definitive statement. To admit this is to recognize an economy of the unsayable and the sayable as the basis of every possible language, every system of saying and defining. Any language capable of making determinate statements pivots on an internal distinction between that in it which, under any circumstances, remains unsayable versus that which it is able to articulate. Yet the mechanism of this pivot remains generally invisible because it is itself below the threshold of the articulable.

It is not hard to see that the import of this issue of the unsayable extends throughout the whole of philosophical discourse, for something unsayable lies in the crease between the extrinsic and the intrinsic, the essential and the accidental, the necessary and the contingent, and every other fundamental philosophical distinction. The distinction between abstract and concrete as well depends on some sort of blind transaction between what can and cannot be said. The concrete as such is infinitely dense and is never adequately expressed. Only its relatively abstract form can be stated in language. And such distinctions are all conceptual creations that purport to be based on realities. The real, however, stripped of all conceptual determination, cannot as such be grasped or said. In the end we make discriminations, such as that between abstract and concrete, on the basis of a judgment that can never be fully justified in words.

Everything in philosophy depends on how these sorts of conceptual demarcations are negotiated. Such negotiations, however, take place behind the scenes by means of silent, pragmatic pacts and tacit understandings that can never be completely articulated or explained but are simply embedded in the conventions of the language we use, and so are implicitly accepted and in effect obeyed. Any lexical terms and syntactical conditions of sense that can be expressly stipulated and so made explicit presuppose others that are not explicit but are necessarily assumed as self-evident. We always need to assume terms and apply rules even at the level of a meta-communication, so as to determine and validate the very rules and most basic vocabulary of our communications. Language always makes sense, then, on the basis of what it does not and, in the end, cannot say.

The classical problems of philosophy, hinging on such distinctions as essence versus accident or intrinsic versus extrinsic or concrete versus abstract—that is, on the most elementary determinations of philosophical thinking—to the extent that they are formulated in language are thus, in untold ways, all implicated in the problem of the unsayable. In this spirit, the following reflections are proposed as bearing on the most general issues that still trouble philosophical thinking today—and that compel it to turn its search in the direction of a philosophy of the unsayable.

Chapter Two

IN THE HOLLOW OF PAN'S PIPE

Unsayability and the Experience of Truth and Totality

> *The Missing All – prevented Me*
> *From missing minor Things.*
>   —Emily Dickinson

i

What we most strongly and deeply think and believe, what we passionately love or ardently desire, inevitably escapes adequate articulation. It is always more, if not completely other, than what we are able to say. This common human experience of butting up against the limits of language is experienced paradigmatically in the disciplines of philosophy, theology, and poetry. All of these types of human endeavor lead inexorably to renunciations of language at critical stages in the attempt to advance toward their goals. Nevertheless, at the same time, this very deficiency of speech, this incapacity of verbal expression, indeed of representation of any sort whatsoever, forms the starting point for rich, articulate, expansive discourses in each discipline, discourses about what cannot be said. What these discourses reveal, I contend, is that we are always oriented in all that we *do* say by what we *cannot* say, so that, indirectly, we are always talking "about"—or at least "from" or "out of"—what cannot be said. If this is true, then all discourse at some level collapses—or blossoms—into discourse "on what cannot be said."

This contention is susceptible of a variety of interpretations that make it by turns either obvious or absurd—a matter of plain self-evidence, or else perfect paradox. On the obvious side, what motivates never-ending human saying of things could only be something that never can be said. The very fact that we go on speaking indicates that something—something that concerns us enough to make us keep on speaking—still remains unsaid. And since there is no built-in limit to the continuation of our speaking, this something unsaid proves, in effect, to be unsayable, at least for as long as we go on speaking. Precisely this predicament is exquisitely illustrated in the incessant, unendable monologues that babble on through Samuel Beckett's works of fiction. And the same problematic is dramatized in theatre pieces such as his *Endgame*.

There is no built-in limit except, naturally, death, to our saying of the things that can be said. And in this respect, death lays claim to being the name, or at least one name, for the unsayable. Yet to say this is to say, one way, the unsayable, to give it a name, and thus to depotentiate it as, precisely, unsayable. A homologous, equally challenging, and in many regards compelling reduction takes place if we name the unsayable "God." Such namings have some validity as interpretations, but they must not be allowed to be definitive and so to end the production of new namings and sayings, since it is precisely the unlimited, open-ended production of denominations and designations that testifies to the genuine infinity—and perhaps even divinity—of . . . what cannot be said.

Death and God are unsayable and as such prevent language from being able to achieve closure. Language, as discourse, is open-ended and goes on infinitely, unable to bring to final presence in consciousness the impossible (non)experiences of death and God. If language, in its saying and naming, is basically a bringing to presence in consciousness, it is radically impossible to "say" death, since consciousness is itself annihilated by death. What consciousness grasps is only some external effect of death, like a corpse, and never death itself as it is experienced from the inside because consciousness is no longer present at the moment of its own death. Likewise, the unsayability of the Name of God, which is enshrined in religious traditions and eminently in the unpronounceable Tetragrammaton

(JHWH), a name for the Unnameable, stands for the impossibility of encompassing God's infinity within any finite structure of human language or consciousness.[1]

It is their operating as unsayable, as beyond the inevitably reductive meanings of their names, that characterizes both death and God as genuinely unsoundable, inarticulable, endlessly provocative mysteries. Whatever is said of "them" is said rather of some image or idol that betrays them in their status as unsayable. In apophatic discourses, all that is said may be said in some manner of death or of God or of both, but we should not pretend to know what these names mean—except to the extent of knowing that it is not any of the things that can be said. Specifically and uniquely, the experience of what cannot be said can take us nearest to the limits of being human, and thereby also to what may open up beyond these limits.

This unsayability is, arguably, what "humanizes" persons and their understandings, what grants them the possibility of relation to singular individuals having some kind of whole and unique meaning that cannot be articulated, since *individuum ineffabilis est.* Unsayability in this sense leads toward something beyond a field of calculable objects, toward the truly and uniquely human. At the same time, it is what *de*humanizes us, for it makes us strangers to ourselves. No category or norm such as "humanity" can accurately express this being that constantly reaches beyond even Being (as the ambit within which understanding by categories is possible), and that by its nature essentially transcends and negates itself. Human beings constantly define and create limits, but this activity itself is not limited, except perhaps by itself, if it so chooses: and to *set* limits is not to *be* limited; it constitutes rather a way of implicitly placing oneself beyond them.[2]

Indeed, anything finite and definable proves in the end insufficient to satisfy and motivate modern, Faustian humanity. For in the historical course of its development, the human spirit discovers itself to be without definable intrinsic limits. Whatever limits it recognizes always turn out, at least in their articulated, verbally defined form, to be limits that it has set and defined *for itself.* Whatever depths and riches of human spirit we can exhaustively state may be highly revealing, but they cannot account for or motivate the infinite passion by which humans— perhaps insofar as they are human—can be motivated, even in this very activity of endless articulation and self-definition.

Human experience, in its unfolding in language and desire, opens—at their limits—into the undelimited and ungraspable. The specifically human element must in the end be recognized as something uncompletable and therefore ungraspable. It is the self-negating and self-transcending movement in which the undelimited capacity for relationship opens the world of finite objects surrounding it to an infinite Beyond. As such, humanity is something radically other to itself, not excluding potentially even "divinity." Such "humanity" is thus better designated as "transhumanizing" (to adopt Dante's "trasumanar," *Paradiso* 1.70)—or as uncontainable within any single, static category such as the human.

The signpost of this "transition beyond" throughout Western cultural experience has most steadily been *apophasis,* the negation of speech. And the only fitting description of such experience has been to characterize it as indescribable. Such a predicament can be most effectively illustrated by means of the various self-subverting or self-unsaying linguistic maneuvers and techniques that make up the repertoire of apophatic rhetoric—devices such as oxymoron, paradox (sorites), ellipsis, contradiction, irony, anacoluthon, litotes, and the like.

What in negative theology is called "God" transcends every finite consciousness and can never become present to consciousness, perhaps because God already *is* presence and consciousness in their absolute infinity, in a way that is immediately lost as soon as these and any other terms, including "divinity," focus and define and thereby delimit God. Of course, Hegel thought that he was able to rethink infinity, by dint of a dialectical reversal, as finite in such a way that it is humanly realized as a concrete, completed whole. He *did* identify God with infinite presence of consciousness to itself and declared this to be realized in the absolute knowing (*absolutes Wissen*) reached by his philosophy. He would leave no holy, untouchable realm for the unsayable. He holds what is commonly called the ineffable to be untrue, an impostor: "what is called the inexpressible is nothing other than the untrue."[3] Or, in another programmatic formulation that comes to the same thing: "The real is the rational."[4] Since the rational is coextensive with language and all it can express, this means that what is not expressible in language simply has no reality. Yet Hegel's *writ-*

ings also provocatively show the limits of this position and point to another possibility, a possibility of infinite difference, of something neither real nor unreal, neither true nor untrue, that would remain forever inexpressible to Logos.[5]

The genius of Hegel, especially as it was distilled by Alexandre Kojève and so passed on to twentieth-century French thought, was to think finitude in its absoluteness. Kojève's reading receives an important impulse here from Martin Heidegger's philosophy of finitude.[6] Absolute truth thereby becomes realizable in the death of God: the infinite and absolute (God) is finally and fully expressed in finite terms by dying. Only what has died can be completely and finally comprehended. Totally realized in the finite, the infinite is no longer an open-ended mystery but is an actually articulable whole, concrete and finite. The unsayable is banished: the real in its entirety is fully uttered and therefore fully rational. This is recognizably a classical Greek ideal that reaches an apotheosis in the German idealism of Hegel.

Although they also attempt to exorcise this idea, Walter Benjamin and Ludwig Wittgenstein are, at certain stages, still haunted by it. Both become apophatic thinkers only by reversing the thinking of the fully articulated whole, in which Hegel excelled. The world, whose factual existence Wittgenstein calls "the mystical," he conceived of initially as a delimited whole ("begrenztes Ganzes").[7] For the early, logical-positivist Wittgenstein, there really is no expressing anything infinite and beyond language—not by apophatic modes of linguistic dysfunction, nor even by silence (which he enjoins, but not as if it indicated or expressed anything). Even for a certain young, still highly Hegelian Benjamin, it is only because world and word alike are fallen that the infinite communicativity of language encounters a limit and comes up against what cannot be said, checked particularly by the muteness of nature. Ideally, in Paradise, name and thing are perfectly transparent to each other, for reality consists in the finite, material particulars of Eden.[8]

Such an outlook is supported by the presumption that only what is determinate and defined can be concrete and real. It forgets or ignores that the "concrete" and "real" that can be said are, after all, linguistic abstractions in comparison with what unsayably is there, concretely and really, before all linguistic delimitations. And both Wittgenstein and Benjamin eventually abandon the tight logic, analogous to Hegel's, of their early writings for more open-ended outlooks on a reality that cannot be comprehended. They thus preserve their apophatic insight from being buried by their penchant for the perfection of the system.

Apophatic thinking sacrifices system in order to let the infinite be undetermined and wholly other to every definition in discourse and every construction of consciousness. We understand always only on the basis of what we do not understand. Knowing arises as a reflexive wave of illumination within a sea of unknowing. The alternative, Hegelian way is to make the concrete and articulated Idea the intrinsic ground for every reality and every idea, including that of the infinite. One starts with this articulated Idea and works outward toward its realization in Nature and History. But to a post-Hegelian sensibility, humanly defined ideas are not the origin of anything. We start thinking always only belatedly. We have already, always already, been thrown into existence, as Heidegger conceives it through the notion of *Geworfenheit* (thrown-ness). We are oriented first and fundamentally to the unknown rather than to the known. What we cannot say, because we never knew or grasped it, underlies and bears upon the sense of everything we can and do say. This is the concrete and real (whatever such terms may concretely and really mean), though we cannot define it—in fact, on the condition that we cannot define it.

One of the few things we tend to be able to agree on today, after Nietzsche, Freud, and Marx—*pace* Hegel—is that the nature of human consciousness is not to exhaustively comprehend what spurs and motivates it. Consciousness is oriented by something that it cannot completely grasp. This may not actually be some *thing* at all but rather the very structure of open relatedness that characterizes and constitutes human existence. It is in this dimension that divinity and death are authentically encountered, if at all. I say "if at all," since in some sense this encounter is inconceivable, impossible, and has to do with what is altogether other than human existence. But that very impossibility is exactly what makes this encounter necessary as an *imperative* of human self-transcendence— an imperative driving human existence toward what it cannot define in terms of itself, and so cannot define at all.

The human capacity, for instance, to sacrifice and renounce the self and its immediate, or even just determinate, satisfactions, in order to in-

vest unconditional care and commitment in something or someone, surpasses the limits of the finite and definable. Such behavior, not for the sake
of any calculable gain or realizable objective, depends on the strange,
incomprehensible human faculty of conceiving something indefinable,
something that cannot be said. Such is the ability that is manifest mysteriously, for example, in what is called love. And thought, too, as the intelligence of love, lives from beyond the same limit to conceptual, categorial
comprehension. What motivates the on-going, open-ended activity of
thinking is precisely what refuses to yield itself up to thought, even while
animating it from within. The source of motivation is something that has
an infinite or indefinite significance for the individual person involved, although this unlimited significance cannot be justified objectively.

The intrinsic openness of thinking, including thought's very thinking
of its own limits, has been worked out theologically in connection with
Anselm of Canterbury's famous ontological argument by Karl Barth in
Fides quaerens intellectum.[9] It is not the concept of God as "that than
which none greater can be thought" ("id quo maius cogitare non potest,"
Proslogion 2) but rather the openness of thought to the infinity that is realized in actually thinking this, and so negating every determinate thought
as still allowing for something more unlimited and therefore greater, that
gives validity to the ontological argument as an actual manifestation of
God's infinite being. There is here no logical deduction of God's existence
from a necessary concept but, simply, the realization of infinite openness
of mind, which is itself the very being of God conceived of as infinite Intellect. This, at any rate, is as much of God in his own essence as can be
humanly experienced under the aspect of knowing or intellect.[10]

For consciousness to conceive of what it cannot define or say is for it
to transcend itself in its very act of conceiving and saying. Such a significance, or ultra-significance, can be vouched for only by the effects it
inspires in human beings, and it can be given a definite content not in
itself and as such but only by human action and emotion, and perhaps devotion. This sort of non-object is what orients and evokes our most powerful passions. It has many different faces, both human and divine, as well
as demonic and uncanny. But all are only reminders of something beyond
themselves that does not accept being defined in any finite terms. Something limitless about the miraculous capabilities of human beings to

"in-finitely" *care* projects infinity onto whatever is being loved—or loathed or feared or abhorred—so that it can no longer be grasped or defined.

Any discourse attempting to signify such an instance will quickly find itself arrested at the limits of what can be said. And yet such passion can hardly be conceived without discourse, without being motivated by a capacity inherent in language to project an infinity beyond everything in the world of definite objects—infinity such as can never be encountered or even conceived of except in a dimension of discourse. Discourse engenders the possibility of projecting this transcendence to a beyond that cannot be articulated. The self-reflexive (and thereby also self-negating) powers of language are crucial to this capability of discourse to project infinitely beyond itself.

The reflexiveness characteristic of human self-consciousness in language—which arguably defines the threshold of the human vis-à-vis other forms of conscious life—is what makes possible the operations of totalization and singularization. Both of these linguistic functions lead by means of self-negation toward transcendence of the definable—of all conceptual definition and verbal determination. They negate their determinate, concrete content by opening it toward an unlimited set of individuals, an infinity that cannot be thought as such. This infinity is nevertheless totalized by a negative concept, for example, as the nonfinite or "in-finite." Or, again, it is singularized as a unique individual taken as such, with no determinate properties and under no delimiting description, designated at most by a proper name with no common or conceptual meaning. In both cases, a thinkable, sayable content is reflected into an infinite and unsayable dimension of open-endedness.

Death and God are both totalizations and singularizations—of a whole individual life in one case and of the unique principle of all reality in the other. In a sense, these totalities and singularities exist only in discourse, but at the same time they raise the question of where discourse comes from and of wherein it exists and consists. They point up the fact that discourse in these operations does not comprehend itself. Its operations, involving singularization, as in the name, particularly the proper name, and totalization, as in the concept, especially the explicitly self-reflexive, self-negating concept, reach toward an infinity which transcends all that could possibly be comprehended in finite, stateable terms.

Such discourse is more than it can itself account for. "There was a myth before the myth began," writes Wallace Stevens in "Notes Towards a Supreme Fiction." "The clouds preceded us." Something we cannot define in our discourse remains the unexpressed point and ungraspable motivation driving all that we can and do say.

Totalization and singularization open up a perspective upon what cannot be given within language but is rather the inexpressible Giving in which language itself originates. They define something finite; yet whence comes this capability to articulate a whole or express a singular individual? These finite forms have been produced by something operative and yet not exhausted within them. All finite figures of totalization or singularization, as soon as they define and finish themselves, demonstrate their inadequacy to the not yet exhausted, not yet finished force that forms them: they are discursive functions within a language that precedes them and brings them to be out of its own life. By realizing their finitude in definitive terms, they at the same time witness to an unrealized, unfinished, on-going process of language of which they can only be the effects. They exist as relations to this "in-finite" that they do not encompass or exhaust. Leveraged in this way from what transcends articulation, totalization in the concept and singularization in the name turn into forms of self-transcendence.

Self-transcendence, so understood, is not just an operation within language but also the operation *of* language as a whole and, even more deeply, an operation *upon* language of . . . what cannot be said. Self-reflexive and self-transcending operations of discourse embody language opening out beyond itself toward . . . . This is the actual enactment of the infinite—beyond simply the saying of the word "infinity." This realization of infinity can be assigned no meaning, except for the negation and attenuation of all assignable meanings. It is this opening up from within of language that witnesses to a sphere of totality and infinity, which otherwise cannot be described. It is pointed up by ruptures in language—Bataille's "déchirements"—as the realization within language of some life or movement that strives beyond it.

I have been speaking somewhat like Gregory of Nyssa, with his notion, called *epektasis,* of the soul or consciousness being drawn endlessly beyond itself toward an unrealizable infinity and even of an open-ended, self-transcending totality of meaning. Yet in recent, postmodern apophasis (with precedents already, for example, in the sixteenth-century Sefardic Kabbalah of Moses Cordovero and Isaac Luria), the tendency has been to emphasize the breaking and shattering of all meanings as that which opens language to intimations of what lies beyond its possibilities of saying. Where discourse ruptures, meaning spills out and spreads without bounds, and in this sense becomes infinite. The cutting and rending of language, so effectively imaged by post-Holocaust poets such as Paul Celan and Edmond Jabès, open it to the unfathomable, unsayable dimensions of the external and infinite. Language is split open to something radically other than itself and all that it can contain or say. When "das Gedicht" (the poem) is turned into "das Genicht" (the noem or no-poem), the word is broken open to let out the nothingness in its midst, and this says something about poetry, language, and everything that is: it insinuates their derivation from Nothing—that is, from nothing that can be said. The essential poem, like the essence of anything and everything, so far exceeds words and concepts (including the concept of essence) as to be nothing at all in their terms.

It has become increasingly evident in our time that this intellectual operation and movement of negation continue down the path of reflection broken open not quite two millennia ago by Neoplatonic thought. The incommensurability with language of an Other, taken especially in an ethical sense, presents itself to Emmanuel Levinas, for example, as an explicit version of the Good beyond Being that Plato famously gestured toward in *Republic* 509b, as well as of the Neoplatonic problem of a One that cannot be said.[11] Radical heterogeneity, as emphasized particularly by numerous authors writing in French, like Michel de Certeau,[12] shows up in relief against this traditional background of Neoplatonic thinking, which recognized the One as irreducibly other with respect to all thinking and being and conceived of it similarly, in terms of the limits of language, as the Ineffable. This movement of ancient, pagan Neoplatonic thought, as it culminates in Damascius (ca. 462–538), will be explored in the fourth essay of this volume.

The fragmenting and shattering of language actually constitutes an opening to an undefined and untamable realm. The inexhaustible mystery and unsoundable provocation of this Other to Thought and Being, to all

that can be said, which figured as the One for the apophatic Neoplatonists, has inspired much recent apophatic thinking, for example, in the
style of Jacques Derrida or Maurice Blanchot. And Franz Rosenzweig,
who is still far too little appreciated for his fundamental contribution to
these currents, worked out for contemporary philosophy an apophatic
grammar of Nothing as prior to the logic of Being: logic applies only to
the world of objects and not to what Rosenzweig expounds as the "proto-
cosmos" and the "hypercosmos," the indefinable, inarticulable dimensions
from which the experienceable world emerges and toward which it evolves.
Prior to the world revealed to us in language is a reality that we can represent only in myth and in art. And then posterior to disclosure in language,
what lies beyond the world of our experience we can fathom only in silent
intimations of an eschatological future—and in the apocalyptic poetry
that this inspires.[13]

A major motivation for turning our attention toward what cannot be
said is that only in this domain, if at all, is it possible for truth in its (always only virtual) wholeness to be touched and brought into contact with
life. Though Truth, especially in its wholeness or totality, is presumably
forever beyond our comprehension, discourses on what cannot be said
bear witness to how it bears upon us and thus to how we can live in relation to and in acknowledgment of this perhaps divine (im)possibility. Partial truth may not be truth at all; the truth is perhaps to be defined simply
as the whole. It was so defined by Hegel: "the true is the whole" ("das
Wahre ist das Ganze," *Phänomenologie,* preface, p. 24).

But to say the whole truth, or anything wholly true, is arguably quite
impossible for a finite human being. Nevertheless, precisely this impasse
to articulation suggests that there is an indistinct conception of something
inconceivably and unsayably "whole" and "indivisible," "simple" and
"total," that preempts our always only fragmentary and finite possibilities
of stating.[14] The source of possibility of all speech seems to be touched
"whole" precisely in proving to be inarticulable. A passion for and fascination with this unsayable something or nothing results in discourses touching upon the true and even the "total" in a wide range of disciplines,
preeminently in philosophy, religion, literature, and the arts.[15] The true
and total remain unsayable, yet in encountering what exceeds all limits of
description or articulation—what cannot be said to be untrue or only

partial either—we are, almost without knowing it and without being able to adequately say so, oriented toward the unimaginable, unsayable sources of our images and words, including those for "truth" and "totality."

Indeed, the overwhelming fascination of the Nothing throughout apophatic tradition flows from the sense that it is somehow pregnant with the significance of everything, yet in a way that cannot be directly or adequately comprehended or signified. The empty void, the silence before speech, is suspected of being incomparably the most significant phase in the whole process of expression—even though saying this, in whatever way, risks belying it. A meaning, or rather quasi-meaning, is suspected of being somehow present in an inkling that is gathered or intimated before articulation begins and that ever after will be irrevocably lost.[16] Indeed meaning can be whole only before being articulated. To be broken into component parts, "arti-culated" into members, is at the same time to be "dis-articulated." However, the wholeness before speech is not the wholeness of a complete ensemble of parts. This latter wholeness is delimited in terms of the parts that make it up. The wholeness of what is not yet articulated is an undelimited, undefined wholeness. It cannot be defined as more real than unreal, more as being than as nonbeing, more true than illusory. It is not Hegel's finite infinity of the completed whole. It is "infinite" and undelimited. To us and our definitions, it is manifest only by its incompleteness. Hegel snubbed this as the "bad infinite" ("die schlechte Unendlichkeit"), but modern thinkers of the fragment, beginning with Hölderlin, the late Schelling, and Kierkegaard, and continuing to Rosenzweig and Benjamin, and then with those thinking in (and out of) the breaking and bursting asunder of the word—Bataille, Levinas, Blanchot, Derrida, Celan, Jabès—have attempted to think through this open-ended infinite that is unthinkable and thereby delimits thought.

Especially interesting and significant is the way that apophatic thought develops historically in tandem with more metaphysical doctrines, qualifying and redeploying their articulations in a different and nondogmatic register. The truth of metaphysical visions is revealed as something other than anything that they themselves had actually stated or even could directly say, let alone systematically expound. Insight that formerly was coded into the vocabularies of metaphysical and transcendental philosophies or theosophies retreats into the refuge of silence and the ineffable. The point of these philosophies lay not so much in anything actually proved or presented by their rhetorics of unity and wholeness: the truth of their discourses was typically invested rather in something more indirectly witnessed to in their silences. Indeed, they often let on, and sometimes even explicitly insisted, that their ineffable meaning was experienced and signified only by silence—which, however, signified all perfectly, as no determinate articulation ever could.[17]

Historically, these traditions in large part were effectively silenced, inasmuch as they were physically and textually eradicated and transmitted only by their opponents, particularly by church fathers combating Gnostic heresies, most prominently Irenaeus, *Adversus haereses,* Hippolytus, *Refutatio omnium haeresium,* and Tertullian, *Adversus Marcionem* and *Adversus Valentinianos.* However, rather than just refuting what these Gnostics said, it is necessary to listen to what they do not say and to how they indicate why this needs not to be forgotten. The Gnostic other world of the *Pleroma* can be represented only analogically and negatively in terms of our phenomenal world. Its "fullness" can appear to us only as "emptiness," literally, the *Kenoma* of "this" world. Hippolytus, in *Refutatio* IV.38, records that their "Ur-principle was held to be inconceivable and inexpressible and unnameable. . . . Others name it with the following name: first as Ur-principle."

We have here an example of a historically immense but suppressed discourse that turns on what it cannot say. In Gnostic literature, a new life and a new status is accorded to myth on the basis of the apophatic shattering of the concept vis-à-vis the inconceivable. Cyril O'Regan speaks of "the nonnotional status of Valentinian narrative grammar," which he excavates from Valentinian narratives of the Hellenistic era.[18] Peter Koslowski suggests how, on such a basis, narrating beyond one's own notional grasp, Gnosis undertakes to tell the origin of all reality following the revelation of the biblical Genesis narrative. It makes a metahistory of all reality in terms of its threefold schema of Origin, Fall, and future Reintegration of the Pleroma. This can be done only in narrative terms, which is the only knowledge possible of the Whole. In effect, for Koslowski, "Gnosis is dynamized and narratized theory of Totality."[19]

In order to account for the whole, one has to include the origin, and that can only be narrated. It is a unique event, not a generality that can be explained through universal principles. Each individual likewise is determined by a history that links contextually to an infinity of relations with other individuals and their histories. An individual event can never be exhaustively explained but can only be represented exemplarily, as in narrative. Plato resorted to myth, particularly in the *Timaeus,* in order to account for the origin of the world, and this has remained exemplary of the predicament of philosophy ever since. There can be no apodictic or purely logical judgment concerning origins; these can only be narrated, not demonstrated, for they are unique and temporal and cannot be subsumed under universally valid propositions.

Accordingly, narrative is ultimately the foundation of judgment and therefore also of system. Koslowski infers that "[t]he narrating judgment is therefore the most universal form of judgment, and all judgments are based on narratives as their deepest foundations."[20] Hegel, of course, does not take his System to be based on narrated judgment, but rather on the pure self-reflection of the concept. However, the real basis of intelligibility of his thought is the epic narrative of Spirit (*Geist*): it unfolds within a specifically Gnostic narrative of a Fall from the Idea into Nature and History and the subsequent struggle to reintegrate all into Spirit. Koslowski agrees with O'Regan and numerous other interpreters, including John Milbank, in reading the metanarrative beneath the logical pretensions of Hegel's System.[21]

The discourses of Gnosticism and Theosophy are best understood as mythical expressions spontaneously arising from the poetic license acquired through insight into the inadequacy of absolutely all discourse about the absolute. The Gnostic system in its furthest reaches is an elaboration of the imagination that expresses in psychological terms our relation to the divinity, who, as such, we do not know. The terms are narrative and analogical, but they are predicated on the unknowable God of negative theology. This is explicitly avowed by Allogenes, for example, in a Sethian Gnostic text: "I was seeking the ineffable and Unknowable God— whom if one should know him, he would be absolutely ignorant of him— the Mediator of the Triple-Powered One who subsists in stillness and silence and is unknowable."[22]

Koslowski stresses that Valentinian Gnosticism concerns the actual self-becoming of God, and that this makes it unlike Neoplatonism and

Kabbalah, in which emanations of the One and *Sephirot* as shining forth from *Ein Soph* leave their transcendent source intact and unchanged (*Philosophien der Offenbarung*, p. 63). However, this is perhaps to forget the *narrative* status of the myth of the *Aeons* and their relation to the *unknown* God proclaimed in texts such as the *Tripartite Tractatus*. It is true that many types of Gnosticism tell a story of God's fall and self-becoming that seems to deny divine transcendence. God's Being is represented as the Becoming of the world. And yet there are also the affirmations of an absolute, unsayable transcendence that is beyond any "God" that can be represented. The Gnostic text *Allogenes* refers to the Aeons as "images" or as "types and forms of those who truly exist." It says, concerning the ultimate One, that "he is superior to superlative . . . . He neither participates in age nor does he participate in time." All positive statements about the supreme, ineffable One in the end cancel each other out in pointing to something altogether beyond statement. Applying Koslowski's principles perhaps somewhat more rigorously than he himself does, we must conclude that Gnostic doctrine cannot quite be identified with any of the myths that it generates.

Gnosticism is undertood by Jacob Taubes as a remythologization of philosophical concepts after philosophical enlightenment and also after the undermining of pagan myth by monotheistic revelation.[23] Mythologoumena serve Gnosticism as building blocks ("Bausteine") that are only instrumental to a true doctrine and can eventually be kicked away like a ladder (*Vom Kult zur Kultur*, p. 107). Wittgenstein used the same image (*Tractatus* 6.54) to describe the dispensability of logical propositions. So conceived, philosophical concepts dissipate at will as mere "white mythology."[24] Such self-consciousness of one's own investment in myth can help to mitigate the potentially deleterious effects of self-deceived forms of adherence to a discourse that is dogmatically fixed in an inalterable figure of indelible truth.

What the Christian church rejected in exorcising the Gnostic threat, on the other hand, was also something vital to its own seeking after truth. I do not mean by this to side with Gnosticism or to deny the extraordinary insight (perhaps even inspiration) displayed by the fathers in the early ecumenical councils in forging a normative Christian doctrine; rather, I mean to read the tension created here in order to understand what orthodox theology was not able to say and yet unconsciously also needed—what therefore frequently came to expression in heterodoxy. In Gnosticism, myth, concept, symbol, dogma, metaphysics, and philosophical thinking are all indiscriminately received and fused together. The exclusions, which may have been historically necessary for the cohesion of the Christian church, cannot be adequate ultimately to the wholeness of Truth that is aimed at: they were expedients, and they caused lesions ("heresies," in the root sense of the word). What is rejected is always also in some way part of the greater whole that the God beyond our comprehension encompasses.

Koslowski insightfully remarks that Gnosticism "through its genetic account of the whole of reality reaches a yet higher systematicity than metaphysics does because it includes negativity and the metamorphoses of reality in its theory" (*Philosophien der Offenbarung*, p. 252). The Gnostic system of theosophy is distinguished as "the most comprehensive of all epics," as "totalistic epic" (ibid.), for it embraces the genesis and eternal destiny of the entire history of Being, including all its negativity in its ongoing dynamic of self-transformation. Such narrative philosophizing leads philosophical thinking outside itself, outside the domain of the pure concept, for no complete theory of all reality, including its origin and end, is possible without such a resort to narrative and imaginative modes of thinking.[25]

It may become possible to understand and, in a sense, recuperate the intelligibility and even the "truth" of some of these ancient forms of wisdom once we recover the necessary ground, or rather background, of all knowing in some form of unknowing, such as apophatic discourses are bent on evoking and adumbrating. And as for Gnostic myth, so also for Neoplatonic metaphysics. After all, metaphysics is not just a system of propositions, certainly not when the negative theological currents that for the most part, at least implicitly, have accompanied it are understood as determining its ultimate purport. In the broader spiritual tradition, metaphysics has generally not been understood strictly in terms of explicit formulas but rather with some sense of its deeper, subtler, and largely silent significance. That is why it has lived such a long, varied, and in fact still vigorous life. Perhaps only in philosophy—in fact, primarily only in academic philosophy—has metaphysics been interpreted narrowly as a deductive system and without regard for its allusive and largely poetical power of vision and for its suggestion of a beyond of all *logos,* a beyond in which something more naked and dumb is revealed. This "something," like *physis* in early Greek thinking, is newborn yet not completely severed from the womb, not yet "arti-culated" but rather *natura naturans,* "nature" in its emergence (φὺσις).[26]

When we allow what cannot be said to be present silently at the center of all discourse, the gap between competing languages claiming the name of philosophy drastically narrows. Virtually all such languages, in different ways, have recognized what cannot be said as at least defining their borders. The conflict of widely diverging statements and stances attenuates when consideration is given to what they were *not* saying and were not even able to say. An intention beyond what they were saying toward what they were not able to say—or at any rate a possibility of understanding them as leaning in such a direction—is inscribed within them, if we learn how to read it. The devotees of such wisdom always had their own ways of reading the words—quite beyond what they were able to say in completely exoteric language to the detached, critical, philosophical mind.

To enable a reconnection of metaphysics and theosophy with critical philosophy, we must bring about a reactualization of the unsaid and unsayable in all these different traditions and foster a rereading sensitive to this silent dimension of discourse. Such a rereading moves against what might be taken to be the main thrust of philosophy since Kant, who aimed to make this border impermeable and so to definitively separate prescientific from critical philosophy. Yet awareness of what cannot be said, if allowed to emerge from eclipse, illuminates the very aspirations to fullness of truth that have driven even this scientifically inclined, science-emulating sort of philosophy, just as much as philosophical inquiries of the most unanalytical types.

With the defeat in the post-Hegelian era of all attempts to claim whole and complete knowledge or even to conceive of things as a whole, we had arrived, especially in postmodern milieus, at a prevailing skepticism that often sneered at such notions as oneness, unity, and, of course, truth and totality. To narrowly rational scrutiny, such ideas prove untenable, for reason's tools can only divide and conquer—or else liquidate by the acid of analysis. But an alternative to the rational, enlightenment mode of thinking that has accompanied and guided Western culture in its unfolding since the Greeks is presented in a range of religious traditions, from mythologies to monotheisms and metaphysics, that furnish a variety of vocabularies for what cannot be said. Rather than basing knowledge all on the Logos, these approaches, in different ways, are based on an openness and abandonment to what is not logical, not sayable. At their limit, they open themselves in silence to what is beyond word and representation—to the ineffable.

Discourses on what cannot be said share in common a structure of opening out beyond all definable, systemic parameters and so of being open to infinity. Meaning and significance accrue to human discourse from motives and passions that cannot be rationally delimited in adequate and exhaustive terms, and this dimension of discourse remains unsayable. Curiously, this structural inability of human discourse to achieve closure in itself makes it homologous to, and even indistinguishable from, certain metaphysical and mythical discourses that have been taken to epitomize closed systems. The analogies become evident when these metaphysical and mythical discourses are read as symbolic languages for what cannot be said.

If we interpret mythic or symbolic archetypes and metaphysical hypostatizations as condensing potentially open-ended, on-going narratives that testify to what can never be adequately or exhaustively stated, then claims about ultimate grounds and origins are claims about the openness and infinity that drive these discourses rather than about objects or essences that are arbitrarily posited as guarantors of fixed and stable significance. Only in terms of what cannot be said, of experience of failed—or at least unfinished—attempts to articulate, and of impasses to expression, can we attempt to think (or to renounce thinking) the openness of experience and life as they inform or *de*form such narratives and expositions, beneath the level of controlled and conscious expression.

Alongside myth and metaphysics, certain types of self-reflexive poetic literature explore language to its limits in order to render intimations of what lies beyond language audible and articulate. Historically, philosophical reflection, too, both in the course of ancient and medieval philosophy and again in modern thought, notably in some of its more esoteric offshoots, has attempted to recuperate this expanded field of experience beyond rational comprehension, seeking for more flexible ways to use reason, so as to allow for what exceeds it, and seeking also to redefine reason in relation to this other-than-reason in a way that would somehow integrate it with rational knowledge.

Indeed, a powerful impulse in just this direction was given precisely by Hegel—or at least arose in his wake. Hegel, and in particular his *Phenomenology of Spirit* (*Phänomenologie des Geistes*), was fundamental to several generations of French intellectuals, including a number who figure among the most salient of modern apophatic thinkers. Lectures on Hegel by Alexandre Kojève in the 1930s at the École Pratique des Hautes Études were attended by Georges Bataille, Maurice Merleau-Ponty, and Jacques Lacan. Similarly epoch-making were the seminars on the *Phenomenology* given by Jean Hyppolite at the École Normale Supérieure and the Collège de France until his death in 1968. This date was signaled by his student, Jacques Derrida, as the time of a "punctuation" in the intellectual life of the French university. In this milieu, Hegel came to be read as the precursor of the discovery of the irrational and the unconscious. Merleau-Ponty attests:

> Hegel inaugurates the attempt to explore the irrational and integrate it with an enlarged reason, which remains the task of our century. He is the inventor of that Reason more comprehensive than understanding, which, capable of respecting the variety and the singularity of psyches, civilizations, and methods of thought, together with the contingency of history, nevertheless does not renounce dominating them in order to conduct them to their proper truth. However, it turns out that the successors of Hegel have insisted not on what they owed to Hegel so much as on what they refused in his heritage.[27]

Hegel thus opens reason to the irrational, but he then absorbs the irrational back into reason, the Logos, and so back into the range of things that can be said. Hegel uncovers—even while he denies—the apophatic origin of all speech and reason. This is the nerve of his disturbed connection with a numerous progeny of postmodern heirs.

Closely related to this is another capital idea that passes through Kojève and Merleau-Ponty, an idea that is likewise crucial for understanding the reversal of Hegel wrought by his successors, namely, that of Hegel's "existentialism," or of death and finitude as the condition of all knowledge, even of absolute knowing. This condition again closes the circle of consciousness on itself rather than opening it to what is beyond its grasp and beyond being and language altogether. Only a finite being can reach absolute knowing—a consciousness in which consciousness and *self-consciousness* are one and the same. Only because of death can the in-itself and the for-consciousness fully coincide. Death is necessary to a fully realized and exhaustively known totality. Man must be mortal and finite to be perfectly comprehensible to himself. Only on this basis can Spirit sublate its ultimate ground to itself. Death, or a prolonged sojourn in its face, gives Spirit the magical force ("die Zauberkraft") for transposing the infinitely negative into determinate being.[28]

This idea has been at the very center of French Hegelianism ever since Kojève's reflections on Hegel and their reception particularly by Bataille.[29] But precisely these interpretations actually break the circle of Being-Logos open to what inevitably evades reason and invades speech in the reverberating shock waves after Hegel. By collapsing the infinite into the finite, the transcendent into the immanent, Hegel made everything totally immanent and totally sayable. Reversing this implosion, the post-Hegelians envision everything that is apparently finite and stateable as breaking apart and exploding into something infinite and indefinable.

Although thus opening perspectives into the other of reason, Hegel himself attempted relentlessly to reduce all that is real to the rational, to bring anything and everything to articulation by the Logos, refusing to recognize any absolute, irreconcilable alterity. His system can tolerate no ineffable absolutes that would resist total mediation by the discourse of reason. Jean Hyppolite lucidly explains how Hegel has to exclude all absolute negativity that is outside language, for instance, in sensation, which can never be adequately or exhaustively expressed, as the precondition for absolute knowledge, to which nothing remains unexpressed or inexpressible.[30]

Hegel frequently inveighs against "the present age" in its denial of the possibility of knowing God in order to turn, instead, to positive, anthropological knowledge of religion by empiricists such as Hume, on the one side; or, on the other, to a noncognitive, intuitive, emotional fideism, the Romantic religion of feeling following Jacobi; or, again, to ethical and psychological reductions of religion in the styles of Kant and Schleiermacher. Particularly Hegel's *Lectures on the Proofs of the Existence of God,* given in 1829, two years before his death, demonstrate his constant determination to vindicate the possibility of actual knowledge of the Absolute, of God. Here Hegel makes unambiguous his definitive adherence to a position that thinks not from unknowing but from an actual knowing of God in and through the concept.[31]

So Hegel's main historiographical significance must be read as enforcing the reign where Logos is law rather than as ushering in the anarchic realm of apophasis. Nevertheless, this distinction actually blurs in Hegel: he is not included in my canon of apophatic authors, despite the enormous influence he has had on it, because of his profile as a systematic thinker rather than a thinker (like Heidegger) of the breakthrough—the *Durchbruch*—through which what cannot be said asserts itself. Of course, a system is first necessary in order for it to be broken through, and so it is difficult if not impossible to imagine contemporary apophaticism without Hegel. Especially the recent renaissance of French apophatic thought would hardly have been conceivable without him. Furthermore, Hegel's paramount importance for opening the turn to religion in philosophical thought of the twenty-first century has been demonstrated many times over by a new generation of theological thinkers.

In an attempt to reverse the prevailing view of Hegel, some critics argue for a Hegel who was open to contingency and risk and against "the stereotypical post-modern critique where Hegel represents the totalizing philosopher par excellence."[32] Mark C. Taylor concordantly explains that as "the impending threat shifts from totalitarianism to sectarianism" (p. 91), Hegel's infinite is coming to be appreciated as a place for mediating differences rather than simply as a totalizing System or monolith. David Walsh similarly remarks, "It is one of the insufficiently understood ironies of the history of modern philosophy that the thinker most notoriously associated with the system took his beginning from the realization that life always escapes any effort to contain it."[33] Walsh takes Hegel as the pivot for the entire modern revolution of thinking that consists in thinking ideas through their manner of existing. Nevertheless, in the end we still have to admit that the main thrust of Hegel's own effort went into building the System.

The counterthrust within Hegel's own works stands out particularly well when he is viewed as the culmination of the mystic tradition of Neoplatonic philosophy.[34] Hegel himself was capable of identifying Neoplatonic mysticism with speculative philosophy like his own: "The speculative Idea is a μυστήριον [mystery], as much for the senses as for the understanding. Μυστήριον, namely, is that which is reasonable; for the Neoplatonists, this term already means nothing but speculative philosophy."[35] However, in his appropriations of Christian mysticism, Hegel also persistently erases precisely the apophatic elements. Cyril O'Regan has shown that Hegel's use of Christian mystics such as Eckhart and Cusanus consistently ignores or suppresses their apophatic dimension.[36] In the end, Hegel rejects negative theology as a reversion to worship of the Unknown God and therefore the antithesis of Christian revelation—particularly as it is proclaimed by Paul on the Acropolis at Athens (Acts 17:23). The truth of Christianity for Hegel (as Protestant and specifically Lutheran) lies in the revelation of all truth in the Word.[37]

Twentieth-century reversals of Hegel, particularly by French thinkers, in their discovery and exaltation of the ultra-logical and apophatic, had been anticipated a century earlier. Kierkegaard, in an early wave of reaction against Hegel, and taking his cues from Schelling's lectures in 1941 in Berlin, which he attended, wished to think passion and paradox in ways inaccessible to reason and Logos. In "The Absolute Paradox," Kierkegaard writes: "However, one should not think slightingly of the paradoxical; for the paradox is the source of the thinker's passion, and the thinker without a paradox is like a lover without feeling: a paltry mediocrity. . . . The supreme paradox of all thought is the attempt to discover something that thought cannot think. This passion is at bottom present in all thinking."[38] Not even the *via negationis* will serve reason to draw near to this other-than-reason, according to Kierkegaard (p. 55). No codified "way," of course, could. Nevertheless, it is telling that Kierkegaard registers precisely this proximity, even in denying it—in a move that itself unwittingly imitates the negative way as a negation of method rather than a method. As such, this negation is indeed a way: it is not itself the destination, and so is destined to be left behind. That is the point about this (and really any) way, as Kierkegaard himself remarks elsewhere: "Irony is like the negative way, not the truth but the way."[39]

ii

Since Hegel has, in effect, become the historical anchor and pivot of this speculative essay, we must try to confront some of the messier issues involved in determining the apophatic in conjunction and also in contrast with Hegel's project, which in any case proves ineluctable. We must consider in more detail exactly how Hegel's most powerful thinking approaches apophasis, even though, conformably with the overriding scientific demands of his age, he turns away from acknowledging anything as irreducibly unsayable. This is what has made him such an obsession—an irresistible magnet but also a target—for so many apophatic thinkers following him, especially those of postmodern persuasions.

Hegel has been crucial in recent philosophy of religion for understanding what drives thinking, including the thinking that goes under the banner of negative theology, toward some sense or experience or acknowledgment of the ideals of truth and totality. Particularly in postmodern contexts, these ideals tend to imply total openness, which in practice demands openness without limit to the Other. At the same time, Hegel shows how genuine apophatic insight can be missed or perverted by the ambitions of absolute knowing. Much of the most original apophatic thinking in the twentieth century, especially among French thinkers, took its bearings by facing off against Hegel. Consequently, a philosophy of the unsayable today can hardly do better than to explain itself with reference to the teasingly ambiguous thinking of Hegel.

Hegel expressed impatience with talk of the ineffable. In the *Logic* of the *Encyclopedia,* he designated this purportedly most elevated and truest theme as the most insignificant and least true of all. He associates it with merely subjective intuition that cannot achieve objective expression and so can achieve no substantial, historical reality, either. "What I only *mean* is *mine* and belongs to me as a particular individual; if, however, language expresses only the general, then I cannot say what I merely *mean*. And the *unsayable,* feeling, sensitivity, is not the most excellent and truest but the most insignificant and untrue."[40] The truth for Hegel must be said and said completely. It is not consummated in silent contemplation, but is eminently articulate and must be realized objectively in the world. As noted by apophatic commentators Massimo Baldini and Silvano Zucal: "Silence is suppressed by Hegel in virtue of the identification of knowing with being."[41] Yet Hegel remains crucial for discussions of negative theology and is arguably himself, at least in certain phases, a negative theologian par excellence.[42]

It is fairly obvious how Hegel's claims to absolute truth and total self-presence of consciousness are the antithesis of an apophatic outlook, which is based always on recognition of limits and on negation of achieved knowledge. What is less obvious—and what I wish to bring out—is how the regulative ideals of truth and totality, when resituated and redefined in terms of a nonassertive groundlessness, actually belong by rights to apophatic thought and vision. Some idea of truth and also of an absolute is even necessary in order to keep us beholden to what exceeds us, and this in turn serves to prevent us from feeling superior to others and especially to predecessors on the basis of our principled resolution to resist the lures of truth and totalization in any form. The idea or ideal of the whole greater than what we can apprehend, of the whole that is yet to come, is actually necessary to keep us from closing the circle of our own little utopia around those who think like us, thereby ignoring the demands of universality.

Hegel was peculiarly receptive to the demand for wholeness. The call of universality is not just a private matter—it is *for all* and must be open to all. In the postmodern context, Slavoj Žižek has advanced precisely such claims in Hegel's name.[43] He has embraced Christianity for the sake of its universalist vision, its opening of salvation to all in a hyperbolic form exceeding classical reason in proclaiming the death of God as initiating a life in the Spirit for all.[44] Still, the manner of wholeness in question in Hegel is crucially different from that proposed by apophatic thinkers such as Schelling and Rosenzweig. From an apophatic perspective, we are right not to completely give up on the claim to universality and even to truth and a kind of totality in our effort to know. However, we must avoid reducing what we know to the measure of our language, and likewise our thought must learn to stretch and open itself toward what is other than and exceeds it. This is the key to relating to the true All (Hegel's "das wahre All") that is not just our own figment. Thinkers such as Rosenzweig have measured themselves against Hegel and taken another route, one that is more unambiguously apophatic in that it reverses wholeness—or rather breaks it open—into a kind of measurelessness.[45]

Hegel's striving for a knowledge of truth and totality is actually not mistaken in its underlying impulse, but he perverts it to the extent that he opts for a totally rational system as the form of its realization. This is too drastic a delimitation. It leaves too much of what mind and spirit seek out of account and unacknowledged. The divinization of Reason and the Subject derives from an Enlightenment humanism that remains enamored of itself and thereby closes itself off from all that is. Hegel's reason is, of course, self-transcending reason. Nevertheless, the other and the non-identical, the irreducibly different, seem in the end—at least to Hegel's postmodern critics—to be excluded by the final triumph of identity in the identity of identity and difference. If self-transcending is *only* that, then it is still centered on self rather than radically open to the other; it is oriented to closure rather than to the unceasing questioning which we are.

And yet Hegel makes clear that the abandonment of self on the path to knowledge must be total. Nothing remains in or with the self as a fixed point or foundation. It must be totally mediated by its other, that is, by what *appears* as absolutely alien to it. Later, this other will be recognized as the self in an externalized, more complete and truer form than the self's mere abstract, immediate intuition of itself. This mediation by the Other proves to be self-mediation on a larger scale and compass than what Spirit previously was able to comprehend.

There is in Hegel's dialectic no fixed or stateable foundation to which everything can be reduced. The identities of particular entities are dissolved into the infinite relations that constitute them. The difference from apophatic thinkers is that surrender of self to the infinite and unknown, the Other, leads back to transparent self-knowledge. The system in its entirety for Hegel forms a completed whole and is *known*. Of course, the total or absolute knowing proclaimed by Hegel's System is a knowing of determinate content. It supposedly comprises the history of the world and the entire scope of the cosmos. This presupposes an interpretation of the infinite as a concrete and whole content. However, this knowing itself, in addition to being a never ending circle, must exist somewhere in time, which continues (the "end" of history notwithstanding), and how could any content remain static or even stable in that case?

Hegel brings everything that exists under rational rule by the Subject. Yet this rationality is not reason as we ordinarily understand it; nor is the subject in the pursuit of whose self-completion this comes about any familiar or given subject. In the preface to the *Phänomenologie des Geistes,* Hegel writes that "everything depends on grasping and expressing the True, not only as *Substance,* but equally as Subject," and he further specifies that "[t]his substance is, as Subject, pure *simple negativity*" (p. 10). Reason and subject alike are broken open and radically mediated by all that is other to (or is not) them. Neither has any content that it can hold on to as exclusively its own; all is subject to a process of infinite mediation. In this sense, Hegel's total immanence is also an absolute transcendence, in that it is open infinitely: it consists in infinite mediation.

There is, then, nothing in particular but rather the system in its entirety that for Hegel forms a completed whole and is *known.* Knowledge is translated into a dimension of "infinity"—it is realized not in discrete atomic units but rather in the endless circulation of Spirit within the whole of the System. Is it not, then, also in some sense an *un*knowing? Certainly there is no possibility here of knowing individual propositions in isolation. Still, Hegel's objective in the end is to attain to absolute knowing. And there is nothing beyond this pure self-positing of absolute knowing: it is a knowing purely of itself.

Hegel defines the True, accordingly, as something *produced.* An "original or immediate unity" is for him pure untruth. Yet that does not mean that he and we cannot be and are not still haunted by it, nor that the capacity to conceive of such an abstraction is not intimately bound up with every concrete production of spirit. In this case, such a conception expresses and symbolizes something about spirit itself and about everything that spirit produces. Here, the apophatic emerges in the belief that something else is going on below the level of what Logos can account for in its own self-conscious terms and that this is manifest in Logos itself— most tellingly, in its tripping up or being spooked. Likewise, the famous ontological argument claims fundamentally, as I previously suggested, that the measurelessness of God (that than which nothing greater can be conceived) is inherent in the nature of thought per se.

Thinking in Hegel is totally beholden to the Other. It cannot possess itself. It must give up all self-possession completely in order to come back to itself and receive itself from the Other of thinking, from being and its history. Hegel's *Philosophy of Religion* defines religious consciousness in terms of spirit's going out from itself and going forth toward an Other ("ein Aus- und Fortgehen zu einem Anderen").[46] Even God must die as abstract concept and undergo a physical Passion in history for the sake of reconciling the world as an exterior phenomenon to its idea. This entails a total realization of thinking and therewith a complete volatilization of things and subjects as particulars and as singular individuals.[47] In the end, in Hegel's System, there is only one true and complete individual: the Whole. Only as the Whole is Spirit fully concrete universality; it then has all its relations *within* itself and therefore as mediations of nothing but itself. This last point is indicative of what has made Hegel's solution unacceptable to poststructuralist thinkers. The complete relativity of thinking to being and vice versa results in the total knowability of the Whole.

From an apophatic perspective, Hegel is not wrong to allow for a unity of all in one, but to identify this unequivocally with total mediation by thinking on the part of an individual subject expresses a confidence in human reason that belongs to his own era: such confidence has not often been deemed sustainable either before or since. The unifying principle of things has more often been admitted in religious and specifically in Christian thought to transcend human comprehension. Hegel is compelling for us in his opening of thought to unlimited negativity as the driving force of the Absolute. There is nothing for Hegel that is not instituted through negation: that is the meaning of his embracing "total mediation." He breaks thought and word open from within to expose them to their own radical Other. This brings things back into unity at a level deeper than the ordinary perception of the world of separate individuals: it reconciles all in one. This idea that a deep unity joins all is not necessarily mistaken. But to claim knowledge of this unity, and to claim this knowledge as exhaustive, is to collapse and end our relation to God as Other. Because this union is conceived as an articulated knowing, Hegel in effect reduces God to world and both God and world to word.

This, too, is not without certain Christian precedents. It embodies the fulfillment of the spirit of reconciliation: in Christ, the Word, God becomes one with man and reconciles the world to himself (2 Corinthians 5:19). To this extent, Hegel's thinking can claim to represent the spirit of the Gospels, especially the Gospel according to John, with its declarations that the Word was God and became incarnate as man. Of course, in achieving the reconciliation of God and the world essentially at the level of speculative thinking, Hegel veers rather into a form of Gnosticism.[48]

In making such a claim—the claim to absolute knowing—Hegel, in effect, realizes an eternal point of view abstracted from time. Hegel borrows the grammar of infinite self-relatedness from the discourse of Christian theism, with its Trinitarian doctrine of divinity; he applies this conception to thought itself, which for him is identical to being, even absolute being, and so ipso facto to God. Thus the doctrine of the Trinity lies at the foundation of Hegel's dialectical logic. Nevertheless, there is a will, deriving from the Enlightenment philosopher in Hegel, to deny transcendence to this Trinity. Because this Trinitarian self-relating is conceived of as an articulated knowing, Hegel in effect reduces God to world and confines the divine to finite, human unity. These equivalences are not necessarily untrue to experience from an apophatic point of view, but they cannot be articulated in language and so cannot be humanly *known*. They can be experienced authentically only as modes of unknowing.

And yet Hegel's total immanence is also absolute transcendence, in that it is open infinitely: it consists of infinite mediation. There is no term that has its identity in itself alone. All identity is produced through infinite mediation with otherness. The identities of particular entities are dissolved into the infinite relations and mediations that constitute them. Thus a necessary transcendence of itself is built into any finite identity whatsoever. Hegel concretely conceptualizes this infinity as a completed whole. It is not simply an open-ended process: the latter is what he calls the "bad infinite." The completed whole for Hegel is *knowledge* rather than *un*knowing, even if there is in it no reduction to a particular known but rather the opening of particular objects to the infinite relations that constitute them. Still, the universe of these infinite relations is conceived of by Hegel as finite. Moreover, for Hegel, the *an sich* or "in itself" must become self-conscious *für sich* or "for itself": and to this extent, knowledge does presuppose closure.

Despite this important difference, the central vision of apophatics consists precisely in the ceaseless negative energy that courses through Hegel's system and not in any hard and fast tombstone erected to the Unknown God. The essential insight is rather that God is traced and enacted and re-acted in the negations through which all achieved knowledge of him is confounded. Viewed in historical perspective, Hegel's System of absolute knowing and its opposite, namely, insuperable unknowing, articulate together a figure of totality and truth. Totality and truth are achieved rather in *un*knowing—which is not exclusive of systematic knowing, nor even of a certain closure that is not deadening or limiting but rather enables further openings. The mistake is only in believing that one has to prove Hegel wrong in order to go beyond him. On the contrary: his structure of thinking calls to be negated, as do all determinate articulations, from the apophatic point of view.

Hegel remains vitally important for suggesting how the apophatic perspective is related to a vision of truth and totality. Apophatic thought has flourished historically in close conjunction with comprehensive metaphysical visions of truth, especially in the various monotheistic religions. The extreme claims for total truth and absolute negation call each other forth. Therefore it is worthwhile to pause and look at Hegel's ambiguous (dis)analogy with apophatic thinking: he eminently exemplifies both apophatics *and* its antithesis.

Hegel is crucial to contemporary apophatics, even though his form of expression images its presumable antithesis, for he opens being and thought up in total exposure to "the negative." His thinking, which is theological in character from beginning to end, does not shrink from the most radical encounter with the negative, and to this extent it realizes itself only by passage through a radically negative theology. Every positive affirmation must be negated. Of course, this negation too is negated, and the affirmation for Hegel comes back, but only as the mediation of its own negation. Any unmediated positivity is abolished. And this is what turns out to be the limit of his thinking.

Here is precisely where Schelling parts company with Hegel and indeed takes up the attack against him. Schelling's "positive philosophy" insists on beginning with "something" (which is equivalently "nothing") that is positively given rather than allowing everything real to be produced only by negation. He posits the purely positive that is not mediated by any negation as prior to the whole process of dialectical negation. This suggests why Schelling has taken on a crucial role in contemporary apophatics.[49] However, simply to embrace Schelling and dismiss Hegel is not adequate to the negative theological insight and import of the latter's thinking.[50] For when we ask *what* is given in a purely positive philosophy, there is no answer. Hegel, too, has an important point to make about what cannot be an adequate answer to this question. What stands outside the system, its Other, cannot stand simply in opposition to it. This Other would then itself be limited and not infinite. This is a reason why John Caputo, following Derrida's own bent, remarks shrewdly that God is only *almost* wholly other.[51] To completely sever the Other from oneself serves to complete its conceptualization but not to remain in touch with and alive to what utterly surpasses us. Hegel correctly sees that whatever is other to the System cannot be manifest to it except as the driving force of the negative at work within it. The Other cannot be delimited as an object of discourse or be articulated by the propositions that make up the System.

This is why Hegel's positive negation is so compelling—because differences that are stated are ultimately overcome as differences and are subsumed into the identity of the Whole. This could be true also in a Christian apophatic view, with the proviso that the Whole is no object of absolute knowing but rather gestures toward the infinity of a relation with the Absolute. Any differences that can be stated and given content could only discriminate among different sorts of creatures. God's absolute difference is not stateable. Even if we say that "he" is other, we must take this back. He is not other in any way that can be understood from the otherness manifest among creatures as distinct, mutually exclusive individuals. In this respect, he is *non*-other. Meister Eckhart bequeathed this idea to Nicholas Cusanus, who made it the fulcrum for some of his most far-reaching speculations in apophatic theology.

For Cusanus, God is different not only from everything that is, but also from every difference and even from difference itself. As pure difference, God is *in*different to every declarable, definable difference, even to "difference" itself as a distinct category of thought or being. God must be thought of as different from every thinkable difference, as other than every specifiable other, and so as non-other, *non aliud*, in Cusanus's lexicon.[52] There is thus no thematic content to otherness or negativity. The determination to negate any and all such content is the only operative criterion.

Seeing how God cannot be *that* either—*whatever* we have characterized him as—generates for us an oblique insight into the divine transcendence.

Accordingly, the exterior or the transcendent must not be set up in opposition to interiority and immanence. What is in question is *infinite* exteriority and *infinite* transcendence; it therefore stands in no definable, finite oppositions whatsoever. Only as such is it honored as God—and even beyond any conception such as "God," at least in the sense we inevitably understand of some particular bearer of this name. Blanchot and Levinas have pursued this dialectic into the neuter and nameless, in which any sort of term or definition must eventually be apophatically abandoned.

Hegel construes our relation to the Absolute as an opening toward truth and totality. But he identifies this truth with the mediations that make up the total system of discourse. Post-Hegelian thinkers today, particularly apophatic thinkers, feel that truth is not this but beyond it—or not *only* this but also beyond it. Truth is not what we grasp and deliver in the end as our final discourse, but what escapes all our formulations and remains in the silence after all is said and done.

Hence William Desmond, after several decades devoted largely to expounding Hegel's philosophy of religion, writes his *adieu* to Hegel. In *Hegel's God: A Counterfeit Double,* he cannot help concluding that Hegel's God is an idol, a creation of speculative thinking that leaves no room for the God that is other than all that we can say, the God who transcends us in a more robust sense than that of merely human *self*-transcendence. This is the God "beyond" that Hegel was never willing to acknowledge. "On the surface Hegel's thinking saturates us with God, but what it saturates us with, I have come to think, is a 'God' who is not God."[53] Desmond's dismissal of Hegel's dialectical sublation of God into the all of "immanent infinitism" (the completed Whole that is realized by human Spirit) is confirmed and extended in his *God and the Between*.[54] Here he calls for exceeding the "holistic immanence" of Hegel in the direction of what he designates as the "reserve of transcendence," which remains always unexhausted by all our human exploits.

Of course, any express totality articulated in language cannot but be a "counterfeit double," in Desmond's terms. The only "true All," as Rosenzweig writes, is one that cannot be expressed in any finite terms. And yet we are obliged, by the energy and élan of thought itself, not to stop at any finite configuration but always to expand our horizon to include whatever Other should present itself. This infinite opening outward is uncompletable for us. It can never be at a final endpoint, but we must imagine that it is complete absolutely in God—if all things are to be related together and not remain insuperably strangers to one another. This is the dynamic that early on in Christian apophatic tradition, even before Dionysius, was approached by Gregory of Nyssa under the title of *epektasis* as a never resolved tension to be one with God. Otherwise reality would not be ultimately one or at least projectable as one, and God would not be experienced. The world would consist in individuals who are not just presented as independent and as psychologically estranged but who, much more fundamentally, *are* ontologically and irreducibly separate and alien. There is no God in such a universe, no overarching bond that unites all that is before and beyond all differentiation and separation. We would be most authentic in fleeing all relations, all bonding and solidarity, as impositions upon our true nature—as impostures, or at least as impertinent solicitations with no basis in reality.

Hegel was thinking essentially the Word that was God and that became flesh and dwelt among us, full of grace and truth, as in the Gospel according to John (1:4). His System should not be denied recognition as an expression of that Word, but unless we also attend to the flaws in this expression, as in any expression, it will become idolatrous. Judged by apophatic lights, the incarnation of divinity in the human discourse of systematic philosophy must always remain provisional and illustrative.

Nevertheless, Hegel has highlighted the way that thinking, by its intrinsic nature and aims, opens upon truth and totality. What is the nature of this experience of thinking? I submit that it is not the full and adequate articulation of science but rather the inarticulate openness vis-à-vis an unmediatable experience of truth and totality that is its primary witness. The System, too, we should grant, is a witness in its own way. Its articulation describes the limits of articulation and does so eloquently. Therefore, Hegel is important for correcting the total mystification of the wholly "Other" and the concomitant erecting of an altar to the idol of the Unknowable. What is unknowable is concretely experienced right within knowing, even "absolute knowing," as its inadequacy and in its *aporiae*. This emphasis on experiencing the absolute *in the midst of life* is found in thinkers as diverse as Rosenzweig and Desmond. It is apophatic in thinking from a middle that remains open at its ends and refuses closure by undefining its ends and objects.

Hegel indeed shows how reason itself is the mystical. Even his so-called "onto-theology" is not just cold logic-chopping, performed on empty concepts of what inevitably escapes logic. Rather, it translates some kind of communication in terms of effects from an unsayable source. Its limitation is in the controlled nature of conceptual analysis, but this very control dissimulates a sense of the unmasterable charge or *energeia* by which this thinking is actually animated. We need not reject the traditions of onto-theology; rather, we need to think them through more deeply— and, above all, in a more timely fashion. There has been a rather widespread tendency today to consign to oblivion, with the contemptuous label "onto-theology," the tradition of rational reflection about God as Being—whether as supreme being or as the ground of being or as the excellency of being. The vanity of metaphysics is often taken today as self-evident. But metaphysical thinking often included a thinking of the limits of reason (in Hegel this is necessary to thinking reason's infinity), and this makes metaphysics still perfectly relevant for thinking through our most intransigent philosophical dilemmas today.

iii

The break with Hegel and with absolute knowing, and thus the focus on what remains necessarily outside all systems of knowledge and even outside conscious, verbally articulable experience and so denies itself to speech, opens a vast new field of inquiry for contemporary thought. It is essentially the field in which apophatic thinking has flourished time and again in the past in the wake of the perennial crises of Logos. The same questions that were struggled with throughout the antecedent apophatic tradition arise again in new guises. Most obviously, one can never finish with asking: How is this "realm" of the unsayable to be conceived? For if we know anything about it, we know precisely that it is not conceivable at all. Can it then be experienced? Can there be some kind of a journey to the other side of knowledge and into Unknowing? Is such experience, then, an experience of language, that is, of the limits of language, or is it, finally, altogether beyond and apart from language?

What cannot be said is often imaged as quintessentially invisible, for example, in the Bible's account of God's refusal to show his "face" to Moses (Exodus 33:18–20). This becomes a fulcrum for mystical theology in the style of Gregory of Nyssa in his *De vita Moysis*. But the unsayable also sometimes figures as what by its nature must "show itself," famously in Wittgenstein's formulation: "There is indeed the inexpressible. This *shows* itself; it is the mystical" (*Tractatus* 6.522). A *showing* of that which exceeds all articulations in language is theorized again, but in quite a different direction, as the "saturated phenomenon," by Jean-Luc Marion.[55] A paradoxical phenomenology of the invisible, stemming in crucial ways from Merleau-Ponty's *Le visible et l'invisible,* is pursued in a theological vein by French philosophers in the wake also of Levinas and his peculiar *ultra*-phenomenology. This makes for quite a significant theological turn in recent French phenomenology as represented by theologically-minded thinkers such as Michel Henry and Jean-Louis Chrétien.[56] The latter's *L'antiphonaire de la nuit* can be placed specifically in the Dionysian tradition of the luminous darkness that calls forth liturgical response and first enables true seeing.[57]

Still more deeply puzzling than the question of whether what cannot be said must in some sense be *seen* is the issue of its relation to language. Is the unsayable beyond language altogether, as mystics often fervently maintain? Does this make it simply nonlinguistic? Or is it the other of language and therefore inextricable from language (Derrida)? Or is it without relation to language (Blanchot)? Or is it language itself, the being or essence of language ("das Wesen der Sprache"), as Heidegger maintains? Paradoxically, what cannot be said can *only* be said (de Certeau): for all we can tell, it is nothing but this verbal negation itself. And yet when Henri Meschonnic argues that the inexpressible exists *only* by virtue of language ("L'inexprimable n'existe que par le langage"), he shows how throughout monotheistic religions the existence of God as the unsayable is recognized specifically through this peculiarly verbal presence.[58]

Many such absolute *aporiae* are generated endlessly by what transcends language, by what cannot be said. This transcendent-of-language can be conceived of equally well as Nothing or as Everything. It entails total incomparability, in virtue of absolute singularity, and at the same time the complete connectedness of everything with everything else, indeed, the deep indistinguishability and ultimate oneness of everything. All these seemingly incompatible possibilities are encompassed by the condition of being unsayable. Frequently in apophatic tradition, for example, in the Sufism of Ibn al-Arabi, the claim is made that total transcendence and pure immanence come to coincide in what cannot be said. Neither ought to be asserted without the other. Both must be held together, even in their contradictoriness, on the verbal level:

> If you insist only on His transcendence [*tanzih*], you restrict him,
> And if you insist only on His immanence [*tashbih*], you limit him.[59]

Admittedly, then, it proves impossible to decide these antinomies in favor of one alternative or the other. The apophatic is the locus par excellence of complete contradiction and paradox, of *coincidentia oppositorum* in a language given currency by Cusanus. Might we, then, envisage an asymptotic point of "indiscretion" at which all such alternatives collapse together and cannot be dissevered or even discerned from one another?[60] Meister Eckhart teaches that nothing can be compared to God because nothing is distinct from him. Absolute distance and no distance at all alike prevent any sort of articulation. Total mediation becomes indistinguishable from sheer immediacy in language, as Benjamin, for another, makes manifest.[61]

The unsayable must be expressed in contradictory forms because it can have no proper identity of its own but exerts absolute, decisive influence in all directions on everything else. If it had any kind of identity, then what cannot be said would be, to that extent, sayable. Nor is it permissible to conceive of "what cannot be said" as a certain something shared in common by all these discourses, giving them the unity of reference *ad unum*. There is no "what" to which discourses of the ineffable refer. Therefore the affinity that is sensed among these discourses cannot be reduced to a definition, for that would be to say what these discourses do not and cannot say. What associates these different languages with one another is rather that each, in its own way, discovers at its limit something that it cannot articulate and discovers this unsayable something as decisive for its own discourse throughout. Yet this unsayable something/nothing is in every case unique and incomparable.

The uncanny kindredness of the discourses of apophasis across the widest range of historical periods and disciplines is itself nothing that can be adequately accounted for. It, too, testifies to what cannot be said. For "what cannot be said" is not a rigorous definition of any subject matter; it is not a definition at all, nor even properly a description. It can itself be specified only in terms of a linguistic operation that negates any possible object and so dissolves the designation of anything definite and identifiable. Nevertheless, the mutual affinity of all these discourses is unmistakable.

Paradoxically, it is the incomparability of what is experienced in each case that invites—and alone allows for—comparison. This phrase "what cannot be said" enables us to unite, as if under one cover, a vast range of texts tethered to vastly different experiences embedded in widely disparate spheres of culture and history. We are compelled to compare these experiences precisely with regard to their incomparability. Intrinsically recalcitrant to any form of expression, the "experience" expressed in apophatic discourse is always totally different and (strictly speaking) completely without comparison. Bataille's "inner experience" could be called upon here as witness.

Whether classical or contemporary, apophatic discourses are about nothing, no definable theme. They have an affinity that consists in precisely nothing, nothing that can be objectively defined: it is rather performed in backing off from every definition and from every objective expression. Essence and truth are intimated only at this remove—not as themes, not as "themselves," but as their negation and undoing. This is not denial or denigration, which must identify something definite as their target, but rather "de-negation," a negation that unsays *itself*—in order to leave alone what cannot be said and therefore cannot be negated either. If it is "deconstruction," the result is not that truth, essence, or totality are unmasked as bankrupt notions and so finally stop importuning us and disappear, but rather that they appear *as* disappearing into the zone of the inexpressible. They vanish under the temporality of all that can be said and represented, leaving only traces that are *not* themselves. These values and idealities are not grasped, nor can they be grasped. They are glimpsed only in their "dis-appearance" into what cannot be said and thus cannot appear directly or as such and in itself, but only in this act of relinquishment—a letting go and turning away from everything that is something, as in Eckhart's *Abgeschiedenheit.*

This glimpsing and relinquishing of such "metaphysical" ideas as truth and totality can actually be the vindication of them, showing how they have really operated all along and showing them to inhabit, or at least haunt, the very limits of all significance. So far from being (simply) meaningless, they force the very possibility of meaning to its limits, illuminating the point where being meaningless and being meaningful first separate into mutual opposition. These ideal concepts may even be recuperated, yet not as secured and grounded, but as open, free, abyssal—and as such "restored" to their true dignity and potency. The spell they have cast historically becomes once again comprehensible. As modalities of the unsayable, truth and totality and other such idealities and virtualities become more credible, more undeniable, more potentially imposing than ever before.

In experience (or consciousness or "revelation"), there is always also something that withholds itself and withdraws from experience, never becoming fully conscious and revealed, something that remains necessarily unarticulated in terms of the experience or consciousness or revelation of which it is the enabling condition. We must let go of all these concepts, in order to let what they cannot express disclose itself. It does so in this very relinquishing of concepts and discourse, in the unsaying that lets what cannot be said show up and, to this extent, "be" nothing that can be said (even to be). The point is that this cannot be said or experienced, and yet in accepting this "miss" in discourse's aim at reality, this naught, and hearing and seeing it in our language as it releases its conceptual holds, we can nevertheless be genuinely receptive and attuned to what this language inevitably fumbles saying and lets escape.

This movement of backing off from any and all articulations is what all apophatic discourses share in common. There are, of course, extremely different motivations for such backtracking of speaking. But, in any case, it is the negative movement of language back upon itself, releasing its grip on itself and on all its definitions, that opens a glimpse into what this language cannot say. Something is revealed concerning a hollowness at the core of language and an open space within all our experiences and within all the "phenomena" that we as finite, discursive beings encounter. Can this revelation suggest some higher *plenitude,* where what we grasp verbally in the form only of deficiency, negation, and difference is whole, intact, and infinitely potent? We are aware of something that cannot be said, but so far as what *can* be said *in relation to* it goes, we seem to be left free. There can be no theory per se of what cannot be said, yet literary forms can nevertheless enable us somehow to "see" it, to give it a form, and this "seeing" (*theorein* in Greek) paradoxically takes place in words—going through and beyond them. Indeed, literary forms, given their "poetic function" (in Roman Jakobson's sense), are peculiarly apt to train attention upon language, where manifestation of the apophatic is taking place.

This anti-logic of discourse which negates and withdraws itself as discourse, or, in other words, apophatic (a)logic, can be seen as underlying and connecting all of its various expressions—mystical and anti-mystical, discursive and intuitive, abstract and concrete, verbal and nonverbal. The full riches of discourse are discovered to be accessible, paradoxically, only in its extreme reduction and virtual vanishing. Only what appears in this disappearing of discourse—albeit as mediated still by discourse—really counts. This is a relatedness revealed by dismantling all relations that can be articulated linguistically, a "relationless relation," to use Blanchot's phrase. It is a purely inarticulable, unsayable relatedness, a relatedness in unsayability. It is therefore a relatedness that is not just artifice, but is revealed rather by the removal of all artifices of language, in order to leave only the unsayable as a miraculously given order—or anarchy—of (canceled) relations.

What discourses on what cannot be said have in common, then, cannot be a common object. The unsayable is not an object at all. Any object *can* be said in some language. To be an object is to be within the purview of some framework for perception or conception. An object is correspondent to and commensurable with some system permitting cognition and articulation of experience. If there is, after all, in some sense, an experience of "what cannot be said," this could only be an experience with literally no content proper to itself. Yet experiences, all of them, have their limits. And although there can be no discrete experience of what cannot be said, it is experienced in *all* experiences precisely at—and as—their limit. To this extent, it occurs within and impinges upon every experience, but it is never experienced as such or properly as an object of experience. And yet this "experience" in the penumbra of experience of all that can be objectively focused nevertheless registers, with peculiar perspicacity, in a variety of discursive modes—those which we call apophatic. These modes have historically generated discourses that open a perspective onto something like a realm of the unsayable, which they present in negative, throwing it into relief. Like a photographic film, these discourses are the negatives made from an encounter with what is not itself objectively present.

Unlike photographic film, however, discourses of the unsayable are without correspondence to any positive object or image that just happens to be absent when the photograph is actually viewed. Apophatic discourse is the negative for which there is no positive that can—or ever could—be shown or presented. This realm can be seen *only* in negative, via the impressions of witnesses who confront the unsayable and react and render their own incommensurable testimonies to what is in itself incommunicable. What these witnesses all have in common is the experience of not being able to say what they are talking about because of the intrinsic unsayability of what is experienced—even though it may be experienced as the source and sum (or inversely as the negation and annihilation) of all that it *is* possible to experience.

Language in this case becomes not description but witness, a bearer not of information but of testimony.[62] What has been witnessed is inaccessible as such and can only be "vouched for." The witness has experienced something in a unique, inimitable, and unrepeatable manner. This "something," therefore, can never be represented as it is (or was) in itself, but only as witnessed to by the witness: it is, in practice, inextricable from the discourse that vouches for it and which is itself the only phenomenon that can make it manifest. Paradoxically, the language by which this witness is borne and delivered becomes, in its very inadequacy, absolutely decisive as the only objective thing pointing to what is utterly beyond verbalization. Only this language, which negates itself as language, enables the otherwise inaudible silence to resonate and so become perceptible. In this way, language is simultaneously devalorized and absolutized. Its supreme significance reposes in the silence that envelops and evacuates it.

Focusing on the apophatic moment, on what cannot be said, since this is objectless, does not prejudice content in any way. It valorizes the contemplation of the (contentless) whole prior to articulation and comprehension. The blind relating to and opening of oneself toward . . . what cannot be said is the most potent—though also objectively the most empty and elusive—moment in any experience. Prior to any articulation of content, there is an affirmative belief in something that is (as yet) no-thing but that nevertheless proleptically orients all possible knowing and eventual speaking. This as yet unbroken, unarticulated whole-nothing that gathers all attention to itself in silence is more potent than any supervening articulation that breaks the silence.

Although this potency is actually Nothing, that is, no *thing*, it absorbs and totalizes attention and orients us wholly to itself, and this is what makes a difference where otherwise none can be made. It makes all the difference *to us*—before any difference can actually be made *in it*, in any objective and stateable terms. It is something that makes a difference because it is *believed* to be all-important, even without itself manifesting any differences in which its importance would consist. To this extent, apophasis has a structure like that of faith: it cannot be validated except in a movement projecting and postulating its own validity. Although the moment before speech and articulation is objectless and completely indescribable, it dictates the concrete, determinate orientations of those who have trained their attention wholly upon what cannot be said, having been pointed in that direction by the limits, by the unsayable "beyond," of some particular form of experience.

This particular form of experience may well be conveyed bodily, in the flesh, for example, in the sacrament of the Eucharist. The infinite and incomprehensible gives itself mysteriously and impossibly to be touched and tasted. Thomas Aquinas was celebrating Mass in the chapel of St. Nicholas in Naples on December 6, 1273, when he fell into the speechless stupor of his last days that made all his writing seem to him but straw (or more exactly "chaff," *palea*). Christian tradition all along, based on the Incarnation of God in Jesus Christ, has particularly stressed the encounter with God in the flesh. This mind-shattering experience has been made the basis for a phenomenology of the flesh and for rereadings of the patristic and medieval corpus in a strongly apophatic key.[63] The apophatic can be apprehended equally in the profane body, on the condition that it is left mysterious—as more than we can ever know.[64]

There is, then, inevitably some measure of belief in approaches to apophasis. This is undoubtedly why apophasis has been mixed up with all manner of metaphysics and mysticisms, as well as with all sorts of theosophies and transcendental philosophies, in the course of its peregrinations through the history of thought and culture. This kinship naturally provokes skeptical reactions. The vacuousness of any determinate formulations need not necessarily be taken as revealing a plenitude of unqualified infinity. Not surprisingly, therefore, atheistic apophasis has often been ascribed to key apophatic thinkers, from Pseudo-Dionysius the Areopagite to Meister Eckhart. Yet this position all too easily falls into making rather too confident claims, if the denials are believed in without being also disbelieved. If denial becomes determinate, it then disbelieves some*thing* and has become just another form of belief in a finite, articulated discourse: it believes in what it says rather than in what it cannot say, and that changes everything. Language becomes an instrument for delivering a definite doctrine, a dogmatic denial, rather than remaining a medium open to mystery and the constant escape of what it cannot encompass. In this case, it becomes easy, too easy, to reject a putatively open mystery like "what cannot be said" as mere mystification.[65]

In opposition to the inexhaustible fascination with the mystery of language in apophatic tradition, there is indeed a more skeptical attitude toward the emptiness and inaptitude of language that devolves from the Sophists. Gorgias comes to the conclusion that nothing exists, and that even if something did exist it would be incomprehensible, and that if it were comprehensible it would have to be incommunicable. It is his sense of the absolute disjunction between language and reality that leads him to these contentions: "If anything is comprehensible, it is incommunicable . . . . that with which we communicate is speech, and speech is not the same thing as the things that exist, the perceptibles; so that we communicate not the things which exist, but only speech."[66] This specifically linguistic motive for skepticism easily induces to a crude nihilism after the motto: there is no God, no essence, no origin, nothing; it is all only language. I do not mean to deny all insight even to this position. In some contexts, it could be the right thing to say.[67] But I remain nevertheless spellbound by all that cannot be said. So do all genuinely apophatic thinkers—not least Derrida—down through the ages. The subtler and more consistent skeptical attitudes toward language in the apophatic tradition cannot ultimately believe what they themselves *say*.

Thus language itself remains a mystery, and so does everything else in its train—a mystery of what cannot be said. Language shows itself, indeed, as the gateway to the mystery of the unsayable beyond language. Rather than knowing that all is nothing because it is nothing but language, apophatic thinking holds that, since all we know is only language, we know nothing about what really is or is not—about the enigma beyond our language that language itself in its mysterious, suggestive evasiveness provocatively points toward. The apophatic sage is skeptical about all that is known—all that is accessible to language—in order to be fascinated by the mystery that language does not deliver and cannot master. In this way, when apophatic writers deprecate language, they have already presupposed its potency to gesture toward what it is insufficient to articulate but nevertheless indicates as lying beyond itself.

To this extent, the unsayable becomes manifest only in the collapse and reversal of all our saying and of the intricate order that it establishes. It is there just below the surface of the whole, linguistically leveraged world and all of its artificially created coherences. Unsayability thereby negates and sublates this verbal order of totality and disclosure of truth—not into the completed Whole, which for Hegel is the truth, but into the limitless Nothing (no thing) of what cannot be said. All the potencies and projections of language, which include the entire knowable universe, are resituated and redeployed as more intimately and originarily invested in the unsayable, albeit in a way that cannot be rationally grasped or said. All the effects in language of truth, order, origin, totality, and the rest that we *can* articulate appear as mere glimpses of these same "values" that in their own nature remain unsayable, undelimited. This is perhaps some kind of Platonism again, but inverted and subverted—that is, with the difference that it is the breakdown and relinquishing of form and order in this world, our linguistically articulated world, that testifies to an ideal world with its own form and order, which remains unfathomable to us. Precisely the rupture of every express form of order for the world makes a (to us) formless, expressionless instance of these ideals compelling. For the form and order are there to be perceived: they are miraculously given—yet always only in their disappearance, and thus as deformed and distraught, as soon as we attempt to define them and fix their identity. Mapping the infinite onto finite coordinates distorts it beyond recognition—at least for finite vision.

Only in revealing its own nullity as discourse does discourse indirectly reveal, without distorting it, something that is not just discourse, and in fact this self-revelation of discourse itself as nil becomes, in a way, indeed the only way possible, the revelation of All. It is by discourse undoing its own identity that all that is can emerge from the straits of identity that has made it disappear into an artificial formalization occluding all that really and unreally—virtually and conjecturally—*is*. In this way, everything is set free from the imprisoning grid of language. In apophatic unsaying, with the admission of the radical inadequacy of all our language vis-à-vis the real, the articulated system of the universe collapses. All vanishes into Nothing—in order to reemerge liberated from the conceptually articulated world that reduces it to an empty formal structure. In terms of language, it is nothing, nothing that can be said, but freed thus to be nothing sayable, all is for the first time open to *all* its possibilities.

In relation to . . . what cannot be said, all things are deliriously open and infinite. They are allowed to open themselves at last to being freely explored without conceptual limit, without being verbally curbed, in a sort of Bataillesque bacchanal. Of course, this is not an achieved reality or any steady state. It is rather a dynamic relation induced by the release from conceptual constraints, in which other possibilities, undelimitable possibilities, come to light in concrete ways *un*determined by the concepts that are being relinquished. Language accordingly unsays itself in proving unable to say what it *would* say. In this unsaying of language, not in what it says but in what it *is* when it unsays itself, the "reality" that refuses and eludes language, after all, appears, or rather is richly witnessed. This is the ultra-linguistic experience of language as world that is variously called "mystical" (Wittgenstein), "magical" (Benjamin), and "miraculous" (Rosenzweig).

Every experience is necessarily limited by some horizon. Yet its finitude, by releasing its grip on itself and even thereby breaking itself open, can open into the infinite, which is nothing (nothing definable or finite, nothing sayable). Language can enact just this opening by breaking apart in itself and can thereby catalyze an opening of experience to the openness at its core and origin. It does this when it bursts asunder the artifices of finitude and escapes confinement by linguistic constructions. So-called postmodern experiences of language, as reflected in oeuvres such as those of Blanchot or Barthes or of other literary thinkers, have highlighted the moment of dissolution and even stressed the finality of dispersion of sense without return.[68] Yet, at the same time, opportunities arise for envisioning this disintegration as the realization of what has long been intuited by the more synthetic, visionary versions of apophatic thinking, in which the devastation and destitution of language clears the way for a true relatedness of all with all. This dissolution and disappearance of language has long been envisioned by mystics as coinciding with the invasion of language by God.[69] God as silence, after His return to Namelessness, is also the culminating vision of Rosenzweig's *Star of Redemption* (secs. 401–6). Such experience has been probed with particular acuteness in literary texts.

With or without "God," the break-down of language opens up a sphere of higher life and awareness, a "rising tide of divine feeling" ("steigenden Flut göttlichen Gefühles"), as Hugo von Hofmannsthal writes in his "Letter of Lord Chandos."[70] When the fictional Lord Chandos loses the ability to simplify things in their raw incomprehensibility through words and through their reduction to the concept, he experiences terror but also exaltation. He experiences a loss of individuation but also a sense of union with all. He experiences his being as flowing out into all others and all existence as one great Unity ("das ganze Dasein als eine große Einheit"), so that "every creature was the key to the others" ("jede Kreatur ein Schlüssel der andern," p. 464), and yet this results in a total loss of coherence in thought and speech. Chandos experiences aphasia and an incapacity especially for abstraction, but also for any judgment whatever. When the enchantment ("Bezauberung") ends, he can say nothing about it ("so weiß ich nichts darüber auszusagen," p. 469). The moments of incomprehensible fullness and of "an unnamed and blessed feeling" ("unbennantes seliges Gefühl") deflate, yielding to emptiness and depression.

> [It is as if] . . . we could enter into a new, intuitive relationship with all existence, if we were to begin to think with the heart. If, however, this extraordinary enchantment falls away from me, then I am

able to say nothing about it; I could then no more put into a reasonable discourse in what this harmony that wove me together with the whole world consisted and how it made itself to be felt by me than I could describe in detail the inner movements of my intestines or the coagulation of my blood. (pp. 469–70)

There is here much palpable romanticization of the apophatic experience of "mute being," "an unnameable Something" ("ein unnennbares Etwas"), that can be the "source of that mysterious, wordless, boundless rapture [Entzückens]" (pp. 470–71). Nevertheless, this description turns idealization toward materialization in the magma of thinking that melts down articulated speech. Thinking is discovered as a "material that is more immediate, more fluid and glowing than words" ("Material, das unmittelbarer, flüssiger, glühender ist als Worte," p. 471). This thinking, unbridled by language, is material and concrete and leads, therefore, not to bottomless emptiness but to the "deepest seat of peace" ("tiefsten Schoß des Friedens," p. 471). Unconstrued sensuous experience comes forward as the raw material of life that furnishes a better basis than does pure intellectual abstraction for apophasis or for training attention on what cannot be said. This makes Hofmannsthal modern, materialist, and anti-idealist in his apophatic creed, although he is still presumably a far cry from the darker modernist accents pronounced by Kafka and Beckett.

The breaking-down and dissolving of language, as it has been pursued poetically and ingeniously displayed by Celan and Jabès—but also by Emily Dickinson, Rainer Maria Rilke, and Wallace Stevens—is in like fashion an allegory (and a realization) of a breaking-down and crumbling away to the nothing-stable-or-definable that characterizes the temporal world, our "reality," or whatever it is that things in time and space are supposed to be. What is revealed is that this order of finite elements is not self-sustaining or grounded in itself. That does not at once make some ungraspable sustaining Ground miraculously appear, but it does open the horizon of the world that is known and articulated to a beyond, to what may be conceived of indifferently as a hidden ground or an abyss—as in Eckhart's *grunt*. The fact that there is anything at all, even in the vanishing of all finite forms, that we can say raises the question of why and wherefore. Whatever is or is not beyond this appearing of disappearing that characterizes our temporal reality is nothing that can be said. For it is experienced precisely in the experience of not being able to say it. This experience binds together classics of negative theology and contemporary apophatic writers in the belief that Nothing is pregnant with Everything—albeit a new, wild everything set free from the nets and webs of language and so no longer corralled by Logos.

Once the unsayable has been encountered, what cannot be said infiltrates and infects simply everything—everything in the simplicity of its *not* being said or sayable, its *not* being "arti-culated" or "arti-culable." And when all that *is* said comes to be considered as a failed attempt to say what cannot be said, something extraordinary happens. The world as it is known and said to be suddenly disappears. All that has been said to be *is* not really at all—except inasmuch as it reveals something else entirely. It is in apophatic language—language which unsays itself and abnegates its own identity and so annihilates itself—that this exposure of the ineluctable "othering" of the world by language happens. It is not just that the language backs off from something, some *thing* too great for its powers. It is language's own self-annihilation that reveals . . . what cannot be said. In this self-destructive movement of language, radical apophasis becomes the full revelation of our whole (un)reality as . . . what cannot be said—which is what mystics were (not) saying about "Reality" all along. This is the removal of the veil of illusion that our language casts over absolutely everything we know and experience. Put somewhat more dramatically, the broken *Logos* that has been crucified and died rends the temple curtain (Matthew 27:51), which is the linguistically segmented, socially ritualized world that we ordinarily see and say, in order to expose the radically other reality of what cannot be said, of what is variously figured as uncanny or demonic or "divine."

The Christian religion identifies God with the Word in Jesus Christ. Jesus alone is the complete and final revelation of God. This doctrine makes a strong statement in support of total disclosure in the Word. Yet viewed especially in the light of negative theology, the divine transcendence must be safeguarded against all idolatrous appropriations.[71] Christ, in the annihilation of death, discloses God fundamentally as love that is beyond all knowing and representation, beyond disclosure and articulation, beyond saying of any logical, discursive type. Beyond all that human discourse can encompass, this Inexpressibility is what Jesus reveals of God.

The total disclosure proclaimed in Christ, the identity of God with Jesus, does not constitute man alone as ultimate reality, as a certain Hegelian humanism developed further by Feuerbach would have us believe. It reveals conceptualizable man in his *un*reality and as *re*-veiling an *other* reality that cannot be fully revealed or expressed in human form.

Such is the relation of the Incarnate Word to the divine Word as second person of the Trinity, the Word that was with God and that was God (John 1:1) from all eternity. The revelation of Christ as "the image of the invisible God" (Colossians 1:15) leaves this mystery of the divine life within the Godhead intact. The destruction of the Word within the world gestures toward an unworldly reality or ideality in which the Word would be whole and total. The transcendent reality or ideality of the Word is revealed only as unrevealed and unrevealable by human words—except in and through the total destruction of the Incarnate Word: the Crucifixion and death of Jesus, the Word, is the dark background and bedrock of the glorious mystery of the resurrected Christ. His annihilation as an historical man is the crux of the story issuing in the message in which this Word is declared infinite and alive, as preached in the words of the Church. The Logos becomes the Word of the Cross (*Logos staurou*, in the language of 1 Corinthians 1:17–31). This is equally the Cross—or even the crossing out—of the Word as we can know and are able to say it.[72]

Even the naked disclosure in the world of Christ the Word as an infant is nothing that words can comprehend. Its first, unmediated presence (as opposed to later enactments in preaching) inspires rather silent worship—emblematically in the adoration of the Magi at the Epiphany (Matthew 2:11). The final disclosure of the Word, naked and nailed to the Cross and then obliterated in the silence of the tomb, consummates this apophatic discourse of the incarnate and ultimately martyred Word. The same discourse continues thereafter as silent testimony in the Eucharist, in the breaking of bread, the Word made flesh. As broken and disseminated, the Word becomes salvific in the eucharistic community in which love silently discourses through charitable *action*.[73]

The visible, finite, corporeal forms that are obliterated in the sacrifice of death make way for the negative manifestation of a glorified Christ who is not, however, visible as a finite object. Even the church as the visible body of Christ is *in*visible as his mystical body. Even as resurrected in the community of the church, in the words of preaching and in sacramental rites and the liturgy, the Word itself as such remains shrouded in mystery.[74] All these discursive and ceremonial forms serve to manifest an unspeakable Word. In all these ways, Christian doctrine epitomizes the apophatic predicament of the word. In this perspective, there is no world without the Word, and indeed (as Hegel insists) "God in Christ was reconciling the world to himself" (2 Corinthians 5:19), and yet the word is made strange and the world is made unrecognizably other by this conjunction, which surpasses understanding.[75]

iv

The "other world" that becomes somehow discernible through sensitivity to the apophatic dimension cannot be objectified. It is discernible only in something uncanny about this one, the supposedly "normal," ordinary world, which is revealed as not really itself. This world shows up as back to back with, and as inseparable and even indiscernible from, an *other,* non-manifest world. This other world is called a "world" only because it concerns *this* world, our world, as a whole, which is to say, as a world, and not because it can itself be delimited as a whole, discrete sphere, such as the term "world" generally implies. It might be called "pleroma," following the metaphysical imagination of the Gnostics. This locution has the advantage of suggesting that the world we ordinarily grasp and encompass with our language is lacking in fullness, that it is defective and defined by insufficiency and lack. Accordingly, the Gnostics call it the "kenoma." In any case, I wish to maintain that the *pleroma* is "world" only analogically and in relation to our world. As we move through our world, defined as it is by discourse and disclosed, in fact, as coextensive with our language, the uncanny, irreducible alterity of this plenitude—its remaining recalcitrant to our saying and proving itself rather to be what cannot be said—projects this double of our world that sometimes gives rise to talk of an other world. What remains stubbornly other to all our articulations of our world opens into the dimension of being itself a "world," a realm of at least virtual experience.[76] Apophasis thus opens up a "world" lying on the outside or the underside of the world as we know it. Apophasis entails, then, after all, an indirect yet ineluctable sort of referential employment of language—even though that to which it points or "refers" cannot be said or at least cannot be objectively articulated.

Language produces all sorts of worlds of intelligibility, but if all discourses are fundamentally missing the really real that they project and aim at, this miss itself becomes the witness to the radically unsayable. It is the crisis of language—its proving *in toto* to be unveridical in its relation to the reality it was supposed to represent more or less truly—that forces us to face the unsayable. Reality itself is unsayable. Conversely, what we *say*—whatever we *can* say—*is* not: in real terms, it can only serve to open us to the unsayable reality beyond it. I will not say that this, the unsayable, is the reality that truly is, since I cannot say anything about it at all. But this other to saying is the attracting pole that we are inexorably related to through all the checks and arrests to our saying that language itself is constantly bumping into and stumbling upon.

Seeing the intrinsic openness in everything to something radically other is perhaps analogous (we might say, indiscernibly close) to a metaphysical vision that sees the Transcendent behind all manifest phenomena. In this perspective, beings are not (only) themselves. Their deeper being is other than they. In speculative thinking, from Eckhart to Heidegger, it is called "Being"—and there is no saying what that is. "Being" is thereby disqualified as an analytic concept and becomes a cipher for . . . what cannot be said. The effort in apophatic discourses to illuminate some invisible ground, or rather background, and to elucidate its silent dictates, or rather its effects, may seem to resemble projects of transcendental critique—except that here no transcendental principles are being articulated. Critical vocabularies are employed here only in order that the "experience" inspiring them may be elicited.

Is this, then, an effort to recuperate holistic thinking and an exaltation of transcendent knowledge? In surpassing the sharp oppositions between transcendence and immanence, between knowing and unknowing, and in bringing out the mutual participation of these determinations in each other, it is not a regression to systems that have long ago died but an attempt to interpret what made them live. The total openness to knowing in question here is most emphatically not a knowing that is exclusive of unknowing. On the contrary, the whole point is to see every knowing as based upon—and as a specific determination of—an all-pervasive un-knowing. Only as unknowing in the face of . . . what cannot be said can any sort of partial, provisional knowing be articulated. There is an element of belief here, but not in a system. It is belief precisely in what no system can catch or get its meshes around—even though a system may sugges-tively point it up by exposing its unsurpassable limits. Hence, again, we recognize the importance of Hegel as the quintessential systematizer in this exposition of the unsayable as it has been progressively discovered in modern thought. Indeed, Rosenzweig, in his critique of German idealism, still aspires to a sort of system in order to peer into the wordless world beyond.[77]

This belief beyond any system—belief that cannot say *what* it believes in—witnesses to the sense of a reality (or irreality) resistant to conceptu-alization, a "reality" that can be experienced only in a negative dialectic—to the extent that it can be experienced or dialecticized at all. Its description can be only negative and therefore is not properly a description. But this thinking of what cannot be said does give an account of the synthetic strivings that have driven systematic philosophy throughout history as consisting potentially in more than just vanity and delusion. There is some strange manner in which everything has to do with everything else. This is the uncanny connectedness of things that engenders wonder, philosophical stupor—ταῦμαζεῖν, as Aristotle baptized it in his *Metaphys-ics* (982b12), following Plato's sense that such "amazement" is the ἀρχὴ or principle of philosophy, and not just its point of departure (*Epinomis* 983a–c). Perhaps an even deeper sense of wonder was expressed by the pre-Socratic thinkers, who were still directly in touch with what rational statements can never adequately grasp. Their unaccountable One-All, ἕν-πάντα, as it was contradictorily called by Heraclitus, has never ceased to elicit every sort of rational explanation and need not be ignored simply because all our verbalizations ineluctably transmogrify it into what it is not. Connectedness that is *said* can perhaps apprehend only the coming apart, the disconnecting, the *dés-astre* of things.[78] But what comes undone here cannot but be *imagined* as connectedness so subtle and intricate in its order and wholeness as to be beyond our grasp and saying.[79] Its own in-trinsic articulation is always in advance of ours, supervening upon our intelligible ordering as a mere artifice in relation to which it remains a mystery in its inexhaustible reality, or at least "realism."

This sort of unsoundable content of experience, considered apophatically, entails not an experience of the whole, as if this could be an object of cognition, nor of any object whatever, but rather an experience of an unconceptualizable connectedness of things, a connectedness ultimately to what is not grasped or conceived, and thus an experience of openness to the unknown and unobjectifiable. It involves being in touch with an undelimited whole of what cannot be said or known. It is a negative experience of not knowing, and as such it is a relation to what cannot be circumscribed or delimited. This unknowing extends potentially without limit to the whole of reality. It is the negative experience of unknowing and unsaying into which truth and totality collapse—and by which all circumscribed experience of truth and totality is encompassed. Truth and totality in this manner are involved in experience that furnishes no knowledge but can, as an experience of unknowing, genuinely open to what has been pursued as truth and totality throughout the ages. This pursuit takes place in various traditional forms of philosophical as well as of theosophical intelligence, which, if too narrowly construed as forms strictly of knowing (to the exclusion of unknowing), vitiate the attempt and deform the very ideals they are pursuing.

Apophatic unknowing leaves intact these ideals of truth and totality and relates to them as infinite and out of reach and yet as impinging on our finite sphere of experience, marking and giving relief to its finiteness and relativity. Without recognition of this unsayable order transcending our knowledge, the sphere of knowledge will close in upon itself and render itself absolute and, consequently, deny and distort its contingent character. In this peculiar way, truth and wholeness are touched in experience precisely in and *as* their own negation.

The unsayable is not an object; therefore, any expression for it can be no more than the indication of an openness, an inconclusiveness, an infinity immanent in all our experience and operative in all our discourse. It is our way of gesturing toward something other than us and our experience right in the midst of it, toward a sort of crack or rift in this experience. Only in this rupture can experience intimate something besides or beyond itself that would be simple or complete, unbroken, whole, blessed. It is the incompleteness of our existence that makes such conceptions pertinent, compelling, and even necessary—as expressions of the inexpressible, the ungraspable source of our open activity of signifying. It is not the object signified in a completed representation but rather the structural incompleteness and the intrinsic openness of the representing itself, as executed by a finite, mortal being, that inform the significance of such expressions. Also, whatever supports this being and representing, so as to enable them to be something rather than nothing, informs the expressivity beyond determinable significance of such expressions.

There is always something "in-finite" about human experience. Certainly its potential for meaning is inexhaustible. But this infinity cannot be positively presented. We express it as what cannot be *said* because our mode of apprehending infinity is, for all we can know and say, linguistic. Indeed, can anything at all *be* infinite without language? Nothing simply *is* infinite, in any sense we can understand, but our saying—with its constitutive negating—makes it so. This is already the case in the very word "*in*finite" by which we negate the finite. We call that which we experience in language, at its limit, unsayable. Still, this "Unsayable" is not any discrete object of experience. It expresses rather the open, incomplete mode of our experiencing itself. Thus this openness, this infinity, is not treated as an attribute of any nameable object, not even of "human experience." In the discourses of the unsayable, the unsayable itself is the space—the linguistic and even ultra-linguistic region—in which anything can emerge as an object. This space of emergence, which remains open to the uncanny and impossible, shadows the world in which we live.

Still, what is in question is not itself in essence linguistic, nor even essentially experience. It *is* at all only in the undoing of all such qualifications. It emerges only as what they conceal, as what the emergence of discrete contents of experience and articulated objects of discourse leaves *un*revealed. Language is, nonetheless, privileged because the movement of backing off from definition is, after all, linguistic. Language articulates this loss or losing that operates paradoxically as an articulation of the inarticulable. It is only in the fault lines in what *is* said that what is neither said nor sayable registers at all. Not the unsayable "itself," then, but its first and perhaps its only witness, is linguistic.

Paradoxically, it is only through language that what is radically other to language can be evoked. To do so, language must be used (at least initially) against its ordinary semantic and logical functions of meaning and referring. Language as representation is indeed dismantled by apophasis. But there are other communicative functions, such as apostrophe, prayer, supplication, and projective imagination, often in the optative mood, that language can assume. It is in these functions that even silence can become superlatively significant. As *situated* in communication and discourse, silence has always different and concrete significance. The silences behind discourse, if attended to, tend to contradict, collapse, riddle, ridicule, and diffuse the pretensions of words. Words' reductiveness is overcome by the breaking through of silence.

Contemporary writers have made us more sensitive to apophasis as the key to discursivity and help us see with new clarity its importance in traditional discourses. The predicament of language as lacking any ability to communicate straight and unambiguously in a temporal world is hilariously dramatized, to the point of eliciting tears, in plays such as *Waiting for Godot* and *Endgame*. The absurdity or, better, inanity of the said reaches such intensity as to "say" purely and lucidly what is not nor ever could be said. Beckett's plays constantly use silence to undo their speech, even while their declared purpose—namely, to end, to finish—fails, as in this "speech" by Hamlet's comic namesake, which drips like a leaky faucet and hints that the nature of narrative is to be water on the brain, giving a simulacrum of purposiveness to the definitionless.

HAMM:
        One! silence!
        (*Pause.*)
        Where was I?
        (*Pause. Gloomily.*)
        It's finished, we're finished.
        (*Pause.*)
        Nearly finished.
        (*Pause.*)
        There'll be no more speech.
        (*Pause.*)
        Something dripping in my head, ever since the
           fontanelles.
        (*Stifled hilarity of Nagg.*)
        Splash, splash, always on the same spot.
        (*Pause.*)

A little vein.
(*Pause.*)
A little artery.
(*Pause. More animated.*)
Enough of that, it's story time, where was I?
(*Pause. Narrative tone.*)[80]

Beckett orchestrates his texts on the basis of precisely timed pauses, so that any statement that is made need only be followed by an insinuating silence in order to instigate its own nullification and crumble to next to nothing. Hence his language can aptly be called a "language of cancellation."[81] Waiting for Godot is the emblem of expecting . . . we know not what, since whoever he is he *will* come, that is, he said he would come, or at least we were given to think so, to think that he would come "here," which might just as well mean *there*, under that tree, or was it *that* one, or perhaps it was rather a bush? We seek reassurance from language, from the stories it tells us, but words always essentially cancel themselves out because their meaning ultimately posits some absolute, unambiguous presence which can never be concretely given in the medium of language. It is the nature of words as signs to indicate something absent from themselves, something they are not. Conversely, what actually *is* contradicts words and all that they can say—its *being* is always more or less than what can be signified. Beckett ingeniously exposes the shifts and denials to which this predicament puts human beings in their pathetic psychological weakness and vulnerability. Whatever is said, in its confident verbal clarity, turns out to be menaced by the uncertainties and ambiguities of what concretely, messily is.

However, while every fixed meaning laughably collapses in the shifting time of life and drama, this time is itself nothing if not a linguistic production. As such, it too must undergo negation, and this engenders openness to permanence and eternity—beyond all we can determinately know—as what cannot be said. Indeed, traditional interpretations of religion and philosophy are full of just such imagery of the eternal. Such imagery, then, is hardly nonsensical, or at least it is not unmotivated, in relation to what cannot be said. Though such words do not *say* what they intend, they make a space for what is other to this reality of ours that we experience as really there and yet as vanishing as soon as we try to articulate it. If we believe that what we can articulate of the flux that we experience is not necessarily all there is, or that its being precariously here now testifies to something more, something beyond our knowledge, then we believe that we are experiencing something not just temporal and not just finite because not exhaustively contained within these conceptual schemes.

Discourse, with its feigned and literally "fictive" truths, is ever and again arrested by apophasis as a silence witnessing to a truth (or untruth, or a/truth) that is covered over by words. Harold Pinter remarked that "speech is a constant stratagem to cover nakedness."[82] In this optic, what comes across most powerfully whenever we speak may be something altogether other than what we say. The words, because of their saying *some*thing, can be seen to be an attempt to dissimulate the nothing (the no *thing*) that is the very nakedness of our being—what we simply, silently are—as much as an attempt to reveal anything. What is really there to be seen in speech, the naked truth, may be precisely what speech covers up. The anxiousness to dissemble it suggests that this nakedness is perhaps a neediness whose silent peal ("Geläut der Stille," in Heidegger's parlance) speech aims to stifle.

Playwrights such as Beckett or Pinter (for example, in *The Dumb Waiter*) or Nathalie Sarraute (in her *Silence*) skillfully show this and so expose us. They often expose the arbitrariness of *what* we have said, whether *this* or *that*—it hardly matters. *That* we are speaking in the first place says it all, beyond all our intentions. And it is perhaps not even so much that we are speaking as that we are trying to speak and cannot abide simply being there, "on stage," so to speak. We must incessantly "arti-culate" ourselves and cannot just let ourselves be. Whatever we say, we are defining ourselves thereby and claiming to be *some*thing, which cannot but be a dissimulation with regard to all the rest of us that it leaves out. The fact that we are trying to speak, trying to articulate ourselves at all, so as not to simply be there, nakedly, dumbly, wholly exposed, is subtly unveiled as forced and evasive and even mendacious at its core. This is an exposing of the unspeakable that we *are* beyond any content of meaning that we utter or consciously convey, whether as covering over or as communicating ourselves. The utter deficiency, not specifically of what we say but of all that we possibly could say, is pointed up by these dialogues or monologues, which are senseless—except inasmuch as they expose a radical senselessness at the root of speaking per se or, more precisely, of the being who speaks. They disclose how whatever this being speaks is but an avoidance of the naked truth, the whole truth—beyond any truth or lie that it can say about itself.

Speaking, then, comes across as a denial of an unspeakable depth or recess into which all that is said slips, as into an abyss. The *what* that is said is but a vehicle for an undefined and indefinable, unspeakable but superlatively, pathetically significant . . . we cannot say what. We are confronted with this unspeakable again and again in the drama of human existence, and we are driven to all manner of shifts and evasions with words in our more or less transparent attempts to master it. It reaches us precisely at the moment when we perceive what cannot be said as the real and vital meaning or meaninglessness of all that actually *is* said.

Such insight into the apophatic way can be approached from out of many different types of experience and disciplinary matrices. Yet it is always unique and incomparable insight. And it is always, therefore, incommunicable. Nevertheless, it seems to be in some sense one and the same—or at least not discernibly different. Its many different instances in the end turn out to be indistinguishable, since each erases all specific content. The circumstances of the approach to it are infinitely variable and concrete, but the negation of all articulable content is shared in common. Wittgenstein observed that all those who have been "enlightened" have nothing to say about it (*Tractatus* 6.521). My reflection in this essay has been an attempt to intimate why not. But my meditation also participates in the effort to somehow achieve this level of insight beyond words. We must use words and use them up—so as to remain with what is left over. For then (and only then) to be without words is—at some level beyond saying—to be open to all in all, to truth in its inconceivable . . . shall we *not* say wholeness? We do—at least some of us, at least in our "moments"— have experience of "truth," even of truth that somehow touches on what is complete and total, though of course any *verbal* formulation would not be the whole truth, nor perhaps even be true at all. This experience comes always in a reversal and release of discourse, in the silence before and after, or right in the midst, of discourse—in what discourse, for all its struggling, does not and cannot say.

If we care about "truth," which we may take, with Hegel, as entailing a coincidence of the real and the ideal, then we will want to look behind the words and interpret what they do not and cannot say. Interpreting the words and what they mean enables us to reconstruct a project and a purpose for which they are being used. But discourses do not always—or perhaps ever—say what their deepest meaning and motivations are. To fathom this "truth" we have to break with interpreting just the words, and yet, paradoxically, only the words are there to guide us . . . beyond themselves.

Sensitivity to the apophatic means learning to interpret our own language somewhat more cannily in its inescapable relation to what it cannot say. This relation, though invisible and purely negative, determines our bearings toward all that we can and do say. In its sheer negativity, it is only a vanishing, a trace, but many thinkers and writers of the most diverse provenances have dedicated themselves to tracing it in its vanishings, and their discourses reflect upon one another in provocative ways. Perhaps we can learn to read them better by reading them together. That is why I have attempted to treat them as constituting a loosely coherent discourse manifest in variegated forms across many centuries—a perennial philosophy of the unsayable.[83]

If we ask *what* is missed and not comprehended in this vanishing trace, there are simply no limits to it. The *relation* to it is unrestricted and is therefore a relation to the unrealized and uncircumscribable as a whole. That is what makes this experience so incomparably compelling. It is a glancing, uncomprehending experience of reality as a whole and in its ground—or *as if* as a whole and in its ground, even without positing that reality unequivocally is a whole or has a ground. The ground of all might as well be *un*grasped metaphorically as a seed, as Malevich suggests: "The miracle of nature is that it all is contained in a small seed, and yet this 'all' cannot be embraced. Man holding a seed, holds the universe and yet cannot examine it."[84] The effects of wholeness and groundedness are experienced in the perception that things, after all, connect together or are spawned and sprout in some manner as related to one another—however far the pattern and principle of it may be from our comprehension. This experience takes place precisely in the openness that ensues upon the failure of every attempt at articulation, in the releasing of the words by which we have stalked reality—in other words, in apophasis.

THE WRITING OF SILENCE IN THE POST-HOLOCAUST POETRY OF EDMOND JABÈS AND PAUL CELAN

i

Postmodern writers and artists of all sorts have developed radical new poetics based on the hidden resources of silence. Poets have focused on silences become audible in the tearing of language and the rending of sense.
To a significant degree, this is a rediscovery of the oftentimes repressed resources in Western tradition of apophatic discourse, discourse on what
cannot be said. "Apophasis" is the Greek word for "negation," and it is
used here, as it has been since ancient times, initially in Neoplatonic am-
biences, specifically to designate the negation, and especially the self-
negation, of discourse. Jewish writers have been particularly important in
this revival, partly because the biblical interdiction on representations of
the divine, denounced as idolatrous ("graven images"), gave Jewish tradition a peculiar attunement to the limits of representation and an especially acute sensibility for the Unrepresentable. Most conspicuously, the
Holocaust experience has become recognized as a cultural code for the unspeakable par excellence.[1]

Edmond Jabès and Paul Celan emerged almost contemporaneously out of widely divergent cultural backgrounds in Egypt and Romania, respectively; nevertheless, they share these coordinates in common. Writing as post-Holocaust Jews, each in a different way lends language to silence in order to give voice to the unspeakable. Moreover, each makes the typically Jewish predicament of ineradicable separateness from other peoples, as well as from a transcendent, wholly other God, into something more universal: it becomes a predicament of life (or oftentimes death) in language as the state of being severed from an ultimate significance.[2] Originating in regions of linguistic diaspora with regard to their respective French and German tongues, moreover, both authors are exceptionally qualified to express the experience of exile as the archetypal condition not only of the Jew but of the postmodern writer in general: this is the condition simply of the human being in language, to the extent that language per se is a signifier forever severed from its signified.

Exemplary, in this regard, of a wide range of contemporary poets, Celan and Jabès fundamentally are writing about what cannot be said. Their respective poetic rhetorics are most comprehensible when placed within the tradition of apophatic discourse. This sort of discourse is best known in its theological expressions, namely, in the millenary discourse of negative theology that originates with Plotinus. It was, of course, anticipated by Plato, not to mention Pythagoreanism, Orphism, and mystery cults, all of which in various ways acknowledge the inexpressibility in language of some kind of divine transcendence. Initiates typically swore vows of silence at least partly in recognition of the futility of any attempt in language to adequately express the transcendent perfection and splendor of the supreme deity. In certain later developments of negative theology, the renunciation of all means of expression demonstrates an incipient skepticism with regard to official, orthodox discourses and a retreat to the inner, silent dimension of mystic experience.

Mysticism, with its powerfully apophatic thrust, in many instances is best understood as a secularizing reinterpretation of supposedly objective categories of official religion in terms of individual experience and existence. This is manifestly the case for Gnostic and hermetic mysticisms that crop up in the crises for rational philosophy and its Logos in the Hellenistic age.[3] In later ages, alongside and interpenetrating these mysticisms, are other, aesthetic sorts of apophatic responses to the foundering of rational discourse. These include certain kinds of poetry and other art forms, as becomes especially evident in more modern times, for example, in the Baroque period, as well as in various versions of Romanticism that reach out by rhetorics of silence and excess toward what lies beyond the furthest limits of description.

Our contemporary world again has been visited by a radical crisis of confidence in language and a concomitant resurgence of interest in apophatic modes of discourse. We have been ardently searching for alternatives to strictly rational speaking and logical expression, since the Logos in crucial ways has proved impotent to disclose our reality and to truly express things as we experience them. In postmodern apophasis, it is often not the divine that proves to be out of reach of language in its failure to attain reality so much as simply the singularity and otherness of the other person. Nevertheless, singularity and otherness have been intertwined with divinity throughout apophatic tradition, and this nexus still obtains in numerous and diverse contemporary authors.

Philosophers such as Jacques Derrida and Emmanuel Levinas, as well as writers like Maurice Blanchot and Samuel Beckett, along with Celan and Jabès, are consciously working in an apophatic vein that is still replete with theological underpinnings. Sometimes the tendency toward negative theology in these writers turns into an impulse to negate theology *simpliciter* and to escape from it altogether. However, whether and to what extent apophatic modes of discourse can be made independent of theology is controversial.[4] It may be that any negation of theology is still beholden to theology. Even if in a negative mode, atheism is still, in some sense, a theism. Jabès expresses such a suspicion, for example, in writing, "You deny God because your love for him removed him from your view—as the light hides from us the light."[5]

Theology may be an inevitable paradigm for any discourse in Western culture that envisages some sort of generally valid truth or universally communicable meaning or verifiable disclosure. Derrida, for one, held that "the sign and divinity have the same place and the same time of birth. The age of the sign is essentially theological."[6] Implicitly theological concepts, such as truth and meaning, presuppose some kind of total presence, as if in or to an infinite, divine mind. The theological postulates of infinity and totality, as in the presence of a divine Mind, may belong to the logical structure of language in its most elementary functions, such as naming and saying. This is so at least to the extent that these operations are conceived of as giving access ideally to the essences of the things. These inevitably theological ideas need not be positively asserted as founding our linguistic acts of knowing or as guaranteeing the success of our communicative transactions. They are operative simply as rendering intelligible the inevitable frustrations and misfirings of these acts and attempts in their approximations to what they fail to convey fully or to unconditionally verify.

Whether it names God or not, language necessarily withdraws from whatever it posits or intends as its would-be object: language *is* not what it means. The movement of transcending all linguistically defined sense or meaning is what characterizes apophasis, and whether this is understood to be a recoiling before the divine or simply before the other person or even just an unspeakable thing or event, it intimates an inviolable otherness such as has been approached from time immemorial, exemplarily through discourse that acts recursively to erase itself as discourse.

This characteristically apophatic movement and gesture of withdrawal is given distinctive definition by writers—especially Jewish writers—attempting to come to terms with the unspeakable horror of the "Holocaust." This term itself, signifying a sacred sacrifice (literally, "whole burnt offerings"), is nearly blasphemous as a term for the genocide of the *Shoah*: but perhaps any term at all would be a sacrilege. Hence the persistent endeavor to express it without or against language, in artfully crafted and situated sorts of silence. In this respect, so-called Jewish Holocaust literature becomes exemplary of the motives of the broader apophatic tradition. The *Shoah* represents one historically specific motivation for language that denies and deconstructs itself vis-à-vis the unspeakable that any language cannot but violate and desecrate.

The challenge of speech after the demise of Logos has been addressed in pathbreaking ways both by poets after Auschwitz and by philosophers after the end of philosophy. The motifs of the singular and the Other, as vestiges of an absolutely incomparable, wholly other God, retain perhaps a certain Jewish accent, thanks to their monotheistic matrix, yet they are also broadly diffused throughout Western culture.[7] The problems of particularity and alterity that transcend language's uttermost ability to express have become urgent and pervasive in modern and postmodern culture as a culture of the word in crisis. The present inquiry bears on the broad question of whether the discourse of what cannot be said, that is, language that takes itself back in its very act of utterance, the apophatic language of *un*saying, can provide a viable approach to the problem of relation to the other and the singular as they have been rediscovered in the provocative texts of Jabès and Celan, as well as of many other recent writers.

Like so many contemporary poets, Celan and Jabès constantly point up the limits of language and recur to the motif of silence. Even more tellingly, they write in an aphoristic, elliptical style that effectively leaves unsaid the main target and intention of their poems. It is only by moving away from and withdrawing before what they intend to say that the unsayable burden of their poems registers at all. Is it the radical singularity or otherness of what they are writing about that so often, perhaps always, at least implicitly, makes them acknowledge that language fails them?

Certainly singularity and otherness are two good reasons why language might run up against its limits. Might this place at the limits of language prove to be the best place for defining or adumbrating what singularity and alterity, or alternatively oneness and otherness, could possibly mean? Although a clear, abstract grammatical sense can be assigned to both terms of each of these oppositions, what singularity or otherness might concretely mean, not just as concepts but as incarnate in discourse and as actually encountered in experience, can perhaps not be elucidated at all, except in terms of the way they exceed language and its furthest capacities to define and describe. The singularity and otherness of another individual are perhaps precisely what I cannot describe about him/her/they/it/what/or whoever. Or at least such abstractions are as much as can be thought and conceived about them. Just this singular alterity is what cannot be appropriated in any general terms, and all our language is general. Grammatically, "I" is every "I." Likewise, I cannot articulate the absolute, ownmost particularity of the other without universalizing it. Classical rhetoric expresses this in the motto: *Individuum ineffabilis est.* It is only in relinquishing the claim of language to comprehend and convey the singular, the other individual, that I can perhaps witness to an authentic experience of their alterity—or rather, it is not even an experience that is witnessed to so much as the *check* to experience, the experience of the impossibility of experience vis-à-vis this alterity. My language can transmit nothing of this alterity or singularity as such. It is only in dismantling its claim to re-present the other that it can create a space for the singular alterity of the other, and so bear witness to it.

This account describes some ineluctable limits posed by language in the relation to another person. No universal concept or Logos can ever do justice to the singular individual. Such is the motive of Levinas's ethical critique of Logos philosophy.[8] Are these limits confirmed by the discourses of the poets, or do the poets perhaps, in the "magic" of poetic language, manage after all to say the unsayable and communicate something of the otherness of the other in its infinite singularity? Might they betray by "indiscretion," as Levinas puts it, what logical language cannot say? Arguably, the rational limits of language can be transcended by poetic language, which is what has given it its peculiar fascination for proponents of contemporary apophaticism, for thinkers such as Blanchot, Derrida, and Levinas himself, even though Levinas aims to establish ethical limits that would not be exceeded but rather confirmed by poetry, especially the ethically engaged and absolutely intense poetry of Celan.[9] It seems that poetry excels only in the expression of inexpressibility and that this alone, paradoxically, becomes the mode in which the sense of alterity and singularity can be communicated. Not by being communicated but rather by being marked as evading all linguistic formulations, the inexpressible is made at least to show up in poetry. As in Wittgenstein's dictum, the inexpressible "*shows* itself, it is the mystical" (*Tractatus* 6.45).

What, then, specifically, are the means by which Celan and Jabès evoke the unsayable as the marker of a singularity or alterity that cannot as such be expressed? One means is simply the function of language as an index—plain, unadorned referentiality in the most basic sense. Although much is often made of the loss of referentiality in poetry like Celan's, in fact the unspeakable horror is often enough pointed to, as if poet and reader alike were on-site, in the fields of the death camps. It is not what the poems say but what they point to and decline to say or prove incapable of saying that bears the burden of their pathos and perhaps even exceeds every pathetic mode of poetic expression in the face of the unbearable and inexpressible.

For Celan, the unsayable is most obviously outside language, in "that which happened" ("das, was geschah").[10] It cannot be expressed but can be indicated mutely, in a sort of pure, absolute reference. Accordingly, Celan counsels his reader in "Engführung" to stop reading and rather "see," and then to stop seeing and rather "go." Context overwhelms text and in fact threatens to cancel it out completely, overrunning and crushing, or else voiding, it. The Holocaust in this way has a very direct, unmasterable pertinence for nearly all of what Celan writes. It is the historical context that gives meaning to his poetry, sometimes even by depriving it of literal sense. The violations of grammatical and lexical norms that make Celan's expressions so often veer into nonsense or a surplus of sense resonate with this larger significance of bearing witness to the incomprehensible in Holocaust history and even mimetically reenacting its destructiveness on a linguistic plane.

The Holocaust experience his poetry revolves around stands as the incomparable, "that which happened" that it is impossible to say or name. But this historical catastrophe is not really accessible as history, and it is not only an event in the past. In its very uniqueness and incomparability, it becomes for Celan the key to interpreting the situation of human beings at all times—that is, simply as in time, in time which is always catastrophic by its very nature. It is the nature of time to isolate moments of "encounter" ("Begegnung") of the wholly Other into their strange, uncanny, incomprehensible singularity. This singular reality can be touched only in a unique, irrecuperable, and incomprehensible encounter.

In "Einmal" ("Once"), Celan approaches something infinitely singular, and he does so literally through annihilations enacted in and upon language. It is by linguistically interrupting and destructing the One and Infinite that an unconditional singularity is allowed first to emerge:

EINMAL,
da hörte ich ihn,
da wusch er die Welt,
ungesehn, nachtlang,
wirklich.

Eins und Unendlich,
vernichtet,
ichten.

Licht war. Rettung.

ONCE
I heard him,
he was washing the world,
unseen, nightlong,
real.

One and Infinite,
annihilated,
ied.

Light was. Salvation.[11]

The cleansing annihilation of the One and Infinite ("Eins und Unendlich") occurs in the break-down of language, its fragmentation into
syllables, imitating time as disjunctive, as producing an incomparable, un-
integratable "once." In this way, the singular once of "Einmal" can wash
the world ("da wusch er die Welt") of generalization and its fictions. This
happens blindly, unseen during the night ("nachtlang")—where language
cannot grasp or reach with the light of its Logos. The word for "annihilates" ("vernichtet") actually engulfs a word for "something," the particle
icht (from Middle High German *iht*, "something," "aught," as opposed to
niht, "nought").[12] Every something is annihilated by the breaking up of
language in this poem. However, *icht* is then recycled to "*icht*en," and then
further relayed to "*Licht*" ("light"), suggesting ways that the break-down
of language into syllables first lets something be and even show itself in the
daylight. This light is itself in turn "salvation" or "redemption" ("Rettung").

These rich connotations, squeezed from an act of linguistic dismemberment and re-incorporation, thus attain finally to a religious register of
meaning. As in the Kabbalistic theory of Creation by divine contraction
(*Tzimtzum*), only the annihilation of the Infinite and One by self-
withdrawal permits *some*thing to exist in its uniqueness. Furthermore, also
embedded in *icht* is the word *Ich*, German for *I*. The *I*, as verbally enacted
by being made a participle (*ichten/ied*) in this poem, emerges in its singularity and is illuminated by the linguistic annihilation of the One and Infinite. The obliteration of the quintessentially linguistic categories or
abstractions of oneness and infiniteness issues in the emergence into the
light of a singular subject—linguistic, lyric, or existential, as the case of

the "I" may be. Celan experiences the radical singularity and incommunicability of this "I" in annihilations of language, of the unity and generality and even infinity (as in the infinitive) that language alone makes possible and imposes on the world. One and Infinite may be the nature of the singular, but paradoxically these *words* must be verbally annihilated in order that the oneness and infinity of singular existence be freed, redeemed, brought to light. This can happen only in a singular moment, "Once." It can happen only in time, in the "once" that only the breaking of language can release and allow to be perceived, "heard."

In his discourses on poetics, Celan speaks of encountering himself by writing from or to a specific date: *his* 20th of January—the day on which the Nazi party met and formally decided on "the final solution," namely, the liquidation of the Jewish race. This time, emblematic for annihilation, is the reality that Celan approaches over and over again in his poems. By breaking out of all constructions that identify us by words, we enter into real time, which is a breaking, an abolishing of every continuous, settled narrative that encloses time between the set meanings of a beginning and an end. Celan parallels (and perhaps depends on) Benjamin's theory of Messianic time as a discontinuous, eruptive "now" or *Jetztzeit*. The poem, as a breaking open of language, first enables this open time of the break to transpire. In this sense, poems are "underway" ("unterwegs"). "Toward what? Toward something open, inhabitable, an approachable you, perhaps, an approachable reality."[13]

This you, however, is radically unknowable and can be designated only as "other": "The poem intends another, needs this other, needs an 'over-against.' It goes toward it, bespeaks it. For the poem, everything and everybody is a figure of this other toward which it is heading."[14] Indeed, the poem and everything in it is to be understood only in terms of this intention moving toward an other that no word can name but that every word intends and adumbrates. Hence what the poem approaches is described as the "altogether Other" ("ganz Andere"). Vis-à-vis this wholly other, language is reduced to silence. This happens in amazing ways in virtually every poem Celan writes. As he himself puts it, the poem today exhibits "a strong tendency toward growing dumb" ("eine starke Neigung zum Verstummen," *GW,* vol. 3, p. 197).

The poem can only approach and bespeak—not say or express—this altogether other. For this, there can be no words. Only the failing and foundering of words—accentuated or seconded by their artfully deliberate dissection and destruction—can express this intention directed toward the wholly other. Language vis-à-vis this wholly other can grasp and express nothing properly in name and concept, but rather "passes through terrifying silence, through the thousand darknesses of murderous speech."[15] The language Celan writes of, and himself writes, "went through. It gave me no words for what was happening, but went through it. Went through and could resurface, 'enriched' by it all."[16] Even growing dumb in relation to unspeakable happenings can enrich language by its brush with a historical reality that it cannot represent or name.

For Jabès, in contrast, it is not the unutterable density or plenitude of the historically concrete, nor even of the personally incarnate, the singular individual, that escapes articulation, but rather the essence and reality of language itself. Everything that is anything is such by virtue of the word, for the word alone gives it definition as *some*thing. In this sense, the word alone *is* unconditionally, yet the word itself is essentially a cipher: it *is* not. Language is an articulation of nothing concrete or given, apart from the positings of language itself. Language is a regress to infinity, what Jabès calls the Book—and as such collapses into what can never be made manifest except in and through the negation of every finite, representable form or object. Living in constant and total relation to the Book, the Jews are exiled from every would-be, concrete, definite reality, every fixed and stable home.

Exile for Jabès means primarily not being a solitary individual separate from others in history, but exile of and into the word. Language opens a space of emptiness, since all that it posits, strictly considered, it posits as absent, as only verbally posited, and therefore as virtual and ideal. The verbal is, in this sense, a "universe of emptiness" ("Le verbe est univers de vide").[17] Bound to and separated by their special relation to the divine Name, the Jews are exiled into the name ("le nom") and become literally "nom-ades." Where the (w)hol(l)y unsayable divine Name reigns, every given, finite form is sacrificed to the infinite, the ungraspable and incomprehensible, the totality of language in the Book. This is a purely virtual totality that is beyond all possibility of articulation. Like God, it is unencompassible in its infinity and is signified only by the silence of the Name of God. Every word, therefore, with its concrete sensorial and semantic content, is given up for—and is beholden to—silence.

The Jews, then, are denizens of the name that is located nowhere, at no stable or ascertainable place in real space or geography. Not only does NOM ("name"), through its incorporation in NOMADE, intimate that language is a nomadic condition of perpetual exile: the word NOM is also MON—the first-person possessive pronoun "my"—backwards.

> (NOM devrait se lire deux fois, de gauche à droite et de droite à gauche, car deux mots le composent : NOM et MON; mon nom. Le nom est mien. Tout nom est personnel . . . . [18]

> ─────

> (NOM should be read twice, from left to right and from right to left, because it is composed of two words: NOM [NAME] and MON [MY]; my name. The name is mine. Every name is personal
>
> . . . .

This convertibility of *nom* and *mon* hints at the way that the name is always an indirect, backhanded sort of appropriation. Whatever is named is in some manner also possessed. Articulate speech begins only with such appropriation, which is ineluctably destruction of the purity of silence abiding at the unsayable center from which language emanates. This silent source of language would presumably be an anonymous foundation for all constructions of names, ultimately the total structure of the Book. Indeed, the common noun for book, "livre," turns out, like the adjective for free, "libre," to be subject to voiding at its center: by suppressing their central letter, LI(V)RE (book) and LI(B)RE (free) are pared down equally to LI RE (*lire*, the infinitive, "to read"), and then, by further hollowing out, eliminating all but the first and last letter in each word, to LE, the singular, masculine, definite article for generically designating whatever is anything at all. But LE reversed is also the Hebrew Name of God, namely, EL. In this manner, the Hebrew name of God, which is in principle silent and unpronounceable, is found at the core of the book and of reading and of naming in general, and so of language itself.

Jabès works with French the way the Kabbalah writers worked with the Hebrew language, finding presumably mystical truths of the universe inscribed within it. Ostensible contingencies of the French language are presented as miraculously revealing the mystery of Creation by the Name of God—the empty and unpronounceable divine Name that creates all from Nothing. But whereas Kabbalists supposed that Hebrew was the language of Creation itself, Jabès uses French to show how the self-subversive forms and fictive powers of a human vernacular mirror an undelimited power of creativity from Nothing. Jabès exposes the operation in language as such of the power of creation from Nothing that was traditionally attributed to the divine Word.

Jabès's thought unfolds entirely within the Book as the boundary and abyss of language, and the Holocaust impinges in the sense that, in any of its manifestations, the Book is inflected as subject to destruction and infinite nullification. As well as being a contingent event befalling the Jews, holocaust is experienced at another level as evacuation of reality by the word as an offering up of beings to the Nothing of language (language by itself being but an empty representation, a mere form). This takes place already paradigmatically in the Book as a transcendent totality that cannot but be absent from any ensemble of words, however "complete" it is, as well as absent from any history and from the world of finite entities. The obliteration in the Book of any immediately present reality unmediated by the word (and its emptiness) is a general condition of holocaust, of annihilation by and sacrifice to the Word, even apart from being a singular historical event.

Jabès's poetics of the inexpressible (in contrast to Celan's) pivot not so much or so directly on an extralinguistic singularity or otherness as on the Book. Like the Neoplatonic One, also an All-Nothing, the Book is infinite and can be manifest only in fragments and finitude, never as a whole and intact. In finite terms the Book is nothing, that is, nothing finite can express it, and every word taken as a word of the Book cannot but be empty. The emptiness of the word, as abstracted and separated from the reality of things and as belonging to the Book, opens into the omnipresent infinity of Nothing. The Jews, by dwelling in this exile of the word, are veritably the people of the Book (*gens du livre*). This infinity and emptiness of the word, as well as its totalization—the Book—is, naturally, unsayable. But it is open in its emptiness, an open question and an open desert for wandering, a space of errancy. Only in this openness is there any room for human expression.

Whereas Celan most often approaches the unsayable from the side of what language cannot say, with the unspeakable of the Holocaust directly present before him and obliterating word and image before they begin to express it, Jabès typically approaches unsayability from the side of language. Jabès's problem is not that there is no language for the singular reality that beggars description, but rather that language, as it can be used by humans, is singularly nothing because it is not everything—not the Book, not God. The singularity that occupies Jabès is discovered first and foremost within language rather than apart from and outside of language and as inaccessible to it. In Celan, the singularities inhering in language seem to function as analogues for the incomparable, unspeakable singularity of a historical catastrophe, the Holocaust that no language can reach or articulate. Jabès, by contrast, seems to acknowledge no outside of language; for him, rather, words themselves are already inhabited by singularity and alterity that nullify every positive content. They possess no territory and stand on no secured soil. They fall away from and destroy themselves and reduce to nothing articulable, to the silence of the absolutely singular and other that is in their midst and at the same time engulfs them entirely.

The allusion to the historical Holocaust is, in this respect, often somewhat more attenuated in Jabès than in Celan. Yet it does surface in the narrative that sporadically but insistently hints at a historical context. There is a sort of story in the *Book of Questions,* which is never actually told so much as commented on from many different angles—though this is a way of not telling it, since, tellingly, commentary is understood by Jabès as a means of silencing, as literally "comment taire" or "how to silence." We infer a tragic love story between a writer, Yukel, and a young woman, Sarah, who goes insane in a concentration camp during the Nazi deportations in France. Yukel, an alter ego for Jabès as writer, is asked to comment on silence as the alpha and omega of all language: "Yukel, speak to us of the silence that is the end and the beginning, being the soul of words as the cantor and the martyr are, at the designated moment, the soul of the world."[19] The Holocaust is thus alluded to by a fictive narrative that is sketchily adumbrated by Jabès. It is indeed at the center of the fiction: history is not left outside but is drawn into the book and its fiction. There is nothing, at least nothing imagined or representable, that is outside the Book.[20]

Celan's language is witness to an event; it is in a state of shock. Jabès seems rather to be witnessing to a predicament; the disaster that he expresses is already, and always, there in language. Jabès's theoretical reflections and the glassy, cool composure, as well as the quietly fiery passion, of his sybilline aphorisms bespeak the disaster of the word as such. Every finite, human word is an annihilation of the infinite, divine Book. This annihilation is necessary to the existence of humanity, of the finite, which is otherwise totally obliterated by the infinite.

There is no such hypostatized infinity of language as the Book behind the infinite otherness of "I" and "you" in the poetic lexicon of Celan. Celan considers the originary disaster from which words arise rather under the aspect of a happening, an occurrence, as in the following brief lyric from *Die Niemandsrose*:

Was Geschah? Der Stein trat aus dem Berge.
Wer erwachte? Du und ich.
Sprache, Sprache. Mit-Stern. Neben-Erde.
Ärmer. Offen. Heimatlich.

Wohin gings? Gen Unverklungen.
Mit dem Stein gings, mit uns zwein.
Herz und Herz. Zu schwer befunden.
Schwerer werden. Leichter sein.

What Occurred? The stone trod out from the mountain.
Who awakened? You and I.
Language, language. With-Star. Next-to-Earth.
Poorer. Open. Homelandwise.

Where did it go? Towards the unsubsided.
We went with the stone, the two of us.
Heart and heart. Found to be too heavy.
Become more heavy. Be more light.[21]

"What happened" here is depicted as a sort of separation and falling away from an inorganic mass, a "mountain." The order of language—in which for the first time there can be relations of togetherness with the stars and of nearness to the earth—creates an openness and impoverishment unknown to the prelinguistic state of burrowing unawakened and unseparate in the rich concreteness and density of the mountain. Awakening to this linguistic order, in which things are now bound together in relation, including you and I, everything is "found to be too heavy." One is burdened with a whole universe that language has made separate from oneself. And yet if language, through which all this has come about, can now be shed or shaken off, amortized, then existence in the freedom of having come unstuck from the mountain may on the contrary be found to be "light," heart to heart, unencumbered by linguistic mediation. One goes toward what is "unsubsided" ("Unverklungen"), a fading sound that has not yet fully finished its vibrations but is drawn toward the arriving silence. This pull of language toward its own extinction is a gravitational force taking "you" and "me" as grammatical pronouns with it. It will allow us then to be light when fully divested of language, when with its cessation we have become open in all directions and there is no longer any determinate homeland toward which we are oriented. We will then have become heavier with the stone's own heaviness, but we will be light because absolved from language. Mute like the stone, we will be weighed down physically, heavy, real, and yet lightened of the burden of consciousness in language and all its mediated relations.

Jabès's route to silence, in contrast, begins and ends with the Book. Whereas Celan imagines the maximum intensity of earthiness and massiveness as a state before and beyond language, Jabès does not relinquish linguistic imagery even in opening toward absolute silence. The absolute openness and emptiness generated by language lead him to the question of the book and even of a sacred Book:

> Il n'y a pas un Livre sacré mais des livres ouverts au silence du Livre sacré.
>
> Écrire, à partir de ce silence, c'est insérer le Livre de l'éternité dans le livre mortel de nos métamorphoses.[22]

There is not a sacred Book but books open to the silence of the sacred Book.

To write, from this silence is to insert the Book of eternity in the mortal book of our metamorphoses.

The absolute Book cannot as such exist, for then it would stand out from other things, be one among many, no longer absolved from all relativity. Yet all our writing must annul its limits and its very existence in opening itself toward this Book, which is not. It is nothing but silence. Of course, "To say this silence would be to say the sacred, but equally, at the same time, to annul it" ("Dire ce silence, c'est dire le sacré; mais c'est, également, l'abolir aussitôt," p. 50). So there is an irresolvable paradox of priority between the Book that cannot be, except as refracted in our books, and our books that cannot be, except as fragments of It.

—Qu'est-ce qu'un livre sacré? Qu'est-ce qui confère au livre son caractère sacré?

—Le sacré dépend-il de nous?

—Un livre de savoir, serait-il un livre sacré? Non, puisque le savoir est humain.

—Nous disons : "Dans ce livre, il y a la parole de Dieu. Donc, c'est un livre sacré." Mais n'est-ce pas nous-mêmes qui, cherchant à la révéler, formulons cette parole?

La Parole de Dieu serait-elle cette Parole silencieuse qui laisserait se rompre son silence en chacune des nôtres?

—Il n'y aurait, ainsi, pas plus de livre sacré que de livre profane : il y aurait le livre.

Mais quel livre? Le Livre absolu de Dieu, le livre inaccompli de l'homme?

—Le livre est, à la fois, présentation—il présente, se présente—et représentation—il reproduit, cherche à fixer.

Mais Dieu n'a-t-il pas condamné toute représentation de Lui-même?

(p. 51)

———

—What is a sacred book? What confers on a book its character as sacred?

—Does the sacred depend on us?

—Would a book of knowledge be a sacred book? No, because knowledge is human.

—We say: "In this book, there is the word of God. Therefore, it's a sacred book." But is it not we ourselves who, seeking to reveal it, form this word?

Would the Word of God be this silent Word that would let its silence be interrupted in each of our silences?

—In this way, there would be a sacred book no more than a profane: there is the book.

But which book? The absolute Book of God, the uncompleted book of man?

—The book is at once presentation—it presents, presents itself—and representation—it reproduces, seeks to render fixed.

But did God not condemn every representation of Himself?

His obsession with the Book gives Jabès a different slant from Celan in his approach to the poetics of silence. Both of these authors write poetry whose standard of success is not its aesthetic quality as such, its bravura in figuring through descriptively apt images, but its capacity to intimate what it cannot figure. It is a negative capability of self-erasure by which both these types of poetry, the one strictly lyric, the other gnomic and mixed typically with prose, excel. For both Jabès and Celan, language is important only for its giving itself up and vanishing, but what it moves from and vanishes toward is differently conceived as "what happened" or as the Book.

Pointing to "what happened" imagines the erasure of language to lead to the outside of language, whereas the figure of the Book suggests that the erasure of all words produces a result that is still determined as linguistic, still encompassed by Language, even if in a purely negative mode. Of course, the Book is but another figure for an absolutely unutterable, unscriptable, unimaginable Nothing. It is not a determination of any essence. But it is nevertheless a verbal road marker and provides a linguistic landscape for the journey from alpha to omega.

This comparison between Jabès and Celan can help us to discriminate between what are historically two distinguishable lineages and logics of apophatic thinking, one based on the ineffability of the singular existence, whether of God or of the individual human person or event, and another based on an ineffability inherent to language itself. The latter is traditionally figured as the unutterable Name of God. The word at the origin of all words, too hol(e)y to be pronounced, is the missing ground or abyss into which all language slips. All language depends upon this ground, which, however, can never itself appear, so that all language that does appear in finite fragments or words is unveiled as really nothing, as a mask for the nonappearing, indefinable Nothing of the infinite language known mythically as the Book.

On the one hand, we have the superabundant fullness of history and existence as manifest in the concretely given otherness of the other person, and on the other, the infinite emptiness of the word resulting in a nomadic exile into the Name, with its withdrawal from lips forbidden to pronounce it—which would be, in a manner, to possess it. These are two distinct motives for ineffability and two distinct roots of apophatic tradition that can be aligned with Celan and Jabès, respectively.

From ancient times, there has been an apophaticism of existence, of the positively and absolutely existing that language cannot comprehend, which from Philo Judaeus to Wittgenstein registers in the fact *that* something is, even though *what* it is cannot in the least be expressed. But alongside this there is also an apophaticism of the Divine Name. In this latter case, it is language, paradigmatically the unpronounceable Name of God, rather than existence that emerges as the prime instance of what cannot be said. Whereas the unsayability of existence or being has been pursued in philosophy from Plotinus and Proclus through Schelling and Kierkegaard to Heidegger, theoretical reflection on the ineffable divine Name develops especially in the Kabbalah and resurfaces recently in philosophical thinkers of language, especially those of Jewish heritage such as Benjamin, Levinas, and Derrida. These two strands of tradition are conjoined and intricately intertwined in the work of Franz Rosenzweig.[23] Rosenzweig manages to blend together both a philosophy of existence deriving from the late Schelling and a philosophical meditation on the absolute, silent Word of Creation in the tradition of the Bible.

The synthesis of existential with linguistic apophaticism in Rosenzweig is a hint that perhaps these seeming opposites may prove not to be separable in any final and definitive way after all. Language, and in the prime instance the divine Name, is perhaps the creative core of being as it is manifest in existence, and the unsayability at the heart of both being and language might therefore, in the last analysis, be indiscernibly the same. Characteristically, in apophatic discourses distinctions posing as ultimate collapse and opposites come to coincide. Indeed, without the word, nothing is left to articulate things into separate entities. In an apophatic universe, all things become equally inarticulate. The fullness of existence as such and the emptiness of the pure word are each equally beyond saying. They are based on radically different, incomparable experiences. But *what* is experienced in each case is inarticulable and comes to coincide in the original indifferentiation that is manifest only in and as the neutralizing of every finite expression, every fragment of word or of being that *can* be expressed. Although these are divergent ways, they lead to what may be indistinguishably the same silence. At least, it does not seem possible to *say* the difference between them, except as a difference that disappears and as a saying that is erased. Apophatic discourses of the most diverse sorts converge upon this point, where the singular has no stateable difference to define it or distinguish it from either All or Nothing. The ineffable concreteness of existence and the ineffable emptiness of language in this manner meet in the silence where being and language grow dumb together.

These two different paradigms of apophasis, as they develop in Celan and Jabès, respectively, can be compared both in their distinctiveness and ultimately their inseparability from one another. For in either case, the claims of difference are driven to their limit and expose its arbitrariness, so that the opposition collapses into indistinction: in different ways, Celan and Jabès both reveal an infinite, indistinct Nothing-All as underlying and swallowing up every finite form of manifestation, every articulation. All history is within Jabès's language, and conversely for Celan language is already itself a holocaust, the actual site of annihilation. Both authors close in upon the ultimate inexpressibility at the origin of language and existence alike—where words and reality are indistinguishably together in virtual emergence—but from opposite directions.

ii

What is in a word? What lies at the core of language? It can only be the silent, empty nothing of the tomb, the pyramid of the dead letter, as in the letter A. For language abstracts from things, it memorializes life, it voids presence. Yet language *says* this nothingness in so many beguilingly soft, sweet, subtle, and insinuating ways. The textures of words make it palpable, their sonorities render it audible, their suggestively shapely letters display it graphically. At the core of a word, beneath the crust of its consonants, is the liquid of its vowels, and these vowels in effect liquidate the word until it flows into the ocean of nothingness. This nothingness is what Jabès finds harboring rapturously in the wings of language, as he parades and stages it in his books. But that nothingness, into which all that is articulated dissolves, is the unity of everything, albeit a unity that is itself nothing. As such, the inexistent totality/nullity of the Book governs every passage of the writing of words. Words are but the unfolding of this total nothingness. It turns them into a universe of emptiness: "Le verbe est univers du vide" ("The word is a world of emptiness").[24]

Jabès breaks language down into its elements in order to liquidate, vaporize, pulverize, and immolate it—so many different ways to reduce it to nothing by violence. He develops, in effect, like Gaston Bachelard, a poetics of the four elements to suggest how all sensible images serve the purpose of pointing to what cannot be expressed in language without being bloodied, killed, and annulled. Language is water, for it dissolves into a sea where meaning is dispersed. Indeed, in some sense, "all books have been

written in the sea" ("Tous les livres ont été écrits dans la mer," *El*, p. 74).
The watery element effects dissolution into nothing, as does also the fiery
element that consumes all, converting static matter to effervescence of energy, while the aerial element, "aérien," refines mass or content to "rien,"
nothing: Jabès hears this word as saying "A e(st) rien" ("A is nothing"). Finally, the earth, the solid element, is the place of errancy ("errer"), as can
be heard in its name, "terre." Earth is a place of wandering until one has
lost all direction and destination and thereby evades every definition.

The Nothing into which all four elements disappear is nothing but
the word, which then is itself erased or scratched out. In each case, the
nothingness of silence is released from the word as its essence. The word
is revealed as hollow and empty at its core. Voided of all determinations
of content, the word echoes precisely in silence. By revealing the word in
this way in its empty inner nature, writing gives birth to the Nothing
("L'écriture est enfance du néant," *El*, p. 74). But this Nothing is also, in a
sense, everything, and the word in merging with Nothing rejoins the infinite, the abyss (for us) also known—or rather *un*known—as God.

By dissolving words into their elements, Jabès's writing returns them
to their purity and transparency, which is to be nothing. "All writing,
then, consists in sending the word back to its initial transparency" ("Toute
écriture consiste, alors, à renvoyer le vocable à sa transparence initiale," *El*,
p. 28). Similarly, we could say that writing sends the word back to the
original soundlessness from which all words resound. Writing releases the
silence trapped within words, freeing it to rejoin the infinite silence of
the ocean, or the hush of heaven (the empty air), or the dense muteness
of earth, or the deafening siren of all-consuming fire.

As Jabès explains, words evaporate, taking wing on their "air" of
"nothing": "aérien" (aerial) releases "rien" (nothing) from its midst. Take
away even this wing, "aile," pronounced as the letter "l," and the word
"voile" (veil) gives way to "voie" (way), opening the prison of the page enclosed by its four margins to a way, an open space of day, but also an infinite emptiness. It is by such elimination and erasure that words reveal the
infinite nothingness that is their secret, silent essence. It is this, their absence, that is God. In fact, the eliminated "l," pronounced "el," is another
avatar of the Hebrew Name for God—El—that Jabès finds omnipresent
as the uncannily omnipotent absence occulted within language. By recog-

nizing the unpronounceable, unspeakable divine Name dwelling in the midst of the word, Jabès restores the word's essential silence. He elicits this silence by decomposing words so that they yield up the Name of God—the unsoundable—as the pearl within their sounding shells.

In Jabès's texts, as in the Kabbalah, letters of the alphabet are disclosed by anagrammatic permutations as encoding mysterious meanings. By dismemberment into their constitutive letters, words release magical and mystical powers. For all letters ultimately represent the Name of God, the unspeakable, the all-pervasive Nothing.[25] Accordingly, the ultimate power of any letter has to be that of disappearing, of erasing its very self, and the meanings revealed have to be approximations to meaning nothing, the all-embracing meaning of language as a whole in its self-erasure, in order that it point beyond to the Unsayable.

Nevertheless, abundant specific meanings and connections of meanings are left by language as traces along the trail of its disappearing. This makes for the great play with words in Jabès's texts. He is constantly finding words unexpectedly hidden within other words, and he elicits them in ways that suggest previously unsuspected intrinsic connections. In other examples just from *El, ou le dernier livre,* Jabès finds "foi" (faith) in "folie" (madness), "nuage" (cloud) in "naufrage" (shipwreck), "orgie" (orgy) in "origine" (origin), "mur" (wall) in "murmure" (murmur), and so on. It appears as if words could all be fit one into another—or conversely all be drawn out of one another—and as if language were nothing but an internal relation to itself. As such, it is a trace, a remembrance of oneness experienced always only as shattered and as the sheer externality of homophonic and homographic coincidences.

All words break down ultimately into the silent nothingness that haunts the Name of God. And since all categories and genera break down in the infinite collapse of every word into every other word, it cannot but be pointed out that "El," when pronounced, is indistinguishable phonemically from the third-person, feminine pronoun "elle." When written, moreover, ELLE shows up graphically as the gender reversal and chiasmic doubling of the Name for God in Hebrew: El. Male and female thus are opposites that are conjoined or coincide in being created one out of the other by symmetrical permutations—by a double inversion—of signs for the ultimate Nothing of the divine Name, the Name that cannot be said.

This type of sensitivity to the graphic and phonemic body of language, as well as to the homologies between words and their component parts, is exploited by Jabès to show what an echo chamber the French language is. A handful of vowel sounds are used to say everything, and all words thus turn out to be virtually the same word but with a marvelously diverse repertoire of inflections and variations. This one word—any word—subsuming all of language reduces further to the letter, any letter, *A*, for example, which is conceived of as containing all the rest of the language. Such a single signifier is itself but the minimal difference disappearing into—and coinciding with—Nothing. We have already encountered Jabès saying just this with his elucidation of the word "aérien" as meaning "A is nothing" ("A est rien," *El*, p. 89).

In *El, ou le dernier livre* a particular geometrical image, the point, is taken as the image of absolute unity vanishing into nothing. It is a traditional image of the One-Nothing, the All-Nothing, used in the Kabbalah of God and his presence among humans, his *Shekkinah*. Every word is such a point ("Ponctualité de toute parole," *El*, p. 94). In this point appears the whole of language, which is the whole universe, but as collapsing and condensing to a minimal, and even infinitesimal, vanishing point, a point which itself is but an inflection or speck of Nothing. This residue of finite, determinate language is erased in the whole of language, which absorbs it like a sea. Without differentiation, this whole itself slips into definitionlessness. This "beyond" of every definition has commonly been called "God."

The linchpin to Jabès's entire enterprise is the idea of God as "the silence of all words." Our words are merely the desert dust into which God's Word has been pulverized. So our words are oriented to the infinity of his Word. This Word, however, broken into mortal finitude in our words, can only be emptiness, exile, and silence. God can be (to us, anyway) nothing besides this infinite absence in our human words. Indeed, Jabès asks whether it could be that "our relation to God is only a relation to ourselves so vast that no word can carry." Not being sayable in any word we can say, this God is detected as "a lack of words within every word we utter."[26]

Everything here turns on Jabès's distinction between the divine and the human word. And yet divine language is characterized by being inaudible except in and through our words. It is like the hollow of a ring: "The divine word is silenced just as soon as it is pronounced. It is on to its sonorous rings, which are our inspired words, that we grab hold."[27] In fact, a divine word is created precisely by its own absence ("L'absence d'une parole divine la crée"). It is created in human words by the abyss that inhabits them, the emptiness at their center. It is, then, human words that create the infinite (insofar as it can be apprehended or articulated at all). Words make absolute what they name and define and thereby annihilate as extralinguistic entities, for they substitute ideal entities, meanings, which language projects, for the supposedly real things. Thus Jabès's rabbis can maintain that anything *is* at all only by virtue of being named: yet this named ideal entity or essence itself is but a delimitation, an inflection of Nothing, the essence of language.

Language is clearly the key to the universe in Jabès, as in the Kabbalah, and silence is the essence of all language. What is true of the universe is true also of the microcosm of the soul, which is likewise an infinite silence suspended upon the nothingness of the human word: "The Soul may be compared to a mountain of silence lifted up by the word. A relaxation of muscles and it falls."[28] The inestimable might, the mountain of silence, in the eternity of ideas is all precariously sustained by the frailty vanishing into nothingness of sounds articulated by the feeble, fallible, fleshly organs from which speech issues. Organically, silence blooms in the flower of the word, in all its fragility, and in the leaf of the book:

> "—Donne-nous à méditer, mon maître, les leçons de tes livres, afin que pour chaque feuille offerte à la feuille, une parole apprise au cœur du silence fleurisse."
>
> (*Livre des questions*, p. 164)

> "—Give us to meditate, my master, the lessons of your books, in order that for each leaf offered to the leaf a word learned in the heart of silence may blossom."

"God," too, comes forth, or is fabricated by the power of naming, from nothing. In this sense, the God that is named is an impostor. Whereas verbal richness constitutes the lie of the language of humans, nudity and poverty are the lies of God ("La nudité, la pauvreté sont mensonges de Dieu,"

Livre des questions, p. 93). The inventive, mythifying power of the word is human in its wealth or flourishing and divine in its dearth, its blankness clearing space for infinity. Still, in either case, language is an artifice, a lie relative to the truth of infinite silence that outstrips it and is always already there where words end. The saying even of nothing betrays it into the guise of something: some sound or sign is given to represent the unrepresentable. And this makes language constitutively mendacious.

Jabès's books are generally spare rather than loquacious, but they give a full repertoire of images—as images for the Unrepresentable. Their words and images are presented as scars and wounds—traces of what they have wounded and scarred by saying and imaging it. Although Jabès's writing does, then, present images, they all efface and erase themselves, and vanish into Nothing—which is what they are meant merely to *evoke.* This at least mitigates the untruth inherent in their apparent attempt to represent the unrepresentable. This shyness, not to say abhorrence, of images is, of course, quintessentially Jewish. The Jews, under the interdiction on graven images, are "the people of Nothing, of the splendid limpidity of Nothing" ("le peuple du Rien, de la splendide limpidité du Rien").[29] This fate is reflected in the stony, dusty, barren, desert landscape common in Jabès's texts.

There are a lot of blank spaces and empty pages in Jabès's book(s). They induce the reader into communion with nothing—as signified and displayed by the emptiness of the white page. Learning to read is a process of learning to see this emptiness within every written page and word and letter. The words and letters signify this emptiness that they cannot say. Jabès takes language literally to pieces in order to show this. He elicits the void, "le vide," from between the cracks and spaces seen in language (*vide* is also "see" in Latin), and this emptiness is the vision of God. Writing makes this divine vision possible through the "Life of the eyes" ("Dieu = Vide = Vie d'yeux," *El,* p. 84) presumably trained on and animating the divine Book through reading.

Jabès's writing is thus also a manner of seeing: it sees and reads the silence in words, the emptiness dwelling in the heart of language. When words are opened up to the void within them, they connect together in surprising ways, discover their affinities, and reveal something absolute in all their ever so contingent relations. They are seen to be all saying virtually the same thing, but differently, as they collapse in concert back into nothing. Jabès contemplates letters in order to see the invisible in them, for it becomes visible where they crack or are lacking. Where language breaks and bleeds, where its sense spills out beyond all boundaries, there the Infinite is intimated. This absolute, this Nothing, has only the form that language in its disintegration and decomposure and disappearing gives it. The word is a nothing, a mere convention, *vanitas voci,* a hollow artifice without any solid substance of reality, but precisely as such it reveals a certain nullity that encompasses and envelops anything at all that emerges into distinct identity and substantial reality. Distinctness, substance, and identity, after all, at least insofar as they are apprehended by us, are always linguistically defined and, to that extent, artificial.

Whatever is (anything) is the result of a word: otherwise it would have no being (or identity). Of course, every identity is but an inflection of the emptiness that infects language as a whole. As Jabès writes, "There is no name which is not a desert. There is no desert which was not, at one time, a name" ("Il n'y a pas de nom qui ne soit un désert. Il n'y a pas de désert qui ne fut, jadis, un nom," *Le soupçon le désert,* p. 131). Yet language, on which everything depends, is itself nothing real or substantial. It is an articulation of Nothing. The linguistic is always a nullification of, but thereby also a reconnection with, the infinite and immortal. For Jabès, "All writing is silence inscribed, crests aligned from beyond-voice" ("Toute écriture est silence inscrit, crêtes alignées d'outre-voix," *El,* p. 14).

Only as a disappearing act is the word able to indicate the silence and infinity from which it hails. It is the word blotted out that bespeaks its birth and death in blankness. It is only in this elimination or erasure that the word as such is perceptible as truly word rather than just an empirical object like any other: "'I no longer see the words, he wrote; I only see the place of their birth and of their death, which is completely blank'" ("'Je ne vois plus les vocables, écrivait-il; je ne vois que le lieu de leur naissance et de leur mort qui est tout blanc,'" *El,* p. 118).

Paradoxically, "Where no letter can be articulated, the word turns into a passage of the absolute" ("Où aucune lettre ne se peut articuler, le verbe se fait passage d'absolu," *El,* p. 118). The letter is already an aphorism, a caesura, an interruption within the word and its discourse. The letter lives by its solitude.[30] The letter must be eliminated in order to set discourse free and let it return to its source. The hidden root of all words in their ramifications and declensions is something "in-finite" and indefinable, something like the Book. This is the impossible, inexpressible One-Nothing to which all expressions are beholden. It is God.

Consequently, any actual finite linguistic expression, word or letter, no matter how minute, by virtue of being *some*thing, betrays God. Although all language is but a refraction of the Book and ultimately of "God," any language for God is a betrayal and any name a misnomer. Thus Jabès writes that the Name of God is against God—it imprisons him, just as writing "God" is "against God" ("Dieu S'écrit contre Dieu"). God, as undelimited, unlettered, "in the exploded word strikes against the hostility of the letter" ("Dieu, dans le mot explosé, Se heurte à l'hostilité de la lettre," *El*, pp. 47–48).

To this extent, language is not really a means of comprehending in order to re-present and assimilate, but rather a way of repelling in order to relate externally to what is other than itself and other to all human transactions. This way of construing language opens it to an infinite outside.[31] Most important about language is not that its structural integrity can reproduce the forms of objects, but rather that its structural incompleteness keeps it open and always on the way to what it cannot represent. Thus meaning slips from word to word, collapsing into an infinite outside, just as the exile or *sol*itude of the Jews slides the soil ("sol") out from under them and leaves them without solace, wandering from place to place.

Jabès's works are all impregnated with the sense of silence as the alpha and omega of a Book into which everything that is anything falls and disappears. Their aphoristic style makes for an open-endedness where the *un*said is evoked on all sides round by the too little, too elliptical, too laconic bit that *is* said. Emphasizing the role of this apophatic rhetoric in the conclusion to her book on Jabès's rhetoric of subversion, Helena Shillony writes:

> An "other" rhetoric is necessary to express a negative theology, which is at once a quest for the divine and a slow deciphering of the absence of God . . . . A different language is necessary to wed the same movement of a paradoxical creation, of an always deferred entry into the Book, of an always renewed attempt to evoke the unsayable, and the poignant sentiment of exile and of lack that is

manifest only in an illusory presence: *"Our absence to the world is perhaps nothing but our presence to the Nothing."*[32]

Jabès's rhetorical techniques are adapted especially from procedures for interpreting the Torah. Reading the empty spaces between words and the concept of interpretation as an open-ended process, an infinite project, are familiar notions for Talmudists. Jabès's writing can thus be understood as a sort of grafting of Hebrew onto French. He expressly declares this analogy between interpretation of the Torah and the task of the writer: "The relation of the Jew—Talmudist, Kabbalist—to the book is, in its fervor, identical to that which the writer entertains with his text. Both have the same thirst to learn, to know, to decode their destiny engraved in each letter from which God has withdrawn."[33] The practice of relating through letters to God's absence is deeply Jewish and Kabbalistic. Indeed, *El* has been read as Jabès's Hebrew challenge to Greek thinking. It performs an absolute inversion whereby not only Being but also the One—which Neoplatonic philosophy exalted as the supreme principle of reality "beyond Being"—are stricken with nullity as a result of the textual productions of the book.[34] It is the writing of the letter that is the agent of this nullification. Yet in the letter, every real existence, every "is," becomes unlimited at the same time as it is eliminated. As with each of the four elements or "letters" with which the Creation is written, each letter vanishes into its own infinity.

Jabès's own writing is, in this manner, a writing of silence. Also at a thematic level, he frequently makes it explicit that his is a writing of silence, absence, nothing. Of course, these (non)themes, being what one cannot say, can be approached only through metaphors. "One does not think death, the void, the nothing, Nothingness; but their innumerable metaphors: a way of getting around the unthought" ("On ne pense pas la mort, le vide, le néant, le Rien; mais leurs innombrables métaphors: une façon de contourner l'impensé").[35] There is here a mystique of the Nothing, the Nothing, however, that contains everything:

> "Je vois un mot qui s'avance ver la mer. Ce n'est pas le mot ciel, ni le mot terre; ce n'est pas, no plus, le mot sel ou semence; mais le mot Rien, mais le mot Néant.
>
> Et je me dis que sel, graine, terre et ciel sont dans ce vocable."[36]

"I see a word that advances towards the sea. It is not the word
heaven, nor the word earth; it is not even the word salt or seed; but
the word Nothing, the word Nothingness.
And I tell myself that salt, grain, earth, and heaven are in this
word."

All words and images are metaphors for the Nameless, for Nothing. Yet, as
metaphors, they do not furnish a handle for this ultimate Nothing, but
rather express the rupture of all expression with the unthinkable: "The
unthinkable has no stem" ("L'impensé n'a point de tige").

Jabès proves particularly fertile in imagining organic, vegetable metaphors for words and their life as cut by the pencil or sickle. Thus, to twist
free of the figures inherent in language is fundamental to his project. Like
Blanchot, Jabès seeks to cancel figures inherent in language in favor of the
neuter, an *il* (impersonal third-person pronoun) without name and without figure.

In this way, metaphor becomes a means of separation rather than of
identification. Shillony analyzes how Jabès's metaphors achieve rupture
and the absence of their intended significance rather than identity and
union: "The characteristic images of the poet privilege moments of rupture and obliteration. The point of intersection between two semantic
fields that create a figure of similarity becomes in Jabès an asymptote of
absence."

In fact, these metaphors are more akin to what Gershom Scholem describes as the Kabbalistic language of mystic symbolism, where there is no
referent for the signifier except the Unsayable. Scholem contrasts the symbolic language of the Kabbalah with allegorical languages, which presuppose an immanent translatability of meanings from signifiers to signifieds:
"While in allegory, one expressible stands for another, in the mystic symbol something expressible stands for something removed from the world
of expression and communication."[37] The idea of the "mystic symbol" as
dominated by "the ineffable" that in seeking expression "bursts and destroys its earthly form, which proves to be too weak a vessel for this infinite and mighty essence," is also articulated by Walter Benjamin.[38]

Accordingly, rather than metaphors serving as bridges toward some
other reality, it is their breaking down in the movement toward what can-

not be represented at all that makes them significant . . . of what they cannot say. And hence renunciation of words proves necessary for traveling to the word of God.

> (*"Dieu méprise la mémoire. Il voyage."*
>
> Reb Haim.
>
> *"Le voyage est le refus de la parole.*
> *On se tait pour écouter."*
>
> Reb Accobas.
>
> *"Tu voyages pour retrouver la parole de Dieu et*
> *jusqu' à elle, tu étoffes tes paroles."*
>
> Reb Benlassin.)[39]

> _____

> (*"God despises memory. He travels."*
>
> Reb Haim.
>
> *"Travel is the refusal of words.*
> *One is silent in order to listen."*
>
> Reb Accobas.
>
> *"You travel in order to find again the word of God and*
> *all the way, you suffocate your words."*
>
> Reb Benlassin.)

The truth, our truth, our God is nothing, that is, nothing definable: it (He? She? They?) is a question. We are ourselves nothing that is not a question, yet precisely insofar as we are nothing, an emptiness in flesh and blood, God is manifest in us.

For Jabès, the unsayable is found within language, a language that wounds and bloodies itself by fragmenting into letters. The word is already a dismemberment of the book, and Jabès constantly further dissects words into letters, so as to expose their structural anatomies as homologous, and thereby lets their meanings bleed into one another. Written or spoken language, any expression whatever, slaughters the wholeness of the Book, which cannot emerge out of latency and be made manifest without being compromised or, to put it more dramatically, murdered: the (human, finite) book is the tomb of God, and writing is the death or even the killing of God. Hence the cry or scream (*cri*) that wells up from writing, "*é-cri-*ture." The significance of the whole—significance as a whole—is at stake in writing, and just this is what God is and always was about.

The unseen, unmanifest Book is presupposed by every stroke on the page, since as a whole it will affect the total meaning that any *iota* can convey. Accordingly, Jabès avows that every work he writes is immediately rewritten by the "book," that is, the whole, unmanifest Book which governs all meaning in the universe of language—but it can only be presented in particular words and letters, or more precisely in their vanishing, thereby leaving open a space for the infinite, though it never appears in itself or as a whole.[40] To this extent, the Book appears only as disappearing and disintegrating, as hacked up and reduced from infinity and wholeness to finitude and fragmentariness. All language seems to be contained in every word, in every letter, as speculated in the Kabbalah—but the containment is immediately a cancelation, an annihilation, an erasure of the word in its infinity and divinity as Book. Whatever *appears* of language in any book is the negation and *erasure* of language as a whole and of the Book as such. Writing performs a cutting from and splitting apart of the whole into unbound, boundless fragments.

Accordingly, language as we know it is but the scar left on the linguistic world of humans by the prey that escapes it into uncircumscribable liberty: "Thus the bird, drunk with liberty, in its flight pierces the nets of the bird-catcher whose universe bears the scar" ("Ainsi l'oiseau, ivre de liberté, pourfend dans son envol les rets de l'oiseleur dont son univers porte la cicatrice," *El*, p. 84). We can have only metaphors for the "Book" or for the divinity that escapes expression, since its "essence" is perceptible to us at all only in this very escape.

Jabès strongly identified with his friend ("mon ami") Paul Celan, who has often been accorded a certain emblematic value as the poet of poetry without images.[41] He wrote that he was united with Celan by everything ("tout me rapproche de lui"), but in particular by "one and the same interrogation and the same wounded word" ("Une même interrogation nous lie, une même parole blessée").[42] Within this common project the two poets take different directions, inwards toward the unnameable Name of God at the core of language, and outwards toward the unspeakable "that which happened." Yet for both alike, language does not attain its object except in canceling itself out: the word is but "the trace that it leaves" (Jabès).

iii

Celan's poetry dwells obsessively on the experience of annihilation, referring everything, as noted above, to "my 20th of January," the date the Nazis decided on the "final solution." Read in the context of his oeuvre, nearly every poem seems to generalize the historical catastrophe of the Holocaust in negative—and in various ways self-negating—images that find this annihilation lurking everywhere and in everything, at the threshold of speech. Celan's unmistakable voice vibrates in the unflinching naming of nothing—or even the negating of naming altogether—in the evocation of a screaming silence in the most intimate core of every experience. This penetrating silence at the same time makes the words of Celan's poetry peculiarly recalcitrant to interpretation. As Aris Fioretos suggests, "What remains incomparable, today, in Celan's poetry, are its traces of words—its remnants of expatriated meaning—which cannot be assimilated successfully in the 'digestion' of any interpretation."[43]

Celan was recognized early on as the creator of an original poetry and poetics in which words verge upon silence. Decades ago, Theodor Adorno influentially wrote that "Celan's poems attempt to express the most extreme horror [*das äußerste Entsetzen*] through remaining silent [*durch Verschweigen*] . . . . Their truth-content itself becomes something negative."[44] Not long thereafter, Maurice Blanchot, in his book on Celan, commenting especially on the lyric "Sprich auch du," powerfully intuited and provocatively expressed the negative poetics of silence and absence at the heart of Celan's poetry in suggesting that blanks, stops, and pauses are constitutive of a "non-verbal rigor" which substitutes a void for meaning, a void that is not a lack but a saturation, a saturation with emptiness: "And what speaks to us in these usually very short poems, where terms, phrases seem, by the rhythm of their brevity, undefined, surrounded by blankness, is this blankness itself; the arrests, the silences are not pauses or intervals allowing for respiration in reading, but belong to the same rigor, which authorizes very little relaxation, a nonverbal rigor that is not destined to bear sense, as if the void were less a lack than a saturation, a void saturated with the void."[45]

However, widely divergent ways of interpreting the silence generated by Celan's language have emerged in the critical literature. On the one hand, his poems are said to evoke a utopic, pure language born from silence ("die reine, aus dem Schweigen heraus geborene Sprache"), which does not exist except as an unheard claim ("unerhörten Anspruch") in every poem.[46] And they are read, accordingly, for their "intentionality focused on language."[47] On the other hand, the silences of his poems can also be read as *deixis,* as pointing dumbly in the manner of an index to contextual circumstances unsayable in their concreteness.[48] Thus, enormous effort has also gone into searching out historical and biographical keys to what Celan cryptically leaves unsaid.[49] So, while Celan has become more and more widely recognized as the poet of unspeakability par excellence, the bases and thrust of this poetic of silence remain in the highest degree controversial. Is Celan's language mystic or anti-mystic? Is it a dissolving of reference or an absolute intensifying of reference in relation to history and specifically the Holocaust?[50]

The very marked mystical affinities are routinely underscored, for example, in readings by Dietlind Meinecke, who concentrates especially on the mystery and magic of the Name in his *Wort und Name bei Paul Celan,* while they are made the key to reading Celan by Joachim Schulze in his *Celan und die Mystiker.*[51] This mystical background is acknowledged by Shira Wolosky, but she insists that, in keeping with Jewish mysticism and the Kabbalah, as against Christian mysticism directed toward silent union beyond language, Celan conserves the highest regard for language as the dimension in which the divine is encountered: "This metaphysically positive attitude towards language, and the structure implied by it, in which, as Scholem writes elsewhere, 'language constitutes the medium in which the spiritual life of man is accomplished,' ultimately frames the function and treatment of language and silence in Celan's work."[52] However, Amy Colin concludes her essay in the same volume with references to Wittgenstein and to Celan's endeavor to overcome "bewitchment by means of words."[53]

Presumably, deciding these controversies for one side or the other would be needlessly reductive. They point to ways in which Celan's poetry places traditional categories under pressure and invites us to look through the cracks of our conceptual armature to other possibilities of conceptualizing and perhaps, rather, of *de*conceptualizing. Deconstructive readings, heavily influenced by Derrida's *Shibboleth* (1986), as well as by Philippe Lacoue-Labarthe, Werner Hamacher, and others, have demonstrated the peculiar aptness of this avenue of approach to Celan.[54] In a further comment, Derrida points out that idioms are in language that which cannot be appropriated ("l'idiome—ce qui ne peut pas être approprié").[55] The most proper language is what most resists all forms of appropriation. Such is the paradox of poetic language as communication of the incommunicable. Accordingly, emptying language of determinate content, as well as dismantling its form, are key to any possibility of answering to the otherness of an untranslatable ownness. Poetry's essential structures are presented by Celan as most essentially empty ("leer"): "Leerformen" ("empty forms," "Die silbe Schmerz"), "Leerzeile" ("empty lines," "Sommerbericht"), "Leertext" ("empty text," "Die Posaunenstelle").

Nevertheless, while crucial aspects of his poetics are illuminated by an apparently deconstructive repudiation of all fixed and stable meaning, Celan still adheres to a language of return, reality, and even eternity and origin.[56] Celan's chief poetological discourse, "Meridian," the Darmstadt address delivered on the occasion of his receiving the Büchner Prize in 1960, works out a description of poetry that pivots on precisely these terms that have often been anathematized by certain deconstructive ideologies. Celan insists on "a sort of homecoming," tracing "the shape of a circle which, via both poles, rejoins itself and on the way serenely crosses even the tropics"[57] where he encounters himself—as an estranged I. The poem is the "connective" ("das Verbindende"), the "meridian," the means of an encounter with what is wholly other, and therefore of encounter with oneself, too, as genuinely human.

Without tightly embracing any particular school of interpretation, we can at least say that Celan's poetry reads, and has been widely read, as a translating of silence into speech and vice versa. One of a numerous company of critics who have dedicated minutely probing study to this subject, Leonard Olschner, for instance, focuses on "the silences from which his poetry emanates, the silences inherently belonging to Celan's sense of language."[58] Olschner, following Adorno in attempting to retrace Celan's "path from horror to silence," reads Celan's career ending in suicide as an unsuccessful struggle against the ineluctable encroachment of silence: "In the course of Celan's development, the texts become increasingly inaccessible and also more numerous, even if generally more terse—as though the poet were writing, futilely, to stem a threatening flood of silence. The final surrender, Celan's suicide in 1970, is also the final silence."

Olschner quotes Walter Benjamin's essay, "On Language as Such and on the Language of Men," to the effect that the communicating process is "a translation of the silent into the audible" (p. 384). The question guiding his inquiry, then, is "How do we define such resistance to engulfing silence, resistance which consists of designating the unspeakable, not in metaphysical categories, although perhaps in metalinguistic ones?" (p. 37). In this perspective, it is imperative to "not relegate silence to metaphysical fictions." Yet Olschner himself focuses on the influence upon Celan of Osip Mandel'shtam's theory of the preexistence of poetry in silence, which, however different, nevertheless evokes a metaphysical, Platonic order. Celan's poem "Argumentum e silentio" translates much from the Russian of Mandel'shtam's "Silentium" into German. And according to Olschner, "Both texts speak of the poetic word by postulating, respectively, its preexistence and its movement toward and then retreat from incarnation. In 'Silentium,' Mandel'shtam attempts to trace the path of poetic speech back to its origins in silence and chaos, thereby considering music to assume a transitional or mediating position; it expresses a longing to regain a linguistic Arcadia, the silence from which language issues forth" (pp. 373–74).

"Argumentum e silentio" posits a word that withdraws from the light of day, a word beholden to night, a silent word that accompanies us alongside our transactions with the world. It is liminal, subliminal, shy of the light, yet also an uncontainable surplus that overflows the sea and overflies the stars.

An die Kette gelegt
zwischen Gold und Vergessen:
die Nacht.
Beide griffen nach ihr.
Beide ließ sie gewähren.

Lege,
lege auch du jetzt dorthin, was herauf-
dämmern will neben den Tagen:
das sternüberflogene Wort,
das meerübergossne.

(ll. 1–10)[59]

Laid on the chain
between gold and forgetting:
the Night.
Both grasped after it.
Both let it prove its worth.

Lay,
Lay down there you also now what wishes to come
up dawning beside the days:
the star-overflown word,
the sea-overflowed word.

The sublimity of this word exceeded by star and sea lies in the contexts
that are silenced, yet glimpsed, in the act of disappearing—as by one frozen by fear with wolves attacking from behind, or like blood *not* running
from the poison of a predatory tooth.

Jedem das Wort.
Jedem das Wort, das ihm sang,
als die Meute ihn hinterrücks anfiel—
Jedem das Wort, das ihm sang und erstarrte.

Ihr, der Nacht,
das sternüberflogne, das meerübergossne,
ihr das erschwiegne,
dem das Blut nicht gerann, als der Giftzahn
die Silben durchstieß.

Ihr das erschwiegene Wort.

(ll. 11–20)

To each the word.
To each the word that sang to him,
as the pack attacked him from behind his back—
To each the word that sang to him and froze.

To her, the Night,
the star-overflown, the sea-overflowed,
to her the turned-to-silence,
whose blood did not run, as the poison tooth
drove through the syllables.

To her the word turned-to-silence.

The word emerges here from terrifying violence and persecution. Its silence is the testimony of terror. Its merest, metaphorical mentionings of violence are there to suggest terrors that are not said. In this manner, the poem argues from silence to evoke unspeakable terror.

Osip Mandel'shtam's poetics, predicated on silence as the origin of speech, in fact on the preexistence of the poetic word in an ideal realm of silence or music, were of great importance to Celan as his translator. Olschner shows the impressive extent to which the themes and very locutions of this problematic can be documented in Mandel'shtam's poetry, including the poems Celan translated, especially "Silentium" and "Das Wort bleibt ungesagt."[60] This suggests how Celan could be paired also with Mandel'shtam—to stay within the ambit of post-Holocaust European Jewish lyric—in an examination of poetry as a means of setting into relief ethically inviolable alterities.[61] For both poets, the sense of respect for what cannot be expressed demands rather a dumbness that becomes the poem's main vehicle of expression. Limits of language and barriers to expression are basic to the imagery and poetic language of either writer. Even though this may entail a sort of remythologization in terms of idealities of language, it seems that poetry excels in the expression of inexpressibility and that this, paradoxically, becomes the mode in which alone the sense of alterity and singularity can be communicated—paradoxically, by *not* being communicated, but being marked in its intrinsic recalcitrance to all possible linguistic formulations.

Getting outside of language, stepping out of its inwoven web, emerges as the purpose of writing in Celan's poems written against—as well as with—language. We saw that this entails writing a poetry in which language "grows dumb," in the terms of "Der Meridian." For by delivering itself over to dumbness, poetic language "sets free" what it intends, that which has been silenced. The silence itself persists as a trace, the only possible trace of what cannot be named or said at all in language. For Celan, words are not names but traces, shattered and scattered remnants of an expropriated, destroyed meaning. If this meaning and the language that bears it remain intact, they can never receive—or communicate—the wholly other. Only in being damaged and destroyed does language testify to the reality that it cannot say. In another closely related poetological meditation, the shorter address he gave at Bremen, Celan describes language in the poem as wounded by and searching for reality ("wirklichkeitswund und Wirklichkeit suchend," *GW,* vol. 3, p. 186).

While "Der Meridian" (1960) outlines a poetics of the wholly other, the "ganz Andere," the Bremen address (1958) speaks of language as having to pass "through terrifying silence."[62] Although language offers no words that can articulate silence, nevertheless it emerges from the failed attempt enriched by assuming a quality of pointing toward something that it cannot say, something that is killed by words. Language's very helplessness as played out vis-à-vis what resists it, its being broken down and crucified, are responsible for this enrichment. Curiously, this is language's remaining "secure amid all losses" (*Collected Prose,* p. 34). The form remains: it remains scarred by the realities that come to pass and disintegrate, the murderous terrors that are passed through, leaving only wounded language behind.[63]

Celan thus defines a poetics of language that is underway toward some reality so other, so strange that it can never be grasped by language. At most, it can only leave its mark on language like a wound. Generally, only the failure of language to adequately express and comprehend witnesses to this miss at the crux of the "encounter" ("Begegnung"). Still, this witness by failure is an indirect sort of approach to the reality of the Other that language—and only language—can be directed toward, even without ever being able to attain it. "Toward what? Toward something open, inhabitable, an approachable you, perhaps, an approachable reality. Such realities are, I think, at stake in a poem" (p. 35). In a suggestive image in his speech at Bremen, Celan described the poem as "a letter in a bottle thrown out to sea . . . ," toward someone, some "you."

This other, this you, is one kind of context that the poems cannot express but strive to relate to through failed expression. Celan's is a poetic of encountering the absolute Other, which is also the self estranged from itself and disabused of the disguises placed upon it by social convention and essentially by language. The wholly Other, "das ganz Andere," can be encountered in no word but only in the word's divesting itself of itself in self-devastation. This otherness beyond verbalization can nevertheless be what is most familiar to us, even something like a human presence. Such a presence is what Celan finds expressed by Büchner's character Lucile, from *Dantons Tod,* when she exclaims, "Long live the king!" The exclamation is "a homage to the majesty of the absurd which bespeaks the presence of human beings" (p. 40). This majestic human presence has no proper name, yet it is encountered in poetry. For poetry is a majestic presence of the human being beyond language—as unsayable and in this sense "absurd." Celan states that the poem leads all figures to absurdity ("alle Tropen und Metaphern ad absurdum"). There is no proper way to represent this encounter with the other, who is you perhaps. It defeats all logical expression.

For Celan, poetry is language that can become the path of an encounter with someone that is no one, some Other, and thereby also with ourselves—as alienated, as nobody. Celan opposes poetry in this sense to "art." For art leads in the direction of self-oblivion: aesthetic vision kills and petrifies after the manner of the Medusa. Poetry, by contrast, leads to an encounter with the Other and with oneself in a region that cannot be aesthetically portrayed or represented at all. This nonrepresentable space is human time. In an "art-free manner," when representation and even language are suspended for the moment of a turning of the breath, an "Atemwende," the poem can set the I—estranged from itself—free in its encounter with the wholly Other, who is likewise set free. Poetry summons us to take a "step," rather than remaining purely within language, and to enter the outside world, the world outside language and representation, where otherness is encountered. In "Engführung," Celan exhorts his reader to read no more but to "look," and then to look no more but to "go," to go into the fields where those who died in the concentration camp lie narrowly together. This spells a way out, a pragmatic exit from language, which in being silenced has led to something that cannot be communicated verbally but can only be directly experienced.

Partly it is his insane relation, as a German-speaking Jew in Romania, to the language of the perpetrators of the Holocaust, which obliterated both his parents, that determines Celan's penchant for violating and annihilating language in poem after poem. More generally it is his relation to the unspeakable context for his defective discourse, the *Shoah,* that registers in the linguistic desecrations of every poem. This context haunts the texts as what they cannot say, making them collapse into grimacing disfigurements. It is as indescribable and inaccessible to comprehension that the context has its effect on the poetry.

Such a context can be detected plainly, for example, in the verbal chemistry of "Chymisch." Language is analyzed into elements, breaking it down so as to reveal the cryptic nature of the linguistic compounds that make it up. It is through this alchemical process that the gold of silence is produced:

> Schweigen, wie Gold gekocht, in
> verkohlten
> Händen.
>
> ———
>
> Silence, cooked like gold, in
> charred
> hands.[64]

Here the historical context of the concentration camp workers is lucidly imaged as the agent producing the gold of silence. The final and perfect state of the historical material the poet deals with is to become this silent context over which the burnt-up names of victims are scattered as ashes bestowing their bitter blessing. This ash is "to be blessed" by the inevitable blasphemy of words:

> Alle die Namen, alle die mit-
> verbrannten

Namen. Soviel
zu segnende Asche.

———

All the names, all those
names
burnt with the rest. So much
ash to be blessed.

As these historical traces go up in smoke—"Finger, rauchdünn" ("Fingers, smokethin")—becoming even "Cinder- / less" ("Schlacken- / lose")—the speaker and hearer of the poem themselves are released or dismissed by this hour ("Nicht wahr, auch uns / entließ diese Uhr?"), and the word of the *you* dies here in "passing beyond" ("dein Wort hier vorbeistarb").

"Chymisch" is imagined in the all too familiar context of the concentration camp. But often the unsayability of the context makes it free of specific thematic content (except incidentally) that refers to the historical Holocaust. All identity is effaced in this poetry of and about nothing (sayable). Of course, other historical catastrophes, such as Hiroshima or the Spanish Civil War or the expulsion of the Jews from Spain in 1492, are sometimes alluded to similarly as codes for annihilation. But apart from the fact that such events are subsumed under the Holocaust experience in which Celan himself, together with his Jewish heritage, is inextricably enmeshed, history is evoked in any event not in order to be represented so much as to vanish into the unrepresentable. The annihilation of language itself is enacted in the poems as a way of performing the Holocaust as that which nevertheless cannot as such be represented.

Language itself must enact annihilation, if reality is to be realized uniquely, "once," as in "Einmal." This means that language must annihilate itself: exiting language and its abstract construction of context is necessary to escape from all generalizing valuations so as to enter into the genuinely ethical sphere of the singular and unique, the One and Infinite ("Eins und Unendlich"), where alone light and salvation can be found. As "vernichtet" ("annhilated") yields "ichten" ("ied"), the singular emerges in the form of a subject, an "I" (ich) constructed grammatically as a predicate participle that is gathered as a fragment from the very word for "annihilated"—as was demonstrated in the first section of this essay.

Language in Celan's vision inevitably works by erasing reality and annihilating things: the word steps out in front of the thing and, by fixing its nature in a static essence, does it to death. It substitutes an inert, inanimate concept for the living vibrations of the thing itself. It must therefore itself be neutralized and dismantled in order to let what things really are show through. Celan typically does this by dismembering, maiming, and wounding words. KEINE SANDKUNST MEHR, for example, trails off in progressive reduction of a verbal compound into its atomic components:

> Tiefimschnee
>
>   Iefimnee
>
>   I – i – e

The original expression means "deep in snow"—a good description from Celan's perspective of almost anything as covered over, whited out, and, in effect, "frozen" by the language that describes it. As the phrase reduces to minimal traces, language melts away, bringing out a syntax of empty spaces between the letters, as indicated by the dashes. As the saturation by language attenuates through the filtering away of heavier, consonantal components, an unspeakable reality of what remains unarticulated between the letters is released from the empty space in their midst.

In this very *dis*articulating of language, Celan's poems expose what they cannot say. Something indefinable comes to fruition in the context of the poetic utterance, as elicited by the poem's retraction and destruction of itself as language. The pressure of context is palpable, even while remaining unspecified, in a poem like "Zwölf Jahre." This context outside the poem perdures and yet changes over the space of twelve years. Not anything intrinsic to the poem and word-immanent, but rather this temporal reality outside it, makes it true:

> Die wahr-
> gebliebene, wahr-
> gewordene Zeile: . . . *dein*
> *Haus in Paris – zur*
> Opferstatt deiner Hände.

The line
that remained, that
became true: . . . *your*
house in Paris – become
the altarpiece of your hands.

Twelve years presumably have elapsed since the writing of the line datable in 1960 that is quoted in the poem consequently entitled "Twelve Years." The original line, in fact from "Auf Reisen," a poem that Celan dated "Vienna 1948," speaks out of a silence, a twelve-year silence at the time of its reinscription. Apart from anything the poem says, it makes this silence audible. This gap, the space of time featured in the title (alluding also to the twelve years of the Nazi regime in Germany), is the express subject of the poem: it is this twelve years' silence that makes the line remain (and thereby also become) true. The twelve-year interval enables a return to the original, bridging the gap of elapsed time and registering it as silence. Not any actual word or positive entity, but rather this elapse of time, this silence, is the bearer of truth.

The original line ("dein Haus in Paris zur Opferstatt deiner Hände") in its reprise twelve years later is broken in pieces and distributed over three lines. The dash in its middle also breaks the line—which is evidently key to its remaining (by becoming) true. The silence, moreover, before and after the poem, any poem, is brought here into its midst and is marked visibly by the gap in the poem's middle section.

Dreimal durchatmet,
dreimal durchglänzt.

. . . .

Es wird stumm, es wird taub
hinter den Augen.
Ich sehe das Gift blühn.
In jederlei Wort und Gestalt.

———

Breathed through thrice,
shone through thrice.

. . . .

It's turning dumb, turning deaf
behind our eyes.
I see the poison flower.
In all manner of words and shapes.

The ellipses in the middle are the enactment of the silence—or rather the growing dumb—on which the poem pivots. At precisely this point (that is, these points), the poem breaks into two.[65] Each part is thereby isolated from the other by silence. The silence of the line cited in the first part is respected even in being reinscribed into a new poetic utterance in which it becomes true. Occurring in cursive, it is not spoken with the rest of the lines, and in this sense it remains unspoken.[66] The other part of the poem moves forward toward the "you" who is addressed, the one to whom the poem writes or ascribes itself ("schreibt sich dir zu"). But this present or future context remains just as quintessentially silent as the past context in which the line was originally written.

Whatever else they *can* do, words cannot remedy silence. Words can only "poison" it, however organically they grow up around this crack in the page. It opens, in effect, as an altar of sacrifice upon which sayable, stateable significance is slaughtered. The poem becomes thereby emptied of significance such as that conjured up in the threefold ritualistic repetitions of the spirit of prophecy ("Dreimal durchatmet") and of the light of revelation ("dreimal durchglänzt"). These rituals immediately precede the break, and their meaning, so to speak, falls into this gap. With meaning exorcised in this way, the poem remains as but the gesture of citation of what has no recuperable content. "Love" itself evades all intrinsic meaning and erases its own name and becomes a mere blanket attribution to the "you" at the end and on the outside of the poem. Time and historicity of context are evoked by this text in order to be left open, unspecified—to be let disappear through the fissure in the middle of the poem.

In general, every word or shape "poisons" that which it is produced to convey. The word is the death of the live impulse that gave rise to it and that it would express, for it fixes this preverbal motion in static conceptual form. Only in disappearing and growing dumb can language indicate the changing and uncontainable, and therefore unnameable, life-forms toward which it gestures. This unsayable nothing-that-can-be-said is itself without word. The concept fixes meaning and thereby kills it even as it blooms. Coming to expression in speech is a blooming that blasts: after being articulated in the word, the indefinable motion of the soul that issues in speech will never again be quite what it originally was. Real love for life and its free, unconstrained growth and movement cannot survive such delimitation. In this sense, love erases names ("Die Liebe löscht ihren Namen"). It gives itself rather to the other in ascribing itself to "you."

> Geh. Komm.
> Die Liebe löscht ihren Namen: sie
> schreibt sich dir zu.

> ———

> Go. Come.
> Love blots out its name: to
> you it ascribes itself.

This struggle between the word and love is already adumbrated in the two terms for truth at the beginning of the poem that is "wahr*geblieben*" ("remained true") because it is "wahr*geworden*" ("become true"). Interrupting its words and isolating its syllables first brings to light the poem's literal word ("wahr- / geWORDene") and encrypted love ("wahr- / gebLIEBEne"): these hidden graphemes emerge retrospectively as planted in the parallel past participle forms at the poem's beginning only after Word ("Wort") and Love ("Liebe") have emerged expressly as key themes by the poem's end.[67] They must be torn out of the words in which they are embedded. Similarly, the prophetic truth of the line from the earlier poem has been made to shine out only by breaking the line into three—hence, again, three times "breathed through" ("Dreimal durchatmet") and "shone through" ("dreimal durchglänzt") by empty space.

Interrupting words and their conspicuously organic unity is often instrumental to revelation of more deeply encrypted, silent meanings. This imperative of silence is expressed by Celan, for example, in his poem for Bertolt Brecht: "Ein Blatt" ("a page," literally "a leaf"). Celan reverses this author's famous lines: "What times are these in which a conversation on trees is practically a crime because it entails silence about so many egregious misdeeds?" ("Was sind das für Zeiten, wo / Ein Gespräch über Bäume fast ein Verbrechen ist / Weil es ein Schweigen über so viele Untaten einschließt . . . ?"). It is perhaps silence alone that is *not* criminal in times where every word risks being blasphemous vis-à-vis unspeakable horror. It is, in any case, by its interrupting and deforming language that the poem becomes expressive indirectly of what language cannot express. In "Ein Blatt," Celan offers Brecht just "a page" torn off from the tree, a trace with no more organic connection to any living, growing source ("baumlos"), refusing grammatically connected discourse. In its isolation from any living tree and vital stream of speech, this fragment of broken discourse echoes with silence like a tomb.

Celan gives an interpretation of such disconnection (. . .) standing at the source of poetic creativity in ". . . Rauscht der Brunnen" (". . . Plashes the Fountain"). This traditional image for poetic inspiration depicts the spontaneous, inarrestible flow of inspired speech. But Celan's words, and along with them the poet, are instead crippled, and precisely that is their uprightness:

> Ihr meine mit mir ver-
> krüppelnden Worte, ihr
> meine geraden.

> ———

> You my words being crippled
> together with me, you
> my hale ones.

Being crippled makes them sound. Any word pretending to be simply straight and whole cannot but be mendacious. So, paradoxically, crutches in this poem are wings: "Krücke du, Schwinge. Wir - -" ("You crutch, you wing. We - -").

The use, moreover, of the personal pronomial forms of address (singular and plural) perhaps insinuates a lack of any possible objectivity in language, as well as an animistic communion with the inanimate. Yet such personal address (both first and second person) becomes so obsessive as to undermine the mystique of poetic apostrophe. It occurs here in conjunction with conventional images—roses—described as worn out, as past:

Und du:
du, du, du
mein täglich wahr- und wahrer-
geschundenes Später
der Rosen -:

And you:
you, you, you
my later of roses
daily worn true and
more true -:

Such a stuttering apostrophe does not issue in the presence of the apostrophized so much as in its perpetual deferral. Truth invoked by words appears not as present but as belated and worn out. Inspiration is diffused. Words are inadequate forms for what requires rather prayer and silence. Breaking the "tear" into two ("Träne-und- / Träne") helps disperse its ready-made sentimental significance. In fact, here the work is done not by the words at all but by the poet's silence. His "silence" cuts like a "prayer-sharp knife" ("ihr / gebetscharfen Messer / meines Schweigens"). Words in comparison are but child's play—"We shall sing the nursery rhyme" ("Wir werden das Kinderlied singen"). As so often, here also Celan breaks words down into their subsemantic components, and the broken bits turn out to be saturated with meaning. In "mit den Men, mit den Schen, mit den Menschen, ja das" ("with the *men*, with the *jen*, with the human being [*menschen*], yes, that"), Celan discovers the English and Chinese words for "man" buried in the German word for "human being." To him this demonstrates that the significant elements of words are dispersed among and between languages, which with their whole structures and systematized codes come always too late for truth.

The goal, whole and intact, toward which words can aim is, in one sense, the you—the one who would receive and thereby gather their sense into one. But this you is, in effect, transcendent—shrouded in an unknowable night:

DEIN
HINÜBERSEIN heute Nacht.

————

YOUR
BEING BEYOND in the night.

Words would fetch this you, make it present, and so be true—though in reality they remain but a waiting upon truth:

Mit Worten holt ich dich wieder, da bist du,
alles ist wahr und ein Warten
auf Wahres.

————

With words I fetched you back, there you are,
all is true and a waiting
for truth.

Calling into the presence of the word is bringing to truth—but to truth as absent. Words do not enable us to see, except in part. We see an organic growth, a bean stalk, but like Jack in "Jack and the Bean Stalk" we cannot see the top toward which it grows. That summit transcends our horizon circumscribed as it is by the window of our consciousness. We only blindly *think* the perspective of one who could truly see this presence that is right beside us in its immanence: we cannot perceive it in its wholeness or transcendence.

Es klettert die Bohne vor
unserm Fenster: denk
wer neben uns aufwächst und
ihr zusieht.

————

In front of our window
the bean-plant climbs: think
who is growing beside us and
watches it.

This is to perceive God partially and as scattered:

Gott, das lasen wir, ist
ein Teil und ein zweiter, zerstreuter:

———

God, so we have read, is
a part and a second, a scattered one

Only in death, in the death of those mowed down (we can imagine the
grass of "Engführung"), does God grow whole. Only by being truncated
in their visible growth do they become whole and infinite in an invisible
dimension:

im Tod
all der Gemähten
wächst er sich zu.

Dorthin
führt uns der Blick,
mit dieser
Hälfte
haben wir Umgang.

———

in the death
of all those mown down
he grows himself whole.

There
our looking leads us,
with this half
we keep up relations.

We look toward this region of wholeness and transcendence and are in relation to it by our looking, but it is the half we do not see. We "have to do" ("haben wir Umgang") with it, but we do not *have* it: what we have and can conceive is but a half, not the whole. Such is our experience of others as others—it is possible only on the basis of our own insufficiency. Although we see a segment of the whole bean stalk as framed by our window and see not above or below it, we are nevertheless directed and related to something beyond what we see.

Thus our predicament in questing for the other, the you, is like digging in ourselves:

> ES WAR ERDE IN IHNEN, und
> sie gruben.
>
> ———
>
> THERE WAS EARTH INSIDE THEM, and
> they dug.

They dig and dig and do not praise God, nor do they think up any language. They simply dig. This activity supplants all other supposedly higher efforts of communication or communion. And, in digging, all individual identity is lost. So this digging within oneself becomes itself an opening to the other and a mutual bond of union, a kind of mystic marriage:

> O du gräbst und ich grab, und ich grab mich dir zu,
> und am Finger erwacht uns der Ring.
>
> ———
>
> O you dig and I dig, and I dig towards you,
> and on our finger the ring awakes.

Only by digging in silence toward each other, that is, toward nowhere ("nirgendhin"), can I and Thou be unearthed and indeed united—at a depth outreaching separate, individual identity.

The fundamental orientation to the unsayable of Celan's characteristically aporetic conversation, his beyond-of-dialogue, is simply and lucidly expressed again in MIT ALLEN GEDANKEN:

MIT ALLEN GEDANKEN ging ich
hinaus aus der Welt: da warst du,
du meine Leise, du meine Offne, und –
du emfingst uns.

———

With all my thoughts I
went out of the world: and there you were,
you my quiet, my open one, and—
you received us.

The "you" on which the poems hinge, in which their significance can happen and take hold, if anywhere, has a certain pressure or weight of reality—
but without any sayable, nameable identity. It is experienced only as being
lost, thus, when "it is no longer" (ES IST NICHT MEHR), and at this
point, "It, like you, has no name" ("Es hat, wie du, keinen Namen").

Celan is seeking a sign that can stand outside of and without language. This means standing alone and unrecognized and for no one, like
the "no one's rose" ("die Niemandsrose"). And yet it means being *with* all
that is there, inarticulately, dumbly, without language. Such a sign Celan
conceives as a raw wound, one that is not understood or clearly marked as
a sign through being inserted within some linguistic code; it is rather a
sign that stands in shadow and up in the air:

STEHEN im Schatten
des Wundermals in der Luft.

Für-niemand-und-nichts-Stehn.
Unerkannt,
für dich
allein.

Mit allem, was darin Raum hat,
auch ohne
Sprache.

———

TO STAND in the shadow
of the scar up in the air.

To stand-for-no-one-and-nothing.
Unrecognized,
for you
alone.

With all there is room for in that,
even without
language.

This image of a free-standing wound that signifies by standing in its own shadow and without language epitomizes the relation to an overshadowing and obliterating context: it epitomizes Celan's poetic language, mutilated and mortified to the point of erasure.

In this as in other images, Celan also emphasizes how language actually bars one from experience of the Other. The weave and mesh of language become a sort of grid of prison bars. Celan is recorded as speaking of this barrier between poet and reader in relation to his poem "Sprachgitter": "I stand in another space—and on another level of time with respect to my reader; he can understand me only 'from a distance'; he cannot take me in his grasp; he always grasps only the grid-bars between us."[68] The language that enables communication also arrests it. This is the impasse demonstrated over and over again in Celan's poems. Only in breaking up and finally breaking away from language altogether do they succeed. Access to the other can come about only in silence beyond identity and speech. This holds whether the other in question is the singularity of *was geschah*—the historical event—or that of the other person in the present tense of direct address in the poem, which is always also an absence. The words of the poem must erase and annihilate themselves in the face of either of these two sorts of context.

Clearly, these examples could be multiplied. They are meant to be illustrative of the workings of the new and peculiar language of poetry discovered or invented by Celan. In the background, we are aware of a powerful historical matrix and motivation: each poem is marked as some-how an attempt to write poetry after Auschwitz. Each opens a way of re-membering that leaves *what happened* unresolved, unintegrated, and as such preserved by its description's being destroyed. In this manner, the whole, intact image that circumscribes and re-presents a whole mean-ing, which would inevitably disguise and belie what happened, does not substitute for the dismemberment of destruction that as such cannot be re-membered. This language is rather a mimesis of destruction in act. It enacts the logic of discourse that cancels itself out: everything in the world is perceived through and from this act of self-negation. That is the poetic act par excellence as it is redefined by Celan's post-Holocaust poetics. It is not the form-giving, great-shaping work of the imagination formerly cele-brated by Romantic poets. Such an idea shows up more as myth against the "decreation" (to use Simone Weil's expression) through self-annihilation that the poetic word enacts, over and over again, in the poems of Paul Celan. Thematically, this refusal of language to express by encompassing and re-presenting an object is translated as silence. Dramatically and de-monstratively, by coming undone and falling apart in itself, Celan's poetic language indeed speaks silence through growing dumb.

iv

Two models of apophatic discourse are at work in Celan and Jabès, as they are throughout the apophatic tradition. They are based, respectively, on the unsayability inherent in being and on the unsayability inherent in lan-guage. The first can be traced from the Greeks: it developed in Neopla-tonic discourses revolving around the One that Logos cannot comprehend. This One is the supreme source of Being as such and therewith also of all beings throughout the universe. Yet it remains itself inaccessible to every effort of knowledge by means of the Logos: it is the ineffable par excel-lence. The other paradigm of apophasis has its matrix in the problematic of the unnameability of God as it devolves from Jewish interpretations of the Torah and, following them, from Christian and Muslim meditations on the revelation of the divine Names. Here, language itself is the starting point, and the divine Name stands as the ineffable instance at the source and core of language. In the first case, the unsayable is figured as lying out of reach beyond language, whereas in the second it is posited as right in the midst of language, in its very origin in the divine Name, though still as ungraspable by any human linguistic means.

How shall we situate Jabès and Celan in relation to these two models? Jabès attributed to Celan a search for unsayable reality as an absolute of language: "His poetry was but the search for a reality. Reality of a language. The real, that is, the absolute."[69] Yet this perhaps describes Jabès's own search best. Both poets seek through words the disclosure, or at least the recognition, of an absolute reality. In monotheistic tradition, such an absolute was often called God, although strictly speaking it cannot be called by any name at all. But does Celan seek this absolute *in* language or rather *outside* language and through its annihilation? Jabès acknowledged this other possibility—not linguistic consciousness at all but rather its refusal: "But the question still poses itself: would the language of silence be that of the refusal of language or, on the contrary, that of the memory of the first word?"[70] The title Jabès gave to his little book on Celan—*The Memory of Words: How I Read Paul Celan*—suggests his own commitment to searching out the source of his words in language itself, in a mythical first word. Jabès tellingly entitled his own original collected verse poems *I Build My Dwelling (Je bâtis ma demeure)*. But the other alternative, that of constantly breaking out of words rather than building one's dwelling within them, in crucial ways aligns with Celan's leaning best.

Still, both the extralinguistic and the intralinguistic approaches to apophasis are clearly discernible in both Celan and Jabès—both poets use these two avenues as intersecting and interpenetrating. The difference between them is a matter rather of emphasis and orientation. Indeed, Greek Neoplatonic speculation on the ineffable One-Nothing and Jewish, Kabbalistic theology of the unutterable divine Name have been tangled together all through Western intellectual tradition. Just as being and language are mutually relative terms, so also the absolute of what cannot be said in the register of either being or language emerges in complementary fashion from the parallel reading of these two apophatic oeuvres.

Differentiated this way into two branches, apophatic tradition has been used here as a general framework to make this juxtaposition of two contemporary Jewish Diaspora poets mutually illuminating. This comparison shows, moreover, something of the widely diverse and apparently contradictory possibilities inherent in the paradigm of apophasis as a mode of poetry and of discourse generally. The passage beyond language seems to be indissociable from an extreme reduction to a practically exclusive concentration upon language. Both movements are unmistakably evident in both poets. Yet, whereas Jabès makes the universe seem to disappear into the totality of language, the Book, Celan characteristically annihilates language in deference to what is outside and beyond it. Paradoxically, Celan's language becomes unforgettable, indeed indelible, precisely in its act of self-erasure before the unspeakable of history. Conversely, the reduction of everything to the Book in the universe of Jabès takes place through the disappearance of language itself, its de-realization, its reduction to Nothing.

Both poets, in fact, speak from the coincidence of language and reality in the All-Nothing and thereby resonate with theosophies such as the Kabbalah and Neoplatonism—a joint heritage that they share in common. Each offers an inimitable testimony to the vitality of both of these apophatic traditions in contemporary and postmodern culture, albeit sometimes transformed and disguised, perhaps beyond recognition, by the writing of silence. At the same time, both these traditions, along with the modern poets that transmit them, demonstrate the incongruity of language with any reality that might be deemed true or ultimate. Any such reality is revealed only by the inadequacy and disintegration of language understood as deflected from it.

We have distinguished two paradigms. In one, the more existential model, reality is unutterable in its concreteness. Real individuals are absolutely singular and other and therefore cannot be expressed in their uniqueness by language, which inevitably generalizes. This is paradigmatically the case for the One or God as the first or even the only ultimately real individual. In the other, more linguistic model, reality is not external but is rather immanent to language. The ultimate instance or essence of language, the divine Name or the first word, proves, nonetheless, to be unattainable in its endlessly internal relays. Again, the would-be real is unveiled always and only as nothing that can be said. This Nothing would be the ultimately real, except that it cannot be asserted as real, or be said at all, any more than it can, as such, be revealed. Precisely the disintegrating, disappearing tendencies of language, which are exalted and exploited in different ways by each poet, become channels for relating to this unsayable Other. Language relates to the unsayable paradoxically by losing all relation to it—through dissolution of itself. In both cases, though for different reasons, language is exposed in its inability to express, and this is its greatest, perhaps its only genuine, expressive power.

Part II

PHILOSOPHY AND THEOLOGY

Chapter Four

APOPHASIS AND THE PREDICAMENT OF PHILOSOPHY OF RELIGION TODAY

From Neoplatonic Negative Theology to Postmodern Negations of Theology

Alles was gesagt wird ist wert genichtet zu werden.
(All that is said is worthy of being annihilated.)

i

The situation of philosophy today makes it peculiarly receptive to a great variety of apophatic discourses, not only to those devolving from mono-theistic traditions concerning the unnameable Name of God, especially in mystical currents, including the Kabbalah and Sufism, but also to those consisting of negative-theological speculations in an onto-theological vein, like the Neoplatonist philosophies revolving around the inaccessible being or beyond-being of the One. Mysticism and negative theology have again become powerful paradigms for knowledge in a postmodern age, which is no longer bound to the rational foundationalism that guided the lead-ing strains of philosophical thought and culture throughout the modern period.

This description suggests already what sorts of reasons may account for such a heightened receptivity. If the quest for foundations is the inaugural project of modern philosophy since Descartes, it has fallen into crisis and in many quarters today is given up for lost. Human rational reflection has proven inadequate to ground itself, despite the best and most determined efforts undertaken from Descartes to Hegel, for whom philosophy is finally absolute self-grounding knowledge of the subject. This failure to prove self-grounding has placed philosophy on an equal footing with other forms of rationality that admit to having their grounds outside themselves. Preeminently, theological discourse acknowledges God as its transcendent ground, and the widespread forsaking of foundationalism by contemporary philosophers of numerous persuasions has contributed in no small measure to the "return of religion" that in our time has been blazoned widely, not least by philosophers themselves.

Neoplatonism was similarly born out of a crisis of foundations in ancient philosophy in Hellenistic times: its historical emergence parallels in certain crucial ways the unsettling of intellectual frameworks that precipitated the turn from modern to postmodern thought.[1] In spite of its well-known penchant for propounding elaborate metaphysical systems, Neoplatonism, profoundly considered, contemplates the impossibility of articulating any rational foundation for thought and discourse. It accepts the radical lack of any articulable first principle for metaphysics, especially as this type of thinking developed from the late speculations of Plato. The impossibility of rational foundations is evident particularly in the *Parmenides*, where it is demonstrated that there can be no discourse or knowledge of the One, on which all nevertheless depends. Knowledge and discourse always entail multiplicity (at least between knower and known, not to mention the inherent duplicity of saying or knowing something *about* something) and thus are contrary to the very nature of the One.

This conundrum plays itself out especially in the more esoteric Platonic doctrines handed down through the Middle Platonic and Neoplatonic sources that claimed to transmit Plato's oral teaching, which was held to be more true and authentic than all that he wrote. These "unwritten doctrines" (ἄγραφα δόγματα), referred to by Aristotle (*Physics* bk. 4, ch. 2, 209b14–15) and by Theophrastus and other pupils, turned on the One, which is the unsayable par excellence. In this doctrine, the ultimate principles of things, beyond even the Platonic Ideas, which were themselves the principles of sensible things, were the One and a Twoness, or Unity and Multiplicity, in which the Ideas themselves needed to participate in order to exist, as Aristotle explains in the *Metaphysics* (bk. 1, ch. 6, 988a10–15).

These unwritten teachings have been made an object of intensive study particularly by the so-called Tübingen school of Plato scholarship. The research of Hans Joachim Krämer, Konrad Gaiser, and others has opened up a space of mystery at the heart of Plato's teaching, the ground of which begins to look less like a rational, philosophical foundation and more like religious experience.[2] The unwritten doctrine, which, according to *Phaedrus* 278d, concerns things more worthy (τιμιώτερα) than those treated in the writings, gestures beyond to "the realm of the completely unsayable" ("Bereich des gänzlich 'Unsagbaren'"), the ἄρρητον. "The knowledge of the principle of being *in itself* is removed from the Logos and is reserved for an intuitive-'mystical' experience."[3]

There is, of course, an obvious contradiction or paradox in maintaining that an oral teaching about the One should be silent or somehow less effable than the doctrines written in the dialogues, as well as in maintaining that a doctrine of the *One* should somehow be anti-foundationalist. What is the One, if not the supreme foundation par excellence? And would not direct oral teaching for Plato be a way of keeping true to the word rather than of discarding and surpassing it? Indeed, Krämer interprets the oral teaching as *supplementing* writing, in the terms of the *Phaedrus*, or as *saying* what could not be rendered in writing, and thus as *against* positing anything as intrinsically unsayable.[4]

However, this argument can also cut the other way: as final ground, a supplement is never sufficient. Just as writing lacks its foundation in itself and must be supplemented by oral teaching, so, too, this oral teaching in the end is lacking in an immanent foundation and can be completed only by what it cannot say, indeed by what cannot be said at all—the ineffable. The fact that the oral teachings were mysterious and secret—not allowed and perhaps not even able to be divulged—reads as a cipher for their unmasterability and elusiveness. These unrecorded teachings, or *agrapha,* are intriguing because they introduce a kind of unknown at the very foundations of the Platonic system of knowledge, which become inaccessible.

A literary corpus that is dependent for its intelligibility upon a theory of the principles given only in an unwritten teaching takes the shape of *logoi* dependent on what they do not contain and cannot say. This arrangement mirrors the structure of Neoplatonic reality in relation to its own "beyond" as suspended from what cannot be comprehended within it, from what lies beyond the threshold even of the conceivable.

We know from the *Parmenides* that absolutely nothing can be said about the One as such, although everything whatever that *is* said is said always in some kind of relation with the One. All that was said and taught concerning it was rather "about" it in a sense that left the One itself unexplained and incapable even of being adequately expressed. This is the predicament that the unwritten doctrines are called upon to manage and to mitigate.

In the name of an ineffable experience at the origin of all of Plato's thought, Christina Schefer has delineated certain limits and aporiae of the Tübingen paradigm. This paradigm rightly identifies the void of the unwritten teaching, which is itself further identified as the theory of principles ("Prinzipienlehre") that concerned a mysterious, undetermined duality (ἀόριστος δυάς). Yet it is constantly faced with the paradox of dealing philologically with writing, even while by its own reckoning all that really counts is what remains *un*written. According to the unwritten doctrines purportedly expressed in Plato's lectures "On the Good" (Περὶ τἀγαθοῦ) and handed down through the tradition, Plato's thinking rested not on one but on two irreducible principles, or two beginnings (ἀρχή), a Unity and Duality (Large-Small), without derivation of one from the other. This is already a contradiction of the idea of a unified foundation, of one principle, the One, at the base of everything. In the end, the Tübingen school itself speaks of aporiae and of an "open system" ("offenen System").[5] The system of knowledge opens, beyond logic and speech, to what Logos cannot grasp.

Schefer takes the far-reaching revisionary interpretations of Plato that were initiated by the Tübingen school a step further by maintaining that not only unwritten doctrines but, more radically, ineffable experience lies at the source of all knowledge in Plato's thinking. This experience she presents as modeled on the Eleusinian mysteries. In Schefer's view, written and oral philosophizing for Plato find their origin and end in cultic experience and specifically in an ineffable epiphany of the god Apollo, the "not-many" (α-πολλον).[6] This, she argues, was an experience of human mortality as recalled by the formula on the temple of Apollo at Delphi— "Know thyself" (γνῶθι σεαυτόν)—and therewith of the inviolable boundary between the human and the divine.[7]

This is the experience that makes Socrates a true philosopher, one who is cognizant of his ignorance, by teaching him that, for all his knowledge, he does not really know anything. Such would be the sense of the oracle of Apollo at Delphi, which is reported as having said that none is wiser than Socrates (*Apology* 21a6–7). The philosopher, as a lover of wisdom, is described in the *Apology* as being in the service of Apollo (ἡ τοῦ θεοῦ λατρεία, 23b4–c1). This initiatory religious experience of the god Apollo leaves knowing without any properly philosophical grounding or rational foundation. Especially in the further development of later Platonic tradition, a gap of unbridgeable transcendence opens up between the world and its ultimate ground. What may have been intuitive certainty for Plato becomes a missing link shrouded in mystery that can be approached only through mystical experience for his followers, notably those in the Neoplatonic tradition.

The premises of inevitable foundationlessness were thus already present, if not patent, in Plato, but it took another historical moment, one removed from the classical era in which Plato lived, to bring the implications of this fully into view. In late antiquity and particularly in the context of the crumbling Roman Empire, Neoplatonist philosophers from Plotinus to Damascius developed Platonism in directions that clearly showed its opening toward a mystical experience of the ineffable and hence its *un*grounding of rational, philosophical knowledge.

Most importantly, Neoplatonism provides, at least implicitly, a general theory for *why* philosophy and indeed knowledge in general *must*, in rational terms, remain foundationless. Its theory of the One as the transcendent, unknowable source of all opens up a fissure in reality that irreparably separates everything that exists from its ultimate ground. For everything that is exists in total dependence on what *is not*, on what has no objective existence in the manner of finite beings, which is to be with and among other beings. The first principle, the One, is beyond being (equivalently to Plato's Good, according to Aristotle's *Metaphysics* bk. 14, ch. 4,

1091b14) and is therefore unknowable, since knowledge consists necessarily in a Logos of being. It might be said that this unknowable ground alone *is* in a higher, truer sense, but there is no telling what *being* in this sense might mean. Such an imputation can at best express only a negative knowledge of the ontological dependence of all that is on what is not and *cannot* be in the ordinary way. All that is known in relation to the absolute transcendence of the Neoplatonic One is that there is an unbridgeable gulf between the world of beings and anything that can possibly function as their ground.

If the One is to ground all that is, it must *not* be, not at least in any way of being that can be known from the beings which are: otherwise its own being would itself have to be grounded. Nothing *within* the set of existing beings can furnish the transcendent grounding that Neoplatonic metaphysics envisages. Knowledge of beings can disclose only the apparently foundationless existence of beings in the world. So far as beings within the world are concerned, there is no ground. There can be knowledge only of the non-self-sustaining nature of beings. No worldly being can serve the purpose of grounding beings in the world. If there is to be any ground at all for the astonishing fact that beings are—and Greek thought had always been profoundly committed to the idea that all that exists is somehow grounded—it must be of a wholly other nature, outside of and beyond the world. Whether or not we hold to the presumption that there is any ground at all for beings, the Neoplatonic conception of the radical transcendence of the only *possible* ground has far-reaching consequences: it means that all knowing opens upon and issues ultimately in *un*knowing.

In this respect, Neoplatonism is based on a critical overcoming and surpassing of classical Greek ontology.[8] Particularly, it discards the metaphysical assumptions of a realist Platonic ontology, or at least treats them as no longer secure, no longer assured by an intuitively certain knowledge descending from above, where the Good, as the supreme principle of all intelligibility, is ascertained with apodictic certainty. The knowability of things in general is undermined and even evacuated by the recession of the first principle out of the world into unknowability, into a dimension to which not knowledge but only a kind of mystical experience can gain access.[9] Viewed from within the world, things are foundationless, and yet *that* they are and even somehow hang together is given as a fact, and to account for this the Neoplatonists still infer or imagine that there is some kind of ground. It is just that the ground cannot be anything within the ambit of beings that we can know.

It follows, moreover, from its not being within the order of beings and thus of things knowable, that nothing at all can be said of the One that must not also, at the same time, be *un*said. It cannot even be said unequivocally to be One. It is rather ineffable. Or rather, it is "not even ineffable," for it *is* not anything at all. The cleavage between a presumably knowable universe and its necessarily unknowable first principle or ground leaves knowledge without foundation—gaping open and suspended upon an abyss. As an important consequence of this predicament, Neoplatonic discourse attains to a highly refined critical self-consciousness of how even its very own discourse must undermine itself and become self-subverting. That the One is one, that it is ineffable, that it *is* at all become problematic affirmations that must at the same time be negated. And yet all that *is* evidently depends upon such an enigma, upon what cannot be said to be anything at all, nor even be said to be.

On this basis, Neoplatonism reaches a penetrating insight into why there can be no knowledge of anything such as a first principle, not even so far as to be able accurately to call it a "first principle." Nothing whatever can be said of it—nothing that must not, in the same moment, be withdrawn. Just this is, in fact, the conclusion demonstrated by Damascius (ca. 462–538), the last of the ancient Greek Neoplatonic philosophers, in his treatise *De principis (On First Principles).*[10] This work represents the culmination of a tradition of thinking the aporiae of any attempt to think the One as the first principle or ground of the universe. At the other end, at the beginning, of this tradition within the ancient world stands Plotinus (205–270), who is usually recognized as the founder of the new approach to Platonic philosophy that we call Neoplatonism. But the seeds of this innovation are to be found planted already in the aporiae of Plato's *Parmenides.*

A very interesting hypothesis, which helps mitigate the abrupt appearance of such thinking with Plotinus, is that Christian Gnostic sources, as suggested by Porphyry in his *Vita Plotini* (chapter 16), may have influenced Plotinus.[11] A role in mediating Plato's *Parmenides,* with its paradoxes of an "unknowing knowing" and its negating of any predications of the One, including being and oneness, to Neoplatonism, has been ascribed specifically and plausibly to the Sethian Gnostic Allogenes.[12]

Plato had hypothesized a One that cannot be, since if being were added to it, then it would no longer be perfectly one (*Parmenides* 137b–144e). This was the principal basis on which Plotinus was to construct his theory of the One beyond being, the first "hypostasis," the source of all that is. The approach of the mind to this highest principle of its knowing and of every being, and even of being as such, enjoins a relinquishing of Logos and of discourse and, with them, of knowing altogether. Such apophatic speculation develops through a line of Neoplatonic thinkers from Porphyry, Plotinus's direct successor, through Iamblichus to Proclus, Damascius's immediate predecessor. In its most mature phase, with Damascius, the apophatic thrust of ancient Neoplatonism is played out *in extremis* and becomes fully explicit and programmatic. It becomes clear that the entire intricate Neoplatonic order of things is suspended from something that is rather nothing (in terms of the things that are) and that cannot be ordered to any articulable principle or belong to any order whatsoever.[13]

While this might be taken to be only an extreme consequence, it results from what was actually most essential to Neoplatonic thinking all along. In what could be considered the seminal breakthrough of Neoplatonism, being came to be conceived of as infinite.[14] And that meant that any definition of its ground, or even of being in its totality, was necessarily inadequate. Any expression for the cause or first principle of being could comprehend only something finite and definable and therefore would have to be rejected in opening outward toward the infinite and indefinable. The result was an open-ended quest, the new style of speculative mysticism inaugurated by Plotinus. This quest can still be characterized as a quest for an ultimate ground; however, it becomes an endless quest because the ground can never be delimited or defined.

The Neoplatonists are widely known for their invention of complicated and artificial metaphysical discourses and systems, but, more deeply considered, they register the late antique crisis of knowing in a classical, rational sense. This crisis issues in a confrontation with the ineffable that escapes every possible discursively articulated system. This Neoplatonic philosophy of the ineffable, commonly called "negative theology," is critical of all rational formulations as inadequate to what they intend to describe. The ultimate principle of the universe remains beyond the reach of reason. Negative theology arises (or rather comes to self-consciousness) at an advanced stage in the development of rational reflection in any given culture, when the founding myths of that culture are called into question. Indeed, lastly language itself, as the foundation of all culture, must be called into question. At this point, language can no longer be used unself-consciously as having a direct grip on reality and as simply handing over the truth. Discourse's constitutive negativity becomes a central theme in Neoplatonism: its self-negating nature and transforming, annihilating powers become a major preoccupation for certain of the Neoplatonists. No longer concentrated exclusively on what language *does* manage to convey by the light of Logos, Damascius attends obsessively to its failures.

In this respect, the hypertrophy of critical thinking that characterizes contemporary philosophical discourse proceeds down a path blazed long ago by Neoplatonic thought. From our position today, Neoplatonism can be seen retrospectively to represent an early apotheosis of *critical* philosophical thinking. It is philosophical thinking that is critical first and foremost of itself. In fact, every thought that can be thought and therefore expressed is viewed as ipso facto inadequate and subject to critique. All that can be thought or said, affirmations and negations alike, must be negated and given up. This critical aspect of Neoplatonic thought reaches its sharpest formulations in Damascius, "the last and most critical of the great pagan Neoplatonists."[15]

The situation of philosophy today, especially of Continental philosophy, is likewise one that seems to know no alternative to unrestricted and endless criticism: every positive doctrine that can be formulated encounters objections immediately. If there is any consensus, it is that there are no given foundations or stable principles for philosophy to work from—although this view, too, as soon as it is formulated and stated in words, proves controversial and difficult, if not impossible, to sustain. The current philosophical milieu of "limitless criticism," to use a coinage that Hilary Armstrong derives from the French Neoplatonist scholar Jean Trouillard, can be illuminated especially well by the negative theology of the Neoplatonic school and its sequels and spin-offs throughout the course of Western intellectual history up to the present. Underscoring how Plotinus's spiritual and religious approach to reality, in the context of Hellenistic mysticism, radically curtailed the claims of natural reason and philosophy to gain access to an intelligible Truth, Trouillard concludes that philosophy is left with essentially a critical function ("il reste à la philosophie une fonction indispensable qui est essentiellement critique").[16]

With negative theology, critical philosophical thinking becomes indistinguishable from religious thinking: it becomes infinitely open, even open to the Infinite, rather than remaining circumscribed by a method or organon. Philosophical and religious belief alike are by rights subject to this criterion of limitless criticism, according to Armstrong, not only in Hellenistic times but again for us today: "A genuine religious faith in our time must be compatible with limitless criticism."[17]

The principle of limitless criticism has a "positive" and even a prescriptive content, although one that cannot be stated. In fact, it cannot be stated because it is so purely "positive." Any statement requires differentiating what is as stated from what is not and thus permits only a delimited positivity. By contrast, the unsayable principle that makes further criticism always possible and any correction never definitive is purely positive and absolutely negative at the same time, indeed, more positive and more negative than any proposition that can be stated. Nevertheless, this ultra-positive, ultra-negative unsayability makes a claim to being normative for philosophical discourse: it is necessary in order to prevent philosophical discourse from absolutizing either itself or any one of its conceptions, including such concepts as experience and openness, just as much as those of matter or substance or structure. The ways of experiencing and of being open and responsive to this indefinable absoluteness are exactly what apophatic thinkers are concerned to defend and explore without prejudice or constraint, and so they must not presuppose "it" as having any known or definable shape or content.

Apophatic awareness, as a form of critical consciousness, entails the negation of all discourses. However, all discourses, from this point of view, can be recognized as themselves, in effect, already negations.[18] Any discourse we start with, anything we conceptualize and say, is itself always already a negation—the negation of reality itself as it transcends all our concepts and discourses. Apophatic discourse is, then, the negation of this negation that discourse intrinsically is. Apophatic discourse intends to point back toward what, as anterior to all statements that negate some-thing infinite and indefinable by stating it, is simply there. It shows up as precisely *not* what any speech can articulate. Apophasis does not presume to say what is real but backs off and leaves it alone—and thereby lets it show itself as what this discourse (and any discourse) is not and cannot say. The specific ways in which language withdraws and is undone in the face of what it cannot say trace images testifying to this transcendent-of-discourse. The ruins of discourse remain as ruins witnessing to what they cannot depict or determine in any reliable or perhaps even readable way. Their very unreadability says all that can be said about the unsayable.

What distinguishes apophatic thought is that its truth is not in what it affirms and articulates but in the . . . unsayable it-knows-not-what that its self-negation simply makes room for. In terms of content, it has noth-ing particular or positive to offer, but methodologically it can play a key regulatory role, given the pluralistic situation of philosophy today, by of-fering a theory as to *why* this pluralism of discourses is necessary in the first place. For when different philosophies are repositioned and redefined as attempts to say what cannot be said, they reflect upon each other as re-flecting a common . . . something/nothing that they cannot say—except each in its own inadequate way, illuminating it in withdrawing, in taking its positive affirmations back, yet leaving a pregnant, indefinable "sense" of what they were getting at. Different, even apparently contradictory, philosophies are revealed thereby as necessary to each other rather than as excluding and as having to suppress each other.

Apophatic thought does, then, have something *normative* to offer to the whole spectrum of philosophical discourses, even without being able to say anything at all directly about reality as such. From the perspective of Christian, Jewish, and Muslim negative theologies—all of them being de-rivative from pagan, Greek, Neoplatonic negative theology as the cradle of apophaticism historically—it is imperative to acknowledge the ineffable "God" as absolute in order to avoid falling into belief in idols.[19] We might think that we need believe in no gods at all. But somewhere in our logic there is bound to be a fixed point or foundation that will, in effect, be our Absolute. And if our Absolute determines itself in any way, it will not be the truly *absolute* Absolute, the one that cannot be said at all, like the "God" sought in vain by negative theology. It will be rather a relative absolute, one conditioned by some form of representation, and as such it will be an idol. We will be tempted to take it for the absolute or unconditioned Absolute, if we do not keep that position open through some discourse about why it must remain empty for us and for all our discourses. Empty though it must be, still, this place of the Absolute (not to say "place" itself as absolute) needs to be kept constantly in view in order to prevent its being falsely usurped. This is the vital role of negative theology as a sort of empty metaphysic and quasi-transcendental logic of the unsayable.[20]

Philosophy without absolutes is an illusion. We always assume something absolute even in denying it. In effect, we contradict ourselves in saying that nothing, *absolutely* nothing, can be absolute. We need an understanding of how this absoluteness impinges on our discourses in order to keep them translucent and open—and in order to keep the absolute and the relative in relation with one another and yet not utterly confounded together, in which case they would become, each of them, imposters. The ancient wisdom of negative theology, from its matrices in Neoplatonic thought, developed just this sort of theoretical alertness and understanding. That is a primary reason why it has so much to offer to our philosophizing today. This wisdom entails self-awareness of the relativity of all our thinking and its articulations, yet this relativity remains, nevertheless, intimately in relation to that which it cannot delimit or in any way relativize. It is affected and disturbed from outside itself, from above (or below, depending on one's angle of vision).

Not only does this type of (post)critical, negative thinking guard against usurpations by false systems of closed, self-sufficient rationality, but it can also help open us to the inarticulable experience of all that is or at least appears, all that tantalizingly escapes the grasp of discourse and reason. For it disabuses us of belief in rational systems that would close off all possibilities outside and beyond themselves. Cultivating an apophatic outlook can train us to look again and let happen what is truly incomprehensible to us, for negative theology is a discourse that, by reflecting distinctly on our discourse, shows and reminds us that it is *not only* discourse but is also symptomatic of something else entirely. It thereby opens discourse to what it cannot discursively comprehend. This special character and virtue of negative theology has been brought out especially by the recent revival of apophatic thinking leveraged from scholarship on Neoplatonist philosophers. I intend now to situate the view I am articulating within this revival and at the same time to take positions differing from some of the current scholarship, based on my sense of the overall thrust and significance of apophatic thinking.

For J. P. Williams, who claims to be following Hilary Armstrong and Denys Turner, apophasis is fundamentally about discourse itself and represents a possibility of "limitless criticism." It makes no ontological claims.[21] Williams differentiates sharply, indeed categorically, between negation that is self-referential, so as to negate even negation, and negation that only qualifies affirmations, revising them into a higher form of affirmation according to the *via eminentiae*.[22] The latter is the doctrine of negation in Thomas Aquinas and in Middle Platonism, and Williams rigorously holds it to be separate from truly apophatic negation in the strict sense of negation of the negation.

Yet these distinctions in the history of philosophy deal with doctrines codified and interpreted in words and not directly with the deeper apophatic intent of the discourses in question. It is not truly apophatic to make any distinctions *in discourse* ultimate. So, granting the heuristic value of the differences to which Williams points and which are in fact commonly evoked in the scholarship on apophaticism, I do not believe that they discriminate between what is and is not authentically apophatic. All discourses in words fall short of the apophatic, as apophatic writers concordantly insist.[23] The attempt to delimit and define apophasis, so as to avoid promiscuous and indiscriminate use of the term, has strong scientific motivation, but apophasis remains recalcitrant to all definition and simply does not lend itself to being made a useful and well-behaved scientific term. My conviction is that it cannot be sharply delineated by any unequivocally stateable formula or concept, but must be discerned through a finer, indefinable sort of sensibility.[24]

I do not mean to charge that this leading interpreter does not understand apophasis—except to the extent that apophasis, by its very nature, withdraws from any and every attempt to understand it. The problem is that the formulation which makes apophasis a discourse about discourse gives it a positive object. Like all formulas, this one, too, must be withdrawn. Apophasis is not about that, either, nor about anything that can be said. As Denys Turner states, "The apophatic is the linguistic strategy of somehow showing by means of language that which lies beyond language."[25] Turner points out, moreover, that negative language per se is no more apophatic than affirmative language is, distinguishing acutely between "the strategy of *negative propositions* and the strategy of *negating the propositional*; between that of the *negative image* and that of the *negation of imagery*" (p. 35). We must, furthermore, also remind ourselves that the negation of imagery is not simply its absence: imagery must in some manner appear in order to be negated.

Sara Rappe's conception of Neoplatonism, culminating in Damascius, as text-oriented and exegetical in essence likewise makes apophatic philosophy essentially a second-order discourse about discourse rather than a discourse making ontological claims.[26] Yet Rappe realizes—and Damascius, on her reading, is well aware—that it is wrong to say that apophasis is *only* about discourse itself. It demonstrates discourse to be insufficient in itself and dependent on what is neither discourse nor susceptible of being incorporated into discourse. There is a strong temptation to interpret apophasis as being only about discourse, since in that case we can say definitely what it is about. But this sells it short, for then apophatic discourse is presented as having no bearing on extralinguistic reality, no ontological import. While apophasis makes no particular ontological claims, its negations do bear on what has traditionally been treated under the rubric of ontology. This realm is redefined by apophasis as the mystery of the real upon which discourse opens at the limits of what it is able to articulate— as what it cannot formulate and determine in terms of itself. This can be figured, among other ways, simply as Existence. The mystery of existence has been apprehended in apophatic terms by existentialist philosophy in the different styles of Gabriel Marcel and Luigi Pareyson.[27] So beyond its necessary self-critical moment, apophatic discourse is all about this something other, other than itself, indeed other than discourse altogether.

Apophatic discourses testify to some dimension (or at least limit) of experience: they are touched by experience that cannot be spoken in words (whether it is of reality or unreality, being or nonbeing, is not finally decidable). Presumably, this experience cannot be made manifest "itself," "directly" at all, for it is beyond representation altogether. Yet, as Wittgenstein put it, the unsayable nevertheless "shows itself" (*Tractatus* 6.522).

There must, by any account, be some way of "showing" or apprehending at least *that* there is something that cannot be said, even if *what* it is can in no way be determined.[28] Still, this indeterminate "it" may actually be, as Benjamin and Blanchot in different ways suggest, more immediate than any immediacy that is caught between the poles of presence and absence, more present than any presence, although the unmediated experience of it could only be madness, or perhaps the bliss of beatitude.[29]

Like ancient Neoplatonic thinking, contemporary phenomenological philosophies also have their apophatic moments, and they are replete with theological underpinnings. Emmanuel Levinas, Michel Henry, Jean-Luc Marion, and Jean-Louis Chrétien all turn toward the Other, to what is inaccessible precisely in its pure givenness, and propose phenomenologies of an unsayable, invisible instance that remains itself unmanifest, even while allowing everything else to be and become manifest.[30] And here again, generally, only withdrawal from representation and even from every possibility of presentation can be allowed to characterize what cannot be said. This is the movement of a withdrawal—which is apprehended only as having taken place always already—from the zone of articulable experience. Language for what cannot be said is in this sense a "trace" that can never be traced back to any origin.

In deconstructive thinking, the linguistic trace of what cannot be said must precede—and in fact constitute—any presencing or evidencing of the unsayable, which is, to this extent, intrinsically linguistic, that is, an effect of language. The possibility of talking about what cannot be said originates with language as its trace, and indeed, there *is* something to talk about as "what cannot be said" only retrospectively—as what has always already vanished, leaving but a trace. Rather than the trace being derived from the presence it traces, the trace is all that ever becomes real and effectual of the presence, which is never manifest as presence itself and as such but always only as some recognizable, specifiable trait, an instituted trace, which refers to what it is not and cannot re-present but can only mark as vanished, absent, inaccessible.[31]

Admittedly, then, all that can be said about apophatic discourse fails to attain anything like its "essence." Such discourse can be defined only by its relation to something it does not comprehend and cannot adequately or commensurately express. It is what this discourse arises in the face of, and in response to, that constitutes its essential, albeit essentially incommunicable, meaning, its inexpressible import. This being "in-the-face-of" can be inexpressibly concrete and singular. But in attempting to name or say it, we can only generate myths and metaphors, such as "Nameless," "Inexpressible," "Secret," or "Ineffable"—expressions that testify to what they cannot say and cancel themselves out as expressions, leaving only a trace that indicates what cannot be represented or characterized or expressed.

This is to understand apophasis in essentially performative terms. Certain verbal performances can hint at what language cannot articulate but nevertheless somehow shows in the very cancellation of its attempts at expression. It is language's faculty for *un*becoming (from Meister Eckhart's "entwerdende") that is the resource enabling it to designate, or rather adumbrate, what cannot be said—the other of everything that *is* anything and so *can* be said.

That is indeed how recent interpreters have instructed us to understand apophatic discourse. Steven Katz observes that apophatic discourse actually does something different from what it says. For the terms used to deny expressibility are themselves laden with descriptive value. He concludes that apophasis is generally only an abstract, programmatic position that mystical discourse in practice belies, or at least qualifies.[32] But precisely this inconsistency has been recognized by other interpreters as the cunning of apophatic reason or discourse and as its distinctive character and strategy. The ineluctable disjunction between what is said and what is concretely realized in discursive practice is exactly what apophatic discourses mean to focus attention on and illuminate. Michael Sells defines apophasis as a "meaning event" in which language unsays itself. His readings of apophatic texts aim to show how they can "perform (rather than assert) a referential openness."[33] Mystical union is imitated in language that effaces grammatical distinctions between subject and object and thereby collapses or displaces reference.

We have arrived, in some strains of our culture, at a predominantly apophatic phase that repeats moments of this loosely coherent tradition reaching back to the Neoplatonists. Apophasis tends to emerge explicitly at a late stage in the development of thought and culture, at a point in an historical cycle where critical faculties are in the ascendant and creative

faculties in comparison are liable to become atrophied. Of course, creation and criticism can also elicit each other and are often inextricably
interwoven. Still, the full weight of tradition is most acutely sensed at a
phase in which philosophy is essentially about philosophizing itself, and
self-criticism accompanies its every act. Yet the characteristic emphasis of
negative theological thinking is to turn this introversion inside out. The
very emptiness of the self-reflexive introversion of thought and discourse
in our late moment of modernity issues in a turn toward the unsayable,
the Other of thought and discourse that discloses their inexhaustible richness as indicators of what no thought or discourse can fathom. Such is the
provocation of apophasis in its very emptiness (of articulable concepts),
which evokes everything: its very saying of nothing suggests all. Discourse
shows itself to be empty not of content but only of conceptual purchase
on absolute reality, while at the same time it is let loose to *express* in crazy
ways all that it could never properly say. This phase turns out to be exceptionally fecund in the invention of discourse reflecting from different
angles—and in its very disintegration as discourse—upon what cannot
be said.

   This openness to apophasis, especially to some of its mystical and religious tendencies is, of course, far from uncontested in philosophy today.
Certain strands of postmodern thought ask to be understood primarily as
the denial of the tradition of negative theology that has been traced here
from its Neoplatonic origins. Much philosophy since the Enlightenment
has understood itself as anti-theology and therefore equally as opposed to
every form of negative theology, which is seen as a sly effort to recuperate
the myth or lie of God that is viewed nevertheless as fatally doomed for
good reason and without appeal. Progressive politics and a revolutionary
ideology are sometimes portrayed as intrinsically antithetical to theology
in any form whatsoever. Of course, this denial of what it *says* is exactly
what an apophatic philosophy expects and invites. To be contradicted is
not so much a denial as a confirmation of its vision of the necessary inadequacy of any discourse whatsoever, including its own. Nevertheless, the
intent of such attacks is to oppose the sort of philosophy of the unsayable
that is here in question. It will be instructive, therefore, to consider at least
one specific line of thought that understands itself as attacking negative
theology for being still a theology and therefore, presumably, the enemy of

free philosophical thinking. Paradoxically, this thinking eventually turns out to be itself one of the greatest achievements of contemporary apophatic thought.

ii

To develop my assessment of apophasis as crucial to the situation of philosophy today, I will first, therefore, respond to one thinker who has taken, at least initially, exactly the opposite tack from mine in interpreting the tradition of negative theology. I respond specifically to Jean-Luc Nancy's masterful and provocative essay "Des lieux divins" ("Of Divine Places"). Nancy's essay appeared originally as a contribution to a collection of essays by thirty-six of France's leading thinkers in philosophy, theology, and literature on the question "What is God?"[34] Addressing this public of mixed professions, Nancy transposes the question concerning the essence of God into a question of the "place" of the divine, thereby making it possible to broach the question of God in a de-essentialized form. He is interested in how divinity, emptied of all content, becomes no more than a place, a topos. As a subject devoid of attributions, divinity as such no longer has any characteristics and is nothing but a place of pure receptivity. This might be thought to put divinity in a place of peculiar power, but Nancy interprets it as bearing only the opposite significance: he wishes to depotentiate theology and render God not just dead but—much more radically and devastatingly—irrelevant.[35]

Nancy acutely analyzes monotheism as consisting essentially in an identification of divinity with Being, or rather with "the excellency of Being," in which all Being is one ("L'idée de l'excellence de l'existence dans l'être—en fait l'essence du monothéisme," sec. 1, p. 254). But he rejects the idea that Being or its unity can in any way be God. For Nancy, Being *is not* at all, but only beings, and so, by the same token, the monotheistic God is not. Of course, the whole tradition of negative theology also insists that God is Nothing, just as much as—or more than—he is Being, since he is rather *beyond* Being. But for Nancy there is nothing whatsoever besides beings. He even chooses to consider beings, not Being or the beyond of Being, as divine, and thus to concern himself not with

God but rather with *a* god or *the* god. But he does not allow these terms any genuine theological content as attempts to conceptualize a divinity transcending beings, since for him there can be no such thing; neither does he accord them any ontological import as designating what somehow conditions beings. The powers, if any, of *a* god or *the* god are none other than those pertaining to just one more kind of beings.

Nancy is above all concerned to deny theology its privilege as the discourse par excellence on the Other, the Infinite, the infinitely other. In our age, he maintains, there is nothing to say about God that cannot just as well be said about elusive things like love, poetry, the "event," and so forth. *D'accord!*—I agree. But it is (and always was) what *cannot* be said about these subjects, or about any subject, that is most important about them. And the word "God"—with its perhaps annoyingly pretentious aura of something supernatural or transcendent—marks this difference. Possessed of no determinate, sayable content, "God" is evidently not the name of a normal subject: God is *not* like the *presumably* familiar subjects Nancy evokes as coextensive and, in fact, as coinciding with everything that God can possibly be.

For Nancy there is really no problem about the concept of God, for there is for him no God that exceeds conceptualization, such as there is for Pseudo-Dionysius and the apophatic tradition following in his wake.[36] What Nancy really wants to deny, like Hegel before him, is what cannot be said: anything beyond word and concept would, in effect, be God, Nancy admits, but there is no such thing. This is not merely a denial that what cannot be said—the ineffable—*is* anything. That much was conceded and, in fact, was insisted upon by negative theologians from Plotinus to Pseudo-Dionysius, followed by Maimonides, Eckhart, and many others. Nancy's point, rather, is to deny any special meaning and pertinence to language about God, since it has no field of reference specific to itself. In Nancy's view—using Hölderlin's phrase—the names of the gods are lacking ("es fehlt heilige Namen"), that is, lacking in gods to name. The gods that were once manifest to preceding civilizations are no longer present or even extant. Modern Western civilization, reason, secularization, and even the Christian religion itself have done the gods to death, as was clearly proclaimed already by Hegel and Nietzsche.

Thus Nancy describes the contemporary situation as one of extreme deprivation of all possibility of naming God. God is no longer even a distinct theme of discourse; theology has been dissolved into ontology, anthropology, cosmology, and the like. The unnameability of God consequently takes on quite different motivations from those of the divine transcendence evoked by negative theologies. God is not unnameable for lack of an adequate concept of divinity or due to divine transcendence beyond the reach of language. The reason is rather that to name God, even by address in prayer, cannot be serious, sincere, or even meaningful. The very function of addressing, whether directed to the divine or to anyone else, has become impossible. Indeed, all names that things or persons can be called have some vestigial remnants of divinity in them, and therefore the very gesture of appellation or address in general has become impossible today, according to Nancy. It is sheer irony that precisely the figure of address becomes the crucial gesture to be found everywhere, the universal mode of relation in Nancy's later and definitive philosophy of "déclosion" or the deconstruction of Christianity.

Nancy rightly admonishes his audience that the extreme destitution, the lack of plenitude and presence experienced everywhere in modernity, should not arbitrarily be called God in a gesture simply of interpreting every negative as infinitely positive. But he seems deliberately to miss the point that the "place" of the divine—to use Nancy's own eloquent idiom—is what is *not* being called anything or being said at all, not even in the calling upon God and in the saying of his Name. The talk of "God" in radical negative theologies attempts to call up this anonymous, unnameable "place."

Nancy is aggressively anti-theological. He proposes in effect an anti-theology, a philosophy of the finitude of being as absolute and final (sec. 29). He scorns and deplores the idea of a return of the religious, about which he admits that there is much ado today. For him, echoing Hegel (though not necessarily in a sense faithful to Hegel's meaning), the death of God is the final thought of philosophy ("La mort de Dieu est la pensée *finale* de la philosophie"). Philosophy proposes this thought, according to Nancy, "as the *end* of religion: it is the thought toward which the Occident (which in this respect excludes neither Islam nor Buddhism) will not have ceased to tend" ["la philosophie . . . la propose ainsi comme *fin* à la religion: c'est la pensée à laquelle l'Occident (qui n'exclut, à ce titre, ni l'Islam ni le bouddhisme) n'aura pas cessé de tendre," p. 551].

Nancy claims to say both what is necessary and also what is no longer possible *for us* to think as belated Westerners ("au coeur de notre expérience, au coeur de notre tardive nécessité occidentale," p. 552) and thus legislates what is a legitimate stance for thought in general ("*la* pensée"), at least today. But by what right is he speaking for us all? This sort of claim could perhaps have been plausible for Hegel, but how can such a "we" be persuasive, let alone meaningful today in the age of shattered subjectivity? Surely a "we" that is "singular plural" (Nancy's "singulier pluriel") should not rule out the possibility of others who think differently.[37] Nancy practically ventriloquizes Hegel, yet without Hegel's respect for religion. When Nancy denounces all talk of a "return of the religious" as ridiculous cant, he asserts in polemical and even dogmatic terms the death of God as an "irrefutable and nondisplaceable" event that has "rendered ridiculous in advance all the 'returns of the religious'" ("cet événement irréfutable et indéplaçeable, qui a d'avance rendu dérisoires tous les 'retours du religieux,'" p. 553).

But how can any thought be final? Is not the very life of thinking invested in constant displacements of every achieved formulation? This has been the irrecusable lesson of French poststructuralist styles of thinking such as Nancy's. With respect to religion, however, Nancy bears down blindly to resist it. His essay in certain moments evinces a deep and personal familiarity with Roman Catholicism and the Latin liturgy. He speaks with a voice affected by this heritage,[38] but when he pronounces his judgment on its theology he seems not to have overcome it sufficiently to be able to take up an objective stance toward it.

In "Des lieux divins," Nancy writes as if the abyss of unknowing—so unfathomable and mysterious and rich in tradition—could be correctly described as a purely human lack, a fragmentation of the human subject that is only mendaciously "baptized" in the name of an unknowable God. A more open tack is taken by Thomas A. Carlson in the programmatic statement of his book *Indiscretion,* where he proposes to leave open the question, perhaps over-zealously closed by Nancy, of the identity or distinctness of the divine and the human. This is the question of whether negative discourse about God is or is not another vocabulary for expressing what can also be articulated in terms of human finitude.

> I argue here that this question can be answered—or, better, suspended and kept open—insofar as one can signal a point at which the negative logic of Being-toward-God within classic apophatic and mystical forms of language and representation reveals a strikingly forceful analogy to the negative logic of Being-toward-death in contemporary (Heideggerian and post-Heideggerian) discourse on human finitude. In and through the development of this "apophatic analogy," the work moves toward a point of "indiscretion" at which the negativity of the divine and of the human, of the theological and the thanatological, can (and do) prove to be neither distinct nor identical—but bound in the radical indeterminacy that haunts the experience of all language and representation regarding an ineffable God and/or an impossible death.[39]

Carlson's rejection of a binary, oppositional logic and his proposal to underscore the forceful analogies between Being-toward-God in premodern apophatic discourses, signally Pseudo-Dionysius's, and Being-toward-death in post-Hegelian and postmodern discourses on human finitude, signally Heidegger's, has guided his work in this area along a more Derridean line. Whereas Nancy takes a trenchantly anti-theological stance, Derrida has been twisting away from such oppositional stances, conspicuously in his deconstructive engagements with negative theology.[40] Mark C. Taylor, too, has explored in innovative ways the space that opens for theology in the very tearing of its text, in the insurmountable check to its discourse.[41] This happens in the face of what he calls "Altarity," or the wholly (or holy) Other, "das ganz Andere," as marked by the surplus ("Überschuss") of the religious beyond all conceptual or even moral meaning. This is the order of significance inaccessible to reason and speech that was characterized as numinous, uncanny, or even monstrous ("ungeheuer") by Rudolf Otto in *The Idea of the Holy*.[42]

Nancy uses many of the same critical and deconstructive insights that animate negative theology and its contemporary interpreters, but he pursues them to opposite ends and purposes, taking these theological ends and purposes as in need of being deconstructed and discarded. One could agree with him, were these ends and purposes articulated or articulable, and were negative theology a positive doctrine rather than a negation even of itself. What negative theology is becomes moot once we admit that it has no essence—or even that its "essence" or pseudo-essence is to refuse and elude every essence. What fundamentally differentiates Nancy's viewpoint from the one I have been at pains to develop is the attitude taken toward the tradition of negative theology. We must decide whether we will resist and resent this tradition or gratefully receive and willingly work with it. These choices are about us—and about our acknowledgment of traditions that exist and that inform us. Christianity is Nancy's own spiritual heritage and cultural matrix, so it is perhaps natural that he should struggle to overcome it. Nevertheless, the result is that, with great insight and acuteness, Nancy is insisting on the impossibility of what he himself has proved, as we have seen in "Des lieux divins," to be an eminent possibility of thinking from age to age. Furthermore, impossibility itself becomes the enabling condition of the kind of thinking that Nancy endorses and endeavors to incarnate in his later philosophical phase.

Jean-Luc Nancy's refusal of Christianity along with all theologies, including negative theologies, is not a philosophical necessity so much as a personal choice and perhaps exigency. Many other thinkers sharing similar fundamental convictions and compulsions enthusiastically embrace elements of the Christian as well as of other religious traditions. Even the refusal is a continuation of dialogue with what proves an indispensable adversary for as long as the discussion goes on. As in Blanchot's "infinite conversation" (*L'Entretien infini*), the reference to theology has never really been erased so long as it is in the process of being erased. Hence Derrida writes aptly of Nancy's "interminable 'deconstruction of Christianity.'"[43] The declared intent to forget theology, and so to cease to be conditioned by it, is pragmatically contradicted by the very discourse that declares this intent. Just this sort of recursive significance of discourse, which goes beyond its explicitly stated intent, must be taken with the utmost seriousness by both the apostles of apophasis and their denigrators.

The larger burden of Nancy's essay is an extremely penetrating analysis of religions and their conceptualizations of God. Yet the method remains purely conceptual. It is a method perfectly appropriate to philosophy, but it cannot begin to sound the depths of theology, much less of religion. It remains willfully blind to the possible revivals of religion that have been witnessed recently and, in fact, have taken place right within movements styled "postmodern."[44] Indeed, a host of thinkers and scholars, many of whom are working within the ambit of Derrida and deconstruction, have given ear to precisely the return of the religious that Nancy here refuses to hear anything about. Such interest found a certain forum, for example, in the series of conferences organized by John Caputo and his associates, starting in the 1990s at Villanova University, as well as in a slew of publications dealing with "the postmodern return of God."[45]

A parallel investment of the postmodern in the rediscovery of the religious in an apophatic key has been fostered in Italy by, among others, Gianni Vattimo, Massimo Cacciari, and Vincenzo Vittiello.[46] Giorgio Agamben, who shares many of the same points of reference in postmodern thinking, is also acutely receptive to the apophatic dimension. Agamben has linked his speculations in an apophatic mode explicitly with the Neoplatonic negative theological tradition of Damascius by beginning one of his books with a reconsideration of this largely forgotten philosopher.[47] Similarly, certain Dutch philosophers of religion have made active efforts to read contemporary thought against the background of traditions of negative theology.[48] Hent de Vries's thinking in the wake of Derrida takes its decisive impulse from the need to explain the return to religion. The "adieu" or "goodbye" to God and religion is in modern times, and perhaps even before all times, a gesture of commending oneself or those one addresses "to God," "à Dieu."[49] De Vries interprets the philosophies of Adorno and Levinas as minimal negative theologies, and he suggests how other modern thinkers and writers can likewise be reassessed through these optics.[50] Yet another approach taking its bearings from a conception of negative theology as the key to envisioning postmodern theology and culture in general emanates from the University of Salzburg and its Institut für Theologie Interkulturell.[51]

Since the publication of Nancy's essay, such trends have become ever more widespread and deep-rooted. European scholarship has produced wide-ranging compendiums of contemporary approaches to negative theology, stressing its relevance to philosophy and assessing the effects on numerous fields of this revolution in thinking.[52] Considerable original activity in this direction is evident in the Anglo-Saxon world as well, by authors such as Kevin Hart, Richard Kearney, and William Desmond.[53] Yet, in the midst of all this ferment, it is Nancy himself who has become, in my judgment, the most outstanding representative of all, indeed, the most original creator of what I call a philosophy of the unsayable. In the next section I show why this is so through detailed readings from his work *Déconstruction du christianisme,* especially the second volume, *L'Adoration.* His work, both in style and conviction, exemplarily enacts exactly what I mean by apophatic thinking.

When we speak of apophatic insight or the unsayable, the question of its positioning with respect to theism and atheism, and to philosophy and mysticism, remains vexed. Nancy is especially useful for my present purpose of demonstrating how the philosophy of the unsayable reaches across all such ideological divides and opens a space of disclosure of truth that is shared in common by virtually all types of intellectual persuasions, at least when the latter are thought through to their final consequences and intrinsic limits. Through this dialogue with Nancy, I intend to show that the scope of the philosophy of the unsayable manifestly reaches beyond sectarian boundaries. Participants in the dialogue are interrogated as to their stance on the question of God (or of the oneness of reality, or of the role of belief versus reason in the justification of knowledge), even if only to reveal a common groundlessness.[54] Unlikely as it may seem, such dialogue is stimulated in the highest degree by what no one can say.

iii

Ironically, in light of my treatment of this thinker in the previous section, it is Jean-Luc Nancy who takes the lead in enabling us to see the intrinsically deconstructive character of Christianity and, conversely, the inherently Christian character of at least a certain style of deconstruction: he shows how deconstruction is essentially a product of a Christian culture. In the first volume, entitled *La Déclosion* (Dis-Enclosure), of his writings collected under the title *Déconstruction du christianisme (The Deconstruction of Christianity),*[55] Nancy articulates a position that is in many ways exactly the reversal of the line taken in the earlier essay "Des lieux divins."

This does not mean, certainly, that the earlier position is recanted, but its development has nonetheless taken a surprising turn. The "return of the religious" ("retour du religieux"), which he had earlier refused, Nancy now recognizes as "a real phenomenon" ("un phénomène réel"). And the idea of curing civilization of religion, as if it were a kind of canker, is now rejected as wrongheaded. We need rather to be emancipated from a certain naïve narrative of emancipation (p. 19), one based on the idea of an autonomous, self-determining subject, and it is Christianity that holds the keys to this liberation.

Christianity turns out to be crucial for opening the world to an inaccessible alterity or "other" ("l'autre du monde"), made paradoxically accessible by this opening or "déclosion." In Christianity—Anselm in particular is invoked here—thought "thinks something in excess of itself. It penetrates the impenetrable, or rather is penetrated by it" ("elle pense un excès sur elle-même. Elle pénètre l'impénétrable, ou bien plutôt elle est pénétrée par lui," p. 22). Christianity indicates "the exigency of opening up within this world an alterity or an unconditional alienation" ("l'exigence d'ouvrir dans ce monde une altérité ou une aliénation inconditionnelle," p. 20).

To this extent, I suggest, the Christian otherworld can represent the other of any and every world. The exceeding and overcoming of itself on the part of the world, the movement of deconstruction ("L'excédant lui-même, mouvement d'une déconstruction," p. 21), is at work in Christianity. In this new formulation by Nancy of his thoughts on religion, Christianity is the agent and not only the object of deconstruction: it is in itself and by itself already a deconstruction (of Western civilization) and thereby also an auto-deconstruction ("le christianisme est par lui-même, en lui-même, une deconstruction et une auto-déconstruction," p. 55). In Christianity, metaphysical reason exceeds and deconstructs itself. Even faith now fascinates Nancy as a relation to nothing, and faith in or as nothing ("Une foi de rien de tout," pp. 89–116) works as an endless opening—unlike belief, which has a determinate object. As such, faith is not necessarily religious, at least not in a positive sense. Its ultimate content or object is not definable—like the God of negative theology.

To conceive deconstruction as "déclosion" reverses the connotation of destroying something and introduces rather the image of opening, or more exactly of de-closing, of *un*stopping or unblocking. This opening or freeing from closure is, in fact, the aim and purpose of deconstruction, as Derrida has often described it, and this is what, *mirabile dictu,* Christianity does in overcoming the abstract truth of metaphysics in favor of historical, incarnate revelation. Accordingly, the genitive in the title "Deconstruction of Christianity" is a subjective as well as an objective one. Christianity is the agent performing the deconstruction as much as the object that is deconstructed because it deconstructs itself and is, moreover, the leaven that deconstructs the whole of the onto-theological, metaphysical tradition and, along with it, the very project and destiny of Western culture since the Greeks. The entire adventure of making the world make sense and then unmaking this sense comes to completion and dissolution in the self-deconstructing act enacted by Christianity.

Nancy's refusal of God in "Des lieux divins" might be compared to the attitude of the most uncompromising, intransigent sort of secular theology or even atheism, in that he rejects theology, demands recognition of the post-theological character of our postmodern age, and polemically denies that traditional theological discourse is any longer possible. At this stage, Nancy refuses to let theology, particularly Christian theology, open up and dissolve or deconstruct itself, along with all closed, finite identities. Yet that is exactly what he does allow in his later writings on the deconstruction of Christianity. In them, Nancy perspicaciously analyzes faith and concludes that "faith . . . leads always to adhesion to the infinity of sense" ("la foi . . . ramène donc toujours à l'adhésion à l'infini du sens"). Faith is "the being-in-act of an infinite sense incapable of being appropriated and which it becomes progressively," and such faith is nothing but "faithfulness to faithfulness itself" ("fidélité à fidélité même"). Perfect self-reflexivity, effecting a kenotic self-emptying, defines the shape of this faith.[56]

In "La déconstruction du christianisme," Nancy explicitly distances himself from all attacks against Christianity in the manner of Voltaire or Nietzsche (and implicitly himself in his earlier essay). He now sees such attacks as outmoded because he considers Christianity itself to be in a condition of self-surpassing. Christianity has ceased to make us live within a general order of meaning shared in common, "the regime of sense" ("Il a cessé de *faire vivre dans l'ordre du sens,*" p. 505). This fate of Christianity may be the fate of meaning or sense in general. It fulfills itself in being deconstructed, and Christianity is fundamentally committed to revealing and realizing this fact.

Is not the abandonment of meaning the quintessential gesture of the apophatic philosophy that grows from traditions of negative theology? Radical negative theology entails not only an abandonment of this or that schema of meaning but also an admission that no discourse can be adequate to God, just as apophatic philosophy leads to the abandonment of sense per se. This is the gesture that makes negation apophatic rather than simply negative, raising it to a higher power of negation. At this level, the strategy of negation becomes a philosophy rather than just a specific intellectual act motivated by local and contingent factors. This abandonment of sense must be the abandonment of one's *own* sense. Does this gesture make sense? That is the question that it must face and somehow finesse. It makes a sense that it at the same time abandons. It is a sense that this thinking itself cannot comprehend. There is evidently a motivation to make this sense, but only on the condition that it not be able to account for itself.

Nancy aligns himself with the analyses of Marcel Gauchet in *Le désenchantement du monde* (1985) concerning Christianity as "[t]he religion of the exit from religion" ("La religion de la sortie de la religion"). The modern world is interpreted, profoundly, as the self-realization of Christianity. The dissolution of Western civilization, accordingly, is the completion of the process that Christianity sets in motion and propels. Christianity works this wonder because "the essence of Christianity is opening, the opening of itself and the self as opening" (p. 508). Nancy takes, or at least interrogates, opening, then, as an absolute "transcendental," or condition of possibility, which overtakes and dissolves all other horizons ("un *transcendantal absolu de l'ouverture* tel qu'il ne cesse de faire reculer ou de dissoudre tous les horizons," p. 508). Christianity leads to an "indefinite openness" ("ouverture indéfinie") without bottom and without horizon.

The dangers of making this "essential property" of Christianity into a transcendental or even "absolute transcendental" have been made more evident through the analyses and trenchant critique of Radical Orthodoxy (see the next essay in this volume). The human positing of transcendentals is fundamentally what Radical Orthodoxy opposes in all secular thinking, and here negative theology shows itself to be paradigmatically secularizing thought. This critique is important for making us aware that even absolute openness should not be taken as a transcendental horizon of experience. Nancy lapses from a rigorously (self-)critical negative-theological thinking by positively declaring the dissolution of sense to be a "transcendental." However, the dissolution of sense of which he writes may still effectively operate to open thought infinitely—hence theologically— without any definable transcendental delimitation of horizons. The infinite openness characteristic of Christianity, precisely in the traditions of negative theology that open all affirmative formulations toward the illimitable infinity of God, is indeed crucial for overcoming idolatry. And it offers thereby a way out of inevitable conflict between the apparently competing theses and conceptualizations of different religions or ideologies.

This infinite self-opening or "eclosion" holds essentially for the Christian vision, beyond all internal tensions between integralism and disintegration within Christianity. Christianity constitutes itself as a self-surpassing by integrating the Judaic, Hellenic, and Roman traditions that it renews, transforms, and transfigures. For the first time in history, a faith understands itself as its own history. Christianity opens the sense of this history, discloses it, and opens the human subject to itself as fundamentally historical. The sense in question, in this historical sense for humanity, is not only an "opening of sense" but also sense as itself precisely opening ("*à la fois* l'ouverture du sens et le sens comme ouverture," p. 510). Sense is per se an opening, and this universal opening without limit is the meaning of sense. It refuses any finite closure; it insists on unsaying itself. This inevitably obliterates all stable, definitively fixed sense. In this totalization of sense, sense is no more. By opening infinitely, sense moves toward its own extinction as a discrete thing. *Nothing,* then, is revealed in the revelation of sense purely as sense, and this precisely is the self-deconstruction of Christianity. It fulfills itself in wiping away every specific, determinate characteristic of its own.

> [T]he idea of a Christian revelation is that in the final analysis *nothing is revealed,* nothing except the end of revelation itself, unless it be that revelation means that sense unveils itself purely as sense, in person [or "in no one": *en personne*], but in one person such that

the whole sense of this person consists in self-revelation. Sense reveals itself and reveals nothing, or reveals it own infinity. (p. 511)[57]

Nancy is keenly perceptive of the way that Christianity dissolves all
sense into the sheer person of Christ who says "*I am* the way, the truth,
and the life" (John 14:6). Nothing means anything in itself anymore except in finally emptying itself out and issuing in this absolute presence,
which is Christ.[58] Christ is the exposure of the personhood of the person
as the Open as such. This entails an appeal to the infinite sense of the pure
person or pure life of relation in the Trinity and Incarnation as the Son's
message of salvation to human beings. Temptation in Christianity consists
in the temptation of attachment to self as opposed to the opening and
even dissolution of self to the point of absorption into the infinite, into
God, beyond any sense we can make of or for him ourselves.

The revelation of sense is thus the revelation of nothing but its own
openness and infinity ("Le sens se révèle et ne révèle rien, ou révèle sa
propre infinité" (p. 511). What is revealed is that God is the revealable,
the Open as such. This is the revelation of Christianity as what Nietzsche
calls nihilism. However, it gives quite a different sense to this nihilism
than what Nietzsche envisaged. Nancy sees Christianity as deconstruction: Christianity shows how deconstruction belongs essentially to Western tradition, and deconstruction is itself traversed by Christianity through
and through ("elle [déconstruction] est elle-même traversée de part en part
par le christianisme," p. 511). Christianity is deconstruction at work in
the Western tradition all along because Christianity fundamentally entails
the distension and opening of itself—indeed, the opening of the self as
such. Despite attempts to deny its own deconstruction, such as the misguided attempt to isolate and return to a presumably original, primitive
Christianity that runs counter to its essence as historical, Christianity is
basically an infinite opening of the sense of being. It is this, among other
ways, through its new and unrestricted use of ontological concepts of
philosophy (such as being, power, and the good), thus infinitely opening
their sense.

The Christian projection of concepts to infinity—already anticipated
in the New Testament with the absolutization of tropes such as "word"
(logos) and "self-emptying" (kenosis)—developed in the patristic period.

It continued in Christian metaphysics through the Middle Ages and into modern existentialist, phenomenological, and constructivist rethinkings of fundamental theology. Pushing concepts to their limits subverts their ordinary, finite content and destroys—or rather, deconstructs—them.

Such critique reveals Christianity's unprecedented power to be the enabling condition and driving force of its own critique. This double-edged critique "of" Christianity, which winds up revealing it and its own unending revelation, has the support of a lineage of thinkers reaching back to Nietzsche.[59] Blanchot is closely associated with Nietzsche as another of Christianity's most implacable detractors, and yet Nancy takes Blanchot as opening a path for thinking beyond atheism as well as theism. The problem is that atheism has always opposed theism by substituting for God some purely human source or figure of sense, some authentic meaning grounded in the presence of humanity. Blanchot (together with Bataille) is taken by Nancy as adumbrating a deconstruction of humanism as the ground of atheism. Atheism must be hammered to bits, just like theism: both are consigned to the twilight of the idols. This, of course, is not intended to justify theism in any way. Nancy praises Blanchot for having remained resistant to the calling of the Name of God and rather adhering to its "call to an interminable *un*naming" ("l'appel interminable à l'innomination").[60]

Thinking, for this style of a/theism, occurs not in the negation of the existence of God but in the absenting and dissolution of sense itself.

> This is why the most precious gift of philosophy for Blanchot consists not even in an operation of negating the existence of God, but in a simple disappearance, in a dissipation of this existence. Thinking thinks only starting from there. (p. 67)[61]

The Name of God is an ongoing self-absenting of sense. It always proves ungraspable, indefinable, even in the act of moving the most powerful emotions. This self-absenting and dissolution of sense is endless; such is the infinity of Christianity in action. "But an 'absent sense' makes sense in and by its very absenting, such that in the end . . . it does not cease not to 'make sense'" (p. 67).[62]

The fully evolved character of apophasis as limitless self-criticism (or self-negation or *kenosis*)—or as the dissolution of one's own sense and ultimately of oneself—that we have traced from a certain Neoplatonic philosophy has been realized in these terms, according to Jean-Luc Nancy, eminently by Christianity. The dimension of the infinite is opened by unsparing negation of all finite formulations. Nietzsche's thought is thereby, after all, against its intentions, turned in the direction of a negatively Christian, deconstructive "a/philosophy" of the unsayable.

iv

Five years after *La Déclosion,* with the publication of *L'Adoration* (2010), Nancy's deconstruction of Christianity has continued to evolve even more decisively in the direction of an apophatic philosophy of the unsayable. Nancy continues to revise his once presumably "final" thought concerning religion to the thought that no thought is ever final. From being a thinker of the insuperable finitude of being, he becomes a thinker of the infinitude of thinking in its passages beyond being and beyond everything else that can be thought, including thought itself, its passing into "another dimension, infinite and not indefinite" ("une autre dimension, infinie et non indefinie," p. 30).[63] This negation of the "indefinite" is a quintessentially Hegelian gesture, but it should not be converted into a unilateral affirmation of the definite: it is rather apophatic in negating the *figure* of the indefinite, which like any figure whatever must be negated in deference to what escapes all figuring. The apophatic cannot be finally qualified as indefinite either: it is made manifest always only in definite, concrete forms—and their surpassing.

Nancy's own writing on religion turns against or undoes itself: it gives up its original assertions in order to relate them to what they excluded, and this, too, is a figure of the apophatic. The paradoxical result is Nancy's opening to the infinite, after his having been so trenchant in his defense of the finite.[64] This finite is now acknowledged to exist thanks only to the infinite and in dependence on it—and in infinite openness, an attitude that Nancy qualifies as "adoration." What Nancy pleads for now is what "adoration" opens toward without restriction and yet cannot define or state. It is, in effect, the unsayable. He now embraces the infinite rather than the finite, yet not as an alternative to the finite, but rather as what is left when all reductive definitions are removed from the finite—or from a certain instance of it, some concrete thing that is thereby opened into the infinity of its relations with everything else.

This approach to the infinite through "adoration" exactly matches the procedure of apophatic theology. It consists in the finite negating—by exceeding and exiting—itself so as to open to, and into, the infinite. The theological idea that all things were created to adore God Nancy understands as signifying that "'God' is but the alias of a pure excess—vain in effect, exorbitant in effect—of the world and of existence beyond themselves" ("'Dieu' n'est que le prête-nom d'un pur excès—vain en effet, exorbitant en effet—du monde et de l'existence sur eux-mêmes?"). What does the name "God" signify except "a pure and simple, infinite relation to the infinite?" ("D'un pur et simple rapport infini à l'infini?" p. 32). Such relation is explained by Nancy in typically apophatic fashion in terms of the negations of self inherent in prayer, praise, celebration, supplication, and so forth. In relation to the infinite, it is but the silent "breath" ("souffle") behind all such orations. Figured in more physical terms, adoration is the ecstatic opening of the body through all of its orifices to what is beyond it: the world opens upon itself as transcendent in its very immanence (p. 32).

The negation of particular determinations of speech or other expressive forms exposes the unlimited significance of the breath or silence that underlies and sustains all these articulations, and this is the apophatic insight par excellence. Apophasis recognizes in the indeterminate background that serves as the medium of whatever form of linguistic determination or articulation, such as the continuum of sound or of visual form or of any other sensible or intellectual medium, the whole intact of that which is communicated only fragmentarily in its articulation. Nancy similarly relates all finite being to an infinite that is obliquely espied in its background and which the finite being is called upon to open itself to in "adoration."

It is the very nature of reason, according to Nancy, to exceed itself and all its reasons and to push itself beyond all limits toward the incommensurable and unnameable, thus beyond all sense that it can make of things, toward "a truth without concept or figure: if it fails to do justice to this impulsion, it atrophies and sinks into a general commensurability and interminable naming in which all names are interchangeable" (p. 57).[65] Like others, including Gianni Vattimo and John Caputo, Nancy offers a postmodern philosophy that deconstructs all its own concepts and finds inspiration for doing so in theology, especially in Christian theology, given its emphasis on the death of God.

Nancy clearly recognizes that this shift to an openness to the infinite places him in continuity with religious traditions and particularly with Christian revelation. The kenotic giving up of self in the Christ event is the enactment of negative theology in the very center of life—all the way to its limit in death. This has been the core of the Christian message for many believers, historically, and Nancy is preoccupied with recognizing the unique and determining role of Christianity in the deconstructive movement that he sees as the essential movement of modern history, while also attempting to avoid the *skandalon* of giving Christianity exclusive rights over the annals and archives of this universal revelation. He also recognizes elements in Judaism and Islam that point to the *déclosion* of thought, which is construed, nevertheless, as the special vocation of Christianity.

The giving up of self for others Nancy understands linguistically in terms of address, of language turned toward an Other, literally, speech or oration (*oratio*) toward (*ad*), the root meaning of the Latin word "adoratio." The sense of life and language alike is accomplished in this turn toward the other in the release of one's self and one's own meaning. In this sense, Nancy equates thought and adoration: both are forms of contemplating all things together, "the totality of existing beings" ("la totalité des existants," p. 27), through annihilation of oneself—in humility. Man (*homo*) is made of dirt (*humus*). Humility (*humilité*) flows from the doctrine of creation *ex nihilo*, according to which God makes use of the lowliest of things, the things that are not at all (echoing Romans 4:17: "he calls the things that are not as though they were"). And humility is crystallized in adoration, which consists in adhering to or "holding oneself to nothing" ("L'adoration consiste à se tenir au rien," p. 25). These are the existential postures of self-negation that epitomize kenosis and apophaticism. The promise of unrestricted vision—or rather relation—of all things in the disclosure of truth is also embraced by Nancy. Truth is disclosed through this opening without limit in self-release as the sense of things. This is, of course, an opening that enacts the deconstruction of truth as objective (not to mention absolute) knowledge. It is expressed most characteristically, rather, in the address.

The "address" or salute ("salut") is what can become our "salvation" ("salut" has also this sense in French). Thus the whole sense of the world hinges on the salute or address: nothing has meaning except insofar as it is meaningful *for* someone. All the signs making up our world are forms of address: they are insistently trying to tell us something. Adoration relates us to another dimension, one which is infinite. It is a dimension that opens from within the world and its circuits of reference, but opens them up and out—without limits. Nancy finds that he cannot quite completely avoid speaking here of "transcendence," even though he is loathe to give any sort of impression of a return to God, who is dead, or to belief in any "other" world (p. 30).

Nancy prefers the word "adoration" instead of "transcendence" (which he considers to be too weighed down with tradition) for "the movement by which an existing thing exits from simple identity with itself" ("le mouvement par lequel un existant sort de la simple égalité à soi-même," p. 30). The important thing for him is to keep language in movement, so as to avoid the sclerosis of a culture that closes itself in a "homogeneity that becomes insignificant for it (or signifying only itself)" ["homogénéité qui la rend insignifiante pour elle-même (ou ne signifiant qu'elle-même)," p. 31]. Against this tendency to the stasis of self-identity, adoration entails attention to the other and to the displacement of sense or to the possibility of an unprecedented address inherent in such attention:

> 'Adoration' means nothing other than that; attention to the movement of sense, to the possibility of an unprecedented address, not philosophical, nor religious, nor theoretical, nor practical, nor political, nor amorous—but attentive. (p. 31)

This series of "neither . . . nor" constructions, of course, employs a paradigmatic form of apophatic rhetoric.

For Nancy, adoration is quite simply address: "*Adoratio*: the word of address [or the word addressed]" ("*Adoratio*: la parole adressée" p. 28). He explains this word as addressed to what it "knows" or rather "touches," without having access to it: "this is the real [le réel] as such turned toward us, open to us and to the opening out of which we address ourselves" (pp. 10–11). Our language, which is our being and our world, "touches and/or is touched by the incommensurable, the non-world, the outside" ("touche et/ou il est touché par l'incommensurable, le non-monde, le dehors"). The world as sensible becomes itself unbounded through being touched by an infinite outside, and thus: "The world is the exposition of that which exists for the touch of sense that opens in itself the infinite of an outside" (p. 11).

Nancy is speaking of an eminently touchable world rather than an abstractly intellectualized one, yet he embraces it as infinite. He finds the infinite in the finite and also finds that the finite cannot exist without the infinite. Existence itself implies its own beyond. It is the finite, after all, that *is* infinite, since by naming the infinite the finite opens an infinite breach within itself.

> The infinite in the finite. The finite inasmuch as it is openness to the infinite: nothing else is at stake. There would not be what we call finitude—mortality, nativity, 'fortuitousness'—if by the very fact that we name it we did not allow the fact that we exist and that the world exists as open upon the infinite and by means of the infinite, to show through. (p. 11)[66]

Nancy acutely draws the inference to infinity from the mere fact of existence. As in the thought of Thomas Aquinas, existence is per se infinite, or unsoundable in its depth, and for Thomas, at least, this infinite existing is God. Nancy similarly stresses that any finite existing is infinite *in its existing,* in the fact *that* it is.

> In other words, the very fact of existence denies that it is 'finite' in the sense in which it would lack an extension beyond itself. This fact attests on the contrary that existence carries, that it brings with itself, its entire extension and full expansiveness. Here and now, between birth and death, without denying or repressing anything belonging to this 'finitude,' since it is this very finitude which *is* in-

finite: between birth and death, each time, an absolute is accomplished. (p. 11)[67]

This latter point concerning the accomplishment of the absolute admits of an Hegelian interpretation. But one might also conceive the manner of the conflation of finite and infinite, in the German speculative tradition, as a *coincidentia oppositorum,* drawing on the negative theology notably of Nicholas Cusanus—and following him, of figures such as Jakob Boehme and Schelling. In any case, this is still a logic for arriving at the infinite through undoing the negation by which the finite essentially is contained.

Like the Jena Romantics, including Hegel and by extension Hölderlin, who were all greatly impressed by the French Revolution and envisaged a political revolution together with a general moral and spiritual renewal, so Nancy thinks in the wake of the revolutionary ideals of liberty, equality, fraternity, and justice. However, he also projects them into a realm well beyond the social. The social is secondary to a more absolute level of being (or beyond-being), in which our common existence consists. This *common* existence is described apophatically through a rhetoric of neither/nor: "The common neither associates nor disassociates, it neither assembles nor separates, is neither substance nor subject" (p. 12). We *are* the common inasmuch as we are in relation to one another. We all share in common, moreover, a certain reference or sending ("le commun renvoi"), a destiny or address, by virtue of sharing a common world.

In this vision of universality as "the common," which is the democratic ideal following the lead of the French Revolution, universality is more than political and social: the common has a sort of transcendence in being reducible to no terms.[68] It is, nevertheless, discerned in the specifically human dimension of language. Language is what makes a totality of the world—it makes the separate being of things consist in relations. Nancy proclaims an infinity of "sense" that no signification can exhaust: it rather envelops, together with human beings, the totality of the world.

Nancy construes this common and universal relation as constituted in and through us by language:

The element of this relay is language. Language orients us all together toward that which it makes essentially arise: the infinity of a sense that no signification fills and that (this time let's say it) envelops with human beings the totality of the world together with all existing things. (p. 12)[69]

Thus the medium or "element" of our common being is language, and I would add that it is surely the zero degree of language—the apophatic—that is the key to realizing such uncommon and incomparable commonality.

Nancy insists (citing Wittgenstein) that the sense of the world exists only outside it. There is no such thing as sense within the world: it arises from the way that existent beings create the "possibility of an opening, a respiration, an address" (p. 12). Nancy wants, however, to exclude the hypothesis of a preexistent or transcendent God. And yet an apophatic God is precisely *not* this or any other concept of God, but rather is encountered in opening to the unconceptualizable infinity to which Nancy, too, opens thought. What this infinity is, we cannot say. But there is also nothing that it is not, not in an absolute sense.

Nancy embraces rather the relation to the whole of being that is made possible by language. What is achieved is not exactly liberation in the form of freedom, fraternity, equality, and justice, as in the aspirations of the philosophical disciples of the French Revolution, but rather a kind of exposure of the human to itself. In the course of history, humanity abstracts itself from what is other to it, including, for instance, "nature," so as to live in a world of its own making that is disembarrassed of gods and emperors and other such "sacralités." Thus, what European civilization has achieved is "to expose humanity entirely to humanity" ("d'exposer l'homme intégralement à l'homme," p. 13). The human (at least in the modern sense) is born in becoming wholly beholden to and possessed of itself. Yet Nancy wishes to warn us that it must at the same time remain open to what it is not: it must therefore negate itself. Its "enlightened" developments, manifest and celebrated in phenomena such as humanism and democracy, need to be challenged by fundamental self-questioning in order to avoid becoming senselessly homogeneous and sterile.

Thus language must become not just a power of relating, in which all becomes enclosed in the human circuit, but a negative capability of opening to what is outside and other, a power of "passing beyond" signification itself ("outrepassement de la désignation, de la signification et de la trans-mission," p. 14). Such language is a self-negating power that "undoes the address and withdraws access" ("déjoue l'adresse et retire l'accès," p. 14). It is not so much a way of binding back (as is connoted by *religio*) as a way of opening out to the Other ("il ne s'agit pas d'être 'relié' mais ouvert," p. 14). Nevertheless, the latter figure of opening is actually no less inte-grated into religious traditions, particularly in their mystical imaginaries.

Nancy's terms are unmistakably those of apophatic thinking. He flushes out the unsayable and unnameable that lie at the root of the pos-sibility of all language and that are indicated by an excess of language be-yond any function, including naming: "This alterity is not to be named; it is indicated in excess beyond every name" ("Cette altérité n'est pas à nom-mer: elle s'indique en excès sur tout nom," p. 15). It forms the juncture of our words, the infinite possibility of sense. "It is not to be reached" be-cause it rather "forms the joining and the junction of our words, the infi-nite possibility of sense" (p. 15).[70] This opening of language to its own "beyond" Nancy considers to be "adoration." It entails turning to (*ad*) and addressing the other at one's own edge or boundary (*ora* in Latin). Precisely that has been the vocation of language ever since the first words of human beings. In such language, the address is "undone" only in that it is "turned toward an outside that is not exterior to the world but rather opens it in itself" (p. 14).[71]

This openness, like sacrifice, Nancy stresses, does not relate only to individuals, but opens the whole world as such. The lost preverbal world belonging to a superior realm is now behind us, and we work out or rather play out our destiny in another world, that of language ("C'est en lui dé-sormais que nous jouons notre destin," p. 15). In this world of words, for Nancy, "Nothing and no one answers any longer to our word" ("Rien ni personne ne répond plus à notre parole," p. 15). In other words, God is dead.

Although the figurations of the gods were perhaps always more or less deliberate attempts to disguise the fact that nothing and no one responds to our word, this is now explicitly declared in our times. On the other hand, everything and everyone now "resounds with the address that we ourselves are" (tout et tous résonnent de cette adresse que nous sommes," p. 15). Humanity has now become fully conscious that it has to rely only

on itself. It is stripped of every other recourse ("démunie de tout autre re-
cours qu'elle-même," p. 15). This is what Slavoj Žižek, in Lacanian terms,
calls becoming aware that there is no "big Other." It involves assuming responsibility for ourselves in the tradition of the European Enlightenment
relayed by Jürgen Habermas or, again, in the vision of John Dewey championed by Richard Rorty.

As for Žižek, the lesson for us today is not that theological tradition
concerning God is irrelevant but rather that it must be rediscovered in its
relevance to our relations *among ourselves.* These relations must be rein-
vested with "adoration," with open relatedness to what cannot be grasped
or defined in each singular other, with adoration of—or opening to—this
incommensurability that, paradoxically, we share in common. Žižek propounds this reprise in theological terms, specifically of the Holy Spirit, as
love among humans. For him, the equation of the Holy Spirit with the
human community united in faith and love is Hegelian in inspiration,
and that is certainly true in Nancy's case too, with a certain accent on the
disquietude of this Spirit.[72] In Hegelian Christianity, the radical Other
dies on the Cross. God is thenceforth unequivocally one of us. What
emerges in place of the radical Other is "the Holy Spirit, which is not
Other, but the community (or, rather, *collective*) of believers: the 'neigh-
bor' is a member of our collective."[73]

This is, for Nancy, what makes our own historical time also, paradoxically, a time of disappropriation of ourselves. No longer beholden to
the gods or to an objective order of things known supposedly through science and on its authority, neither can humanity have any confidence in
itself. "Our time is a time of de-propriation ("Notre temps est le temps
d'une dépropriation"), and humanity discovers itself to be deprived even
of itself ("L'homme s'y trouve dépris de lui-même," *L'Adoration,* p. 15).
"Being no longer entrusted either to the gods or to science, neither does
humanity find its confidence in itself" ("N'étant plus confié ni aux dieux
ni à la science, il ne trouve pas en lui sa confiance," p. 15) but must rather
of necessity learn lack of self-confidence as a new virtue.

Nancy is turning the Enlightenment emancipation narrative in an
apophatic direction: the discovery by humanity of itself as independent of
gods and other metaphysical supports is a discovery of what it *is not.*
Human history is no longer seen as a heroic narrative of growing up into
full possession of oneself, a *Bildungsroman* of the human spirit coming of

age and confidently taking charge of its own destiny. Rather than finding its confidence in itself, humanity learns that it must rely on what is other, or rather, since there is no big Other to rely on, that it must rely or entrust itself "otherwise" ("Il apprend qu'il doit se confier autrement," p. 16). It has nothing and no one on which to rely, not even itself. And just this objectless reliance opens it to a new dimension of the infinitely open.

Nancy understands this predicament apophatically. It is manifest in the failure of names, of names like God or the Tao or Mystery or Nirvana, but also of names in general. All of them fail to name the other, the true life or "vraie vie" of Rimbaud, and are obsolete insofar as they communicate no truth or revelation. Yet Nancy, with his discourse on the spirit that awakes ("l'esprit qui s'éveille"), is aligned with the Rimbaud of the *Illuminations*. Awakening is a metaphor of enlightenment, of expanded human self-consciousness, but Nancy opens this movement of enlightenment to the dimension of the unknown and incommensurable. Spirit is "the inequality to itself of the awakening that opens to the incommensurable" (p. 9).[74] To conceive human reason or thought in terms of spirit as infinity and openness to what is other than it is to move into the dimension of the apophatic.

This is again where Nancy shares something crucial in common with the early Romantics at Jena (including the young Hegel), who restored a religious spirit to the emancipation of the Enlightenment through their opening up of human spirit as reaching beyond calculative reason to the Infinite. He is intent on sensing or "touching" (Nancy's preferred term)[75] what cannot be verbally or rationally comprehended. Still, he is lacking in the profoundly religious inspiration of authors such as Novalis or Schleiermacher or even Schelling. He does rigorously follow out the apophatic logic of thought giving itself up and thereby opening outward without restriction. This degree of insight can be reached philosophically. However, it is fulfilled only in and through a sensibility that is also irreducibly religious.

Giving oneself up is not only a matter of how one thinks but also of how one acts and concretely relates to others. It can be done in recognition of the mutual bondedness of all or even of an an-archic being responsible for the other, à la Levinas. Some such anterior being-together-in-common that precedes our individual being has been cultivated in multiple forms of culture, but the history of humankind has been marked in this regard especially by religious traditions. Nancy, in fact, recognizes this amply in the rich references to religions by which he constructs his reflection and decks out his exposition, but he nevertheless attempts to position himself outside this religious aspect of human experience and history. He plunders the historical archive of religious imagery without generally wishing to acknowledge directly the "minimal theology" (to borrow Hent de Vries's term, based on Adorno's language) to which this commits him. He prefers not to confess to any kind of religious belief.

Strikingly similar to Nancy's view on essential points, yet turning on just such a confessional acknowledgment, is the deconstructive outlook of Gianni Vattimo.[76] For Vattimo, too, Christianity becomes the protagonist in the historical drama of Western culture on its trajectory from idealist metaphysics to "enlightened" nihilism.[77] Its force is intensively secularizing, and modernity turns out to be the realization of the Christian vision in its effective working in the world. Like Nancy, Vattimo offers a postmodern deconstructive version of apophatic thought that sees Christianity as incarnating the dissolution of metaphysics and thus of sense: it does so through an unlimited opening to infinite, ultimately indefinable sense.

Christianity, as Vattimo sees it, makes religious truth a purely spiritual and ultimately a private affair of conscience and thereby liberates the social sphere from religious dogmas in order to become a secular sphere of lay communication and activity. Christianity is universal and missionary, but what it exports in principle is not concrete power—whether political, ethical, or administrative—but a purely "spiritual" truth. This is written into evangelical *Leitmotifs* such as "My kingdom is not of this world" and "Give unto Caesar what is Caesar's." This universalist vision has been compromised, of course, by the histories of colonialism and imperialism, but they are nevertheless completely contrary to its spirit and truth, and Vattimo urges that a purged and deconstructed Christianity rediscover its true vocation as universal, self-giving Logos in the sense of hospitality, of heeding the other and surrendering oneself, one's own identity. He exhorts Christianity to take up and pursue its civilizing, modernizing mission in this form. Christianity should tender the solution to the conflict of cultures and be a source of reconciliation rather than becoming a party to the conflict. Its role should be "to recover its own proper universalistic function without colonialist, imperialist, or Eurocentric implications . . . accentuating its missionary vocation as hospitality and as religious foundation (as paradoxically as you like) of secularity (of institutions, civil society, and the religious life itself of the individual)."[78]

The end of the assumed normativity of Western culture and of Christianity alike has ushered in a new and heightened awareness of their violence against other civilizations. With the shipwreck of Western rationalism in the postcolonial age, Christianity, too, seems to be discredited, and it seems that secularization can no longer be viewed as the evolutionary goal of all societies.[79] The lay space of the modern West was opened, Vattimo affirms, within the unique religious space created by Christianity. Yet even if Christian universalism was tainted by colonialism and imperialism, Vattimo nevertheless asks whether there is not still room and indeed a call for a universal human civilization. Christianity must not be a sect asserting its own dogmatic, fundamentalist identity but rather become the agent of an opening of society in the direction of modernization. By virtue of its kenotic vocation to modeling weak identity and self-surrender, or self-deconstruction, Christianity lays down the condition of possibility of a lay society. This is the authentic meaning of its missionary ideal. By discovering truth in tradition and in contingent historical events, moreover, Christianity liberates from the metaphysics of objectivity. The Christian God is the end of metaphysics. The Christian universal community is thus dialogical rather than dogmatic. Such religion is spiritual and leaves a space for lay society tolerant of radically different religious convictions.[80]

Christianity so conceived is first and foremost a hermeneutic phenomenon, an interpretation, and salvation is an interpretive event. Vattimo interprets our culture of interpretation today as a result of the religions of the book and specifically of the message of Christianity. The productivity of interpretation in its historical applications, he argues, is rendered possible essentially by the Christian Logos as the Word made flesh. Our modern, Western, scientific, technological culture is nothing but a secularization of Christian revelation, where "secularization" means not negation of and detachment from this religious matrix but rather interpretation and application of it. Classical culture or classicism through the ages is conservative: it attempts to recover and reproduce the original, whereas Christian culture is essentially transformative. Of course, the Greeks, too, had a culture of the book based on interpretation of Homer and Hesiod. Vattimo ignores the pagan, Neoplatonic, allegorical interpretation and philosophical appropriation of Greek myth and epic in propounding his thesis that specifically Christianity revolutionizes interpretation by making the original event no longer an historical past but a living present. In contrast, I prefer to see Christian culture not as unique but as especially transparent and revelatory in this regard—and hence as exemplary of a truly universal vocation of many and perhaps, in some sense, of all religions and cultures.[81]

Like Vattimo, Nancy is a thinker of the postmodern dissolution of knowledge as a liberation that is propelled by Christianity as the religion of the dismantling and dissolution of religion. Along just such lines, Christianity has shown itself in the course of history to answer to a deeply deconstructive and apophatic vocation. Naturally, this is a *certain* Christianity, which for Nancy is of Protestant descent—not Roman Catholicism or Eastern Orthodoxy—and it differentiates itself also from Jewish and Islamic monotheisms. Of course, these later, too, have fostered their own kinds of "adoration" as mystic or universal opening, but for Nancy it is particularly a radical, self-annihilating Protestant Christianity that drives the secularization characteristic of the modern world: "I maintain that of the three religions one alone has undone itself qua religion and has in a way transformed itself into a system of irrigation of the modern world and culture (its morality, its jurisprudence, its humanism, and its nihilism)" ["je tiens que, des trois religions, une seule s'est défaite en tant que religion et s'est en quelque sorte elle-même transformée en système d'irrigation de la culture du monde moderne (sa morale, son droit, son humanisme et son nihilisme)," *L'Adoration,* p. 50].

This Christianity, which breaks with society and its institutions and behaviors, "deconstructs itself and enters into a relation of mutual disclosure and opening with modern reason" ("se déconstruit lui-même et . . . entre en rapport de déclosion mutuelle avec la raison moderne," p. 51). Taking his cue from this sort of Christianity, Nancy proposes, in effect, a philosophy of "sense" as opposed to essence or substance of any kind—social and ethical, no less than material. Sense is not foundational but rather relational—a reference or even a "sending" ("renvoi"): fundamentally things are transumed into their sense, yet there is no definitive or "last" ("dernier") Sense, no sense of sense ("il n'y a pas de sens du sens").

The practice of thought incarnate in the body "opens all the senses to the infinite" ("ouvre tous les sens à l'infini," p. 23). And yet, "that does not mean that all would thus flow into [débouchent sur] one unique sense that would subsume them all" (p. 23). Sense creates *tensions* toward relations and meaning, but, ultimately, it is empty. It is infinite. Every thought moves toward it, yet finds in sense its dissolution. Thought opens all sensorial, corporeal, sentimental sensations and senses to the infinite. It does this specifically in language.

Nancy's anti-logic of sense shows itself to be exactly what I have been calling "apophatic," when he stresses that language works in the mode of address turned toward what it cannot conceive or say. What we know on the basis of language, which forms the whole basis of our being, is that

> language addresses itself and addresses us to this outside of communication and of homogeneous signification. . . . It is there for this alone, it does nothing else: it addresses, it calls, it summons the unnameable, the strict obverse of every possible nomination. This obverse is not a hidden face of the world nor a 'thing in itself' nor a being nor an existing thing. It does not exist: it is from it and to it that every existing being opens itself. 'Him' or 'it' or 'that' or 'nothing': *the thing itself* which is no thing but the fact *that there are things, and a world, or worlds, and us, all of us, all existing beings.* (p. 10)[82]

We cannot but remark the submerged echoes here of the liturgy of the Church, with which Nancy is surely familiar by dint of his Catholic background as a youth and his Christian cultural heritage, for example, in a phrase such as "it is from him and to him that every existing thing opens itself." This reads as a rewriting of Paul's hymn to Christ, the divine, creative Logos, in Colossians 1:16–17: "for all things were created by him, and for him . . . and by him all things consist." Indeed, Nancy relies on vocabulary with just this kind of religious, liturgical resonance right from the very first word, the title of his book: "Adoration."

With regard specifically to the divine Name, Nancy employs the terms that have been basic to negative theology since Pseudo-Dionysius. He even finds a place for the Name of God, the "unnameable name" ("nom innommable"), as the name for what is common to all, all beings in their common uniqueness as singular individuals. The name "God" "[b]ecoming thus all names, becoming the unpronounceable of all names, that which in every 'proper' name remains unnameable because not significant" is the name for that which is unnameable in all that is. In this sense, it is the name not only of all humans but perhaps of all beings whatsoever (*L'Adoration,* p. 92).

Nancy thus follows negative theology in its most classic form of the Name of God as naming everything and nothing: it names the unnameable in everything that is. This omni-comprehensive Name names nothing in particular (God cannot be only this or that) and so subverts the statute of the name by absolutizing it. To know God's Name is to know everything, but thereby also nothing at all, since it affords no determinate knowledge of any referent. Nevertheless, Nancy does not want to identify his thought with that of a "learned ignorance" ("*docte ignorance*") or with any other form of "not knowing that would seek to regain assurance by means of the negative." He wishes to admit only "the simple, naked truth that there is nothing in the place of God because there is no place of God" (pp. 93–94).

But this sort of categorical statement is perhaps too simple. At least, it can be verified only by shifting from a register of universal philosophical enunciation to one of personal confession. And Nancy really wants to be speaking not just for himself but for "us" in embracing what is, after all, a critically conscious ignorance:

> And our ignorance is aggravated by the fact that we do not know if it is appropriate or not to name this common and singular property of all names—for example, by naming it "God" in some new currency (an other, a wholly other god? ...). Or else in giving it all our names. Or else by risking the word "unnameable," which not by chance has become for us, with Beckett, a master-word, or better, a master-name. (p. 94)

Nancy has his own interpretation of the emptiness named by the name. He calls it the "fortuity" or contingency of the world: "Adoration is achieved in naming, in greeting the unameable that the name conceals and that is nothing other than the fortuitousness of the world" (p. 93). But to really open to and greet the unnameable, the event of what we cannot say, is not to limit oneself to one interpretation of the world and to decide simply that it is "fortuitous." To define it thus gives a specific, determinate content (one claiming, moreover, to be objective rather than confessional) to the unconditional openness that is the pragmatic philosophical commitment of Nancy's thought of *déclosion,* as well as of all negative theology interpreted radically. There is indeed something infinitely inexplicable and fortuitous about the world and the fact *that* it exists. But also about the fact that it is in some way ordered and miraculously hangs together. This hanging together, too, is utterly astonishing. Why should these facts not deserve to be acknowledged and even to be interpreted philosophically and theologically? The inventions of mythologies and mysticisms and metaphysics the world over witness that such interpretations are indeed humanly compelling. They interpret the universe's fortuitousness *and* its even more astonishing qualities of harmony and order rather than merely declaring it, finally and definitively, to be "fortuitous"—as if that description, in preference to all others, were right and sufficient.

Being open to "God," or calling whatever one opens oneself up to "God," is more radically risky than simply calling it the fortuitousness of the world. "God" is richer with possibilities of what might be demanded of us, of what we might encounter beyond our own powers of qualifying it as contingent or as anything else, since we are no longer exclusively in the subject position vis-à-vis God. It is not just that the world is fortuitous for us, but also that our being there at all is *for someone else,* that makes us the more radically contingent. It is not just that there are no necessary reasons which we can assign to things, but also that we might ourselves *be* assigned an intrinsic purpose and be defined by something or—yet more disturbingly—*someone* else.

These are, in any case, possibilities that are not to be excluded, especially if one wants to be in communication without restriction with potentially all others and to take seriously their ideas about and experience of the world and its wherefore. Nancy understands the God of monotheism as being *with* (*avec*) human beings more than *over* them or *beyond* them. Pagan deities belong to and appear from a superior order of beings, but in monotheism God reveals himself immanently in history and humanity and, for the first time, as *with* humans—most fully, of course, in the fraternal figure of Jesus. For Nancy, God is finally revealed as nothing but this *with* itself: "'God' is no other thing—if it is a matter of a thing, and it is perhaps *the thing* itself—than this 'with' itself" ("'Dieu' n'est autre chose—s'il s'agit d'une chose, et c'est peut-être bien *la chose* même—que de cet avec lui-même," p. 61).

Of course, the meaning of this "with" and of monotheism or revealed religion generally is to be understood primarily in relation to the sign and its infinitely multipliable powers of signification. All that distinguishes revealed religions is that in them, "the sign of the Infinite, which is itself infinite, sends itself from itself" ("le signe de l'infini, lui-même infini, s'envoie de lui-même," p. 61). Like the one God, the sign, or the infinity of signification, is not referred ultimately to anything but itself, and monotheism realizes this as the infinity of God. All is engendered from the self-engendering self-relation of the sign—hence God's self-sufficient, all-powerful character. And all religion is an infinite "desire for infinity." It is unlike all finite knowledge of some particular thing, all "information" or "instruction," which does not open us to the "inexhaustible ground of things" (p. 61).

Monotheism, or revealed religion, is achieved essentially in the emergence of the *sign* as that which unites the uncounted multiplicity of things into unified *sense*. But it is particularly the suspension and interruption of sense in the inarrestible references of signs to always further signs that characterizes revelation. Revelation is thus infinite and is revelation *of* the infinite. No object or signified can exhaust it. And yet our finitude, grasped as mortality, "configures our access to the infinite" ("cette finitude configure notre accès à l'infini," p. 61). We relate to it as *in*accessible.

Revelation through such relation is thus greater than all figuration or representation. The infinite truth revealed in signification exceeds every determinate sense and suspends sense itself. "Revealed truth" ("La vérité révélée"), as Nancy understands it, contains no teaching or dogma or content: "It is simple infinite truth of the suspension of sense: interruption, because sense does not complete itself, and excess, because it does not cease" (p. 62). This revelation does not teach anything in particular but rather calls all to respond to all: "Call and response . . . of all to all, of each to each, just as for greeting one another: nothing more, nothing less, but thus breaking open paths and voices without end between fortuitous existences" ("Appel et réponse . . . de tous à tous, de chacun à chacun, comme pour seulement se saluer : rien de plus, rien de moins, mais ainsi frayant des voies et des voix sans fin entre les existences fortuites," p. 62).

In taking these Derridean positions regarding the impossibility of arresting sense, Nancy embraces a philosophy of literature—or philosophy *as* literature. Literature he understands as speaking from the "interruption of myth" (p. 62). Myths signify a sort of fatality, whereas this significance is reversed by literature, as based on individual expression, into personal freedom. Sense is made in this interruption, and it is continually remade in the variety of mobile, plastic, ductile forms that succeed one another as "configurations of the 'with'" ("l''avec' se configure indéfiniment," p. 62). In literature and art, signs point beyond sense to the infinite ("les signes renvoient à l'infini," p. 63), to all possible relations *with* as generating ever new sense.

It is, therefore, especially the language of literature, as well as of song, that is necessary to express the opening that is astir in "adoration." When the divine spirit becomes physical, real, and present in language and song, infinity becomes actual and incarnate. This actualization was conceived by the theological idea of all nature as the "mystical body" of Christ, through which "I touch the world in its entirety, in the totality of its force of expansion" ("je touche au monde en son entier, à la totalité de sa force et de son expansion," p. 106). Literary and liturgical expressions are manifest in all their paramount importance when we are primarily oriented to relating to others in the world through unrestricted opening of the linguistic address (hence "ad-oration" as meaning "to" or "toward" oration or orality).

Literature is Nancy's model for this type of projection of oneself through unknowing into relation with the impossible. Literature employs fiction in order to relate to what is not real or even necessarily possible in a rational sense. Immortality of the soul or self is impossible in terms of life as we know it, yet precisely this has been a particularly persistent and tenacious belief in religious traditions. Nancy brings the discussion of his book to a climax in its final pages on the question of immortality. He believes that we have a sort of eternity *in relation* to all other things: I *am* the totality of my relations to all things, and only through them can I relate to myself (p. 135). This is what Spinoza considered to be the relation to God or to the totality of what exists seen under an aspect of eternity (p. 135).

Feeling this total relatedness gives us the sensation of our eternity "in relation to the rest of all being and thus to the incommensurable (which Spinoza names 'God') in which we can have joy but not knowledge" ["à tout le reste de l'étant et ainsi à l'incommensurable (que Spinoza nomme 'Dieu') dont nous pouvons avoir joie mais non savoir," p. 135]. According to Spinoza, we feel and know that we are eternal (*Ethics*, Part V, proposition 23). For we can feel this totality of our relatedness with all in joy, but our "knowledge" of it is a feeling and an unknowing knowing.

For Nancy, the relation that adoration actualizes is unconditional and opens to the infinite. This makes the relativity of relation absolute "because the relative is thought only on the basis of the 'absolute'" ("car le relative ne se pense que sur un fond d''absolu,'" p. 108). And that opens relation in its intrinsic relativity to All. Being-with (the Heideggerian *Mitsein*) is an existential condition beyond all categories that apply to beings: consequently, relation is greater than being. Relation opens us to the infinite rather than only to beings in their finitude. The latter places us rather within a web of determinate means and ends in which everything is bound to serve a function.

In fact, Nancy becomes a thinker of relation and of relation specifically to (and in) Christianity as the driving force in Western history. This impulsion drives toward "déclosion," in which humanity and the world consummate themselves in relation to the Other in their very midst. Infinite relation to the infinite rather than unsurpassable finitude becomes Nancy's perspective and approach in his deconstruction of Christianity. Rather than opposing religion and especially the Christian religion, he sees Christianity as exemplary and as laden with destiny in its own operation of deconstructing itself together with the entire civilization of which it is the heir—and also the undertaker.

Nancy thinks the unlimited opening or *déclosion* of reason to its other, which other is itself thought, on the models of Trinity, Incarnation, and Resurrection. He sees how these doctrines archetypally express the claim of infinite relation to others that is inherent in language itself. He explains how these Christian doctrines make relation the successor of and substitute for every form of essence or substance in classical metaphysics, with all its hierarchies and oppressions. His central metaphor of "adoration" signifies an opening of eyes or mouth—orifices—to relation with others, in which the self as an enclosure is overcome.[83] Relation to the Other that began in the form of sacred sacrifice in Western religion is transformed by Christianity into relations with others in the Spirit. This, as we have seen, is a Hegelian interpretation of history and of Christianity's salvific role in it. For Nancy, salvation—"salut"—is nothing otherworldly in nature but consists fundamentally in greeting others or "saluting" them.

The relation to or with others is where the sense of any of our own communications is determined and realized, since their meaning depends on their reception. Such sense is infinitely open to the infinitely other, since there is no limit on the others who can be addressed. This infinite opening effects a deconstruction of sense, which is never anything definable or achieved. It must always be related to what is yet other— in which relation it will be further changed and possibly even reversed. Yet this is also the apotheosis of sense, its opening toward the infinity of sense, the achievement of the meaning (and unmeaning) of history and humanity without limits. In an unsystematic manner, Nancy intends his philosophy to encompass human history, from prehistoric Mediterranean cultures through Christianity and capitalism, in a comprehensive interpretation of how human rationality realizes and then surpasses or deconstructs itself—inasmuch as it all hinges on the indeterminate or infinite: it hinges on what cannot be defined and yet is determined nevertheless non-objectively as opening without limit to what calls, or to the calling of the call. The specifically human and linguistic phenomena of relation or sense, understood thus, are totally open to truth as disclosure, revelation, "déclosion," yet in no linguistically or conceptually determinable form. This way of thinking is quintessentially apophatic. It cannot escape being a sort of faith.

There is a sort of faith necessary to reason in its exceeding itself in the opening of self that constitutes adoration. Nancy distinguishes it from belief, which remains attached to a *representation* of what it believes. By contrast, "Faith, in all rigor, would be without any representation" (p. 128). Faith is belief in what cannot be known or represented but is apprehended rather in the collapse of knowledge and representation. Faith requires holding oneself in the suspense of relation to sense, yet without knowledge or representation (p. 130). Faith, for Nancy, is a kind of self-subversion and annulment of knowledge ("annulation de toute espèce de savoir"), just as sense, as Nancy understands it, is a relation to or sending toward an annulment of sense ("'comprenant' le sens ainsi—comme rapport à ou comme envoi vers une annulation du 'sens,'" p. 130).

In this peculiar form of faith, Christianity and atheism are inextricably intertwined. Living in the world yet outside it, being *in* the world but not *of* it, within time and yet beyond it, characterizes Christianity in particular, but therewith also the West as a whole. Christianity opens life to the death in its midst, breaking down the opposition of the two in the Greco-Roman world and thereby bringing life out of death. Resurrection conquers death and triumphs in eternal life experienced here and now as a saved life or a living of salvation. Christianity effects a deconstruction of life, folding death into its midst. In this manner, Christianity brings on atheism: it secularizes the world and deconstructs religion and its myths. It "desacralizes and demythologizes and secularizes itself" ("le christianisme se désacralise, se démythologise et se sécularise," p. 39).

Nancy understands in atheistic terms the disclosure of truth in history that has been driven particularly by Christianity, through its idea of divine Incarnation. For him, Christianity is thus inhabited from its inception by the possibility of atheism. Christianity affirms the presence in this world of the divine alterity in death here and now in the Christ event (p. 43). Christ by his death opens this world to death in its midst, somewhat the way the death of Socrates did for the philosophical life. In both cases, death opens up in the middle of the world rather than remaining banned beyond its borders and off-limits for those immersed in life. Both Christically and philosophically, death is rather *lived* by anticipation.

The becoming-atheist of Christianity and of religion in general realizes what Nancy calls "déclosion" (p. 45). There is no other world: the infinite openness of sense must all be understood with reference to "this world" ("ce monde"). But why should Nancy so resolutely exclude other worlds opening from within this one? One might just as well say, "La vraie vie est ailleurs!" ("The true life is elsewhere"), as Nancy himself acknowledges, with this citation from Rimbaud, who is also given the honor of pronouncing the last word in a kind of postscript to Nancy's book. With a closing quotation from "Génie," Rimbaud is resurrected as the prophet of a dawning—or at least a desired—new age of "Adoration."

Atheism is presented by Nancy as a historical necessity and as following from the historical course of thought as such in its breaking itself open to the infinite in the movements of *déclosion* and *adoration,* but this choice of atheism is rather his own. He recognizes at other moments that it is pointless to advocate atheism: such advocacy falls into a counter-dogmatism made in the image of what it seeks to defeat. He possesses insight into the fact that atheism itself is undermined by the breaking open of reason in postmodern times, and thus that atheism has no more rational grounds to stand on than does theism.[84]

What is peculiarly provocative in Nancy's intellectual and perhaps spiritual itinerary is its demonstration of the lack of philosophical justification for the decision for or against God, for or against religion, for or against belief. The apophatic logic of Nancy's thought can be separated from his personal convictions on these matters, even though for him as an individual facing his own death, the two are hardly separable. We are all placed as individuals before the question of what we believe about death and its sequel. This personal choice has not quite been disentangled by Nancy from the question of the general logic of *déclosion* and *adoration.*

To define his own type of faith, Nancy aligns himself tellingly with Freud. He takes Freud as the breakthrough thinker who reinvents humanity by means of a new story, one which envisages neither creation by an act of God nor human auto-production in accordance with some Marxist myth. Rather, Freud's evolutionary vision re-narrates human beings' provenance in terms of drives that come from beyond the control of any subject. These "pulsions" (Freud's *Triebe*) hail from an elsewhere ("ailleurs") that is in us and not from a transcendent "beyond," as theologies have claimed, nor from a simple immanence, as is maintained by the atheistic inversions of these theologies. This "impulsion" or "élan," which we more deeply *are* than we can measure or fathom, is being itself that is infinitely open and beyond all categories: it is "a being which no god, no nature, and no history would be able to fill with sense" ("un être que nul dieu, nulle nature et nulle histoire ne sauraient combler de sens," p. 145).

One understands Nancy's preference for this narrative, but only because of what it is not: it is not compromised by the theological traditions that Nancy rejects. And yet the fictional elaboration by these traditions of the mystery of the provenance of the human (Creation, Fall, Redemption, and so on) is hardly inferior to Freud's or Nancy's own fictions. Indeed, Judeo-Christian theology fundamentally informs the imaginary from which the latter both draw. Not unlike Nancy in *Adoration,* Freud, near the end of his life, in *Moses and Monotheism,* had to come to terms finally with the theological premises of his thinking against religion. Each apparently anti-religious thinker offers a negative articulation that turns out to proceed, still, from the domain of the religious.[85] Nancy has his convictions, and he is justified in developing them in continuity with his exposition of an apophatic mode of thought, but not as if they were imposed by that type of thinking per se—except in that it creates the freedom to embrace such convictions . . . *or their opposites.*

Nancy's advocacy of a this-worldly attitude at every juncture, as if it were the only critically reflective and defensible view, is a prejudice of his own. It might be effectively criticized by critical theory in the style of the Frankfurt school, which is certainly as modern and materialist as Nancy ever becomes. Adorno writes in *Negative Dialektik*: "Negatively, by virtue of its consciousness of nothingness, theology is in the right against this-worldly belief" ("Negativ, kraft des Bewußtweins der Nichtigkeit, behält die Theologie gegen den Diesseitsglaubigkeit recht").[86] There are "reasons" for belief in other worlds—beginning with the inadequacy of all reasons whatever grounded in *this* world. We might say that the orientation to other worlds is written into language itself as always structuring the world into something other than what it simply is and even more radically as turned toward the unnameable—as evoking ultimately what it is impossible for language to comprehend.[87]

This motif of the other world (and the world as other) inscribes another profoundly Christian anticipation of the postmodern world. Might not Nancy's thinking on this further bogey of religious superstition conceivably take a similar turn and allow him finally to become the thinker of the other world par excellence? We have noted more than once the irony—in light of Nancy's earlier denial of the possibility of address or apostrophe in our world today—that just such appellation becomes the crucial gesture to be found everywhere, the universal mode of relation, in Nancy's later and definitive philosophy of the deconstruction of Christianity.

In the turn (it is tempting to say the *Kehre*) of Nancy's thinking, appellation becomes the all-important manifestation of his thought precisely *because* it is impossible. For this very reason it is no longer to be dismissed and discarded, but rather recommended and commended. He accordingly finds a place—and what a place!—for calling upon the impossible Name, the Name of God, the unnameable name ("nom innommable"), as a name for what is common to all, all beings in their common uniqueness of being singular (and therefore ineffable) individuals. It is the divine Name that opens sense to the excess from which all sense comes. The name "God," practiced religiously as an exclamation of joy or an acclamation of grandeur ("'quelle joie!' ou 'quelle grandeur!'" p. 113) expresses paradigmatically the purely "pulsional" function of language. This Name is a "salute to the incommensurable by naming no being but designating only itself as salute/salvation" ("salut à l'incommensurable ne désignant aucune sorte d'être, se désignant seulement soi-même comme salut," *L'Adoration,* p. 113).

Nancy arrives through philosophical reflection on language and its limits at descriptions of the divine Name as paradigm that perfectly repeat and creatively imitate the negative theology of the divine Name, with the characteristic linguistic play that animates it in speculative and mystical traditions from the patristic period to the baroque. He continues his meditation on the "salut" thus, in a fragment:

> Mais salut surpris, pris dans la parole par surprise, en deçà de toute phrase et portant à la voix plutôt qu'à la parole proprement dite une nomination de l'innommable ou du nommable par excellence— par excès, par cette profusion que chaque nom recèle. (p. 113)

> But salute/salvation surprised, found in the word by surprise, from below the threshold of any phrase and bearing in voice rather than in the word properly speaking a naming of the unnameable or the nameable par excellence—by excess, by this profusion that each name covertly harbors.

Moreover, Nancy sketches a doctrine of the positive excess of language beyond silence, the hyperbolic language that silence is and that develops in effect the positive expression of apophasis or of the "reserve of sense exceeding the words and rich with language's secret, with its intimacy" (p. 99). And this enables him apophatically to reflect that "[t]o return to language beyond silence means to come back to what in language, nearest to it, neither declares nor names anything properly, yet without as a result disappearing at the approach of an Unnameable" ("Faire retour au langage au-delà du silence veut dire qu'on revient au plus près du langage, à ce qui, en lui, ne déclare ni ne nomme proprement sans pour autant s'évanouir à l'approche d'un Innommable," p. 99).

In these terms, Nancy develops what I call a philosophy of the unsayable and does so with recurrent reference to the unnameable Name of God. As the dark ground or "fond" of language, the Name of God even permits the speaking being, the human, to relate to the totality of existents in the world (p. 100). In fact, Nancy sees the necessity of embracing both approaches to apophasis—through language and through being—that were distinguished in the previous essay. The two are, in apophatic terms, complementary sides of a common silence.

The excessive word expresses itself, Nancy recognizes, in literature, particularly in the exuberance of literary inventions (p. 100), but by its excessive, endless speech it no longer has anything to say—its sense becomes infinite. This can be expressed by saying that the gods are speaking in us or "make us speak" ("ce sont les dieux qui nous font parler," p. 100). Language itself is even divine in that it comes from an indefinable beyond, an "outside" ("Le langage est divin en ce qu'il vient du dehors," p. 101), and it returns to an outside that it itself opens up in us and in the midst of our world. That means that the gods themselves are language in the forms of myths, names, and calls. Nancy points out that in all three monotheisms, God is essentially one who speaks. He is effaced behind this function so as to become the Unnameable. And here we find Nancy articulating a central thesis of the philosophy of unsayability sketched in my second essay in this volume, namely, that all saying opens upon the unsayable:

> [T]here is no nomination except on a background of the unnameable and the latter is nothing other than that which is said in every nomination . . . . Naming opens to the unattainable, to the irreducibility of the thing, the real, the existent. Only language gives this opening, but it alone also designates it as gaping open upon the infinite, as outside language and nevertheless always newly repeated, asked for again in the word. (p. 101)[88]

This marks quite an advance over "Des lieux divins." This discourse becomes a language for what is beyond concept, for what escapes the concept and its grasp (the *Griff* of *Begriff*), as Nancy plays with and thinks from the linguistic form of words broken open to what they do not name—infinitely. Having played the part of a prosecutor indicting all religious thinking as suspect, Nancy converts to being a fervent advocate of a thinking that cannot account for itself by itself alone but is open to what it cannot think and is filled with—or rather is emptied by, is kenotically self-emptied into—in adoration. A kind of negative "religion" or bonding beyond what reason can encompass and control is necessary, after all: prostration is required for reason to open up to what surpasses reason infinitely. In other words, "only reason in adoration is fully rational and reasonable" ("seule la raison adorante est pleinement rationnelle et raisonnable," p. 116).

Thus conceived, thought is, for Nancy, "sensibility to the unnameable: to that which exceeds thought and renders it possible" ("sensibilité à l'innommable: à ce qui l'excède et la rend possible," p. 137). Thought is our "pulsion," a drive that "exceeds itself" ("déborde elle-même," p. 137). Nancy admits that this is a matter not of knowledge but of affect—"of an élan which does not take itself for a semblance of knowledge but rather opens in the impossible the possibility of relating oneself to it" ("d'un élan qui ne se prend pas pour un semblant de savoir mais qui ouvre dans l'impossible la possiblité de se rapporter à lui," p. 137). By releasing one's hold on things through knowing and naming them, one finds oneself suddenly in an unlimited relation to and with them, indeed, with the "totality" of what is and even with the "incommensurable" from which they "come." This lies near to the traditional idea of a source of things in God. The nuance of difference is that things are now understood as coming from the measureless not in an objective sense but in the sense that it is by our ceasing to set any measure to things that they come to us in all their unlimited potentiality and strangeness and even impossibility—as beyond what we could imagine or intend.

The career and the *Kehre* of Jean-Luc Nancy's thought illustrate the historically recurrent strife between the ambiguously religious thinking of negative theology and the militant styles of secular thinking in the tradition of the Enlightenment that take their inspiration from the refusal of theology in any form. The trajectory of Nancy's thought twists away from such antagonisms and infiltrates into the dimension of the infinite and unsayable—or what I call the apophatic. The unsayable is shown to be the place or topos to which critical philosophical reflection leads, whether it follows the path of a critique of positive philosophical rationality or of an unlimited, radical, self-critical negation of positive theology.

Understood in these terms, Nancy exemplifies one of the most significant paradoxes of contemporary philosophy of religion. He evolves from a rigorous proponent of the thought of finitude to a proponent of an unrestricted opening to the infinite. Of course, the infinite cannot simply be opposed to finitude. Still, in key respects, the emphasis and the direction of approach of Nancy's thinking are reversed from its earlier to its later stages. Moreover, whereas he attacked Christianity and religious approaches broadside in his essay on divine places, in his two-volume *Déconstruction* Nancy accords Christianity a unique place as the key to the overcoming of illusion and oppression in all its most dehumanizing forms. Religion, especially Christianity, leads to a deconstruction of the entire metaphysical tradition of Western philosophical thinking and therewith a revolution of human culture. Nancy's thinking is now fully attuned to the apophatic sources and subtleties of religious thought in general and of monotheism and Christianity in particular.

Nancy turns from a negation of theology in the sense of simply refusing it and trying to end it, to an opening or *déclosion* of theology, which turns it toward its other and makes it a negation in an apophatic sense. Theology is not rejected as such but rather only in its positive, dogmatic forms and as limited in its power of opening toward an absolute Other. At this stage, authentically negative theology shows itself to be an indispensable means of directing thought beyond its intrinsic limits.

In fact, like Nietzsche and Lacan, Nancy was always keenly aware of the daunting power of religion and preeminently of Christianity. He has shifted his position in that rather than fighting against Christianity, he now elects to work with it—with and for its own exemplary self-deconstruction or dissolution. One might say that, somewhat like pagan Rome becoming the seat of Roman Catholicism, he has been conquered (or contaminated) by what he attacked yet also assimilated. In his later work and in true apophatic style, he pushes always toward what is beyond the finite and deter-minate ("au-delà du déterminé," *L'Adoration,* p. 72). He does not want to talk glibly about God, but he does project his thought of impulsions ("pulsions") to the infinite and indefinable, and he recognizes "God" as an incomparably significant Name in this regard. Similarly, he projects the order of the world to infinity, where it becomes another order and, in ef-fect, an other world. He opts for an "order with unlimited rights of sur-passing, with infinite thrust" ("l'ordre du dépassement en droit illimité, de la poussée infinie," p. 72). The existence or opening of the world is "the first and probably the only mystery, the one that contains all other myster-ies in itself" ("L'ouverture du monde est le premier mystère, sans doute le seul ou celui qui contient tous les autres," p. 70).

Impulsions are related to desire and hope and all that makes "sense" in the human symbolic order. Like giving priority to the infinite, the thinking of everything in terms of relation is a mode of thought that has passed in the West through theological channels. It was developed by Hegel in conjunction especially with Christian tradition, and this is Nan-cy's heritage, too, even though certain of Hegel's approaches tend to be re-versed in postmodern appropriations and disappropriations of his thought.

Rather than speaking of God, Nancy speaks of "pulsion" (impulsion) as the mysterious source of infinite openness toward which humans aim with their language that relates to the totality of beings. Impulsion or *Trieb,* drive, as Freud understood it, makes us speak beyond our own in-tent and understanding and thereby opens the sense of all to all. The un-nameable is the opening in language that puts it in contact with the "totality of beings and, thus, with the infinite opening which shares them all and reunites them all" ("totalité des étants et, ainsi, avec l'infini de l'ouverture qui les partage tous et les réunit tous," p. 103).

In the spirit of monotheism, Nancy admits that the impulsions, which are the myths of post-mythological man, and hence pure myths, are united into one obscure impulse ("'les' pulsions, pluriel d'une unique, ob-scure poussée indefinie," p. 105). They are united to and in nothing but this opening, which is the world. And this enables Nancy again to define adoration: "Finally, that which I here name 'adoration' means: deciding to exist, siding with existence, turning away from nonexistence, from the closure of the world upon itself" (p. 104).[89] In order that sense remain infinitely open, Nancy's adoration resists reductions—including those of the hermeneutics of suspicion against ideals of the absolute and unconditioned (p. 104). Truth and totality, too, have their role in our apophatic philosophies, just as in our mythologies.

Of course, Nancy's terms finally are those of negation and apophasis "inasmuch as language does not cease to name the unnameable" ("en tant que le langage ne cesse de nommer l'innommable," p. 137). He "believes without believing or as a 'denial' (translating Freud's *Verleugnung*)" ["croire sans croire ou bien comme le 'déni' (traduction da la *Verleugnung*) de Freud," p. 137]. Such negation is "a category which is not even one [a category] but is nonetheless a real and substantive mode of feeling" (p. 137).[90]

Sometimes, however, Nancy is tempted not just to feel but to *know* that there is no other world than "this" one: "I know well that there is no other world" ("Je sais bien qu'il n'y a pas d'autre monde"). In this regard, he resembles Caputo, who similarly announces himself assured about this, although I think that such declarations can be persuasive only because all that religions say about the other world is richly revealing *also* with regard to "this" one. In the end, are not these registers of interpretation complementary? Consequently, should not this-worldly thinking deny itself as such and acknowledge its covert affinities with traditions concerning other worlds? Like Vattimo, Nancy finds that he believes, or at least desires to believe, even if it is in nothing (that he can say): "but I believe, I want to believe, I allow the formation of a schema of a possible or rather a not-impossible, of an unheard-of way of making sense, or not even sense but simply of holding on and of holding to—nothing, nothing but this desire or nothing *as* this desire itself to believe" (*L'Adoration*, p. 137).[91] This is belief letting go of itself and desire that desires just itself in its infinite openness to others. And it is exemplary of religious belief understood apophatically.

Of course, there are also millions of people of various faiths who think that they know well that there is indeed another world and who relate to everything and everyone through such a conviction. We should not cut off our relation and our openness to them by refusing to entertain such belief in our presumption of *knowing* the contrary. More immediately telling than any representation or conviction concerning the other world is the relation realized here and now to others. Nancy would be most consistent with his own apophasis of unrestricted relations by opening infinitely, without limit, in adoration toward all others and even toward honoring the possibility of their beliefs, at least as forms of belief in or of holding to the (to him) impossible. Any nihilist interpretation of his belief in nothing is far too narrow to exhaust its gesture of infinite opening in "adoration."

In its closing gestures, Nancy's book *Déconstruction du christianisme* raises again the question of the position of apophatic philosophy between theism and atheism. This question has been recurrently crucial for apophatic thought at historic junctures, such as the trial of Meister Eckhart, whose defense ("In agro domenico," 1329) confounds the conventional polarizations. The same question also fuels the debates revolving around Radical Orthodoxy today. As a position of *un*knowing, apophaticism would seem to be an agnosticism. And yet it is not the position as such but rather the moving away by negation from any position in which knowing can rest secure that is most characteristic of apophaticism. It does not remain within the limits of any knowledge or even of any definite and achieved state of unknowing—as if that way the question could be resolved once and for all agnostically.

Nancy's anti-religious convictions remain unchanged, but he has understood, like Vattimo, that atheism is undermined as much as is theism by the collapse of all forms of strong thought ("pensiero forte") in the postmodern age. Nancy has his beliefs, which happen to be anti-religious and contrary to those held by all who entertain belief in God and the afterlife. But he shares a faith with at least some of these believers in what exceeds our capacities to know and believe alike: we believe rather in what exceeds our belief, not to mention our knowing. In our opening to what exceeds us immeasurably, we share a common faith. This faith is based on an insight into the inability of our reflection to ground, account for, or even to circumscribe its own activity: it is always in excess of itself, of its own rational self-understanding. This recognition is an enactment of the unlimited self-critique that has been traced here from its sources in Neoplatonic reflection, in which philosophy turns to "religion" in the sense of an orientation to what is beyond its reach. Nancy is right that "religion" is inadequate, as is any term, to describe this turn of reflection in language toward its own "beyond." But neither can he qualify it as secular or irreligious or atheist. The term "apophatic" is intended to gesture toward this beyond of all categories, since it is characterized by the release of all definitions, just as the Name of God is the name for that which in all names absolutely exceeds naming.

Thus my conclusion is that philosophy, thought radically, does turn ineluctably into religion of sorts—just as it was religious in its Greek roots, with Heraclitus, Parmenides, and other pre-Socratics.[92] Nancy formerly attempted to deny this, but his own efforts, ironically, turn out resoundingly to confirm it: his own philosophy becomes an exemplary model of what I call a religious philosophy of the unsayable. Philosophy or reason, thought through, dissolves itself and opens toward its Other in "adoration." This I take to be the quintessence of religion or of the original impulse that inspires religious modes of thought and expression. The philosophy of the unsayable, as I see it, is religious thinking in the sense of opening to the infinite relations of *religio* and finally to relation with the Infinite. This is the vocation of all thinking, as Nancy, in his inimitable style, suggests. Thinking philosophy through apophatically leads beyond the possibilities of thought—and opens to the embrace of what cannot be thought. This Other has been interpreted most profoundly, I believe, by theology in its apophatic form as negative theology and analogously by apophatic forms of literature and art, which in effect embody negative poetics and negative aesthetics.

v

My own belief is that apophatic or negative theology holds in its keeping a key to the perennial vitality of philosophical reflection that does not simply define and then exhaust arbitrarily laid down, heuristic limits for its thinking. The willingness to let go of all definitions, to negate all its own formulations, opens thought to what is moving within it, beyond or beneath the definitive grasp of words and concepts. Philosophy at this level is not merely cognitive but also shades into and merges with other dimensions of human experience and being, such as the affective and conative (or willful). In the ancient world, notably among the Neoplatonists, philosophy was so understood as a spiritual exercise involving all the human faculties of intellection and sensibility and praxis.[93]

Damascius presents the ripest fruit—some would say over-ripe—of the philosophical reflection of the Hellenistic Age. Philosophy is by nature critical, critical especially of itself. I have exalted as a perennial and necessary development in philosophy the phase of hypercritical and even self-crippling reflection that makes a virtue of self-deconstruction, recognizing in the self-subversion of discourse an unveiling, or at least an indicating, of a radical Other to all discourse. But this might also be deplored as the fall from grace of the genuine philosophical spirit and as the extinguishing of the inspired radiance that first dawned in archaic Greece. In this latter historical metanarrative, philosophy in its classical form is thought to have abided within the appropriate bounds of reason but then in postclassical times to have turned grotesque. Hellenistic forms of art, with their overemphasis and distortion of nature, may be seen analogously as illustrative of what happens in thinking that forsakes the measure of nature, stretching ideas to extremes, until they become no longer plausible. Such thinking, on this line of reasoning, oversteps the limits within which it was originally useful and creative.

There must be some truth in this assessment, too, if we consider the widespread appreciation for classical models of thought and art and the periodic reassertion of these models as incomparably to be preferred over all others. Yet such classicizing phases, too, always prove to be passing. So we also need to understand why Hellenistic forms of conceptual mannerism have had such a prominent place and exerted their appeal repeatedly in the cycles of the history of philosophy and again in today's culture and philosophy. This is crucial to the task of understanding the predicament of thought at the present. We can thereby better see postmodern thought in historical perspective and perhaps move beyond it. The point here is not to argue over what is *the* right paradigm for thinking, so much as to explore the furthest potential of each framework, including our own, so as to be able to carry it further and eventually to surpass it. Accordingly, I want to acknowledge the limits of Neoplatonic thought as it can be represented in a contemporary context. Its positive metaphysical program may not have the same direct claim upon us as it had in late antiquity. It is rather the apophatic underpinnings of such thought that are crucial for us today.

The philosophy of the unsayable advanced in these pages may come across as an apology for metaphysical and mystical currents of thinking that are valorized for their appeal to critical reason and more broadly to "philosophy" as the love of wisdom. The revaluation of Neoplatonism as a philosophical critique that turns itself in metaphysical and mystical directions is merely exemplary of similar reassessments that could be made of other philosophies thinking beyond the limits of word and reason. I have sketched out some nodal points for such a history of thinking in the general introductions to *On What Cannot Be Said*. Much more work has been done—and is being done—by many others. The next essay considers how John Milbank, for example, brings out relevant theological undercurrents in thinkers such as Vico, Hamann, and Herder, currents which were submerged beneath the dominant rational paradigms of the Enlightenment.

The thrust of such philosophies of the unsayable is not to undermine reason but rather the contrary. Recognition of the limits of reason as Logos or word restores reason to its proper place at the center of intellectual illumination and yet shadowed at the same time by the circumambient penumbra of what it ignores and cannot penetrate. Its light shines within and even thanks to this darkness (again, *Denken* proves to be *Danken*). Indeed, rational critique has proved essential to discovering the philosophy of the unsayable in Neoplatonism, as well as in every subsequent or simultaneous avatar of apophatic thought. Reason has constantly been called forth by the call of this Other that it cannot comprehend. The eminently rational philosophies of Aristotle or Hegel are not dismissed or diminished in the perspective of a philosophy of the unsayable. Quite the opposite is the case. But just as both these thinkers showed unprecedented understanding for their own predecessors, their philosophies too, for all their fully systematic articulation, should be viewed in the end as indispensable moments within the movement of thought that forges irrepressibly ahead, eventually beyond thought itself, beyond any determinate formulation of thinking in speech, beyond anything that can be said.

RADICAL ORTHODOXY'S CRITIQUE OF TRANSCENDENTAL PHILOSOPHY AND ITS MISTAKEN MISTRUST OF NEGATIVE THEOLOGY

"Unspeakable! who sitt'st above these heavens
To us invisible, or dimly seen
In these thy lowest works; yet these declare
Thy goodness beyond thought, and power divine."
—Milton, *Paradise Lost*, V.156–59

i

One of the fascinating but perhaps also puzzling aspects of the so-called Radical Orthodoxy movement is that it liberally appropriates poststructuralist theory into its own discourse, finding there the essential tools for relaunching theology in a new, postmodern and specifically postsecular key, while at the same time remaining caustically critical of postmodern philosophy and culture *en bloc*. It makes no exception even for

theologically-minded philosophers such as Jean-Luc Marion and religiously relevant thinkers like Emmanuel Levinas. Jacques Derrida was
once targeted as the principal source of the trouble, and all have been
tarred as purveyors of various alloys of postmodern nihilism. Even in ap-
propriating a semiological outlook and a deconstructive hermeneutic,
Radical Orthodoxy theologians (with admittedly varied nuances) condemn all these contemporary styles of thinking as dependent on false ideologies or as idolatrous faiths. Such thinking may employ technically
useful tools, in their view, but it is invariably predicated on a desertion of
the fundamental theological truths of orthodox Christian belief, which
alone is deemed able to stem the growing tide of nihilism in modern
times.[1]

Phillip Blond, in his introduction to the collection *Post-Secular Philosophy*, presents one of the most radical and, in any case, most aggressive
statements of the program of Radical Orthodoxy. He begins from the ob-
servation that the promise of secular humanism since the Renaissance has
not been fulfilled. Human beings have shown themselves *not* to be the
measure of things; they have proved unable to "provide their own calibra-
tion."[2] The evidence of this is all about us in contemporary culture, in
which every imaginable variety of nihilism flourishes. Blond adduces the
violence and perversity of current history and especially consumer culture
to demonstrate the vanity of any mind-set not based on recognition of
theological transcendence, on faith in one God. With regard to philosophy, the various secular proxies for a transcendent ground or principle
of reality—Blond lists language, pragmatics, power—all collapse back into
immanence as pure projections of a human will to be the master of oneself
and to dominate the world. The attempt consistently proves futile in its
narcissism and circularity: it makes manifest only the nothingness of
human existence in the absence of a truly transcendent ground.

In this manner, Blond argues, modernity in general denies the only
true transcendence, that of God the Creator, by putting various a priori
principles in His place. These principles claim to be transcendental conditions of discourse and to adjudicate claims to truth, although they are
nothing but projections of the human minds by which they are made. To
this extent, they are fully of a piece with the idols of human handiwork
abominated by the prophets of the Old Testament. By such transcenden-

tal (generically Kantian) thinking, human beings usurp for themselves and their conceptual artifacts the transcendental status that belongs by rights to God alone. And the wages of such usurpation are death and nihilism.

> Nor apparently, according to these late moderns, can a transcendent value escape any of the contemporary surrogates—language, pragmatics, power—which transcendental thinking has engendered in order to preserve itself. These proxies . . . foreclose upon any other possibility. No, their advocates say, 'your values are ancillary to this, in respect of this discernment everything else is subordinate, this is the prior discourse that secures our descriptions, and we, we who ascertained this, we are the authors and judges of this world and there is no other'. (*Post-Secular Philosophy*, p. 1)

This is obviously caricature. But whether or not it is persuasive, the dialogical style is in itself highly significant. The point of such self-styled "postsecular" philosophy derives in good part from its polemical negation of the type of thinking that it characterizes as secular and accuses of "self-mutilation." We will need to ask whether such a wholesale dismissal of modern culture is not itself something of a self-mutilation. Blond often takes up a contemptuous tone and an embattled stance, which are very unlikely to produce the harmony and reconciliation envisaged by Christian faith as he conceives it. He begins his introduction to *Post-Secular Philosophy* by asserting, "We live in a time of failed conditions. Everywhere people who have no faith in any possibility, either for themselves, each other, or for the world, mouth locutions they do not understand. With words such as 'politics', they attempt to formalise the unformalisable and found secular cities upon it" (p. 1).

Blond's reference to the "unformalizable" is a first significant clue as to the intellectual stakes of Radical Orthodoxy's critique, namely, its argument concerning how a theological vision of transcendence can be recuperated in our time through acknowledging the inadequacy of all our human formulations of an unformalizable transcendence. Hence the accent on the "indeterminacy" of theological representation that is a keynote, in the first instance, of John Milbank's writings. What this expression points to is that which secular reason cannot positively define. It is the object of faith and conjecture and has traditionally been the peculiar concern of negative theology. Around it, Nicholas Cusanus developed a conjectural epistemology of "learned ignorance" in *De coniecturis* (1443). However, Blond does not turn to these paradoxically positive resources of negative theology within Christian tradition. He prefers to proceed polemically by attacking and attempting to demolish all forms of secular rationality.

Even in proclaiming a positive, phenomenological gift and an original basis in theological perception, a theological "sensorium," it is with constant reference to what it rejects that such a radically orthodox philosophical theology profiles and justifies itself. The irony of this approach is that reconciliation and harmony are the goals touted by this self-confessed Christian philosophy. How is harmonious reconciliation supposed to come out of virulent attacks against modern culture as a whole and against the greater part of philosophical thinkers of religion today? Critical sense would tell us rather that it is necessary to show another face of Christianity, one reflecting its self-abnegation (as in the negative theological tradition), so as to enable the Christic spirit of reconciliation through kenotic self-emptying to overtake the crusading spirit of self-justification and self-aggrandizement that have also been so much a part of the history of world religions, Christianity being no exception.[3] An openness to others that withholds nothing, and an acceptance of others in spite of differences and even of what may be recognized as sin, first in oneself, is perhaps more the genius of Christianity, the religion that Blond ardently aims to valorize. The disturbing rift that Blond opens up between secular and theological culture is bound to make dialogue impossible, unless negative theological insight and sensibility are deployed to forestall such an impasse and so to advance tactfully on the basis of self-critique rather than of attack against others.

Expressions of indignation turning to contempt naturally provoke reciprocal retaliation. A correspondingly patronizing tone is used even by one of the philosophers of religion who, among those working today in the wake and under the spell of Derrida, is most thoroughly imbued with traditional Christian thinking. John Caputo remonstrates: "Radical Orthodoxy is a movement that turns on the quaint and (self)comforting idea that everything is either a Christian metaphysics of participation (that is, Radical Orthodoxy) or nihilism, by which they seem to mean variants of their version of Nietzsche or Derrida, which for them means that human existence is awash in an irrational flux. So Radical Orthodoxy, which gives us a choice between being Cambridge Thomists or nihilists, needs to expand its horizons."[4]

Such condescension is understandably engendered by disparaging, antagonistic, exclusionary statements. However, I maintain that Caputo himself takes what is at root a Christian, kenotic, and, I will argue, apophatic approach to religious philosophy and that he is thinking out of the same postsecular revolution in theoretical thinking as is Radical Orthodoxy. This last argument, with its thesis concerning "secular theology," which in becoming "radical" actually turns *post*secular, will be complete only with the ensuing essay. The current essay is intended to expose the insufficiently acknowledged premises of Radical Orthodoxy in negative or apophatic theology (sections ii–iv) and to interpret apophatically the kataphatic forms of expression in which this theology necessarily issues, particularly the hymn (sections v–vi).

ii

Looking beyond this type of ideology-driven dispute, I turn now to Radical Orthodoxy's critique of secular culture and philosophy, in order to freely construct an interpretation of its essential motives. My aim here is to discern in Radical Orthodoxy the logic of a properly theological critique of culture and to understand why, in its view, theology alone can provide the untrammeled critical perspective that all militantly, exclusively secular forms of culture lack. The gist of Radical Orthodoxy's intervention in current cultural debate, as we have just seen, lies in its peculiar insight exposing the presupposed "transcendentals" implicitly advanced by secular thinking in all its varieties: they inevitably absolutize some particular structure of finite, human thinking or some elect concept of human making. Since these absolutes are not God, they are rather idols. All such philosophies collapse into various forms of nihilism because of the vanity of the transcendentals they posit. Not being grounded in the truly transcendent God, the only true Being, these transcendentals are actually, in Radical Orthodoxy's view, just contorted forms of nothing.

The transcendental philosopher par excellence is Immanuel Kant: his thought remains in key ways the paradigm of modern secular Enlightenment philosophy. Reason finds *in itself* the constitutive principles of knowledge and experience. It knows the conditions of possibility of all experience in the form of transcendental principles deduced from reflection on its own operations. Radical Orthodoxy indeed condemns all such transcendental principles derived from secular forms of critique, and John Milbank finds Kantianism everywhere in modern secular systems of thought. Even "modern theology" has been thoroughly invaded by the Kantian construction, and Milbank's purpose, accordingly, is "to indicate how pervasive are its transcendentalist presuppositions and to suggest that these be eradicated."[5]

The Thomistic alternative that Milbank propounds consists in knowledge that is without epistemological foundations but is based rather on ontological participation in divine Being. Being open to an infinite future and destiny in relation to infinite Being (God) is the presupposition, in this perspective, of any possibility of knowing.[6] This Being in which we participate exceeds our grasp: it is not known, and hence Thomas's "agnosticism" vis-à-vis the supreme Being, so different from Kant's with respect to things-in-themselves. Kant, nevertheless, thinks he can establish precisely the boundaries of knowledge, whereas for Milbank this cannot but be a metaphysical undertaking. Kant's metaphysic, for Milbank, is dogmatic "since it no longer subordinates itself to theological faith which surrounded *all* 'known' objects with a certain halo of agnosticism" in medieval theological ontologies (*Word Made Strange*, p. 10).

In other words, we never completely "know" the things that immediately surround us, and only theological revelation completes our understanding of them through offering, in narrative form, an interpretation of Being as such. Kant pretends to know too much in claiming apodictic certainty concerning at least some aspects of knowledge of the finite, while his complete theoretical agnosticism concerning metaphysical reality is based on an artificial and illusory division between the worlds of phenomena and of noumena. For Milbank, our knowledge is rather always analogical—situated between the finite phenomena that we know in part and an Infinite that "creates" them but cannot itself as such become directly an object of our knowledge, which is always merely finite.

This means that we have no transcendental knowledge, not even of the world of finitude. Kant's project and that of modern philosophy after him was to secure knowledge in this finite or phenomenal realm, placing it on the firm and certain foundation of a science, by clearly demarcating it from all pseudo-knowledge of the Infinite, or in other words from purportedly metaphysical knowledge claiming to know "things-in-themselves." But for Milbank and the Catholic tradition of thought that he relays, all our knowledge, of the finite and infinite alike, is "analogical." We cannot know anything in the finite world aright without reference to the Infinite, who is God. And conversely, what we do know of finite things speaks to us analogically of their source and origin in the Infinite that is not properly or univocally an object of our knowledge. Expressed more in ontological than in epistemological terms, what things really *are* is fully disclosed only in the light of Being itself, and there is no *true* being but God's. This is also why for Milbank all of the claims of secular sciences to autonomous knowledge in their particular spheres are vain pretensions. True knowledge can be obtained only on the basis of theology, which is the "science" of the one true Being from which beings in all domains derive. In effect, there is an implicit theology, an unexamined conception of Being as such, in every form of secular science concerning whatever kind of beings. The limitations of these covert theologies can be measured by their respective distortions of ultimate reality, or Being as such, following from their limited views of it based on only one or another kind of being. They are not based on analogical relation to (and participation in) infinite Being, which cannot be known objectively or scientifically. Theological "knowledge" is always necessary to complete and to ground them.

As Aquinas realized and as Milbank insists, all our knowledge can only be analogical. But this means that it follows not only a *via negativa,* denying its equivalence with things themselves (as Kant, too, realized), but also a *via eminentia,* along which excess or hyperbolic language can be a way of expressing and participating in the (divine) Being which exceeds our knowing. To this extent, Milbank defends the *via negativa* in the form in which it is found in Aquinas and as not to be confounded with Kantian transcendentalism (*Word Made Strange,* p. 8). The *via negativa* must be united with the *via eminentia.* For Aquinas and orthodox Christian theology generally, sense arises from being, which is always, at bottom, the one and only divine Being beside whom there is no other that is fully true and real. This true Being is known in limited ways according to the being of the knower, or in other words by "analogy."[7]

The inevitably analogical status of our knowledge makes *poiesis* the proper mode of its expression. All knowledge has a poetical character in being a human construction rather than a direct reflection of absolute reality. Milbank acknowledges that "*poesis* may be the key to a retrieval of the *sensus eminentior* and to a post-modern theology" (*Word Made Strange*, p. 32). The "eminent sense" is one that can be conjectured from the finite in its tension toward the Infinite, in which alone its origin and end are to be truly found. Milbank embraces the earlier, *pre*-Kantian form of the sublime, as formulated, for example, by Nicolas Boileau in his *L'art poétique* (1674), in which there is a continuity between the sublime and the beautiful, with its representations to the senses, and not the Kantian interdiction of all representation of the metaphysical. Before the Kantian sequestering of the sublime from the beautiful, the sublime entailed "the represented rupture and 'suspension' of our reaching towards transcendence" (*Word Made Strange*, p. 31).

This gives a poetic and, inseparably, a theological status to all our knowing. Milbank takes this poetic form of knowledge "not as transparent and complete within the supposed 'bounds' of our finitude (the Kantian modern), nor yet as ecstatically indeterminate (the skeptical post-modern), but rather as an utterly concrete allegorical outline, which remains, precisely by that token, all the more a mere sign of that mystery into which it must still enter in order to define itself" (*Word Made Strange*, p. 32). All that we "know" of things in the world of finitude makes reference to the Infinite, "God," from whom all comes and toward whom all is destined as its final end. This is the basic condition of the intelligibility of our world. Establishing principles of "pure reason" in order to ground this intelligibility (Kant's project) is for Milbank illusory and idolatrous.

Whereas Blond, who offers the most stridently ideological formulation, denounces transcendental principles of language, power, society, and so forth, Milbank lists the principles of nature, freedom, utility, power, and *eros*.[8] They operate as (Kantian) transcendental principles determining everything that can come about in the world (and so be offered to experience). As variously deployed in secular theologies, they thereby serve in the manner characteristic of Kantian epistemology as a general framework for knowing that establishes necessary conditions a priori for what can be experienced and so be known to exist. Since they define the ultimate parameters of what may be considered to be real, such transcendentals, in effect, are elevated to the status of substitutes for God. And, as such, they are idols.

All "secularizing immanentism," in Milbank's phrase, is idolatrous and even "malicious."[9] This critique by Radical Orthodoxy of idolatry, particularly in modern political and social ideologies, is comparable to other critiques situated in the interstices between the secular and the sacred.[10] Philosophical concepts are idolatrous to the extent that they claim knowledge by immanent means of a universe that can only be understood by reference to a wholly transcendent reality. Any philosophy claiming to afford knowledge of reality renders it immanent, immanent to the mind of the knower. For anyone who believes in God as transcendent reality, this cannot but be idolatry. But even without any such positive belief in divinity, the critique is valid and has been practiced widely, particularly since Nietzsche, for example, by Heidegger and Derrida. As Bruce Ellis Benson suggests,

> Western philosophy has at least tended toward idolatry from its very beginning. Indeed Nietzsche thinks that the whole history of philosophy has been more or less one idol after the next. . . . traditional philosophical concepts have been idols in the sense that they are images of our own creation which we hold up (and sometimes venerate) as 'true' reality. In other words, philosophy has tended to assume the possibility of an unmediated immanence in which 'all that is' can be known directly and completely.[11]

This critique of philosophy as "idolatrous," which is advanced here even by supposedly secular thinkers, perhaps owes something to theology, specifically to negative theology. Nietzsche—and Heidegger and Derrida—in undermining secular reason, with its presumption of immanence, may in some sense be religious thinkers after all. In any case, they show up in this light as critics of the modern "idolatry" of reason. The more explicitly theological versions of this critique, like Radical Orthodoxy, therefore, are actually kindred to radical philosophical critique and may be apt to reveal its bearings even more transparently.

Radical Orthodoxy's alternative to the secular outlook of a world defined and circumscribed by some positive, human construct, some gnoseological principle or other, is theology and its faith in a transcendent Creator and Redeemer God. No human efforts, however earnest, of transcendental thinking, but rather openness to and faith in the Transcendent as revealed analogically in creation and history, are constitutive of the vision that Radical Orthodoxy espouses. Of course, even "the Transcendent" cannot be positively conceived without itself becoming an idol. Hence the recourse to poetry and hence the ongoing debate with secular thinking, which becomes indispensible in order to point to the dimension of the theological.

According to this outlook, all that is relates to the *Theos* that no human conceptuality, no noetic structures whatever, can adequately comprehend. The relation is one that no thinkable *principle* can master, though theology *conjectures* it in terms of analogy. This is, then, a poetic type of "knowing," or rather not a *knowing* at all in the strict, scientific sense, but rather a "making" and performing—or a participating and a receiving—in which true knowing consists in becoming one with the known. It is also an "imitating," where the resemblance to what is imitated remains purely conjectural or "constructivist." Only by projecting ourselves into the world as open infinitely and as somehow beholden to an Infinite do we avoid delimiting experience and eclipsing its truth by confining it to the measure of some criterion of our own fabrication. This open projecting and unlimited giving up of self, rather, is the analogical measure by which we can conjecture and construct an image of the divine.

This kind of analogical intuition may be proposed as a valid model for all human knowledge, while all supposedly more solid or apodictic scientific foundations for knowledge must be suspected of resting on idolatrous illusion. That is what the poststructuralist critiques of epistemology seem to have shown, not least in Milbank's postsecular understanding of them. However, Milbank finds the postmetaphysical, meta-epistemological breakthroughs of poststructuralism (following Heidegger, in effect) to be anticipated already by several centuries in Christian thinking of the word and its poetic-creative capacity as conceived on the analogy of the divinely engendered Word that creates all things. Orthodox Christian thinkers, eminently Giambattista Vico, in his *New Science* (*La scienza nuova,* 1744), have paralleled the rise of modern science without falling into the transcendentalist trap of modern metaphysics. Milbank's thinking, like Vico's, is based on the metaphor of *homo creator*: man is a maker in the image of God the Creator.[12] This theological grounding for human creativity makes it a metaphor for divine creating that it cannot comprehend but can perhaps, nevertheless, imitate and thereby mediate. This means that divine creating is accomplished and completed through human making, in ways that exceed the theoretical grasp of humans in their very creativity.

Thus, for Radical Orthodoxy, beyond this analogical form of participation in divine life, there is no transcendental *principle* that can comprehend all things and unify them in a formula, but rather the decisive *difference* between God and the Creation. This distinction is presented as completely different from any other formulable division between the One and the many, or the Transcendent and the worldly. It is considered by Robert Sokolowski, even independently of Radical Orthodoxy, to be "the Christian distinction," and part of the "strangeness of the distinction" lies in the fact that God is not other than everything else: he has no other.[13] Nothing is apart from or outside of him, and in fact, God plus the world is not greater than just God. As Anselm formulated it in his *Proslogion,* God is that than which no greater can be thought.

It is not easy to bear this in mind and to realize that God is *not even other* than anything we can define—although that is precisely what has been affirmed by the tradition of negative theology from Pseudo-Dionysius to Meister Eckhart and Nicholas Cusanus, particularly in the latter's *On God as Not-Other* (*De li non aliud,* 1461). This check to any representation might—indeed *must*—reveal itself through a plurality of expressions. Expressing God becomes pure analogy, since there are no concepts adequate to his absolute transcendence. This inevitably issues in radical heterodoxy, I suspect, since no way of representing God can be certifiably right. Yet Radical Orthodoxy is, in any case, right about what is at stake in this play of symbols: it has an accurate critical consciousness concerning the relation of representation to transcendent reality, and it can therefore effectively critique all claims to knowledge and their implicit reductions of transcendence to represented structure or forms. However, in this regard,

Radical Orthodoxy is indistinguishable from negative theology. Precisely negative theology has been the source of insight within traditions of theological revelation that have produced the representations most efficacious for pointing beyond representation. The negative-theological, critical, and indeed *self*-critical consciousness of discourse has been nurtured all along in the bosom of orthodox monotheistic theologies—precisely in their self-critical, negative-theological undercurrents.

So far this essay has been my free construction of the philosophical-critical foundation of Radical Orthodoxy, a way of understanding its seminal insight as really a negatively theological insight. This critique exposes what is wrong with (or rather self-contradictory in) secular thinking, which attempts to think everything immanently in terms of the world rather than to open it all toward (and in dependence on) an unthinkable transcendence, which one names with the inevitable misnomer "God" and can represent only analogically. This move, furthermore, divulges my hypothesis as to what a well-conceived negative theology in this perspective entails. Theology, on this view, depends on poetic expression as necessary for us to accede to an authentically theological dimension of existence. God is grasped, or rather reflected to us, always only in relations—right from "his" own Trinitarian essence. Not as an object but rather as a relation, the divine nature can be known only in relational or in Trinitarian terms, and such knowledge cannot be expressed objectively but only poetically. In expressions of such experience of unconditional relatedness and dependence, the ineffable mystery at the core of reality is mediated in poetic ways by human powers of imagining.

Milbank frequently emphasizes that Christian theology is based on a narrative that cannot "prove" its truth over against alternative narratives. Its truth is essentially poetic, although that implies no restrictions, since *all* truth is poetic, including the highest truth, the truth of being and reality itself. Christianity, like other worldviews, proposes a narrative that may convince or not, but there can be no direct looking at reality behind the narrative discourses in order to tell whether or not they are true. They can be accepted and even be understood only on the terms that they themselves furnish. The truth proclaimed by Christianity is motivated ideally by the desire for peace—or for reconciliation of all with all through the

Cross. This narrative harbors deep reasons for being embraced by those who want to work in the world in order to make of it a just and harmonious order.

The argumentative strength of Radical Orthodoxy is to be found especially in its ability to critique the history of Western thought and culture and to expose its nihilistic and agonistic assumptions and tendencies. Radical Orthodoxy, moreover, startlingly brings out the crucial role that theology has to play in a critical understanding of philosophical thought throughout the Western tradition. What I have tried to demonstrate is that this theological critique is the resource particularly of negative theology. This is where the critique of idolatry and its philosophical extension in the form of "transcendentals" is originally formed. Monotheistic religion is born of the negative theological insight that rejected pagan idols in order to safeguard the transcendence of true divinity beyond all representations, all "graven images," and this movement continues in contemporary philosophical critiques of conceptual idolatry.[14]

Historically, this tradition of critical or negative theology comes to one of its maximum peaks in Meister Eckhart. An alternative to Eckhart's negative theological approach to thinking God arises contemporaneously with the univocal thinking of being by Duns Scotus and the nominalists. This marks the crucial turn to modern secularist thinking and the loss of authentic theological awareness, according to Radical Orthodoxy's intellectual and social history of the West.[15] I would add that specifically what is lost at this point is the fine sense and understanding of negative theology that had prevailed earlier, for example, in the thought of Aquinas and Bonaventure. Rolf Schönberger has demonstrated in detail that Scotus's rejection of negative theology took place against a background of a precipitous eclipse of references to Pseudo-Dionysius and Maimonides in the fourteenth century.[16]

Radical Orthodoxy, as Milbank construes it, denies adequate analytic (univocal) knowledge of God or of being itself or of anything whatever that could be the first "principle" of knowing. All knowledge for Milbank depends ultimately on analogy—our only way of knowing God, the origin and principle of all that is. Descartes's inaugural move of establishing self-conscious subjectivity as a universal first principle that is known with certainty was anticipated already in the Middle Ages by the nominalists and particularly by Duns Scotus, inasmuch as he made Being, *esse,* a transcendental principle affording a formal knowledge of all things, even of God. This was an idolatrous knowledge, since God was comprehended in terms of a creaturely category of being as used to comprehend the common run of beings. For Thomas Aquinas, this being that could be grasped by human intellect is only the common being—*ens communis*—of all things. God's Being is for Aquinas categorically different and cannot be circumscribed by this category or by any other. Since properly and uniquely theological knowledge of God was deemed by Scotus to be no longer necessary in order to understand the nature of being and beings, Milbank contends that "Scotus inaugurated a metaphysics independent of theology" (*Word Made Strange,* p. 45). Scotus initiated modern metaphysics as a scientific knowledge of universal being, whereas for Augustine and Aquinas the only true "science" of being was theology.

In the Augustinian or Thomistic view, without theology human intellect proves helpless to understand the true and original nature of beings, for they originate in the divine Being.[17] Scotus, in contrast, maintained that being could be understood in a purely existential sense, without reference to God, who then could be understood as the first instance of being in the same sense of being as applied to existing things generally. This pure knowledge of being—without theological presuppositions—is metaphysics in the sense of "onto-theology": a knowing of God as an instance, the supreme instance, of being, which is known *univocally* by human intellect.

For Aquinas, by contrast, God can be known only through a higher science, theology, and theology is in its primary sense God's own knowledge of himself (*Summa Theologicae* I, q. 1, ad 2). God can then choose to share this knowledge, to the degree possible, with human beings by means of revelation. Accordingly, the realm of metaphysical knowledge is evacuated by theology, since only theology can secure knowledge of the principles on which all beings depend for their very being.

In this typically medieval perspective, beings understood as separate from God disintegrate into nothing, since their true being is given them only by participation in God's being and is not possessed by them autonomously. Neither is their being autonomously intelligible; it can be known only in its dependence on God's transcendent Being. Ignoring this dependence of all things for their very being on God—or treating them as having independently intelligible essences—is for Milbank the crucial step across the threshold into the modern, specifically secular world. A science of being that is independent of theology ("metaphysics" in the modern sense) leads from Scotus through Suarez (*Disputationes Metaphysicae*, 1597) all the way to Jean-Luc Marion's phenomenology (at least in certain of its formulations). For Milbank, all such theologically emancipated philosophy or phenomenology must be abandoned in favor of a knowledge that recognizes itself and all knowing as dependent on God's self-giving in Creation and Revelation rather than on any autonomous form of being and knowing. In Milbank's radically Christian view, knowing is grounded in relating, and that means relating ultimately to an ungraspable transcendence, a transcendent Other—or even more accurately, in precisely negative-theological terms, non-Other (*non aliud*). In this sense, only theology overcomes metaphysics because it avoids imposing a *mathesis* that makes a human (and therefore idolatrous) principle into a transcendental condition of all being.

Once they had forsaken the intellectual resources of analogical vision, Scotus and the nominalists tended to understand God's reality essentially in terms of Will rather than of Intellect. As William of Ockham in particular emphasized, God's infinite Power was in principle unknowable, since it was pure freedom and could not be bound by any reasons or intellectual principles. The intellect thus could have no rational knowledge of God, not even by analogy. The Supreme Being, therefore, was arbitrarily posited as the ground and principle of all that is by a sheer act of faith. Already this was a form of transcendental thinking in which human reason established principles for itself by abstraction rather than relying on an actual participatory relationship to the divine transcendence that revealed itself analogically. Passing from Scotus through Ockham, this nominalist outlook led to Francis Bacon and the scientific revolution and even to Luther and the modern secularist worldview. It resulted eventually, for example, among German Idealists beginning with Fichte, in an unconditioned, groundless, "free" human will making the universe in its own image. Knowledge thenceforth was based on positing formal principles fashioned by the human mind and forged into systems.

Milbank deplores these developments as having broken the analogical connection between the finite and the Infinite. Previously, our finite experience had been understood to be an analogical revelation of the Infinite, which transcended our knowledge and yet was indirectly, analogically revealed therein. Knowledge was not a matter of accurate representation but of becoming one (*unio*) with the known. This intrinsic connection based on ontological derivation and participation ultimately eludes analytic thinking because the relation of finite and Infinite is predicated on their incommensurability: it comes about without being able to be justified or thought through conceptually.

All this is a redeployment of the core insights of the apophatic tradition. The fundamental lesson here is that we can approach oneness with the Infinite only by letting it happen to us rather than attempting to grasp and master it in an adequate representation, for that would inevitably reduce it to our measure, to finitude. And yet, as with Adorno, Levinas, Rosenzweig, and many other major apophatic thinkers, Milbank is reluctant to identify his thought with negative theology. In his case, the reluctance is evidently due to the circumstance that negative theology has also been appropriated by numerous forms of postmodern "nihilism" (see my next essay).

There are, nevertheless, many telling phrases in Milbank that evince his de facto reliance on negative theology. He notes that negative theology preserves the alternative perspective, in which human beings do not substitute concepts of their own as transcendentals for the infinite and inconceivable being or mystery of God. Negative theology thereby avoids making God's being commensurate with our finite thought and in this sense "univocal." Milbank writes: "In brief: univocity breaks with the entire legacy of negative theology . . . the term 'being' has now become a logically transcendental place holder that precedes any existentially actual reality."[18] This is, in effect, an admission that "negative theology" names the essential insight that has been lost through secular "enlightenment" in modern thought. Rather than all our knowing being situated within and suspended from an ontological mystery, the unfathomable actuality of God, all being is now subsumed under a transcendental concept of being that operates univocally as knowledge of the ultimate principle of reality.

In modern times, one thinks of being in terms that are definable and comprehensible. Descartes makes this demand explicit in refounding all our knowledge on clear and distinct perceptions of a perfectly transparent self-consciousness.[19] This separation of beings and their opacity from the clear and distinct conceptions that science needs and abstracts from things can be traced to Scotus and Ockham and more generally to nominalism, which represents an origin of modernity more remote than Descartes. This proto-modernity is based on the power of abstraction of oneself from the mystery of being in deference to technical definitions that can be managed and manipulated by human ingenuity and so afford us an apparent power over things. Things are reduced thereby to what fits into man-made schemas rather than being apprehended in the fullness of their being, which is unsoundable in its intrinsic mystery. This unfathomable mystery is what negative theology recognizes and insists on: we cannot define it, but we can nevertheless recognize and even reverence it.

Milbank's reference to negative theology and to the way of eminence or "eminent attribution," whereby being and all its perfections are attributed to God eminently—in a sense that transcends our experience and comprehension of being in all its finite manifestations—is a hint of his recognition of this perspective of negative theology as what is fundamentally eclipsed by the (for him) deleterious main thrusts of modern, secularist thought. Negative theology has made an impressive comeback in postmodern thought, particularly through its critiques of claims to purely rational, systematic knowledge: exemplary is Adorno's critique of conceptual idolatry and his proposal for thinking non-identity, or again, Levinas's thinking the instance of the Other beyond the grasp of the self and the same. Radical Orthodoxy has capitalized on these radical postmodern epistemological critiques. However, the application and diffusion of negative theology throughout postmodern thought is typically viewed by Radical Orthodoxy as nihilistic. In his essay "On Theological Transgression," Milbank charges that negative theology lends itself to serving the purposes of postmodern nihilism, for example, in the figure of the "hybrid void/God":

> for many 'postmodern theologians,' it appears that this void may very easily, or might just as well, be named 'God,' such that at last we have a kind of universal rational theology, independent of creeds and institutions, but in line with a supposed 'separate' tradition of negative theology within Christianity. It is often unclear here whether 'faith' is required in order to name the void 'God,' and if it

is, then further unclear why such fideistic re-naming should make any intellectual or practical difference. (*Future of Love,* p. 157)

Milbank has defined Radical Orthodoxy as contradicting secular thought in virtually all its manifestations. However, I am suggesting that it is especially secular philosophical critique that is needed in order to vindicate a truly radical theological outlook, one that can escape idolatry. It is when the principle of critique releases all positive presuppositions that it becomes truly radical in the negative theological sense that has actually guided orthodox theological tradition all along. Orthodoxy needs to open itself to the secular, its other and apparent nemesis, just as secularism needs to recognize its derivation from (negative) theology—its ostensible opposite and adversary. Only thus can either one of them avoid the lapse into idolatry that otherwise stalks and inevitably captivates each.

In effect, I submit, negative theology is not confined to theology, at least not in a confessional sense: it is a general critique of all knowing that *begins* emblematically from theology as embodying the self-critique of thought and discourse (logos) par excellence vis-à-vis the unfathomable mystery of Being.[20] For human logos is at its weakest and is most readily undermined in the face of "God." Indeed, all forms of hegemony of any human discourse are undermined in this relation. This is realized in the form of self-critique first and foremost by theology—as negative theology. Theology, in this form, remains relevant and exemplary today as historically the first and arguably the most radical form of self-critique on the part of human understanding. Critique as such might well be considered to begin with the condemnation of idolatry by monotheistic theology.[21]

Milbank, in fact, recognizes the essential continuity of theology with other forms of human self-critique. In the essay "Faith, Reason, and Imagination: The Study of Philosophy and Theology in the 21st Century" in *The Future of Love,* he argues *against* the unequivocal elevation of theology above philosophy as *theologically* misguided. It was introduced as a theological expedient in the face of secularization that began with the rediscovery of Aristotle's philosophy in the West. Avicenna and Averroes and, following them, Christian theologians adopted the notorious "two-truths" approach in order to preserve revelation intact, even while admitting the autonomy of reason in the secular order. This destroys, however, the unity of knowledge and creates artificial divisions. It is a technical maneuver designed to maintain rational control over a defined sphere of being, even while leaving a space to the transcendent and divine that remains still inscrutable to human reason. These technical solutions divide up the field into the knowable and the unknowable in order to keep some semblance of control over the former.

Human self-confidence is thereby comforted and reaffirmed within its sphere, defined as the whole realm of the mundane that is available to mastery by human intellect and industry. And natural knowledge of religion is kept thus "within the limits of reason alone," as Kant piously proposed. The sphere of the supernatural is still recognized, but it can be approached only fideistically—by sheer belief in a revealed word that is not in any way verifiable by reason or experience. One discerns here the beginning of a process that leads to Luther and Protestantism in their radicalization of faith as a pure positing by the will, without need of cooperative validation by the intellect. But this is an artifice. It is a rational human apparatus presaging Kant's pure practical reason that makes God merely a pragmatic postulate without theoretical relevance. It treats reason as a circumscribed sphere of delimited operations upon a field of defined objects, while withdrawing from real contact with the divine and its mysteries, for such contact would open reason to itself and to reality beyond its control, as into an abyss.

An attempt to recover the unity of nature with its supernatural grounds was staged, directly following the age of Kant, by European Romanticism in its revolt against the civilization that had been created by the technologically-minded culture that has largely dominated the course of modern Western history. M. H. Abrams's *Natural Supernaturalism: Tradition and Revolution in Romantic Literature* (1973) traces especially in literary history this revolt against the "dissociation of sensibility" that divided aesthetic-religious intuition from scientific and analytic knowing. Milbank probes a related pivot point in intellectual history, particularly in his work on Henri de Lubac.[22] De Lubac highlighted as belonging to authentic Christian doctrine and heritage a natural desire for the supernatural that is constitutive of creaturely being and not an extrinsic imposition of grace upon a nature already complete in itself. This natural desire for the supernatural must be explained "ultimately in terms of the ineffable," as Milbank admits in a perfectly apophatic idiom and manner of thinking.

The natural orientation to the supernatural in human beings and angels entails freedom as an integral expression of personhood and of the deep substance of humanity rather than a faculty separate from cognition, as becomes the case for late Scholastic voluntarism (*Suspended Middle*, p. 28). Beings exist only as the longing—each in its own mode—for God. This is a natural desire that cannot be frustrated (according to the Aristotelian principle) and yet paradoxically requires a necessary gift of divine grace in order to be fulfilled. As Milbank puts it, we *are* a pure gift of radical gratuity. The key here, I submit, is to reason *from* God as alone real, although unknown, except analogically, *to* our reality, which is experienced as all gift and as *in itself* nil. This reasoning expresses a radical skepticism of orthodox Christianity vis-à-vis the *human* taken in and for itself.

Philosophy and theology paradoxically require each other, and de Lubac thinks in the "suspended middle" between them, to employ the poignantly apophatic phrase that Milbank borrows from Hans Urs von Balthasar's interpretation of de Lubac for the title of his own book on this theologian. Von Balthasar remarked how de Lubac "moved into a suspended middle in which he could not practice any philosophy without its transcendence into theology, but also any theology without its essential inner structure of philosophy" (Milbank, *Suspended Middle*, p. 11). Philosophy cannot be autonomous, since there is no object or field of objects among created beings that does not need to be understood fundamentally as divine gift, yet there is no positive knowledge of the theological that does not require philosophical reflection to be humanly appropriated. Theology in this sense requires a philosophical foundation, which paradoxically is unavailable, since there can be no philosophy founded in itself rather than in theology. There can therefore be no philosophical theology, no genuine philosophical knowledge of divinity founded philosophically rather than *given* theologically. The paradox of de Lubac's thinking is that the natural desire for the supernatural can only be fully recognized by faith, not by natural reason (p. 47).

The unparalleled importance for Milbank of de Lubac in theology results from his understanding of the non-autonomy of the secular, of the interpenetration of nature and grace in such a way that neither can be grasped except through the other in an analogical manner. This, too, makes all true knowledge or understanding begin from God yet depend, nevertheless, entirely on finite being that is externally manifest in history in the form of signs of the transcendent. This vision coincides with the classically Catholic, Thomistic approach of ascertaining the existence of God only through his effects in the world. However, God is infinitely in excess of all his effects, and poetry is necessary to register this divine excess. Human spirit, in its poetic self-making, becomes the production of this excess by receiving it as inspiration. Milbank writes: "Spirit is the paradoxical supplying of a poetic 'necessary extra' because it is the recipient of the divine 'necessary extra'" (*Suspended Middle,* p. 103).

Milbank, surprisingly, does not advocate an unambiguous hegemony of theology and even warns against any sort of unilateral elevation of theology (see "Conflict of the Faculties" in *Future of Love*). Theology must rather remain open to mediation by philosophy—though not as if it could be grounded philosophically: there is no human foundation for knowledge, which as such remains only conjectural. Theology is, after all, a kind of philosophy that claims to interpret universal truth and generally valid norms following from the nature of being as such. Theology thus does the same thing as philosophy, with the difference that it admits to having no knowledge of being as such, but claims to be turned toward God as the supreme Giver of being, the One through whom alone being can be known. Nevertheless, we have no natural knowledge of God—except of an analogical nature, since God is present and active in everything that is. While we naturally have no direct knowledge of God's Being, we know something of him analogically through the beings that are his effects.

Accordingly, revelation is not simply imposed from above but rather affirms itself in and through rational inquiry into our world as a created order. Literary studies, too, and culture generally are also inextricably part of a Christian theological education in the program Milbank has helped to shape at the Nottingham Centre for Theology and Philosophy. Historically, Christianity, especially Catholicism, has always recognized the embeddedness of revelation in history and in human culture. The transcendence of reason by revelation can be grasped only analogically: like the divine Being at the heart of worldly beings, revelation is not present to human beings as self-identical or univocal. Our discourse captures it only in multiplicity and never with final accuracy.

An implication of this is that revelation is not a sharp alternative to rational knowledge but can be found (I wish to add) in the latter's self-transcendence toward an ever more complete, yet never entirely graspable, totality. It is especially the lacunas and impasses in reason that point it beyond itself to a possibility—namely, revelation—that it can conceive of only negatively, but which nevertheless is its own consummation and grants it the completeness it inevitably fails to attain by itself.

iii

Milbank's assertion of the truth of Christianity is, contrary to appearances, not so much dogmatic as eminently philosophical. This becomes more apparent the more we realize that philosophy itself is to be understood historically as a critical or negative turn of thought taking place paradigmatically within (negative) theological reflection. However, no philosophy has terms universally valid outside the context of the particular culture and history within which it has originated and evolved. Christianity, like any philosophy, is true for Milbank only on its own unique terms, which are incommensurable with those of other religions and their own inherent ways of thinking. This unique truth is what Christianity, like any other philosophical or religious doctrine, must attempt to promulgate throughout the world by the persuasiveness of its narrative of reconciliation and peace. From the point of view of Milbank's Christian philosophy, moreover, there is no neutral philosophy that is not already theologically determined. Philosophy always already has made some decision as to how to take the gift of being and has construed the overall relatedness of things in some fashion that is not theologically neutral. Furthermore, the truth of theology is not different in kind from that of philosophy: it attempts to give a convincing interpretation of the whole of being. It does so based on a certain narrative—in this case, the Christian story. For there is no *naturally* authoritative account.

For Milbank, there is thus no pure religious experience that is humanly and rationally neutral, such as is posited by John Hicks and others.[23]

And with this I agree. But Milbank sees the mission of Christianity as one of maintaining and asserting *itself* and its own truth rather than, like Nancy, as a matter of breaking down—or at least opening up—all such exclusive structures, through which peace and reconciliation might more plausibly be achieved. A crucial caveat here is that the proposed melt-down concerns not the structures per se of a culture or religion but rather exclusionary and other-deprecating manners of adhering to them. Realizing the infinite relatedness of all things, beyond all invidious and divisive identities, is arguably an eminent realization of God—the divine Event. In this realization, one must let truth be attained finally through the release of all determinate doctrine—yet not to the detriment of highlighting how effective Christian dogmas, such as the Trinity and the Incarnation, together with tropes like kenosis, can be in bringing about an unmasterable apocalypse of truth beyond all sectarian divisions and as unbound by any definitive limits set down by doctrine or definition.

The way for us to this giving up of our *own* identity, the true *via crucis,* could hardly be demonstrated more powerfully than by Christ and his Crucifixion. Beyond all the positive symbolic insight to be gleaned from Christian doctrines, they, like all doctrines and formulated teachings, have their limits. However far their persuasive power and illumination reaches, these discourses will at some point be forced by confrontation with other discourses to admit their internal contradictions and so to allow their contraries their due. It is in releasing their own defined contents into the infinite beyond definition and conception, in an infinite giving (up) of oneself in love, that they consummate the Christic gesture of self-abandon to the point of death (Philippians 2:8).

There is an absolute "truth" in the vision of negative theology, just as in that of Radical Orthodoxy, but it cannot be articulated as a discourse, not even as the discourse of theology. Nonetheless, Milbank perhaps has some reason to prefer theology, not because it has natural or absolute authority as such, but because it preserves the recognition of discourse as itself subordinate to an Absolute or a Truth that transcends it. Theology recognizes an Absolute alongside—or rather above—all necessarily relative mediations. Thus it cannot simply be reduced to one more rational or human symbolic system. It remains mindful of something else, some other kind of truth altogether, which, however, remains finally ungraspable.

The problem with secular reason (at least when it has not become the equivalent of negative theology through its own limitless self-critique) is that it inevitably absolutizes itself. It invariably makes itself in some guise into a transcendental condition or criterion of all knowledge. And this is idolatrous. There is, to be sure, a true transcendent criterion for knowledge, but it is none of the standards that our human discourse can define. They are rather always themselves under judgment, and they become demonic when they arrogate to themselves the role of being ultimate Judge—which they inevitably do, as history repeatedly demonstrates, when no Other is recognized, at least dimly and imperfectly.[24]

In Milbank's vision, no discourse has inherent authority: thus, secular reason, with its idol of science or pure reason, is dethroned. Moreover, theology offers a complete interpretation of reality from its ultimate grounds and can position all other discourses within its purview at least as well as they can position it. One decides what to believe on the basis of the reasons given and the stories told, and the task of Christian theology is to rationally justify and emotionally motivate its outlook as the most compelling. It must demonstrate and open access to what is most rewarding in life—for example, love and peace—in what it says and, above all, through the community that it fosters. It must not simply appeal to the authority of revelation or of blind faith—except perhaps inasmuch as these appeals correspond to something true to humanity and recognizably unavoidable by reason in its inherent limitations and weakness, its liability to inescapable contradiction with itself. One must examine reason historically to determine what it can and cannot do and where it is effective or rather needs to acknowledge other, higher powers and authorities than its own. These higher instances, however, are not simply given to it a priori. They can be accepted always only within a certain discourse, for one can never validate them from outside of *all* discourse, as if one could determine the true and real independently of any discursive apparatus whatever.

Milbank thus levels the playing field between all discourses vying to assert authority, whether for reason or for revelation or for any other contender. But how, then, can he affirm theology's preeminent rights? What is distinctive about theology? Only, I would suggest, that it opens to an object or rather an Other who precedes it as subject—or, in other words, that theology's true end is not to know its object so much as to be known by it.

Theology is, properly speaking, God's own self-knowledge. As such, it is essentially and in its core, for us, negative theology, since God in his self-knowledge, his *scientia Dei,* is "utterly ineffable and beyond our grasp" (*Future of Love,* p. 308).

Milbank's history of theology describes its decline from being a participation in God's self-knowing—and thus from a theologically determined knowledge of being—to a knowledge reflecting on data as given in some prior, neutral determination of being. Philosophy then dictates conditions to revelation and circumscribes its possibilities, and consequently theology is denatured: it is no longer itself the event of divine disclosure "of God himself through his creatures" (*Future of Love,* p. 309). Theology in these circumstances seeks a foundation in positive knowing rather than in receiving being itself as revelation—as given from God, quite apart from rational foundations or conditions of possibility. The presumed positivity of knowledge is characteristic not of theology per se but of the modern age, in which theology—and along with it knowledge as a whole—has become corrupted and perverted. Milbank's ideal is rather the negative theological outlook of the Latin Middle Ages—before Duns Scotus. Duns Scotus was famous in the late Middle Ages for his statement that he did not prize negations highly ("Negationes non summe amamus"). We noted earlier that scholarship on Scotus finds in him a source of the widespread fourteenth-century rejection, or at least abandonment, of negative theology. Milbank concordantly observes that, "where the term 'infinite' was traditionally a negative description of God, it now, in the late Middle Ages, became a positive definition of his *essence*" (p. 309). Before its secular denaturing, the true nature of (theological) insight was not a positive knowledge of essence but rather a negative unknowing that was open to the source of beings in "in-finite" Being.

Theology, so understood, is based on what we do not know; it is a not-knowing. As such, it runs parallel to Socratic wisdom. Accordingly, and contrary to the dominant tendency of Radical Orthodoxy theologians, I would stress the continuities in this regard between Christianity and other religions and philosophies. In the end, it is not the positive formulas of Christian dogma, by which it is nominally distinct from other doctrines, but an intention directed beyond all positive formulations, that distinguishes theology and gives it priority as exemplary of the ability of human discourse to connect with something beyond it, something that is absolute and not merely its own projection.

In the last instance, the superior authority of theology lies simply in its more radical capacity to sustain the self-critique of reason. Theology, given the transcendence of its only real Truth, does not possess autonomous, rational truth and therefore does not allow reason to abstract from the existential and social matrices in which thought takes place and from the relations by which its notions are constituted. Rather, it opens these contexts and relations without limit. There is also a positive content of theology, but it must always be understood as symbolic interpretation based on the infinite openness that lies beyond any circuit of discourse and any positive terms. This infinite openness is the only framework and background that can lend truly holy authority and power to any discourse whatever. Theology, so understood, attempts to interpret the whole of being, which is beyond finite grasp, rather than circumscribing any objective field that it can dominate.

Milbank shows how, historically, theological decisions covertly determine the main philosophical insights that open the way to modern, secular culture. This suggests the lack of real autonomy for philosophical reason, even though modernity typically understands itself as an emancipation from the theologically dominated past. Still, the only irrecusable claim of theology remains fundamentally negative. Theology excels in critique and especially in self-critique, in *dis*claiming final truth for all its knowledge, inasmuch as it is only human and so not able as such to grasp the truth of beings, much less of Being. As primarily and fundamentally negative, theology participates in exposing the fallibility also of reason, its lack of neutrality, its being conditioned by culture. Theology has a keener critical recognition of all this because it can never misunderstand its own authority as being autonomous—on pain of falling prey to the lures of idolatry. And in that case it becomes mere ideology and, in effect, antitheological. For theology, rightly considered, nothing in the realm of beings is truly autonomous. Theology sees all as infinitely indebted in relation to an infinite, divine Giver.

How, then, is it possible to keep knowing genuinely open to otherness rather than having it become a means of reducing all to one's own measure? Theology, particularly negative theology, as the search for the absolute Other who exceeds and surpasses us always and in all ways, is a name for arguably the most thoroughgoing form of this search imaginable. Indeed, it requires an unceasing, never satisfied effort of the imagination. This makes poetic imaginings of the cosmos and its Creator crucial for theological vision.

Milbank rather insistently asserts Christian "hegemony"[25] and does so because the relation to transcendence must not and cannot be absorbed into any neutral form of secular knowing. But does not every other theological logos have the same right and duty to assert its hegemony in defiance of the deluded claim to neutrality on the part of secular reason? Certainly Islam advances its own claim to hegemony. Yet if we think apophatically and so rigorously critique all idolatry, hegemony can be legitimately claimed not for any given narrative or doctrine, but only for the absolute that they aim to mediate in their own inevitably relative language. An authentic (divinely sanctioned) hegemony is properly due to a symbol system not in itself but only on account of its ability to evoke the absolute beyond its own and beyond all discourse. It is only as preeminently self-negating that theology can play this role and occupy this leading position. Milbank rejects talk of a reality wholly outside of discourse, since we have no access to it, except through discourse. But negative theology is not outside all discourses so much as it is a negative, critical dimension within and at the limits of Christian theology, as well as of other religious and philosophical and literary discourses. Essential to negative theology is the faculty to enact its own self-abasement and kenotic self-emptying in recognition of the absolute, in the Face of God, vis-à-vis whom one is nothing. Such self-critique and dissolution is ostensibly closer to Nancy's deconstruction of Christianity: however, it is paradoxically bound up with and necessary also to Milbank's polemical-apologetic assertion of Christianity.

Milbank's theology, I contend, pivots on negative theology. He realizes that apophatic insight, considered speculatively, is indeed the crucial, radical insight of the entire Christian theological tradition up to Eckhart and beyond, for example, when he writes, "Therefore, in Eckhart's phrase, *esse est deus* (not the other way round), Being is the utterly unknown, and in this sense indeed it is more than Being."[26] According to Milbank, Duns Scotus loses this insight and digresses in the direction of onto-theology, which is a purported knowledge rather than an *un*knowing of Being as God. Scotus forgets the ontological difference that is preserved and safeguarded particularly by negative theology. And without the sense of this difference, modern thought quite generally becomes idolatrous. In other words, "Being," as apprehended by Scotus, falls far short of the theological mystery of Being.

Authentic theology, however, transgresses the principles dictated by the modern scene of secular reason. It illuminates Being—or allows Being to be illuminated—from a light other than that of reason alone. From Milbank's viewpoint, modern transcendental thinkers in the wake of Kant and even of Heidegger and Derrida are all setting rational limits to what can be thought and experienced. Their God is a transcendental Nothing. They belong fundamentally to the Scotist, modernist project. Scotus invented modern ontology "by arguing that Being could be grasped *prior* to theology as the bare existence of any single existing thing, whether finite or infinite; all thought, he argued, assumes such a grasp of being as a *univocal* term. Thereby, at a stroke, Scotus anticipated transcendental philosophy, idolized God, obscured the ontological difference, and implied (unlike Augustine or Aquinas) that any being can be fully 'present'" (*Future of Love*, p. 159).

Of course, God can never be fully present to any finite perception or experience. A disastrous consequence of this, for Milbank, is that postmodern theologies generally fail to distinguish God from the empty void. In his attempt to avoid this result, Jean-Luc Marion relinquishes being altogether; he gives it up to the realm of "onto-theology." He attempts to think God *without* being through a pure phenomenology of the gift (pure of any presence of being). Milbank, to the contrary, on the basis of the analogy between infinite and finite being, endeavors to approach Being, or ultimate reality and actuality, through "the moods of faith, hope, desire, and love" (*Future of Love*, p. 158). These modalities of being offer an analogical access to God as source of being and as being itself (*ipsum esse*). However, once we admit that this analogical knowledge is not knowledge of God as an object or as *a* being, it is no longer clear that the experience of God as nothing is not also revelatory of something essential, nor that the "nihilism" of postmodern theologies is necessarily exclusive of faith and revelation rather than an expression of the typically Christian dark night of the soul. This so-called "nihilism" may prove necessary, too, for exploring all the registers and the limits of the analogical experience of God.[27]

Milbank has often shied away from negative theology in order to more clearly condemn secular culture and its alleged nihilism, yet his own position, radically considered, like any Christian theology thought from its roots, is deeply committed to negative theology, and this becomes more openly and emphatically the case as his project continues to evolve in its engagement with secular philosophies. One telling sign of this development is his use of the expression "ineffability" in relation to the mystery of the unknown. In critiquing the continuity of postmodern thinkers of difference with Scotus and his principle of univocity, Milbank points to "an ineffable third path between difference and identity" (*Future of Love,* p. 160). This path, he claims, permits participation and mediation—unlike the contemporary French thought of difference that refuses mediation as a form of fusion.

One can trace through Milbank's recent work a recurrent resort to the negative theological insights of a line of theologians stretching from Pseudo-Dionysius and Eriugena to Eckhart and Cusanus in order to illuminate the theological paradoxes and aporiae that he brings to bear, for example, in debates with atheists such as Slavoj Žižek. Throughout Milbank's contribution to *The Monstrosity of Christ,* the texts he cites to demonstrate his most radical insights are drawn consistently from the most radical of negative theologians in ancient and medieval tradition.[28] He gives a profound exposition of the apophatics of Eckhart, quoting from the latter's Sermon 71: "If God is to become known to the soul, it must be blind." Milbank remarks that thought is,

> as Eckhart also pointed out, a kind of nullity. . . . To think something is kenotic—it is to let that thing be and not to try to be that thing, even not to try to be oneself when thinking oneself. Hence we can see color only if our eye is colorless, come to know something only if our mind goes blank and receptive; it follows, therefore, that if God contains all being within his simplicity, he must be hyperintellectual and therefore the most empty. (*Monstrosity of Christ,* p. 173)

This is the language and the (a)logic of apophatic thinking, to which Milbank now resorts without reservation. Of course, he still wishes to mark his difference from the negative theological moves of his secular opponents, but he cannot do this without misreading those opponents and particularly their postsecular nuances. In effect, Milbank misreads Derrida the way Derrida misreads Pseudo-Dionysius—by misprisioning his radical negative theology, by holding the opponent to a position that in each case is adopted strategically and heuristically and then is recursively given up in accordance with the unsparing self-critical thrust driving each in their radically apophatic, self-subverting performances.

Milbank uses the apophatic language of "aporia" in describing the foundational theological mysteries of Christian revelation, emphasizing here the recognition of mystery "and thereby avoiding a postmodern hypostatization of *aporia* à la Derrida, as though dilemma should itself be the object of a religious cult" (*Future of Love*, p. 159). But Derrida would, of course, be the first one to wish to avoid such a cult. Once the opponent's position is understood as a sort of negative theology, it must be taken not simply at its word but rather for what those words enact and attempt to release. We must pay attention to the strategy at work in the words beyond what they are able simply to say.

Milbank draws freely from Eriugena and Cusanus, appealing to this often underground tradition of Christian theology, yet not fully valorizing it as negative theology, presumably because such acknowledgment might lend itself to a nihilistic misconstrual. In contrast, Milbank generally gives a nihilist spin to those he considers unredeemable secularists, such as Hegel and Žižek. Derrida, too, is essentially a secular nihilist for him, even though the thrust of Derrida's thought in the end is to think beyond secular reason.[29] Hegel and certain of his followers (as discussed in my second essay, section ii) are most interested in how pure negativity reveals itself as absolutely positive and productive of the multifarious phenomena of the secular world. Žižek, too, thinks in a negative theological manner out of what he calls the gap of "parallax."

The centuries-old attack of secularists against religion and especially against the very Christian ideas by which their own thinking is nevertheless vitally nourished can provoke anger, and understandably so, from those invested in Christian faith and its symbols. Yet the more consistently

Christian response is not to counterattack but rather to absorb critique and participate in it through limitless critique turned, first, toward oneself and only then also toward others—to the extent that it can be a service to them. With this ideal and strategy in mind, in the next section (iv) we will look back at the polemic of Radical Orthodoxy against secular culture, now with an enhanced awareness of the insufficiently stated negative theological premises of its thought, before going on to explore the positive development of negative theology by Radical Orthodoxy in terms of analogical language (section v) and particularly the hymn (section vi).

iv

Its critical program rejecting the false forms of transcendence typical of secular modernism and postmodernism represents Radical Orthodoxy at its most relevant, at least from the point of view of those who do not subscribe to its particular presuppositions of faith. And this critique was made possible above all by the structuralist and poststructuralist critique of language, as Milbank's work clearly shows. Particularly the metalinguistic critique of thought, exposing the verbal constructions that inhere in all forms of rationality and that make them relative to culture and ideology, has broken down the pretensions of the philosophy of the Enlightenment to possess the unique, universal truth and has opened a space for irreducibly discursive, narrative-based forms of thought such as theology. Without the presumed hegemony of reason, theology can be recognized once again as a viable approach to apprehending universal and cosmic truth. More exactly, however, it is *negative* theology that critiques the idolatry of every relation of accounting for and grounding that uses a univocal language about all that is, including beings and God. This critique, moreover, is not the exclusive privilege of orthodox theologies, radical or otherwise. It can be thought radically by philosophers as well, for example, as the "other" or "inverted" theology suggested by Adorno in following up hints by Benjamin and Kafka.[30] The radical negative theological critique of knowledge is pursued vigorously today on both sides of the divide of faith: this has already been shown in the case of Nancy in my fourth essay and will again become a focus in counterpoising secular theologies and orthodoxy in the sixth and final essay.

We have also seen that the idolatrous grounding discourses of secularism actually begin in theology. They are traced historically by Milbank and his collaborators—following Hans Urs von Balthasar and the wider Thomistic tradition—to a point of origin in Duns Scotus. In order for God's being to be humanly knowable, Scotus refused the equivocity of "being" as applied to God and beings, whereas Thomas negotiated these senses of being analogically. Scotus elevated being to a higher ontological level that included God and beings alike. This initiated the modern idolatry that posits a synonymous (or univocal) ground for God and beings in the category of being itself.

In *Ordinatio,* Book 1, questions 1 and 2, Scotus postulates the univocity of Being and God. He thereby makes both into objects of thought rather than allowing for any reality transcending all conception. He conceives being as an essence that includes or comprehends individual beings, even the highest. This is what was previously treated (for example, by Thomas Aquinas) as "common being" and was opposed to Being itself (or God), which could be known only by analogy. In effect, the cosmos is turned into a concept—and its divine Ground along with it. This conceptual shift then ushers in the modern metaphysics of the thinking subject and its corresponding objects.[31] Metaphysics is founded as an autonomous science of being, and theology becomes pure, positive revelation divorced from physics and the experience of the world. Knowledge of God is thenceforth founded on love, as in Ockham, rather than on intelligence, as for Thomas.

This interpretation of Scotus, however, is one-sided. There is also a nonknowing of God and of everything else that is accentuated by Scotus and that opens toward a new type of apophatic thought, revolving around singularity as the ineffable par excellence in modern thought. While Scotus does abandon the way of analogy, he pioneers what will emerge as a more modern path of apophasis, one leading through finitude and fragmentariness to an openness without limit. The horizon of finitude of human *intellect* forces human *will* to open toward what it cannot comprehend, and so to discover the infinity of love. Milbank champions analogy and polarizes it from the path of the will, but he thereby turns away from certain modern experiential approaches to apophasis, paths that are in crucial ways anticipated by Scotus.

Specifically, Milbank fails to recognize that Duns Scotus also marks the inauguration of a new kind of respect for otherness, a new and acute sensibility for alterity, with his notion of *haecceitas* or "thisness"—a dimension of transcendence of *this* particular, this singular individual that is inaccessible to rational comprehension. This constitutes a displacement and a new opening for the mystery of nonconceptualizable "being," in which modern thinkers will eventually recognize something transcendent or even divine. Apophatic theology does not actually end with Scotus: it rather turns toward some of its more characteristically modern forms. Ineffable singularity and otherness remain sanctuaries of the holy incarnate in particularity and the body. Divinity will come to be recognized in the singular person (and perhaps only there) by numerous, otherwise integrally secular, thinkers. Here, if anywhere, they acknowledge, perhaps as a "minimal theology," a mystery transcending reason. In its materiality and corporeality, precisely the flesh has been recognized as a privileged locus of divine revelation, from John the Evangelist and Tertullian (*De caro dei*) to Merleau-Ponty and Michel Henry (referenced in my second essay, section iii). This is, of course, a kenotic revelation from negation leading eventually through suffering and destitution to a negative theology of the Cross.

What we find, then, in Scotus and the Franciscan movement could be seen as a shift toward a different kind of apophasis rather than a complete rejection of it. Scotus is pointing the way toward more explicitly secular forms of apophasis. Indeed, the ideology-free truth at which theology and rational critique alike aim is to be found in neither theism nor atheism, neither religionism nor secularism, but rather in apophasis—in what neither of these alternatives and no discourse whatever can comprehend or state. Radical Orthodoxy always places the emphasis on *mediation,* for example, between the beautiful and the sublime, or again as operating in the *allegoria amoris,* which forms a bridge between the finite and the infinite.[32] This sort of expedient is legitimate, but it is a bridge to what remains as such unknowable and transcends human concepts and language, however much it gives itself to be known and touched in incarnation and in the symbols and materials of the liturgy.[33] These are indeed concrete realizations in human flesh and created matter, yet still with reference to what transcends all finite forms. Mediation is still *mediation* and therefore, despite all experience of intimacy, remains distinct and even infinitely distant from the divinity with which communication is believed to take place.

What Scotus fundamentally loses is the sense for unknowing knowing, that is, for the analogy that makes something which is in itself unknowable nonetheless indirectly an object for us through a relation in unknowing that takes on determinate form in and through this relation. This relation is lost on a theology that takes a scientific turn toward detached rather than involved knowing of its object and that homogenizes knowledge into one rational structure. This is the modern figure of knowledge that Scotus had such an important part in shaping. And yet Scotus still has great respect for the unknown, much like Kant: both clearly define the boundary between things known (objects of science) and things beyond human ken (objects of faith). Indeed, Scotus's emphasis on *haecceitas* was destined to foster a new motive of apophasis in modern and postmodern thought. The singular individual is eminently unknowable and indefinable, as Levinas and Derrida, among many others, would stress. But the unknowable in this guise of singularity loses its relation to the cosmic whole: it shows up now only in fragments, as the medieval metaphysical worldview sinks into eclipse.

Scotus thus ushers in a dissociation of sensibility between intellect and will that deeply scores the destiny of modernity. Intellect becomes an instrumental, calculative faculty, separate from the will and its adventure of love open to the unknown and even unknowable. Scotus begins to understand negation, moreover, in terms of logic instead of hermeneutics: it concerns propositions rather than the interpretation of Names, whose function with respect to God is first to praise, to enter into a relation of reverence, not to objectively describe or analyze. He consequently moves away from the pragmatic, dialectical orientation of the preceding negative theology, which is concerned with the negation not of positions but of *oppositions* and results in "neither-nor."

One of Scotus's most symptomatic enunciations is that knowledge of God requires affirmations: we know no negation of God except by means of affirmations. This signals indeed the loss of the traditional negative-theological or analogical outlook and its replacement by a new paradigm of positivistic theology. The relation with a giving Creator is broken and will not be recovered except by a return to the traditional insights of negative theology, based on a real relation with the divine in and through fecund and inventive unknowing. Even the theological relation of giving and acknowledging the gift of being can escape secular metaphysics and conceptual idolatry only once it has passed through a negative theological critique.[34] This is what I find to be insufficiently acknowledged in certain expressions of Radical Orthodoxy, for example, in Blond's argument that "[t]he relationship that pertains for theology with respect to ontology is one of absolute superiority" (*Post-Secular Philosophy,* p. 12).

We can agree with Blond that ontology, as the philosophical discourse about beings in general, must remain aporetic, for it can never find the ground of beings in its own immanent sphere of being. This is basically an argument that can be traced from Plotinus, who recognized the inability of the order of beings to achieve closure and grounding except through a principle radically transcendent to being (see the previous essay). Classical ontology is thereby surpassed: there can be no ontological account of ultimate origins. Perhaps only theology can provide that—just as Milbank argues that only theology overcomes metaphysics. Ontology must end in the silence of apophasis. Yet theology, too, is based finally on apophasis. It cannot logically articulate its ultimate ground. The divine Word in itself or as such, behind all its manifold utterances in creation, remains inaccessible to human words. This can be demonstrated, for example, from the orthodox theology of Augustine. An emblematic moment is the vision at Ostia recounted in book 9 of his *Confessions,* in which human dialogue (with his mother) is transcended into the ineffable presence of the eternal Word.

Of course, in some ways, negative theology would belong to the "deconstructive strategies and skepticism" that Blond in particular is determined to combat. His advocacy of a "perceptual faith" is meant to move a step beyond the negative theological faith in an invisible God. The question is whether negative theology is not, in spite of Blond's suspicions, an indispensable step toward a theological phenomenology, empiricism, and realism of the kind that Blond proposes. Blond lays down stringent conditions for countenancing any sort of negative theology.

> There are those who think that theology can only be defended in a negative fashion and indeed that this form of negation or doubt concerning grounds is the only discourse that will allow a theology

at all. However, these theological sceptics (if I can call them that), lack a cataphasis. They lack an understanding that the *via negativa* itself requires a positum, a positum reserved for theology alone. . . . Negative theology requires a positive discourse about God, if, that is, this form of negation is to be recognizably about God at all. Only then can negative theology take its place in the peculiar grammar and comportment of religious affirmation. (*Post-Secular Philosophy*, p. 5)

Blond's interest is entirely focused on the positive discourse of orthodoxy, and he does not allow that negative theology is not a defense of a minimalist religious belief possible even for skeptics but rather, quite to the contrary, the key to releasing the total vision and force of theology as unlimited—as itself a word in the image of a truly infinite yet inconceivable God. Theology in its essential negativity is not just the truest among competing discourses, any more than God is just the most powerful among beings. What is required is rather the negation of the orders of discourse and of being, respectively and reciprocally. This precisely is how negative theology opens a dimension of infinity in the midst of the finitudes of being and language.

But still, Blond's main point is basically right and has been acknowledged by negative theologians ever since Pseudo-Dionysius, who emphasizes as a cardinal principle the necessary interweaving of apophatic and kataphatic methods in theology (*Divine Names* 872A). Blond's prescription, in contrast, fails to acknowledge how any affirmative theology must equally be conditioned by negative theology. It appears to take the *positum*, if not as pure plenitude, nevertheless as purely given. And although I do not want to rule out a priori an experience that gives itself in these terms (or in any others), miraculously as it were, the terms themselves as they are grasped and defined by us must be acknowledged to be, in a sense, the negation of the experience—just as discursively recorded experience cannot but be a mediation, a negation, and perhaps a distortion of whatever reality may (and perhaps must) be projected as unmediated.

This brokenness of language in relation to such a reality is proclaimed exemplarily by the Christian revelation of the crucified Word. Only in being mortified and eucharistically dismembered and disseminated is the divine Word fully revealed as Love. If we follow Milbank, we find that the semiological consciousness of the difference and absence intrinsic to the sign and therefore inextricable from language inscribes a negative moment into all theologizing. This is to bring negative theology close to deconstruction in the way that Kevin Hart does. Hart is careful not to confound the two and to respect Derrida's insistence that deconstruction is *not* a negative theology. Nevertheless, he affirms that negative theology is an *application* of deconstruction, and vice versa.[35] Both fundamentally place in question the sign as a means of recovering presence.

Hart emphasizes how Derridean deconstruction shows that any discourse, and in particular the discourses of theology and mysticism, can call their own metaphysical assumptions into question (p. xi). Deconstruction traces the effects of the exclusion of mysticism from philosophy. However, the goal still seems to be "the development of a non-metaphysical theology" (p. 21), even though the illusoriness of such a purging is constantly registered. My strategy is to concentrate not on such exclusions but rather on the inclusive (non)vision, which requires faith in a "God" who is only negatively known and defined and therefore in this sense is above all discourses about whatever principles or origins. This is also to move beyond the elevation of one *discourse* above all others. This viewpoint exposes, rather, the motivation for making such exclusionary distinctions and their limits. This (non)vision of God—or, as Franz Rosenzweig says, the nothing of our knowledge of God—before all polemical expressions against discourses that deny it, is what is passionately provocative, even though it cannot as such be delivered in any discourse but can only be signaled by the way any discourse intrinsically comes undone.

Our examination of Milbank and Blond has made evident the way in which the movement of Radical Orthodoxy has become possible only on the basis of a general critique of knowledge and language as never capable of attaining to reality as pure presence. The negative condition that seemed, in classical, critically reflective theological discourse, to be the peculiar liability of theology becomes the common predicament of every discourse concerning reality. This frees theology to come back as a metaphorical discourse on a par with all other discourses claiming truth: all are attempting to describe reality, with no better claim than theology to attain their respective targeted realities. None can present the "thing itself," none has any more positive a datum to present as a foundation for its particular domain of discourse. The true and ultimate concern of each is always beyond verbal articulations.

Thus, my contention is that Radical Orthodoxy articulates the positive theology that has been made possible by postmodern negative theology in the wake of deconstruction. It becomes intelligible (even for unbelievers) not in terms of its positive affirmations of dogma as such, but rather in terms of the specific space and modalities of *unknowing* that the negation of the modern dogmas of Enlightenment reason opens up. This gives rise to a Christian apologetics in which dogmatic truth or discourse cannot be understood to be categorically superior to poetic expression. This does not make such dogmas less true or precise. It only qualifies the kind of truth and precision that can and should be expected of them.

Radical Orthodoxy, with its revival of theological aesthetics and poetics (following von Balthasar and, more recently, Olivier-Thomas Venard), is best understood as a metaphorical discourse of the kind Vico showed all discourse to be. Discourse per se was seen by Vico as having originated with names of God invented as theological metaphors.[36] There is no literal discourse underlying it, but there is a critical discourse that delimits it and reminds it of its status as metaphorical. And precisely this is the discourse that has been gestated in the matrices of negative theology.

This discourse of negative theology is the critical counterpart of metaphysical discourse and even of a dogmatic discourse such as that affirmed by theological Orthodoxy (whether Western or Eastern). The positive discourse of Orthodoxy needs to be heard against this background of negative theology. Its metaphysics then become metaphorical, a poetic expression of what cannot be expressed by any proper language, a human embodiment in thought of a transcendent dimension of existence. This is the form in which "truth" concerning ultimate matters is represented in religion. This is why hymns in particular have been interpreted by Radical Orthodoxy as lying at the root of the possibility of theological language (as will be seen in section vi below). In fact, the critical discourse of negative theology has been paired with such poetic expression throughout a pluri-millenary tradition of contemplating language as inhabited by the mystery of God.[37]

Radically orthodox theology, at its most lucid, accepts itself as the affirmative correlative of a prior negative theology that has deconstructed the pretenses of transcendental systems by proving them to be, in substance, idolatrous. On this basis of the void cleared by negative theology as a deconstructive sort of critique, Radical Orthodoxy goes on to expound the world of beings everywhere it appears, in nature and history and art, as the analogical expression of God. All that is participates in God precisely to the extent that it *is*. However, the concept "God" does not operate as a definable principle in terms of which all else is grasped. The relations among things must be grasped immanently. And only then do their limits and deficiencies reveal also their openness to something undefined and infinite. And then the miraculous being-there of things and their being in excess of every "sufficient reason" or rational determination becomes indeterminately revelatory.

Radical Orthodoxy returns inevitably to the *indeterminacy* ultimately envisaged by any approach to thinking, however determinate or even dogmatic, that it endorses or applauds. This is where *Theos* can be non-idolatrously located—in a signifying function opening to indeterminacy. This radical openness to an indeterminate universal that is the deepest implication of a radical theological outlook contrary to the secular outlook that envisages a closed world, a *saeculum,* is being rediscovered in all sorts of ways in the postmodern world, through the "implosion" (to use Graham Ward's term) of secularism.[38] Even the natural sciences, from astrophysics to cell biology, in rediscovering the indeterminacy of chaos in their midst, are in underlying agreement with this theological outlook.[39]

Thus, theology may in this regard be infinitely superior to philosophy and to all other secular discourses—but only because it refrains from claiming any finite object that it can circumscribe and definitively know. It is in giving itself up as a determinate discourse and in gesturing beyond its own and every logos that theology perhaps reaches toward a higher level than any human discourse can attain. Of course, secular deconstructive discourses may have the same merit and become themselves negatively theological. Indeed, in this sense, as *negative* theology, theology is the work of secular critique as much as of theological reflection. Rather than opposing theology to secular language, I would prefer to find it intrinsic to all language (as discussed in my second essay), specifically, in language's negative structures of universalization and absolutization and in the ability of language to evoke the "In-finite" by negation. Here the vision of secularization as a form of theological revelation has been prescient.[40] One of the most significant and surprising results of this investigation is the recognition that a theological dimension is present throughout language, in all discourse: it is so present as an ineluctable negative theology.

This critique is similar to those of such thinkers as Adorno and Levinas, who criticize secular rationality in the Enlightenment tradition without expressly positioning themselves within a theological perspective, even though their critiques have affinities with theology and lend themselves to being understood as "minimal theologies." Hent de Vries (with Adorno, Levinas, and Derrida) agrees in seeing a "minimal theology" as present throughout the realms of human discourse.[41] This "critique of secular reason" we might equally well see as the full, self-deconstructing realization of secularization, as Nancy suggests.

The peculiar insight of negative theology brings to light the fact that it is theological discourse that most radically negates every other, every human sort of discourse, but also that "the theological" (or the Other or the non-identical) can be grasped by any logos only negatively. Negative theology is not just another logos. It is rather the self-suspension and self-subversion of its *own* logos: it is this act of kenosis as modeled in the Crucifixion that for Christian theologies such as Radical Orthodoxy counts as "God reconciling the world to himself" (2 Corinthians 5:19).

In my view, then, and contrary to a certain strategy that has characterized Radical Orthodoxy, it is not so much by driving a wedge between secular and theological cultures that the truth of Christian revelation can realize itself. Most deeply at stake is not a cultural identity, such as Catholic orthodoxy or secular humanism (even if some such cultural language must be assumed—if only to be discarded in the end), but the "God" or rather the Beyond-Name that is sought and longed for verbally throughout numberless specific human cultures as their unfathomable source. This is the "God" that unites humanity in shared purpose and common life. He/She/It is manifest in the giving and giving *up* of self and even of sense itself. Jean-Luc Nancy is right, in the end, to see Christianity as dissolving the very sense of sense. While concepts and Christian tags may be jettisoned by this movement of secularization, it is nonetheless the way in which

God can become all in all (1 Corinthians 15:28). And then perhaps there is no more "God." In this sense, Meister Eckhart, in his sermon "Beati pauperes spiritu," prayed to God to deliver us from "God."

v

Radical Orthodoxy has absorbed postmodern critical theory as a necessary and valid form of critique of the unchecked reign of reason proclaimed by liberal ideologies, and this sharpened critical consciousness emboldens it to position theology in a new, more self-confident and outspoken way. Empiricist and rationalist dogmas of the Enlightenment find themselves both effectively undermined by the new, broadly deconstructive criticism in which pretended universals have been exposed as strategic mechanisms for perpetrating violence against individuals and groups that they inevitably exclude. This exposure has been going on now for decades, starting, in at least one intellectual style, with the theoretical challenges of Foucault and Derrida, which opened the way, in more recent times inflected by cultural studies, to countless concrete claims of particularized identities asserted against all manner of monolithic norms.[42] Not all truth can be held hostage by the one purportedly universal Truth promulgated by rational science and its empirical methods. Consequently, the religious perspectives and belief systems that had been discredited by modern Enlightenment ideology as lacking in rational foundations find that they can breathe again in the ambience created by postmodern and, specifically, postsecular critique.

It is largely on the basis of this postmodern critique of philosophy, led especially by a first generation of French thinkers of difference, including also Emmanuel Levinas, Gilles Deleuze, Maurice Blanchot, Michel de Certeau, Luce Irigaray, and Julia Kristeva, in the wake of the so-called linguistic turn in philosophy, that theology has found a new footing for itself in the outlook of Radical Orthodoxy.[43] In France itself, the postmodern critical paradigm has fostered a new generation of theologians, including Jean-Yves Lacoste, Louis-Marie Chauvet, and Olivier-Thomas Venard, who have succeeded the "nouvelle théologie" of Henri de Lubac and Jean Daniélou in the attempt to rethink the basis of Christian belief in an era in which the metaphysical dogmas of religious and secular culture alike seem to have collapsed under critical scrutiny.

A crucial part of Milbank's work focuses on rereading modern culture and its critical revolution with emphasis on theological thinkers such as Hamann, Herder, Jacobi, Vico, and Kierkegaard, who were marginalized by their more secular counterparts, particularly Kant, Hegel, Feuerbach, and Marx, at least up until the recent turns of poststructuralism. With their language-reflective outlook, the theological thinkers are the ones who, under the sign of the Creator Word ("by whom all things were made") and Word Incarnate ("the Word became flesh and dwelt among us," John 1:1–14), were already thinking through language in a way that in the twentieth century, with its "linguistic turn," would become the general paradigm even for secular thought and eventually provoke the upheavals of postmodernism.[44]

The critical insights on which Milbank builds are found in radical thinkers of Christian tradition, particularly in the eighteenth century and *its* linguistic turn, with Hamann and Vico and with other "profoundly orthodox Christian thinkers."[45] This is a central pivot of Milbank's rereading of the history of Western culture from a theological viewpoint. Christian thinkers first take the step beyond metaphysics and the substances it posits toward the relationality inherent in language as a form of address and communication. The fundamental nature of reality is conceived of not as inert substance but as speaking being. In Milbank's estimation, as argued in his essay "The Linguistic Turn as a Theological Turn,"

> The oscillations in eighteenth-century linguistic theory between empiricism and rationalism are not, however, what is really interesting. Both philosophies were confined within the inherited metaphysics of substance. More truly significant was the break-up of this thinking, the steps towards a modern 'linguistic turn', beyond linguistic instrumentalism, foundational reason and nominalist empiricism. Yet what is almost never attended to is the fact that these moves were not made by an unambiguous 'enlightenment', but rather by profoundly orthodox Christian thinkers—by Robert Lowth, Johann Georg Hamann, George Berkeley, Giambattista Vico and Johann Gottfried Herder. As an experiment, I now choose

to interpret this linguistic turn not as a secular phenomenon, but rather as the delayed achievement of the Christian critique of both the *antique form* of materialism, and the antique metaphysics of substance. (*Word Made Strange*, p. 97)

Milbank then traces how orthodox Christian thinkers ever since Gregory of Nyssa and Augustine had already undermined substance metaphysics in semiotic terms by a Trinitarian understanding of reality as founded on the Word and therefore on a paradigm of relations. They had, in effect, anticipated the linguistic turn taken by philosophy in modern times, thanks to the Christian doctrine of the divine Word. This turn entailed an opening to unlimited "semiosis" or proliferating resignifications that cannot be reduced to simple prelinguistic facts: "Christian theology has been able, like sceptical postmodernism, to think unlimited semiosis" (*Word Made Strange*, p. 113).

Of course, for Milbank there is also a crucial difference. In the Christian view, this unlimited semiotic activity is a manifestation of something theological in essence: it is concerned with something transcendent and is not consumed merely in and with itself. But this is a difference in interpreting the unlimited semiosis that is shared in common by Christianity and poststructuralist thought. For Christianity, semiosis opens toward the Infinite or God, whereas for postmodern "nihilists" it gapes open to a great emptiness: "The contrast with postmodernism lies at the level of metasemiotics, where the nihilists seem only able to think of signified absence in terms of a necessary suppression, betrayal or subversion" (*Word Made Strange*, p. 112). In interpreting postmodern emptiness as violent and malicious, moreover, Milbank does, after all, accord a certain superiority to theology in terms not of rights but of its effects (*de facto*, not *de jure*). Theology alone preserves real difference that is not reduced, that does not collapse into the indifference of everything being constituted only by signs, but remains absolutely positive and real, a mediation of true being, which (for it) is divinity: "For theology, and theology alone, difference remains real difference since it is not subordinate to immanent univocal process or the fate of a necessary suppression. Instead, the very possibility of substitutive transference is here held to be a peaceful affirmation of the other, consummated in a transcendent infinity" (p. 113). This virtue of respecting and preserving (divine) difference or transcendence lends theology a negative superiority in terms of what it does *not* claim and vigilantly guards against claiming: it does not claim univocally to know its object. Such is the indispensable basis for affirmation of transcendent divinity.

Signs emerge, in the tradition Milbank outlines, as mediations of the real as absolute and as theological. There is the mediation of signs in all our knowledge, which never constitutes direct possession and presence. This cuts against Kant's epistemological subjectivism, which makes the sign merely arbitrary and consequently makes all our knowledge only transcendentally related to things-in-themselves as their condition of possibility. Milbank proposes rather a realist metaphysics or theological ontology, one that does not need to be overcome. With reference to a theory of George Berkeley's, he makes the point that *"semiosis* now involves real relations, substitutionary transitions which though inscrutable, are more than arbitrary; the signifying relation becomes also symbolic" (*Word Made Strange*, p. 103). Thus, the signifying relation is not empty: the *symbolon* betokens the other half of what it has been broken off from, whereas the postmodern secularist, in contrast, is left with nothing to symbolize. Although there is no reality that can be made present independently of signs—a point on which Derrida has insisted—the reality of signs themselves can be received as authentic mediation of a reality that remains indeterminate in terms of signs but is nevertheless mysteriously manifest and present in the ongoing, open process of semiosis—particularly in its indeterminacy.

This view that there is in the mysteries of semiosis a "call of the Other," however, is not inaccessible to poststructuralist thought: it is actually crucial for Derrida himself. *L'appel de l'Autre* is indeed, by his account, the wellspring of the entire deconstructive project. Along these lines, John Caputo has done much to bring out the religious undertow and overtones, the "prayers and tears," to be heard and seen in the margins of the text of deconstruction.[46] Milbank ignores or minimizes these tendencies in order to radicalize the choice for Christ that carries his own conviction.

Nonetheless, Milbank goes a long way in adapting the techniques of postmodernism to thinking theological presence in a deconstructed manner. This presence is an invisible image and is evoked by a shattered, broken sign. These terms help him to reformulate Christian doctrine on the far side of the poststructuralist critique of the sign and its breaking up of the relation of reference. Christ crucified turns out to be the key to this postsecular semiotics: "One paradoxical reason for our recognition of Christ as the true sign is that all the signs he offers us are broken signs that offer their own asymmetry as a testimony to their own inadequacy and to the infinite distance between humanity and God."[47] Christ's death, together with the drama of the Last Supper that frames it, in which Christ institutes himself as a sign to be transmitted through the ages, opens into universal meaning that is, however, as human, continually underway and not crystallized in a finite, definitive signification. It can therefore be "overtaken" by divine meanings: "The words of Maundy Thursday and the acts of Good Friday together compose a poetic act characterized by an 'overtaking', such that the intention of the sign is only realized in the full outcome of its explication." Jesus commits himself to "death as the reality of sign *qua* sign," since the sign can become complete and defined and thereby totally significant only as "a *function* of its lifelessness" (*Word Made Strange,* p. 138).

This death alone enables Christ to be properly identified as the Word of God, though the signified identity remains mysterious. The signifier is concrete, while the signified or "universal" is invisible and remains indeterminate:

> Christ is our proper word for God and for true humanity. This proper word is finally taken up into, included in, the eternal *Logos* of the Father. When we see Christ in the flesh, we already see this invisible centre, because our whole perception is informed by the gift of the Holy Spirit, a *sensus communis* inaugurated in us by Christ as an adequate sense of metaphorical judgement that is— though it is generated *through it*—the necessary transcendental condition *for* the adequate concrete universal. That the concrete universal is ultimately an invisible image is already suggested to us, we may venture to say, in the diversity of reports about Christ and the sheer number of traditions that are invoked to build up this *figura*." (*Word Made Strange,* p. 140)

Milbank's Christological poetics are informed here especially by Vico's idea of the judgment of common sense or imagination, which perceives a concrete universal.

God in Christ remains per se an invisible image. Any determinate image, even of the life and works of Christ himself, yields its full meaning only through further images given by subsequent agents—from Saint Francis of Assisi, for example, to the mentally disabled child, perhaps—in a series in which its infinite meaning remains ever open and determined anew from further angles of vision. Milbank borrows from Hans Urs von Balthasar the idea that the doctrine of justification can only be presented as the history of the saints.[48] Salvation history thus unfolds as the "quest for the representation of the unrepresentable." Such is "the dialectic of human and divine history" (*Word Made Strange,* p. 131).

"Representation of the unrepresentable" is an exact description of apophatic discourse. Milbank stresses that its inadequacy in human terms is "overtaken" by divine action making it adequate, even though the human appropriation of such making can only be, in a broad sense, "poetic." God's perfect utterance of himself in his Word is given to us completely and adequately in Jesus. Yet our apprehension and representation of this God-man remains still always metaphorical:

> It is as this divine-human person, who has both finitely and infinitely the character of a representation, that we finally recognize in Jesus the divine overtaking and fulfilling of all human purposes. As the divine utterance Jesus is the absolute origination of all meaning, but as a human utterance Jesus is inheritor of all already constituted human meanings. He is a single utterance in his unified fulfilment of these meanings, such that he becomes the adequate metaphoric representation of the total human intent. (*Word Made Strange,* p. 136)

Even as an adequate representation of the unrepresentable, Jesus is known always in partial and personal ways that are expressed in language that can be considered adequate not scientifically but rather metaphorically—or as personal witness.

Milbank is applying Vico's ideas of all language as metaphorical and of metaphor as the original language of humankind. In general, the semiotic vision of reality as constituted by signifying relations is basic to his radical (Trinitarian) rethinking of Christian revelation. This leads him to recognize infinite semiosis without original, pure presence as literally *crucial* to the poetic making of revelation. It is a *negative* semiology, since it is axised on the absolute, on God, the Infinite, who can never be adequately represented by any finite sign. This also means that he recognizes what, in relation to determinate signs and language, is a void at the center and origin of all that can be revealed. Or rather, the void inhabits determinate signs that are not part of an ongoing history of revelation of something beyond signs and beyond all human productions.

Milbank uses the Aristotelian idea of *poiesis* as producing something of value beyond the act itself, beyond *praxis,* to suggest how God and providence, as well as sin, work in determining the meaning and value of our actions in constructing our lives. What becomes of what we do and become reaches far beyond our own intentions and direct enactments. Even before we do them, our acts are conditioned in countless ways. In this sense, they "occur to us" and so are open to grace (as well as to distortion)—they are mediated before and after the act in ways both human and, possibly, divine.

Eucharistic action brings with it a sort of theological insight that has been missing from other postmodern attempts to critique and overcome metaphysics. However, Milbank's essay "Only Theology Overcomes Metaphysics" suggests that even the rigorous efforts of Jean-Luc Marion to escape the metaphysical determination of God by Being are fundamentally vain.[49] For Milbank, Marion's phenomenological approach to God as beyond Being, as pure Gift and Giving, remains idolatrous, indeed metaphysical, in its assertion of the autonomy of philosophy. Marion takes being as univocal in the modern, idolatrous way that has prevailed since Duns Scotus—albeit *only* since him. Metaphysics, both in antiquity and in the Middle Ages before Scotus, was not independent of theology. The ultimately equivocal sense of being could only be *revealed*—and hence had to be known theologically, not just philosophically (or phenomenologically). Metaphysics was to this extent a poetry based on the being of God given analogically in creation but not directly grasped by human reason.

The experience and manifestation of a metaphysical God could only be poetically performed, not adequately stated in conceptual or logical terms. Theology, unlike philosophy, is receptive to the revealed Word, most profoundly through a Christological poetics. Theology thereby receives an extra-cosmic, vatic Logos and performs it poetically. Philosophy, in contrast, aspires to be autonomous, self-grounding knowledge. "Philosophy in fact *began* as secularizing immanentism, an attempt to regard a *cosmos* independently of a performed reception of the poetic word."[50] Only philosophy pretends to state what things really are in their true being. Theology is based rather on a poetics of being that is expressed primordially in the hymn of praise.

Similar critiques of the kind of thinking that conceives itself as independent of theological revelation apply to Levinas. He, too, employs the transcendental method of phenomenology in an attempt to disengage thinking and an ethical consciousness of being face to face with the Other that is prior even to any subject and to what can be called "thinking" from being and its essences. But for Milbank, this is still not theological revelation and therefore reduces to immanence, to merely human reflection. Milbank is unwilling to acknowledge the potential for self-subversion and transcendence of such discourse. In my view, postmodern thought can be theological in a negative sense, when it opens in infinite self-criticism to the Infinite. Levinas, as a thinker of phenomenological transcendence, thinks a dimension that is open to and invites symbolization as theological, even if all representations and objectifications are inadequate for what remains always more truly infinite than any finite terms can say. Maurice Blanchot, in dialogue with Levinas, is similarly obsessed with this other dimension *outside* representation—*le dehors*.

The problem, as Milbank correctly insists, with transcendentalist approaches that claim to escape theology is that they set up some criterion defined by thought as determining what is beyond the range of human fashioning and thus, presumably, of idolatry. But all these criteria are inevitably made in thought's own image. Pure "presence" or pure "giving" or the infinite obligation to the Other beyond and before all categories of being simply substitute other categories that are still humanly thinkable and thought. They are idolatrous determinations of divinity. "God" is allowed to escape from being and the categories of onto-theology, but if transcendental phenomenology or philosophy supplies some other normative principle, then God is still measured by a humanly comprehensible standard.

Only if these transcendental philosophies are interpreted apophatically—as providing metaphors that we do not understand properly with reference to the transcendent but only in terms of our human experience—is the regime of a semantics embracing God and creation alike broken up. I take Levinas, Blanchot, and Marion in this sense: they are pointing to the absolute alterity of what we cannot characterize in our language. We can only note where it breaks open our language and the circuits of its sense. Kevin Hart also reads Blanchot and Marion in this way.[51] It is such negative theological reading that can save them from an otherwise devastating critique by Radical Orthodoxy. They fall under this critique only to the extent that they are committed to "modernity," in which ontology becomes autonomous from theology and thereby becomes bad metaphysics.[52]

Milbank argues that Aquinas's *esse* is not, in this sense, metaphysical. For Milbank, Marion confounds divine *esse* with common being, *ens commune,* which is indeed for Aquinas the subject of metaphysics. To this extent, it is the equivalent of Heidegger's *Sein* (*Word Made Strange,* p. 43). In aiming at a rigorously philosophical thinking, Heidegger and Marion might seem to be united in a refusal of analogy and conjecture. And yet Heidegger's "hints" (*Winke*) are surely conjectural and signal an apophatic side of his thought that Milbank erases. Milbank finds rather in Gregory of Nyssa the right relation between ontology and theology that enables being to be thought by analogy and conjecture, and it is indeed apophatic: "in Gregory of Nyssa, 'Being' is allowed the common divinity of the Trinity precisely because it is an entirely apophatic term indicating nothing of 'how' God is" (p. 46).

Marion, by rejecting the language of Being, seems to be seeking some other language that will not have the same defects and so will not be contaminated by onto-theology, but will rather be adequate to what he calls the "saturated phenomenon."[53] But the deeper apophatic insight is that no language whatever can be factually or descriptively adequate to God. All language can operate only as metaphor in divine revelation. Does this, then, set another transcendental criterion for veracity of human speech about God? It can avoid doing so only to the extent that it remains apophatic and accepts its inadequacy to speak of God—and, consequently, of being and everything else. It needs to be conjoined externally with an analogical, kataphatic language in order to say anything at all. This is how, I believe, Marion can most profitably be read.[54]

Derrida's turn to religion in his later writings is based on this realization that no critical, philosophical language whatever could be adequate to the religious.[55] One can be, nevertheless, within the discourse of the divine, even though this discourse is then necessarily expropriated and made strange to itself when it comes to be expressed in any human terms—it becomes Milbank's "word made strange" or even, in a yet more provocative formulation, Christ made "monstrous."[56] There is no standpoint outside metaphysics for a discourse about God. Yet within human discourse, God can act, when this discourse is no longer controlled by human agency but is opened up by the advent of the Other within it. I find that Levinas, exemplarily in *De Dieu qui vient à l'idée,* together with his predecessor, Rosenzweig, in *Stern der Erlösung,* points the way toward this type of religious discourse, which I designate "apophasis."[57]

Likewise Radical Orthodoxy itself needs to be interpreted according to its apophatic sense in order not to fall an easy prey to its opponents and despisers. If it believes in its own affirmations more than in what exceeds and ultimately confounds them, it becomes idolatrous itself. But its truth, I submit, is not to be found in any discourse or formulas that are flatly affirmed. Radical Orthodoxy does not just invoke ecclesiastical authority to back up its theological positions. Quite the opposite. Milbank defends them philosophically and maintains that unorthodox positions, including those of the Protestant Reformation, deform not only the truth of Christian revelation but also anthropology and cosmology and so belong to the general errors and perversions of the modern world. Theology, as we have seen, for him goes terribly wrong with Duns Scotus. The lineage that for Milbank has maintained a true comprehension of God and the world is, in effect, that of negative theology—from Proclus and the Greek fathers to Augustine, Pseudo-Dionysius and Maximus, Aquinas, Eckhart, and Cusanus. This truth proves itself to rational reflection in pursuit of the basis for a peaceful and harmonious creation. Theology offers a narrative and a worldview that has to defend itself by making philosophical sense. Ecclesiastical authority can be a way of safeguarding and dissemi-

nating true doctrine, but the truth of doctrine must remain open to philosophical reflection. Of course, reason must be self-critical enough not to
take itself for self-sufficient or autonomously grounded: faith, hope, and
love, together with all intelligent faculties, are potentially relevant to discerning the truth as well.

Philosophical thinking, in any case, has a relation and a responsibility
to what is outside the range of thought—it does not take place in a
vacuum. This social and communitarian context of truth evokes a dimension that is represented in Christian culture by the church. But the church
for Milbank is not necessarily "a particular Church since the Church is
not particular, not primarily an institution at all, but a dissemination of
love which is the repetition of the occurrence of complete love in the
world, a bearing of evil and death within humanity to the point of exposure of their predatory unreality by the divine *Logos* itself" (*Future of Love,*
p. 166). Receiving the gift of love as given by God is what defines the
church before and apart from any and all ecclesiastical structures or institutions: "To already receive charity, and so to have the possibility of repeating it, is to be within the Church" (p. 166).

Negative theological tradition especially has recognized that all
human claims to authority are undermined by recognition of God's authority. Divine sovereignty is the negation of every human claim to sovereignty. The church constitutes itself Eucharistically by receiving its body
from outside itself; therefore it is never self-governing. "This means, not
'theocracy' in the sense of men claiming to rule with divine legitimacy, but
the very opposite, since all claims to legitimate sovereignty are theocrati-
cally tainted. It means rather the gradual *end* of human self-government,
a kind of ordered anarchy" (*Future of Love,* p. 167).[58]

This is where it becomes plain that Milbank's orthodoxy is indeed
radical. He condemns secular culture and thought, not because it offends
against the codified morality of the church, but because it violates the nature of humanity as open to infinity and divinity as its own "beyond," and
so prevents humanity from receiving a gift that it cannot comprehend or
command. This uncircumscribed openness is betrayed by secular transcendental thinking and the conceptual idolatry it engenders. The Eucharist, in contrast, embodies an ideal of openness to transcendence beyond
all human appropriations.

Thus the Eucharist "is not one more particular cult. Here, we offer all fruits of nature and work to God in sacrifice, and he takes everything—all of creation, all of us—yet instantly gives all back in the mode of himself, to everyone, without distinction" (*Future of Love,* p. 167). There is no "brokerage" here and no hierarchy, since the transcendent is at a distance "more distant than any hierarchical distance" (p. 167). Monotheistic divinity makes the absolute difference that undermines all human discriminations and exclusions and abolishes privileges and oppressions. Yet it can be manifest only as "a cult against cult, a sacrifice against sacrifice, but still necessary, for resistance to exclusive cults needs itself to be encultured. Why? Because the merely abstract resistance of reason to cults repeats in its rational self-autonomy, without the excess of desire or of gift, precisely that cultic self-government which cannot turn itself inside out" (p. 167). Turning itself inside out is a kind of self-negation that opens cult and sacrifice, in the case of the Eucharist, to what absolutely transcends all such human practices.

All knowledge, furthermore, as Milbank argues in "The Invocation of Clio," is suspended from "an unthinkable prior relation to knowledge and to thinking which we cannot know and we cannot think. Yet at the same time we must constantly seek to think and to know this relation, if we are to have an inkling as to the character of the call of truth itself, or its gift-in-earnest of our future reward" (*The Future of Love,* pp. 177–78). This is bona fide negative theology, with its imperative "nevertheless" or *quand même* in the face of the impossible: it puts all the weight on what escapes the grasp of all our knowing and yet impresses itself on the forms of our unknowing.

Radical Orthodoxy seems to be completely identified with a specific, confessional discourse, even though orthodox theology in its radical representatives has constantly and classically resorted to the principle that no discourse on God can be adequate. Christian (and more generally monotheistic) truth cannot truly be located in any discourse but only in the beyond of all discourses. This orientation to the unsayable is expressed by Radical Orthodoxy's affirmation of the Neoplatonic tradition and of language as basically hymnic. It entails ties to the negative theological tradition that should be fully acknowledged and that lead beyond *exclusive* identification with a certain discourse that would absolutize *itself* rather than what it aims at beyond all discourse. Such exclusive identification leads to fractious oppositions with other discourses claiming equally to be religious and revealed. Dogma and its definition and defense have their role in propagating a religion, just as certain postulates serve as enabling conditions for any system—and certain motifs for any narrative. Yet they must be apprehended in their poetic and performative potency, and thus not as exclusive of other, different formulations of truth. It is necessary to aim past all positive formulations, to set one's sights beyond what can be said, in order for the power of the message to be made manifest without the self-defeating constraints of all-too-human appropriations.

Apophatic philosophy, even in its ancient, specifically Neoplatonic guise, resorts to poetic expression—particularly in the form of the hymn. This is the positive counterpart of its necessarily negative discourse leading ultimately to silence. Under pressure of the inadequacy of statement and reference in relation to God, another way of using language emerges. It creates a relation that is not conceptual so much as affective and projective, one that is geared to what it cannot conceive of except as beyond all created beings: beings are hymned only in order to be surpassed in the direction of their source and ground.

We have already studied how poetic language approaches the unsayable in Celan and Jabès. The same goes for theological language, and it is not less true of orthodox theological language.[59] I have suggested here that in Radical Orthodoxy an attempt can be found to think the positive counterpart to negative theology. In the next section I attempt to explain this potential for lending expression to the apophatic dimension of speech specifically in terms of the hymn as it is seen in a perspective reaching from Neoplatonism to Radical Orthodoxy. Any form of significant expression whatever, stretched to its limits, can probably be used to evoke the apophatic, but hymnic expression has a particular history of such employment that can be traced back as far as the ancient Egyptian "Great Hymn to Aten." Written in the fourteenth century B.C. by Pharaoh Akhenaton, this hymn is taken by some scholars to be the earliest expression or original seed of monotheism.[60] We can recognize an implicit critique by negative theological reflection of the idolatrousness of polytheistic worship already in its exclamation: "How many are your deeds, Though hidden from sight, O Sole God beside whom there is none!"[61]

vi

Attending to the form of the hymn will help us track metaphysics, the knowledge and discourse of being, to its source in unknowing and unsaying vis-à-vis an infinite "reality" that can neither be qualified by language nor be adequately known, and which is, to this extent, "ab-solute"— literally, absolved from speech and concept and thus from the grasp of the knowing subject. We admit that metaphysical "truth" is unsayable, yet it must also have some form of expression if it is going to register at all.

As proponents of negative theology from Pseudo-Dionysius the Areopagite to Denys Turner concordantly insist, every negative theology presupposes and is inextricably interwoven with a positive or kataphatic theology.[62] Pseudo-Dionysius writes of the inexpressible (ἀρρήτον) being woven together (σύμπεπλεκται) with the expressible (τὸ ῥῆτο). I wish to explore briefly how the poetic and prayerful form of the hymn gives positive verbal expression—or theologically we could say *witness*—to what cannot be expressed in terms of conceptual knowledge, or knowledge to which the Logos can be adequate.

The final movement of this essay, accordingly, deals with the positive theology that always doubles and indirectly lends voice to the otherwise inaudible negations of apophatic theology. Through conjugation with a positive, hymnic form of expression, apophatic discourse is able indirectly to *evoke* what it cannot properly *say*. On this interpretation, metaphysics turns out to be a poetic discourse and even a sort of religious witness to a reality transcending objective expression and articulation.[63] This perspective is crucial for understanding how apophatic thinking entails not an overcoming of metaphysics (as in Heidegger's "Überwindung der Metaphysik") but rather an ungrounding of its language. Such language is thereby made free and is relaunched in a sphere beyond the reach of objective reference and other standard pragmatic linguistic functions.

The hymn reaches beyond discourse. The priority of this dimension beyond the discursive can be discerned at the very origins of philosophy in the sacred cult, with its rituals, including pantomime and dithyrambic.[64] The hymn and its use and theory from antiquity also hew closely to the apophatic matrix of philosophical reflection. At the other end of this historical trajectory, Radical Orthodoxy's emphasis on "the liturgical consummation of philosophy" likewise points toward the apophatic. I wish now to demonstrate the profoundly apophatic character of Radical Orthodoxy, beginning from its rootedness in Neoplatonic tradition, specifically in terms of the sublation of theological discourse into the hymn. This will bring out the essentially apophatic thrust of both forms of theological reflection, covering a span from the ancient theological hymn to postmodern philosophical theology.

It will help to have a particular hymn before us as model. An ancient Neoplatonic hymn can serve as a touchstone, since I propose this final excursus on the hymn as a way of binding Radical Orthodoxy to its roots in the Platonic and Neoplatonic tradition by a specifically negative theological link: their common exaltation of the hymn as a vehicle of theological knowledge highlights a fundamental, shared inspiration in negative theology for these two historically distanced forms of religious thought.

Ὕμνος εἰς Θεόν

Ὦ πάντων ἐπέκεινα· τί γὰρ θέμις ἄλλο σε μέλπειν;
Πῶς λόγος ὑμνήσει σε; Σὺ γὰρ λόγῳ οὐδενὶ ῥητός.
Μοῦνος ἐὼν ἄφραστος· ἐπεὶ τέχες ὅσσα λαλεῖται.
Πῶς νόος ἀθρήσε σε; Σὺ γὰρ νόῳ οὐδενὶ ληπτός.
Μοῦνος ἐὼν ἄγνωστος· ἐπεὶ τέχες ὅσσα νοεῖται.
Πάντα σε καὶ λαλέοντα, καὶ οὐ λαλέοντα λιγαίνει·
Πάντα σε καὶ νοέοντα καὶ οὐ νοέοντα γεραίρει.
Ξυνοὶ γάρ τε πόθοι, ξυναὶ δέ ὠδῖνες ἁπάντων
Ἔμφὶ σέ· σοὶ δὲ τὰ πάντα προσεύχεται· εἰς σὲ δὲ πάντα
Σύνθεμα σὸν νοέοντα λαλεῖ σιγώμενον ὕμνον.
Σοὶ ἑνὶ πάντα μένει· σοὶ δέ ἀθρόα πάντα, καὶ θοάζει,
Καὶ πάντων τέλος ἐσσί, καὶ εἷς, καὶ πάντα καὶ οὐδέν
Οὐχ ἕν ἐὼν, οὐ πάντα· Ἀνώνυμε, πῶς σε καλέσσω
Τὸν μόνον ἀκλήϊστον; ὑπερφανέας δὲ καλύπτρας
Τίς νόος οὐρανίδης εἰσδύσεται; Ἵλαος εἴης,
Ὦ πάντων ἐπέκεινα· τί γὰρ θέμις ἄλλο σε μέλπειν;[65]

Hymn to the Transcendence of God

O you, beyond all things! For how else is it fitting to sing you?
How can words hymn you? For you are expressed by no word.
You alone are unutterable, though all that is spoken is from you.
How can mind perceive you? For you are grasped by no mind.
You alone are unknowable, since all that is known is from you.
All that speaks and does not speak proclaims you.
All that thinks and does not think honors you.
For all desires and all travailings of all things
are directed towards you. All things pray to you, and to you
all who know your cipher sing a silent hymn.
In you alone all things abide, to you all together rush.
For you are the end of all, the one, the all, the nothing,
being not one, not all. Nameless, what shall I call you?
The only unnameable? What celestial spirit
could penetrate your more-than-light darkness? Be gracious,
O you, beyond all things! For how else is it fitting to sing you?[66]

Understood apophatically, metaphysics consists in *un*knowing and *un*saying, and for the Neoplatonists working in the *Parmenides* commentary tradition, this negation of language registers by being expressed especially in the form of the hymn, which is thereby valorized as an indispensable vehicle for metaphysics. In fact, Plato's dialogue the *Parmenides* was itself taken by these commentators to be essentially a hymn. Proclus calls the first hypothesis of the *Parmenides* "a theological hymn by way of negations to the One" (ὕμνον διὰ τῶν ἀποφάσεων θεολογικὸν εἰς τὸ ἕν, *In Parmeniden* VII.1191.34–35).[67] Again in *Theologia Platonica* III.23, p. 83, lines 22ff., Proclus writes of the One in the first hypothesis, the First, in which there can be no participation, as "being hymned" (ὕμνηται). The second hypothesis, too, is interpreted by Proclus in *Platonic Theology* I.7, p. 31, lines 25–27 as a "theogony," that is, a hymn celebrating the generation of the gods.[68]

Plato's own dialogues define themselves at key junctures in terms of the hymn. *Timaeus* 21a1ff. introduces the tale of Atlantis told by Critias as a panegyric in praise of Athena in a hymnic mode (οἷόνπερ ὑμνοῦντας ἐγκωμιάζειν) offered on the occasion of the Panathenean festival in which the dialogue is set. *Phaedrus* 265c1 calls Socrates's recantation in the second part of the dialogue a "mythical hymn" (μυθικόν τινα ὕμνον). *Phaedo* 61a3ff. classifies philosophy among the musical arts, indeed as the greatest of them. Proclus infers from this that human philosophy consists basically in the imitation of the hymns of Apollo:

> By means of this art [namely, philosophy] the soul is able to honour all things human and to sing hymns to the gods in a perfect way, while imitating the Leader of the Muses himself, who hymns his Father with noeric songs and keeps the cosmos together with indissoluble fetters while moving everything together, as Socrates says in the *Cratylus* (*Rem publicam commentarii,* I 57, 11–16).[69]

Thus Proclus is following Plato in describing philosophical discourse as hymnic in nature, and it is plausible to extend this description to metaphysical discourse in its highest and deepest reaches. The most inspired discourses of the *Phaedrus* and of the other dialogues on love have an easily recognizable hymnic cadence and character. In Proclus's understanding, Platonic metaphysics quite generally consists in composing hymns to the gods. R. M. Van den Berg develops in detail the thesis that philosophy and particularly its metaphysical discussions were understood by Neoplatonists, especially in the Athenian Academy, as a matter of singing hymns to the gods and thereby assimilating oneself to divinity. Through careful philological examination of Proclus's hymns, as well as of his use of the word "hymn" in his commentaries, Van den Berg comes to the conclusion that "[t]he distribution of ὑμνέω and related forms in Proclus's oeuvre squares with the suggestion that for him metaphysical discussions are as it were hymns to the gods. Such verbs are virtually absent from works that do not primarily deal with metaphysics" (p. 27).

It must be admitted that the word ὑμνήσει as it occurs, for example, in the second verse of the "Hymn to the Transcendence of God," is not commonly taken to indicate properly the singing of hymns (ὑμνῳδία). The word "hymn," particularly in its verbal employments—ὑμνεῖν and a variety of derivative forms, including ὑνυμνεῖν—has a wide range of meanings, such as "say," "mention," "maintain," and is not typically considered by scholars to retain the root sense of "hymn" as "to sing songs [ὑμνῳδεῖν] in praise of divinity." However, against this view, Van den

Berg argues that "ὑμνεῖν never entirely loses a special sense of celebration, as can be learnt from an analysis of its occurrences. My claim is that the members of the Athenian Academy used it on purpose because they were convinced that by doing philosophy, or rather metaphysics, they were, as it were, singing hymns to the gods" (p. 26).

Even without subscribing to the contention that the word never lost its root meaning, it is altogether plausible that the etymological meaning would have become, in some measure, conscious again for the philosophers, given their characteristically probing and highly reflective use of language. For example, when Proclus employs ἐξύμνησειν in the sense of "extol" in *In Euclid* 211.27, it is difficult to imagine that the meaning would not resonate with the sense of hymns of praise. The word for such hymns is contained transparently as a component within this locution, and similarly for the other such compounds incorporating the word "hymn."

It appears, then, that for Proclus and for the Athenian school of Neoplatonism generally, philosophizing at a certain level becomes identical with the making and performing of hymns. Plato's dialogues, especially the *Parmenides* and the *Timaeus,* as we have seen, interpreted themselves explicitly as hymns. To this extent, metaphysics can be understood as hymnic in essence, beginning from the Neoplatonic philosophers and even from the Platonic sources themselves. The Platonic dialogues' hints are developed subsequently by the Neoplatonists into a far-reaching metaphysical program for lending speech through hymns to what, at the summit of contemplation, remains in itself inexpressible.

The hymn is best taken simply as a prayer praising the gods, whether or not the text is sung. In this broad sense, the hymn as a genre continues to be recognized as an indispensable frame for metaphysics throughout the metaphysical tradition, particularly in its apophatic or negative-theological strands. Anselm's so-called ontological argument in the *Proslogion* is among the most philosophically significant and historically influential of metaphysical meditations in the Middle Ages, and all its syllogisms are in a certain sense couched in the language of hymn and prayer that frames the entire meditation. This moment of celebration and supplication does not remain merely external to the argument. The *Proslogion* begins with a prayer expressing desire to behold the Face of the Lord ("Quaero vultum tuum; vultum tuum, Domine, requiro"), echoing Psalm

42:1–4: "As the hart longs for the water course, so my soul longs for thee, O God . . . . When shall I come and behold the face of God?" Anselm's discourse similarly ends on a doxological note of blessing for the Trinitarian God that echoes psalmodic language: "until I enter into the joy of my Lord, who is three and one God blessed forever. Amen" ("donec intrem in gaudium domini mei, qui est triunus et unus Deus benedictus in saecula. Amen").[70]

This liturgical framing is less pronounced, of course, in the Scholastic *summas,* but even Thomas Aquinas's oeuvre has to be contextualized by the genre of the hymn, particularly the four hymns he authored for the *Corpus Christi* liturgy, notably the *Pange lingua.* Thomas himself, near the end of his life, saw all his Scholastic science reduced to so much straw or, more accurately, "chaff."[71] He became silent. After a staggering vision, he famously confessed to his secretary that he could not go on writing: "Reginald, I cannot, because all that I have written seems like straw to me compared to the things I saw revealed to me."[72] All that remained was his awe and reverence in face of the divine, and his hymns express this sentiment most directly. Drawing on Olivier-Thomas Venard's poetical-rhetorical reading of Aquinas's theological and metaphysical thought in *Thomas d'Aquin poète-théologien,* Milbank judges that even in his scholastic prose, Thomas's laconic style and concision "can serve to evoke mystery and a horizon of the unsaid."[73]

In the end, even hymns cannot express in words what nevertheless remains as the burden of what they somehow convey without actually saying it. There is, of course, an obvious tension, if not an outright contradiction, between apophasis and the verbal hymn. The one requires words, whereas the other requires forsaking and renouncing them. But for the Athenian Neoplatonists the highest hymn is in fact wordless, a pure contemplation and silent assimilation of the self to the One. It would take a Christian mentality to fully valorize the incarnation of philosophical wisdom in the language of the hymn.

Van den Berg underscores this difference between pagan and Christian authors:

> both Porphyry and Proclus stress that we should not celebrate (the highest) God by means of verbal hymns. To them, the idea that an absolutely transcendent God could be worshipped by sounds (i.e.

in a material way) is nothing less than utter blasphemy. Our hymn can only consist in becoming like god. For Synesius, on the contrary, not only silent, noeric, hymns but also verbal ones are appropriate forms of worship, as his hymns testify. (p. 32)

In Christian authors, such as Synesius of Cyrene, who became bishop of Ptolemais in A.D. 410, the kataphatic counterpart to apophatic negation can take on verbal and material form, as it does in the hymn. The Christian revaluation of the material creation as a gift of God is, accordingly, crucial in order to make physical sounds sung in hymns a worthy means of worship of a God who surpasses all material vehicles. Hymns were, of course, for Proclus a theurgical practice, a kind of spiritual technology for turning us back toward our first, unrepresentable Cause via the intermediate causes that can be symbolized. For pagan Neoplatonists, the hymns constitute a kataphatic theology that must necessarily accompany apophatic theology. Nevertheless, the ultimate hymn for them does not consist in words but in transformation of oneself into the likeness of God (*theosis*). As a practice performed through symbols representing spiritual and material elements by linguistic forms, the hymn is used in order to approach and unify with God. The lower gods, according to Porphyry, can be honored by hymns consisting in words (τὴν ἐκ τοῦ λόγου ὑμνῳδίαν), but Proclus makes clear in his *Chaldean Philosophy*, Fragment 2, that hymns to the Father (ὕμνος τοῦ Πατρός) can consist neither in words nor in rites, but only in becoming like him (τὴν εἰς αὐτόν ἐξομοίωσιν). As Van den Berg explains, "Proclus holds that reverting directly upon the highest God is of no use for the soul that tries to ascend. The soul should initially revert upon its proximate cause, not on its ultimate cause. Hence his hymns are directed to pagan deities that rank low in his hierarchy of the divine. It is precisely because of their low ontological status that they can be invoked by means of verbal hymns" (p. 32).

This makes for a stark contrast with Synesius's—and generally with Christian—uses of prayer, and consequently hymns, as means of direct approach to the supreme and only God. Whereas "Proclus' hymns are theurgical instruments," in the sense that Proclus "believes that the incorporation of (a small range of) inspired poems in his poetry will attract the gods he is addressing," Synesius "just seeks to honour God by composing hymns that are as beautiful as possible" (p. 33). Van den Berg thus distinguishes Synesius's from Proclus's philosophy on the grounds that "Synesius assigns to the Christian gospel the crucial role in the process of salvation that the later Neoplatonists accorded to theurgy. Proclus, on the contrary, follows Iamblichus in his valuation of theurgy as *the* way to salvation" (p. 32).

In light of this, it seems unlikely that the "Hymn to the Transcendence of God" would have been composed by Proclus or by any pagan Neoplatonist. From this standpoint, its attribution to the Christian theologian Gregory of Nazianzus, as noted in my citation of the hymn, is not wildly implausible after all. Pseudo-Dionysius has also been suspected of being the author. In any event, the hymn bears the marks not of a theurgical exercise but of a pure offering of praise to the highest divinity, indeed, to the only and absolutely ineffable God ("you alone are unutterable . . . you alone are unknowable . . . the only unnameable"). It thus bears most in common with the hymns of Synesius of Cyrene, who became a Catholic bishop for the last four years of his life. He never gave up the Porphyrian Neoplatonism that he had learned and adhered to in Alexandria, but he maintained a hybrid philosophy compounded of Christian and Neoplatonic elements, much as did Pseudo-Dionysius.[74] I know of no reason why the "Hymn to the Transcendence of God" might not be the lost work of this author, even though it is not included in the collection of his hymns.[75] It may have been preserved in some separate document from his death in A.D. 413 down to the time when it was attached to Gregory Nazianzus's corpus of writings. This hypothesis, in any case, is consistent with the way that apophatic metaphysics develop new possibilities of expression in relation to inexpressible divinity within the perspective of Christian, creationist monotheism. At all events, the (Neo)Platonic problematic of a necessary transcendence of language in the approach to this highest instance remains indispensable to the intelligibility of such a metaphysics. Elsewhere, in a famous passage, Synesius writes of those initiated into the Mysteries as undergoing an experience that has nothing to do with discourse (ἄλογος) and that transforms rather their state.[76]

In our own day again, within the cadre of Platonism encountering Christian theology, and particularly of the current identifying itself as Radical Orthodoxy, the hymn as a model for philosophical language in general has moved back into the forefront. The philosophical stakes of hymnic language as found in Neoplatonic and originally Platonic sources have been brought to focus in a provocative way by Catherine Pickstock in *After Writing: On the Liturgical Consummation of Philosophy*. Pickstock takes "doxology," or liturgical praise, and thus the hymn as perhaps its primary instantiation, to be the necessary foundation for language in general, at least to the degree that language is genuinely meaningful. Her overarching thesis is that "language exists primarily, and in the end only has meaning as, the praise of the divine." This bold thesis entails as an equally astonishing correlate that "liturgical language is the only language that really makes sense." As Pickstock writes in the opening statement of her argument:

> This essay completes and surpasses philosophy in the direction, not of nihilism, but of doxology. It shows how philosophy itself, in its Platonic guise, did not assume, as has been thought, a primacy of metaphysical presence, but rather, a primacy of liturgical theory and practice. This same primacy, it claims, was developed, and more consistently realized, in medieval Christendom.[77]

By bringing the fundamentally doxological character of language in Neoplatonic and Platonic sources into confrontation with contemporary, especially poststructuralist theories of language, particularly those of Derrida and Foucault, Pickstock, in effect, proposes a rewriting of the history of philosophy from the standpoint of the liturgical, doxological word that she claims is the fundamental condition of possibility of the meaningfulness of all human language.[78]

There are significant parallels, but there would presumably be serious tensions as well, between the positive affirmations of theological orthodoxy and the negations of apophatic philosophy that I have found, for example, in Nancy. Nancy thinks of all language as opening in address to the inconceivably Other, or as "adoration." Structurally, this is not necessarily different from all language's being thought of as spoken in praise of God. It is the choice of traditions and allegiances that determines the divergent tonalities and purport of one or the other pronouncement. I wish to show the homologies in underlying logic and to leave personal choice of religious identity—whether with the Dionysius of Christian tra-

dition or the Dionysios of Nietzsche—to personal preference and responsibility. Decisive in either case is the apophatic moment, in which the
logical pretensions of discourse are abandoned or are at any rate relativ-
ized, so as to give precedence to the more fundamental vocation of discourse to recognizing an Other that it cannot as such characterize or grasp
but must move toward in a gesture of self-abandon and self-opening. This
self-transformation is true praise, not just lip service, and it embodies
"adoration" in the full sense of the word that Nancy seeks to restore.

Certainly, apophasis exposes liturgical language to its underpinnings
in indeterminacy, and such language might, as a consequence, no longer
be an adequate basis for the claims of orthodox theology, if these are understood dogmatically and not poetically, that is, if the one interpretation
is taken to exclude the other. However, Pickstock, too, is centrally interested in the way that liturgical language (like the hymn, which I am taking
to be its epitome) is actually an *un*saying of language, at least of language
as it is known within a rationalist, secularist epistemological framework.
She argues in particular that the medieval Latin Rite must be revived in
order "to overthrow our anti-ritual modernity" and its secularized theory
of language, which culminates in Derrida's absolutization of writing.
She celebrates a certain "apophatic liturgical 'stammer' and oral spontaneity and 'confusion'" as inherent in this rite and as in need of being
recovered (p. 176). The Vatican II reformers "ironed-out the liturgical
stammer and constant re-beginning; they simplified the narrative and ge-
neric strategy of the liturgy in conformity with recognisably secular structures, and rendered simple, constant and self-present the identity of the
worshipper" (p. 176).

Pickstock's outline for a more radical reform of the liturgy turns away
from criteria of rational simplicity of argument and from adherence to
a presumably literal, extralinguistic, nonsemiotic reality, that of the supposedly primitive rite of the Eucharistic meal, which is present in the
background of the Mass as an original event of an everyday nature. She
valorizes rather the estrangements (or "defamiliarization") of the medieval
rite (prior to its more artificial baroque excesses) as embodying genuine
arrivals of a holy otherness, the arrival of the transcendent in the immanent, an actual occurrence of the impossible in the plenitude of Christic
mediation.

> Indeed, unlike the view of reality implicit within immanentist lan-
> guage and the power of its textual permanence, the recommence-
> ments and stammer of the liturgical text are supremely but ineffably
> 'ordered' through genuine mystery and transcendent 'distance,' and
> are by no means devoid of cohesion, purpose, or genuine surprise.
> In contrast to the purified asyndetic 'advance' of secular discourse
> structure and its claim to apprehend the 'real' without encum-
> brance, the liturgical stammer bespeaks its admission of distance
> between itself and the transcendent 'real.' It is this very admission
> of distance which permits a genuine proximity with God. (*After
> Writing*, p. 178)

This stress on distance from the transcendent as the condition of its
proximity sounds, somewhat surprisingly, Derridean. Derrida, too, in his
studies of apophatic philosophical thought, has recognized the essential
moment of prayer and apostrophe, as well as of the hymn, emphasizing its
role especially in Pseudo-Dionysius the Areopagite's mystical theology.[79]
However, even though Derrida pays careful attention to the hymnic framing of the apophatic theology of Dionysius, he does not acknowledge the
full implications of this hymnic character of metaphysical utterances. He
still, in practice and in theory, interprets apophatic thought as containing
propositions claiming objective cognition, even hyper-onto-theological
knowledge of a supra-being, and therefore as vulnerable to and in need of
deconstruction. This has become the chink in his armor through which he
has been attacked by Pickstock, who wishes to make the doxological character of philosophical language and of all language foundational for its
very possibility of meaningfulness.

Pickstock argues against Derrida that Platonic philosophy, starting
from its supreme principle, the Good, is based not on metaphysical presence but on a liturgical word that interrupts presence by opening it toward
the transcendent:

> But the good is precisely "beyond" the distinction of presence and
> absence. Its transcendence does not signify emptiness, nor that Der-
> ridean postponement which reduces absence to objectivity, since the

sun which shines light onto being is present in the gifts of insight, truth, and beauty. The fact that it cannot be grasped by a *mathema* and is unsayable does not identify it with absence. Rather, its mode of 'presence' is articulated through the gifts which it bestows, the beyond-being which, as difference, gives things to be, and which (in Derridean terminology) *disseminates.* This contrasts with the *différance* of Derrida, which is assimilated in turn to his notion of writing. And it contrasts also with a perpetual postponement of an impossible giving and a radical disjunction of giver and gift. (*After Writing*, p. 12)

Against Derrida's reading of Platonic metaphysics as the exclusion of otherness ("health and virtue . . . always proceed from within"), Pickstock points out that Plato stresses the infusion of the transcendent in beings as an exteriority penetrating into immanence, into the sphere of interior knowing and reflection. Metaphysics thus turns out to be a powerful way of relating to transcendence. This is the metaphysics that is realized in the liturgical act of praise. The transcendent makes itself present in and through its gifts, eminently in the language of the hymn, exemplarily in our "Hymn to the Transcendence of God." The sacrifice of the self and of all its words, furthermore, as in apophatic discourse, is integral to the gesture of offering oneself up in hymns of praise.

This is a powerful critique; it points up a serious limitation of Derrida's reading of Plato. Derrida tends to identify the Good—or presence or God—with pure presence. And pure presence turns out always to be necessarily absent. But the effectively present supreme good, or divinity, is neither present nor absent in a strict sense; it cannot be identified with anything finite—except perhaps, incomprehensibly, in the Incarnation—for it is not humanly identifiable at all, but rather repulses all such identities. Similarly, the liturgical word is pried open to its apophatic underpinnings because it faces the incomprehensible divinity before which it can only stammer. Yet Pickstock develops modes of mediation in the deployment of Christic creedal discourse and refuses the resort to "asyndeton," the omission or removal of connecting syntax, in modern revisions of the Anglican liturgy.[80]

Derrida, in contrast, emphasizes such breaks and ruptures in every kind of discourse as pointing to something heterogeneous and unassimilable. But Derrida also argues that no hymn or prayer is actually free of predication concerning the God it praises. He distinguishes the moments of apostrophe and encomium in the prayer (or hymn), but suggests that in the end they cannot be separated. Prayer is never completely pure apostrophe; it always also presupposes some conception or description of the divinity it praises and so is to a degree idolatrous. Simultaneous with its first moment of pure apostrophe to the indescribable Other, prayer inevitably slips into a language of predication, assigning some attributes to the One that it praises. For Derrida, prayer "preserves an irreducible relationship to the attribution" ("Comment ne pas parler," p. 572).

Derrida may not be right about this, since attributes can be negated or suspended at the same time as they are assigned or evoked. The "Hymn to the Transcendence of God" does this, for example, in praising "the one, the all, the nothing / being not one, not all." It is not what the hymn *says* that finally counts, but what it does not and cannot say. The spiritual movement of opening in adoration toward an Other that cannot be comprehended yet must be praised is a kind of existential act, not a cognitive content, and this makes it a link to a transcendence that cannot be said. Like the Derridean trace, then, the hymn would have a referential structure, yet no referential content. Referring to what never was nor ever could be purely present, it is nevertheless an effecting of presence, a tracing or arrival of transcendence within immanence. Radical Orthodoxy and deconstruction actually agree on this point.

At this apophatic point of "that which cannot be said," the effect of presence is perhaps indiscernibly theological and atheological, indiscernibly a manifestation of divinity or an intimation of nothing—nothing that can be said or comprehended. This, at any rate, is the point I have wanted to bring into the open by returning to the Neoplatonic matrices of apophatic thinking and in particular to its hymnic realizations. This orientation to the hymn has been taken in contemporary philosophy in opposite directions—as either compromising philosophical rigor vis-à-vis ineluctable nothingness or as manifesting and materializing the positive gift of divine revelation. My purpose is to recommend adherence to the apophatic insight that is neither the one nor the other but rather opens up both of these perspectives.

Taken negatively, for what it lacks, godlessness might be a state potentially as open and revealing of the religious as singing the liturgy and reciting orthodox symbols of faith. It would seem that Derrida best manifests this in his "prayers and tears," increasingly in his later works.[81] Pickstock's critique of Derrida and the secular city and its nihilism and death fetish is based on his early work, particularly on "La pharmacie de Platon,"[82] and takes little account of what Derrida was doing in the 1980s and '90s, in texts which provided the fulcrum for the turn of philosophy to religion that can be traced in elaborate detail across the numerous writings of this period.[83] Especially pivotal Derridean works for this purpose, in addition to "Comment ne pas parler," are "D'un ton apocalyptique adopté naguère en philosophie" (1981), "Donner la mort" (1992), *Sauf le nom* (1993), and "Foi et savoir" (1996), which finds an appeal to faith ("appel à la foi") in every act of language and every address to an other ("toute acte de langage et toute addresse à un autre").[84] These texts leave the question of religion undecided. Radical Orthodoxy affirms religion on the basis of the breakdown of secular reason, taken to be the enemy of religion. The convergence of these ideological opponents, each with their radical challenges, on the apophatic elements as subtly subversive currents within the metaphysical tradition, is provocative.

The rewriting of the history of Western philosophy proposed in my work from the point of view of the apophatic, of what logical language cannot say, is the ineffaceable margin where even radical orthodoxy and radical deconstruction cannot exclude each other but find themselves contaminated by one another. Both of these antagonists demonstrate indirectly the renewed viability of metaphysics in the Neoplatonic tradition, once we learn to take its affirmations apophatically, which entails giving priority to their poetic and religious registers, as in the hymn. Of course, the hymn is not an isolated example. Apophatic stammering is not confined to liturgical language but is crucial across the full range of revelatory, religious, or "prophetic" modes of language.[85] These modes may be understood to comprise even contemporary poetic language (as my third essay has illustrated). Venard interprets the medieval, specifically Thomist sense of language grounded in an ineffable metaphysical Absolute as parallel to modern French poetry since Rimbaud and Mallarmé, in its quest for an immediate relation with the Absolute, for an ecstatic experience of "L'Éternité." The cult of mystery in literature (as in Mallarmé's "Le mystère dans les letters") endeavors to renew the lost verbal magic or "al-chemy" of an omnipotent creative Word.

In my final essay I will continue to play postsecular religious revivalist philosophy, particularly Radical Orthodoxy, off against its apparent antagonist in postmodern secular theology, even in its atheistic or a/theist forms, as a way of bringing out their common basis in critical, apophatic insight into the generative source of reality, culture, and language and as calling to openness to the "radically Other." Even this designation, however, must be withdrawn for that which, like God, cannot finally be determined even as "Other" but is already in everything everywhere—in our thoughts before we think them—and in this very utterance.

APOPHATIC THOUGHT AS THE MISSING MEAN BETWEEN RADICALLY SECULAR AND RADICALLY ORTHODOX THEOLOGY

Glücklich, die wissen, daß hinter allen
Sprachen das Unsägliche steht.
(Happy they who know that behind all
languages lies the unsayable.)
　　　　　　　　—Rainer Maria Rilke

i

One of the important gains for the perspective of negative or apophatic theology that I have developed up to this point is its potential for enabling uncircumscribed dialogue among religious faiths and, perhaps even more importantly, between religious faith and secular culture. In order to demonstrate this potential, it will be instructive to pay close attention to what are apparently deeply opposed approaches to contemporary thinking in

271

philosophical theology and the philosophy of religion. Postmodern approaches to religion are, of course, myriad, and I am going to mention only a small selection of them. However, the issues raised are representative and are played out along similar lines across the whole range of philosophies and cultures in our postmodern world fractured by competing, sometimes warring religions and their perennial sworn opponents. I argue that a contemporary philosophy of the unsayable, extending the traditional insights of negative theology, can serve to break down and disarm these antagonisms, which reflect and foment potentially violent and destructive conflicts in society today.[1]

On the one hand, we find secularized approaches to theology stemming from the Death of God movement of the 1960s, particularly as pursued by North American religious thinkers such as Thomas J. J. Altizer, Mark C. Taylor, Carl Raschke, Charles Winquist, John Caputo, and others, including more recently Clayton Crockett, who stress that the possibilities for theological discourse are fundamentally altered by the unprecedented conditions of our contemporary world. Our world today, in their view, is constituted wholly on a plane of immanence, without need of reference to "God" as a transcendent reality, to such an extent that traditional appeals to faith in an omnipotent, wholly other divinity or in an other world and afterlife become difficult to take as more than willful self-deception and deliberate blindness to our actual human condition. This American trend has certain affinities in its secularizing emphases with European philosophers such as Slavoj Žižek, Alain Badiou, and Giorgio Agamben, who also think essentially out of the death of God that was announced by Nietzsche. This announcement had been anticipated by Hegel and was followed up in influential ways by Heidegger, with his program of a deconstruction of metaphysics or, more precisely, his taking up the task of a "destruction of the history of ontology" ("die Aufgabe einer Destruktion der Geschichte der Ontologie") declared in paragraph 6 of *Sein und Zeit* (*Being and Time*).

On the other hand, we hear the proclamation of a new lease on life for theology based on its traditional affirmation of divine transcendence over against the putative arrogance of all assertions of human autonomy. This proclamation is advanced provocatively by theologians leagued under the banner of the so-called Radical Orthodoxy, discussed at length in the last essay. Emanating from England, originally from the University of Cambridge in the 1980s and '90s, this movement includes in its core such theological thinkers as John Milbank, Graham Ward, Catherine Pickstock, Rowan Williams, and Phillip Blond. These theologians have linked their approach with that of the predominantly French *nouvelle théologie,* beginning with Henri de Lubac, Jean Daniélou, and Hans Urs von Balthasar in the mid-twentieth century and followed up by Catholic theologians such as Jean-Yves Lacoste, Louis-Marie Chauvet, and Olivier-Thomas Venard today. Both the Anglo-Saxon and the Continental versions of this outlook stress that theology, as embedded in traditional Christian belief, is not only crucial for interpreting the past but also continues to offer a privileged and uniquely penetrating discourse on the true nature of reality even in the postmodern world. These theologians hold that it is necessary to start from theological revelation as expressed in the Christian vision and its narrative in order to understand the world—and not the other way around, as is the common conviction of secular theologians. Starting from the world in its actuality—*this* world as it reveals itself in human life and society, without externally imposed metaphysical and a fortiori theological constructions—is the bottom line for secular theology. Radical Orthodoxy counters this by rejoining that we are always already within some narrative in encountering the world and that the Christian narrative is preferable to alternative narratives—even just in its account of this world, let alone of the next or of any others.

Programmatic publications from each of these two camps have included shrill accusations against the other. Curiously, both tend to reject negative theology, although I intend to show that an underlying apophatic turn of thought is precisely what they share in common. My contention is that both of these postmodern philosophical theologies, at least until quite recently, have been living somewhat in denial of their intimate proximity to the apophatic tradition to which they are in fact deeply and inextricably indebted, albeit in different ways. They have been suspicious and even fearful of it for reasons that I wish to elucidate and dispel. It is not that they are unaware of negative theology and of its nearness to their own positions, but they are not exploiting it as much as they could and perhaps should. Neither approach acknowledges that its own essential insights are ones that have been engendered and nurtured to maturity in the matrices of this tradition over millennia. By exposing certain misprisions of negative theology practiced by each of these camps, I endeavor to reveal apophatic thought as the missing mean between them. I claim that the common root—indeed the radicality—of both radical secular theology and Radical Orthodoxy is a not fully acknowledged apophaticism.

I further contend that the implicit apophatic underpinnings of both approaches are also what make each of them vital avenues of theological reflection in postmodern times. In taking this position, I align myself with what might be discerned as another strain of postmodern religious thinkers—one including Hent de Vries, Gregor Hoff, Kevin Hart, Thomas Carlson, and Elliot Wolfson—who think deliberately and explicitly out of the various historical reservoirs of negative theology. Remarkable work in this vein is also being done by feminist theologians such as Catherine Keller and Elizabeth Johnson. Other religiously inclined philosophers, including Gianni Vattimo, René Girard, and Richard Kearney, can be aligned with aspects of either the secularizing or the theologizing approaches to religion, but all are fundamentally inspired, I maintain, by apophatic insights.

My aim, then, is to situate apophatic thought as key to some of the most challenging developments and disputes in the philosophy of religion today. Such a positioning is meant to mediate and unblock the deadlock between secularizing approaches, on the one hand, and theologizing approaches, on the other. Apophasis (the classical Greek word for "negation" and the generating source of negative theology) is the missing link that would enable both of these strands of thought to be woven together around what offers itself as their common—even if mostly covert—heritage. They share in common a radical insight into the structural negativity of human experience—and of all its expressions in language—as turned toward and dependent on an Other, on something that or someone who the human mind cannot comprehend or say. Apophasis, furthermore, lies at the source of their common concern with elucidating how religion is vitally relevant to our self-understanding in a postmodern age. Religion is always deeply concerned with what cannot be adequately stated, and any discourse that attempts to speak for it or out of its concerns cannot but falter, unless it acknowledges and embraces a dimension of unsayability at its core. Indeed, such faltering itself demands to be read as an at least inadvertent manifestation of the apophatic.

Of these two apparently conflicting currents within contemporary philosophy of religion, the one has often articulated a wish to terminate talk of theological "transcendence," while the other rails against the modern "immanentist" reduction of religion. An informed acknowledgment of the mutual implication of transcendence and immanence, as well as of affirmation and negation, an interweaving which is thought most originally and intensely in the theological tradition of apophasis, is the perspective that can best accommodate and valorize the strengths of each of these approaches, without excluding those of the other. Both currents finally agree in the recognition of insuperable limits to any human knowledge of the truly or ultimately real, and both appeal, consequently, to theological symbols and concepts and structures or patterns of thought. This is the common focus from which they emanate their respective insights. Such insight is always subtly powered by what it cannot quite say and is illuminated from beyond what it can grasp or comprehend: and specifically the apophatic tradition has insisted on just this predicament of human knowledge as beholden to *un*knowing, especially concerning things ultimate or "divine."

My purpose is not to appropriate and assimilate these two different directions or currents of thought about religion, but to facilitate flow and cross-pollenization of ideas between them, in the interests of making apophasis emerge more clearly as the perennially dynamic, revolutionary, revelatory, and perhaps even miraculous factor in radically theological thinking of very different stripes. Indeed, negative or apophatic theology is at once the most traditional and the most radical of theologies: it spans and unifies these mutually opposed orientations. It is there in the earliest emergences of theological reflection, whether in Hesiod and Parmenides or in Moses and the prophets; it is coded into the secret, silent rites of paganism (signally in Eleusinian pantomime) and into the mysteries of monotheism alike. It also represents the perennial vanguard of religious thinking that periodically undermines all settled doctrines by returning to the Unknown from which they have been spawned.

Certain manifesto-like collections of essays have helped to define the debate as a facing off against each other of modern and postmodern *secular* theology, on the one hand, and *postsecular* theology and philosophy, on the other. The latter, in some regards, has appeared as *anti*-modern in repudiating the mainstream, secular, modern Enlightenment that follows

Kant. In introducing his edited volume *Secular Theology*, Clayton Crockett recognizes the intellectual sophistication of some of the proponents of Radical Orthodoxy, but he accuses them of being conservative and closed to the modern—and especially the contemporary—world:

> the conclusions of Radical Orthodoxy can appear very simplistic and one-sided . . . the wholesale rejection of modernity, secularity and philosophy in favor of what sometimes appears to be an idealistic and romantic notion of Catholic Christendom can be frustrating to thinkers and theologians with a much more complicated understanding of modernity and/or postmodernity. These conclusions can appear incredibly simplistic: modernity is bad, postmodernists deconstruct modernity but end up in nihilism because they accept the basic presuppositions of modernity; the only way out is a leap (*salto mortale*, death leap) back to a place anterior to modernity and all of its discontents.[2]

Secular theology is then portrayed as a far preferable alternative, as a way of responding to the challenges of the modern and contemporary worlds "on a much deeper and ultimately more fruitful level." For secular theology, in contrast,

> allows a much riskier and transformative discourse to take shape, one which is not simply concerned to argue point by point with Radical Orthodoxy, but which constructively imagines alternative appropriations of Continental philosophy and constitutes more complex, nuanced and ambivalent understandings of secularity, modernity and postmodernity. (*Secular Theology*, p. 4)

On the other side, exactly the same claim, but reversed, as in a mirror image, is made by representatives of Radical Orthodoxy. *Their* more complex and differentiated understanding of theological tradition enables them to avoid the sweeping generalizations that have characterized the wholesale rejection of theological transcendence as metaphysics by contemporary secularist thought, a rejection that leads inevitably to nihilism, since it (purportedly) undermines the basis of any affirmation of the real.

Graham Ward praises "theological realists" for taking the more "difficult path" rather than falling into step with the "aesthetics of nihilism." He champions anti-secular thinkers who are on a relentless quest for "another city, a kingdom of God, founded in diremption."[3]

In this vein, proponents of Radical Orthodoxy have come out with several important collections of essays taking stances against secularism in theology and in culture generally. The movement-making volume *Radical Orthodoxy: A New Theology* begins with its complaint against "the dismal promenade" of postmodern ontological nihilism. Secularist thinking in the wake of Foucault, Derrida, Deleuze, and the like—prime instigators for secular (a)theological perspectives—is painted with a broad brush as responsible for the supposed decadence of postmodern culture. More specifically, in the introduction to their flagship collection of essays, John Milbank, Catherine Pickstock, and Graham Ward denounce postmodern secularism's "lack of values and lack of meaning. In its cyberspaces and theme-parks it promotes a materialism which is soulless, aggressive, nonchalant and nihilistic."[4] Remonstrating against secularism and its evils as so many expressions of nihilism, these authors describe their project in a way that initially distances it from negative theology: at least as this type of theology is commonly construed, it seems to be conflated with the pervasive trends of a nihilistic secularism.

> [N]or does it [the project of radical orthodoxy] indulge, like so many, in the pretense of a baptism of nihilism in the name of a misconstrued 'negative theology'. Instead, in the face of the secular demise of truth, it seeks to reconfigure theological truth. The latter may indeed hover close to nihilism, since it, also, refuses a reduction of the indeterminate. Yet what finally distances it from nihilism is its proposal of the rational possibility, and the faithfully perceived actuality, of an indeterminacy that is not impersonal chaos but infinite interpersonal harmonious order, in which time participates. (*Radical Orthodoxy*, p. 1)

The positive terms offered here are all anchored to an "indeterminacy." This indeterminacy is how divinity can be apprehended, at least by us, who can only participate in its mysteriously harmonious ordering of things through time, not *sub specie aeternitatis*. This idea of indeterminacy as a paradoxically anarchic harmony, a living order of persons rather than of abstract principles, exemplifies the substantive imbrication of the negative upon the positive, and vice versa, in a manner that exactly mirrors the mutual co-implication at a methodological level between apophatic and kataphatic theologies ever since Pseudo-Dionysius the Areopagite defined them in this reciprocal way. The indispensable interdependence and cooperation of the negative and the positive methods of theology were patent already in his immediate precursor, Proclus.[5]

Radical Orthodoxy profiles itself as unequivocally affirmative of theology. It is openly defiant of secular modernity's strictures against confidently professing one's religion, and it claims that the suppression of a religious perspective condemns modern culture to emptiness and valuelessness. It is thus understandably reluctant to present theology—much less human thinking generally—as fundamentally and ineluctably negative in nature. Negative theology is taken to be a misconceived paradigm of the secular culture that is directly under attack, and as such it is censured as complicit with the very worst perversions that plague and corrupt contemporary culture.

Nevertheless, Radical Orthodoxy cannot quite completely ignore its own deep indebtedness to negative theology, even while spurning the current forms of it as "nihilism."[6] There is actually an extensive and fundamental use of apophatic or negative theology by Radical Orthodoxy, which has been explored in the previous essay, in spite of a certain official position that tends to shun or at least to circumscribe it. We may grant that negative theology *would* become nihilism if it took itself or simply negation or emptiness to be a transcendental hermeneutic that provided the "mathesis" or general framework for all knowledge. In that case, the human mind would have constructed a world around its own conceptions, taking "nothing" as the ultimate principle of the reality that it knows. This is indeed what Derrida and company are accused of doing: "The void itself as a static given assumed by knowledge is the *mathesis* par excellence" (*Radical Orthodoxy,* p. 3). But that is exactly what Derrida is determined to avoid: following Levinas, he constantly warns against all appropriation of the Other to the measure of the Same and the known. Moreover, precisely this avoidance is what he profoundly shares with negative theology. The critical thrust of negative theology, which challenges by its rigorous critique all idols, including the conceptual idols that substitute themselves for the unthinkable God, lies at the very heart of Derrida's deconstructive enterprise.[7] And in this regard, negative theology must be recognized as the best antidote to nihilism.[8]

The remonstrances against deconstruction as purely negative and nihilistic are surely a misconstrual of deconstruction and indeed of negative theology.[9] They miss the point, which admittedly became clearer as Derrida's thought evolved, that deconstruction is not an attempt to master the world by some transcendental principle, but instead aims precisely to give up that fantasy. We noted already in the last essay the turn toward overtly religious thematics in Derrida's later thought.[10] These pivotal Derridean texts raise explicitly the issue of whether Derrida's thought reproduces the conceptual moves and rhetorical strategies of negative theology. Although he still denies or resists any such identification, paradoxically, Derrida's denials can be read as a manner of saying and doing exactly what he denies he is saying and doing.[11] To this extent, they realize what I call a negative theology, inasmuch as they evoke but then back off from an unlimited field of significance beyond what they can conceive by negating their own comprehension of it. As Derrida himself suggests, his continual postponement of a full explication of deconstruction's crucial and undelimitable relation with negative theology may itself be considered a sort of performance of negative theology—once it is admitted that any rigid definition of the latter is impossible (*Psyché*, p. 546).

It was Derrida's contemplation of the negative theology of Meister Eckhart and Silesius Angelus that led him to salute the "democracy to come" and to avow that it would not be possible without what he calls negative theology. Derrida's envisaging, in *Save the Name*, of a "démocratie à venir" along negative theological lines has, in some respects, a distant ancestor also in Nicholas Cusanus's negative theological prescription for harmonizing world religions by emptying them of inevitably conflicting positive claims concerning a transcendent deity that by its nature escaped being known properly by any religion.[12] In aiming more at unblocking passages between different religions or ideologies than at harmonizing them, deconstruction, like negative theology, is not a platform or stance so much as a capability of always backing off from all positive forms of assertion, in order to create space for what is always left out of account by them and is infinitely other than all that they can grasp. Why, then, does deconstruction—and with it secular theology—not embrace negative theology as at least a pertinent genealogical lineage for its own type of vision and insight?

Derrida's long-promised disquisition on the question of deconstruction and negative theology, his address "Comment ne pas parler: dénégations" ("Denials: How Not to Speak"), in which he would presumably justify his denial of this lineage, draws attention to its highly symbolic venue, its taking place in Jerusalem, at the point of confluence of the three major monotheistic religions that, especially on their mystical fringes, have all contributed mightily to developing negative theologies. This address, which marks an important point of departure for current secular theologies, thereby places itself in the midst of traditions that have been bound up with theology and with its constitutive apophatic negations and reversals all along. Derrida's discourse has lent itself to theological appropriations by secularists and anti-secularists alike. Various sorts of orthodox theologians, too, have found penetrating and liberating insights in Derrida's work.[13] Both orthodox and heterodox or secular currents are indebted from their birth to negative theology; indeed, both emerged historically from their cradles in the apophatic cultures of monotheism.

And yet both these contemporary theological tendencies continue to hold in suspicion and to shun at least what they generally understand under the rubric of negative theology. I detect here a hint that negative or apophatic theology may hold the key to what really gives rise to thought, especially theological thought and especially when it is radical. The unmasterable origin of thought must be avoided in the interest of sustaining a discourse of a predictable and coherent or at least assessable type, like that required for the functioning of public institutions such as the church and the academy. And yet secular and orthodox theology alike, following Derrida's lead, remain aloof from the negative theology that is nevertheless at work in the midst—and in the middest—of each.

In the lead essay of the volume *Secular Theology,* in outlining the prospects for a "postmodern secular theology," Charles E. Winquist cannot help but highlight the crucial role of negation in identifying a radical otherness within language that distorts it:

Postmodern theologies work against the totalization of thinking also by attending to extreme formulations, even in traditional theologies, that convolute the discourse of any symbolic order instantiating a radical negativity that marks an "other" within and of language. That is, postmodern theological analyses seek incommensurabilities within discursive practices that are internal traces of the "other" in the subjective fold of discourse. (p. 29)

Moreover, Winquist gives a perfect description of apophatic discourse and its rhetoric of "fissures, gaps, paradoxes and incongruities" (p. 29). Yet even with this acknowledgment of the affinities and proximities, he turns away from embracing this tradition:

These aporetic formulations facilitate a negative theology that could possibly be a clearing for apophatic disclosure or could simply be a negation of meaning within a discursive practice. It is not always clear what is valued by deconstructive theologies about an *aporia,* an impassable passage. Is it that it is a passage, or that it is impassable? Negative theologies emphasize impassability but there are other strategies that emphasize passage even when they articulate themselves in figurations of rupture, fissure or gap. (p. 29)

The common tendency to divorce negative theology from the positive discourse with which it, in fact, always necessarily works in tandem operates here to effectuate what is, admittedly, a relatively gentle dismissal of negative theology, at least as an appropriate label. Only if apophatic theology is severed from its kataphatic counterpart and complement, which is not really possible in theological practice, is it liable to the objections that Winquist advances. In substance, Winquist is accepting and affirming what negative theology has always done and continues to do, but he does not wish to make common cause with it or to align his thinking with this current. He does not wish to see the enterprise of postmodern theology, which he advocates, as a continuation of this tradition. Although this posture of his comforts a certain demand for originality and newness in one's theories and theologies in the public arena today, I think there is more to be gained by seeing Winquist's type of theology in its naturally close association with and descent from traditional theologies of "unsayability"—to give it a more postmodern-sounding name, one closer to the terms of theology since the linguistic turn.

Repeating Derrida's distancing maneuvers, radical secular theological thinkers such as John Caputo and Clayton Crockett frequently warn against confusing or conflating their position with any form of negative theology or apophatic mysticism, which seems to them to pull in the opposite direction from radical, especially politically radical, theology. There is typically a will to deny any connection with this tradition and its archive, since it seems to fold thought back into a past that they prefer to treat as superseded rather than as opening to new and unknown horizons. I maintain, however, that this stance is a misprision of the tradition that has continued to propose precisely radical openness to the unknown. This includes specifically the openness to the future in its apocalyptic "impossibility" that such thinkers themselves wish to celebrate as if it were a new discovery. In fact, the event of the apophatic is always "new" because it is always unique and without compare.

In Caputo's discourse, negative theologians are liable to come in for witty dismissals and withering irony: "the negative theologians would present a long, verbose, and particularly perplexing discourse on behalf of silence."[14] Caputo rejects negative theology because he views it as complicit with the project of metaphysics. He presents negative theology as attempting to salvage the "strong God" of metaphysics: "But in a 'strong' theology—which is pretty much what 'theology' *tout court* always is or wants to be, including negative theology—God is the highest being in the order of presence (overseeing and ensuring the presence of order), who presides over the order of being and manifestation" (pp. 8–9).[15] Yet for any valid negative theology, all these affirmations and any strong assertions whatsoever must equally be denied and withdrawn. In presenting it this way, Caputo ignores Derrida's reminders that negative theology cannot positively *be* anything, that it does not "exist," and that there can be only a negative theology of negative theology (*Psyché*, p. 546).

Caputo sees negative theology as integral to the overall project of onto-theology, but this is not representative of the real inspiration of this most ductile of currents of thought. Negative theology *can* appear in a metaphysical guise, but only when metaphysics has been transformed from a dogmatics to a poetics, from a dogmatic system of doctrine claiming to describe how things really are—which apophatics renounces—to a metaphysical poetic expression in a language that undercuts itself as realist description and rather endeavors to open into a transformative event in which the unsayable and unthinkable can become astonishingly manifest.

Negative theology's deep affinities and genealogy are more kenotic than metaphysical. Omnipotence in this perspective cannot mean exerting superior power as one force among others in a field of opposing forces, although many images, even ones drawn from the Bible, for example, the Lord's outstretched arm smiting the Egyptians, naively interpreted, seem to suggest such a picture. Through denying all positive power and even every attribute to God, apophatic thought has led throughout theological tradition—and still in the present, for instance, in René Girard's readings of Jesus and Job[16]—to the insight that God's power can be apprehended and experienced by us only as a weak force (to adopt Caputo's own terms), one that lays a claim on us—without enforcement—in the name of God or of justice.

Caputo makes a brilliant contribution to thinking of God in terms not of prevailing force but of the weakness and the impotence of the call to justice that has no power whatever to impose itself—and thereby calls *us* the more urgently and irrecusably. This is indeed *exemplary* of thinking God through negations in the tradition of negative theology. Caputo's theology is highly traditional, even though Caputo thinks it in an original manner out of his own context in contemporary Continental philosophy. At the same time, he also harkens to Scripture and its radical, revolutionary annunciations of the Kingdom of God, which are central to the inspiration of Christian negative theologians such as Meister Eckhart, whom Caputo often echoes. Caputo's thought of weak divinity is not as incompatible even with radically orthodox theology as he seems to think, once the negative theological basis of the latter and of his own thinking alike has been brought into the open.

Caputo would have to agree that nothing can be positively and unequivocally affirmed of God, unless, of course, he wants to insist on affirming that God does *not* exist. But would he want to confidently *affirm* what it is to exist? Or would that not be another way of claiming to know the true and real, and thus an affirmation of what one, for all practical purposes, takes to be God after all? Everything Caputo writes shows that he is very far from any such self-deluded pretensions: he is, above all, an adept master at the deconstruction of all such claims to really know what's what, whether in the order of the cognitive, the metaphysical, or the ethical.[17] Caputo persistently expresses himself in exemplarily apophatic terms: "I cannot discern the event that concerns me ultimately, and that failure is my success, my most vital sign, my passion, the passion of my non-knowing (*passion du non savoir*), my prayer" (*Weakness of God*, pp. 294–95).

Caputo's pungent and original formulas are consistently of an apophatic turn: they are paradoxically puissant coinages of negative theological thinking. In this, they resemble Derrida's "religion without religion," modeled on the language of Meister Eckhart. In "Quasi stella matutina," Eckhart adapts such expressions from Augustine, whom he quotes to the effect that "God is wise without wisdom, good without goodness, powerful without power" ("Sankt Augustinus sagt: Gott ist weise ohne Weisheit, gut ohne Gutheit, gewaltig ohne Gewalt").[18] Caputo, frequently harping on Derrida's *sans* (without), is full of similar formulations and variants, such as "Religious truth is a truth without Knowledge."[19] Caputo also uses the characteristically apophatic language of "hyper-realism" (for example, in *Weakness of God*, p. 123), reminiscent of the "beyond being" and "beyond all things (*res*)" of Dionysius, to suggest that what "God" names calls us beyond ourselves and our world and all that is given therein toward what is impossible on any present terms, toward what is other to all that we can imagine. We open to this beyond by negating whatever *is* possible for us to imagine and conceive. Interpreting Derridean undecidability along the negative-theological lines of Dionysius's mystical theology of the dark night of the soul (traceable forward to John of the Cross and well beyond, for example, to Geoffrey Hill in *Tenebrae*), Caputo writes: "Undecidability is the place in which faith takes place, the night in which faith is conceived, for night is its element" (*On Religion*, p. 128).

And yet Caputo is unwilling to associate his radically negative rethinking of theology with theology of any traditional sort but prefers instead to style it a "theology of the event," for which he finds precedents or premises in Continental philosophers such as Heidegger and Derrida and in radical feminist theologians such as Catherine Keller. Nevertheless, his points read perfectly well as astute and creative inflections of the insights that have guided apophatic tradition all along. The philosophical and specifically phenomenological tradition from which Caputo hails is itself steeped in theological debts. It generally reverses or negates theological doctrines—exactly as negative theology itself has always done.[20]

The similarity of negative theology to atheism has often been remarked: negative theology denies all concepts of God, that is, it insists on their inadequacy, since any authentic God is always beyond what they can grasp. The aim is rather to leave an open space for what one calls "God" or "freedom" or "justice," or whatever one calls whatever it is in which one most deeply and unconditionally believes. Gilles Deleuze lucidly recognizes that theology as such leaves completely open the question of *what* one believes, although he conflates this with the question of belief *tout court*. He presents theology as a kind of pantomime of reasoning, in which nothing is actually affirmed but rather thought structures are laid out and left in suspense:

> [N]otre époque découvre la théologie. On n'a plus du tout besoin de croire en Dieu. Nous cherchons plutôt la 'structure', c'est-à-dire la forme qui peut être remplie par les croyances, mais qui n'a nullement besoin de l'être pour être dite théologique. La théologie est maintenant la science des entités non existantes, la manière dont ces entités divines ou anti-divines, Christ ou antéchrist, animent le langage, et lui forment ce corps glorieux qui se divise en disjonctions.[21]

> [O]ur age is discovering theology. There is no longer any need to believe in God. We seek rather the structure, that is, the form which can fill our beliefs, but which has no need of being in order to be dubbed theological. Theology is now the science of nonexistent entities, the manner in which divine entities or anti-divine ones, Christ or anti-christ, animate language and form this body glorious which divides into disjunctions.

What Deleuze ignores is that believing in what one cannot say or think is, nevertheless, essential to opening up the space that theology inhabits. Indeed, *not* believing in God is *not* leaving the question open. Accordingly, the bona fide apophatic theologian does live out some kind of belief, even though it may well take the form of Derridean desire for the impossible. The secular theologian is borne on a belief of this order toward a beyond that cannot be fathomed, except in hope and desire and love, in prayer and pleading, and in action inspired by such passions. For such theologians, "God" can have sense and indeed is perhaps the very sense of sense as a cipher for what they cannot understand or define. They may then recognize the continuity of their approach with theistic tradition, taken together with its apophatic twists. But such recognitions have until now remained potentially fraught with conflict or controversy, rather than fostering a spirit of understanding for differences in belief and, consequently, of readiness for dialogue. I believe that this fractiousness is not founded in irremovable differences, and that this becomes clear if we grasp the submerged apophatic basis of thinking today across a spectrum embracing the factions that we presently see ranged in opposition to each other.

"Secular theology," just as it becomes "postsecular" in postmodern times by following the Enlightenment's self-negation, modulates into "radical theology," and in both these regards—being postsecular and being radical—it happens to coincide with Radical Orthodoxy, its ostensible opponent. At this postsecular stage of secular theology, the apophatic common ground becomes more important than their respective differences; it upstages the programmatic announcements of either rival by revealing the essential wellsprings of both, at least in their most significant proposals. Both forms of postmodern thought and theology, orthodox and heterodox alike, emerge with regard to their deep structure as thinking out of apophatic resources and along negative theological lines. This means giving precedence to what they do not and admittedly cannot define and to what exceeds all premises and paradigms that they can and do articulate. Only thus can they remain unconditionally open to the future and to the changes it will inevitably bring.

In more traditional theological terms, this same openness has meant giving precedence to "God" and to "his" possible/impossible advent. But in any case, by thinking radically without limits, each theology— radically orthodox or radically secular, as the case may be—undermines its own stated premises and turns upon itself, entering into contradiction with its own concept. It thereby exceeds adequate conceptualization altogether. Radically orthodox theology turns out to be deeply one with what have often been treated as heterodox tendencies within its bosom, while secular theology, thought radically, cannot help but recognize itself as postsecular—as the very opposite of its initial defining concept. It, too, achieves its radical insight only by abandoning its own founding conception and reaching out toward what it cannot conceive. This is what makes it essentially a negative—and most importantly a self-negating—theology.

The nonetheless persisting ambivalence of secular theologians toward negative theology seems to come from its being associated with traditional metaphysical theology in the Neoplatonizing style of Dionysius the Areopagite and with its mystical—perhaps even mystifying—component. Thus it is suspected by secularists for reasons opposite to the ones that render it suspicious to Radical Orthodoxy. Whereas Radical Orthodoxy sees negative theology as too ambiguously close to heterodoxy and as too easily appropriated by modern secularist thinking, the secularists characteristically take negative theology as simply a subtle and sly reformulation of the old onto-theological tradition that they wish to terminate. And both are partly right. My point is that negative theology is indispensable to both intellectual "confessions" and indeed lies at the source of the creative intellectual energy released by each. Recognition of this derivation and debt requires each persuasion to gain insight into the strength and necessity of the other, as not excludable but as intrinsic to its own proper form of insight.

This requires, of course, a broader and deeper understanding of the apophatic than has typically been attained in modern times, although high medieval and late- or postmodern cultures (following Kafka, Beckett, and so on) are particularly steeped in a pervading sense of what ineluctably escapes definition and opens thought and desire in the direction of its unnameable and yet inexhaustible source. The negative way (*via negativa*) is a nonassertive way of relating to everything that is or is not—indeed, to anything whatever and to all things together. It does not abstract from finitude and the concrete, embodied things of creation—except in order to allow them to re-concretize freed from the conceptual constraints we ordinarily impose on them.

Much is being done currently by apophatic thinkers across numerous fields to bring out negative theology's potential for playing into a radical affirmation of what is called world, the body, and life, and thus to counter the *merely negative* image of negative theology that is all too common and that traverses even Caputo's text. Negative theology is not just an abstract metaphysics of denial, nor is it condemned to remain simply in the desert. That, too, would become idolatry by limiting apophaticism to a certain register of reasoning and a fixed imaginary repertoire rather than opening it without limits and without any unsurpassable conceptual boundaries. Hence the elaboration of apophatic discourses concentrating on bodies—on their social and political dimensions, among other things—and on beauty. The current renaissance of apophatic thought celebrates apophatic bodies and abounds in apophatic aesthetics.[22]

Another radical theological thinker in whom secular turns of thought turn postsecular, even as the apophatic cast of his thinking comes more clearly into the open, is Clayton Crockett. Up to his most recent work, secular theology for him had been practically synonymous with a rejection of a transcendent God. However, rounding on the customary (and his own former) rejection of transcendence by radical secular theologies, Crockett now writes, "One question I am raising here is whether it is possible to imagine a fully immanent theology, or whether theology necessarily refers to transcendence."[23] He finally finds the position that suits him by resorting to the apophatic rhetoric of neither/nor: his radical theology entails "neither an embrace nor exclusion of transcendence" (p. 164). Rather, he would "venture to name freedom as that which now passes for divinity in the wake of the death of God," and he highlights specifically "the freedom of theology to think matters of ultimate concern—political, moral, existential, cosmological—without the constraint of tradition, authority, or the presumed certainty of dogmatic answers" (p. 17).

This naming of divinity as "freedom" certainly captures something essential, but it will also prove reductive if it is taken as *the* true name of God or even as absolutely more appropriate than any others—rather than simply as one more relevant to the chosen concerns of the author in question. The solution toward which these formulations of "radical theology" are groping is an apophatic solution: the name of freedom is enlightening not so much in opposition to, or exclusion of, other names but rather as exemplary and so as standing for them all. In the end, God is not simply "freedom" any more than he is simply "being," even though both names open vistas for glimpsing, or rather for freely imagining, something essential about the mysterious nature of divinity.

Were Crockett to identify God with freedom as a known quantity, his theology would be reductive and idolatrous. It would simply substitute a human, worldly name—"freedom," indeed the idol of Enlightenment—for the transcendent deity. Instead, Crockett "ventures" a "name," namely freedom, just as Caputo ventures names such as "justice" for God. Yet it is not by virtue of any precise, human definition of freedom but rather, I would venture, as an open vessel of possibilities, that the name of freedom can serve as a good approach for naming God, who remains by rights and by the nature of the case unnameable. In apophatic tradition, God is *omninominabile* (*Corpus Hermeticum* V.10). Every name, like every aspect of creation, says something about him, but all that all together can say nevertheless falls short: neither is God *only* freedom or justice or being or anything else.

Crockett adopts Žižek's trope of "parallax" in refusing the either/or of ideology or theology (*Radical Political Theology*, p. 26), and in so doing he in effect adopts an apophatic neither/nor. For the "parallax gap" is another exemplary figure of apophatic rhetoric: it involves a "constantly shifting perspective between two points," such that "no synthesis or mediation is possible" (p. 27). Crockett eschews definitive answers and opts for Derrida's "religion without religion" (adopting another quintessentially apophatic trope) "rather than a determinate theology, which would necessarily take the form of an ideology" (p. 40). He defines "secular theology" as "an open-ended discourse about value and meaning in an ultimate sense" (p. 27). Opening discourse to the indefinable but ultimately important is about as close to a defining gesture of negative theology or apophasis as can be produced.

Crockett admires Žižek's atheist belief as "the pure form of belief deprived of its substantialization" (p. 40), and, drawing on Agamben, he argues that the task of political theology is resistance against "all positive sovereign power in both political and theological terms" (p. 45). Benjamin's idea of a "pure law" or "law beyond law" helps him to think justice according to Derrida: it "not only exceeds or contradicts law but also, perhaps, has no relation to law" (p. 115, quoting Derrida's "Force of Law"). This, too, is radical apophaticism, reminiscent of Blanchot and his "relation without relation." Crockett draws the conclusion, following Derrida in his famous essay "Force de loi," that "Justice exceeds law; while every particular or determinate law is deconstructible, justice itself is not deconstructible" (pp. 115–16). Using a word closely related to and, in some respects, practically interchangeable with "apophatic," Crockett himself terms this an "aporetic foundation" (p. 116).

Crockett, furthermore, defines his idea of radical democracy in terms of an "indefinite, or infinite, eschatology" that forms "a permanent counter-conduct or counter-governmentality that serves radical democratic action" (p. 102). Such opening to an infinite and indefinable eschatological dimension is what I call the apophatic. "Indefinite," moreover, is a word often indicative of the apophatic move of *un*defining that is indispensable for Crockett's formulations, just as for those of Radical Orthodoxy. "Indeterminate" functions similarly. Taking inspiration from Lacan and Deleuze, Crockett proposes to "think law productively beyond determinate and conscious law" as unconscious event (p. 114). Giving precedence to the indeterminate as presupposed in all determinations and as in some sort containing them immanently in itself is crucial to what I call negative theology—provided that it does not mean hypostatizing indeterminacy as another idol but rather letting what we cannot determine be unconditioned and sovereign and letting it manifest itself *as* unconditioned in all that is determinate.

Still, there is much ambivalence about negative theology among secular theologians, since it can be interpreted as *either* the radical splintering away from orthodox theology in heretics such as Meister Eckhart *or* as a form of thought nevertheless always recuperable by orthodox theological thinking. In the latter case, negative theology appears to be just a way to attempt to repair the theological edifice that secular theologians ardently wish to demolish. The trick, however, and the real task of thinking theologically at the present and toward the future, I submit, is to think the crossing and even the coincidence of orthodoxy together with heterodoxy in terms of the deeper source of each in what neither can say—in what inspires each discourse precisely in its radical thrust.

We have seen that a similar ambivalence toward negative theology has characterized Radical Orthodoxy. Negative theology seems to threaten orthodoxy, as if from within; it turns orthodoxy against itself, casting its positive certitudes into doubt. This provocatively parallels the path along which secular theology turns postsecular by following its own principles to their radical conclusion and reversal. In a statement that serves to suggest what orthodox theological thinkers fear about apophatic or negative theology, Derrida tellingly captures its apparently subversive, *un*orthodox aspect:

> An immediate mysticism, but without intuition, a sort of abstract kenosis liberates it [negative theology] from all authority, from every story, from every doctrine, from every belief, and at the limit from every *determinable* faith . . . whence this odor of heresy, these trials, this subversive marginality of the apophatic current in the history of theology and the Church.[24]

In this light, it is not surprising that Radical Orthodoxy should be reluctant to embrace negative theology, inasmuch as it wishes to affirm itself as orthodox. And yet in pursuing its vocation to a radical reformulation and reawakening of the faith, Radical Orthodoxy cannot help but find fellowship with precisely this current and its corpus of writings. More orthodox than any official orthodoxy that defines itself can be— because adherent to its roots in a mystery that escapes capture by discursive formulations—negative theology remains the unacknowledged source of inspiration of orthodoxy, precisely in its will to be truly and *radically* orthodox. Just as the radically secular turns out to be *post*secular, and so to contradict its own original formal definition, so the radically orthodox turns out to coincide with the heterodox because, as radical, it reaches to the principles that exceed all positive, exclusionary formulations and to the God infinitely in excess of our words and concepts.

In terms of essential commitments, then, from where does all the friction between Radical Orthodoxy and radically secular theological thinking come? It is not so easy to answer, once we admit that secular theological currents, too, turn postsecular: the dispute does not boil down simply to a choice for or against the secular. Neither group wishes to affirm a secular world as "cut off" (*sectus*) and autonomous, or as intelligible wholly on its own terms; both stress rather the world's inherent openness and its being beholden to an Other, or at least to others. Neither does the principal difference of Radical Orthodoxy from deconstruction lie in philosophical positions, for example, on language, where they actually have much in common.[25] Graham Ward uses Derrida's "quasi-transcendental" thinking of *différance* to oppose Gnostic deformations of the relation between language and silence that he finds in George Steiner and other modern thinkers. Catherine Pickstock interestingly invokes Derrida against Eastern Orthodox theologian Andrew Louth, in order to defend the primacy of language and specifically of textuality in liturgy.[26] Both types of theological thinking under examination here are powered by the same post-Saussurian ideas about language and the semiological revolution that they produced. Both types of thinking are based on an embrace of "radical linguisticality."[27] Both build their revisionary movements on radical thinking of the linguistic turn in philosophy and theology, respectively. Both accept the radical contingency and constructedness of all our experience and knowledge as mediated by language. What separates them is rather the positive Christian theology that Milbank and company assert as the only, or at least the best, way to approach a God who must remain indeterminate in our language, versus an indeterminate openness that refuses or seeks to avoid naming God at all.

Accordingly, Radical Orthodoxy emphasizes the positive, analogical theology that expresses a relation to what to us remains conceivable only as the divine indeterminacy. This gives a certain apparently realist basis for the positive affirmations of orthodoxy. But again, this theology is not purely positive in the sense of being revealed without mediation. Revelation is viewed as an intensification of rational understanding, a sort of Thomistic "illumination" of the intellect.[28] It entails intelligent perception of creatures throughout the whole order of Creation. And this valorization of the world and of worldly knowledge actually coincides completely with secular theological perspectives—with the proviso of seeing the finite as a negative reflection or inflection of the Infinite. But that last twist makes this a negative theological insight. Both ostensibly opposed currents emphasize precisely the *world* as the arena of knowledge and of possible encounter with the sacred. To this extent, Radical Orthodoxy's postsecularism is, after all, "secular"—an affirmation of the worldly, just as, symmetrically, secular theology is *post*secular: it too takes its distance from antitheological construals of the world as pure immanence and as excluding the sacred. Both forms of theology are intent upon salvaging and revalorizing the world, but both do so indirectly through the insight opened up by apophatic thinking into the negativity of all determinate forms in which the world comes to us already defined and categorized.

Radical Orthodoxy coincides with secular thinking in critiquing "a Christianity which *never* sufficiently valued the mediating participatory sphere which alone can lead us to God" (*Radical Orthodoxy*, p. 2). This sphere is the created world, and for the sake of its mediating a relationship with the Creator, Radical Orthodoxy theologians admit "Platonic participation" as a "central framework" for their theological outlook. Indeed, they claim that their outlook, framed in these Platonist terms, is "the only non-nihilistic perspective, and the only perspective able to uphold even finite reality" (*Radical Orthodoxy*, p. 4).

The embrace of "Platonic participation" purportedly places the proponents of Radical Orthodoxy in continuity with the seventeenth-century Cambridge Platonism of Ralph Cudworth and Henry Moore, which has also served as an essential intellectual heritage for one of the great revivers of apophatic philosophy in recent times, namely, A. H. Armstrong. That the Radical Orthodoxy movement was originally centered in Cambridge emerges in this connection as something more than just an irrelevant accident. The historical entanglement of the movement with Platonizing negative theology is deeply rooted in its own cultural home ground.

There is in Radical Orthodoxy a strongly assertive, even aggressive tone, an "unprecedented boldness," as its authors themselves declare, that is ostensibly the opposite of apophasis, with its typically self-effacing style, punctuated by ellipses and suspensions and characterized especially by withdrawal from even its own inevitable affirmations. Nevertheless, Radical Orthodoxy is best understood as expressing the positive, assertive theology that is made possible only on the basis of the broader postmodern rediscovery and revalorization of negative theology and its thoroughgoing critique of all idolatry.

Since Radical Orthodoxy's real and original insights, at least in a philosophical register, are of a purely critical and negative nature (they, in fact, coincide with negative theology), it often seems, like deconstruction, to need an opponent in order to gain traction, so as to have anything at all to say. In this regard, despite all its proclamations of plenitude, it perhaps turns out to be essentially parasitical—a critical discourse dependent on a host, which it cannot help but attack and destroy.[29] Without such a host, it would run the risk of remaining simply a private language of pure devotion. It has a message for others who do not sympathize with its beliefs thanks only to this negative component in a critical language demanding public assent. Its polemical edge, which gives this discourse its point, is particularly pronounced in Milbank, just as it is in Blond and Pickstock. For his part, Derrida, too, is finally not polemical without also being parasitical with respect to the speculative theological tradition that he deconstructs.

With Radical Orthodoxy thinkers, we seem to be in the midst of a war of competing perspectives. This is their challenge to modern and postmodern culture. Yet it is my conviction that, in vying for the soul of our contemporary world and its future, we must also offer something besides self-assertive programs and polemics. We also need a nonaggressive, nonassertive way of thinking that is more consonant with the pluralistic mood of the times and yet no less determined to make intelligible the outstanding vision and insight of theological tradition, not least of Christian revelation: theological knowledge is not to be consigned to a definitively outmoded and obsolete worldview. The opposing constituencies I arraign here actually agree on theology's indispensability to our contemporary self-understanding, even though theology is not understood by secularists in the same sense as it is by orthodox thinkers to be based on divine revelation. Still, in either case, theology opens the space of desire to an embrace in faith and love of what infinitely surpasses us. From that point, the choice of narratives used to interpret this space is a contingent matter and depends on personal choice. But the dimension of the theological and the kind of reality and unreality, or rather ultra-reality, that it alone fathoms is something that both approaches honor and defend.

Crucial in the vision of both outlooks is not only the world but also its negation. This entails taking the world not as simply given and real in and of itself but rather as opening toward a dimension beyond itself, to a reality that it cannot encompass or comprehend—except perhaps mythically, for example, as Giver. Thus the world *in its negativity* (as constituted by language and therefore by difference) is indeed foundational for both these approaches and their respective proponents, who turn out finally to agree more than either realized. To understand how this negativity opens up as a breach in the midst of the world, we do well, in addition to listening to poets like Celan and Jabès, to contemplate Neoplatonic ontology. Historically, as discussed throughout this volume, Neoplatonism was crucial to the development of negative theologies in the West. For this reason, it can illuminate what makes both these theological approaches radical by exposing the negative theology that is, in fact, their common root.

A recovery of the Platonic and more specifically Neoplatonic vision of the cosmos, and especially of a beyond that transcends everything within our experience, proves crucial to the critique and renewal that have become possible and imperative in our postmodern cultural crisis. Radical Orthodoxy sees itself as advocating a kind of Platonism *redivivus* turning on the participation of all finite, created being in infinite, transcendent Being. What it has often overlooked or declined to acknowledge fully (though there are increasing signs of correction here) are the profoundly negative-theological underpinnings of the (Neo)Platonic doctrine of the revelation of the infinite in the finite, even though this was crucial historically to the appropriation of Platonism by monotheistic, particularly Christian, tradition. It was especially God's transcendence of all discourses, as described by Plotinus and his followers, eminently Proclus, that enabled the graft of Greek philosophy onto Christian theology.[30]

ii

It is vital to understand that apophasis, for all its constitutive negativity, is not opposed to the kind of affirmative discourse on God proposed by orthodoxy, whether this orthodoxy is traditional, "neo," or radical. On the contrary, apophasis requires this elaboration of affirmations in excess—to the point of collapse. It is through affirmations about God, and through affirmations of whatever kind understood as in some oblique way about God, that the insufficiency of all our affirmations in language is most readily brought into evidence. Such affirmation is necessary for language to become a sign of something radically other than what can be determined linguistically. Taking his cues from Dionysius, Eriugena exalts the metaphorical discourse that arises in the wake of unreserved negation vis-à-vis the divine supereminence.[31] In the tradition following Dionysius and Eriugena, "the impossibility of imitating the divine curiously becomes a source of poetry."[32]

Denys Turner, speaking from a position firmly grounded in the Dionysian apophatic tradition, effectively emphasizes that negative theology's reticence and silence go hand in hand with a maximum of prolixity apropos God. Theological language must talk itself out to exhaustion in order to enable the apophatic to become manifest. The excess and superfluity of the kataphatic must exhaust itself, and then, from within its insufficiency even *in extremis,* the space of apophasis opens. Moreover, this inevitable excess of affirmation can be seen as inherent to discourse per se. It is only the negation of all merely finite, terminal sense that reveals an infinite or "religious" dimension to language:

> For it is common belief among Christian theologians today that there is, as it were, a domain of human discourse which is specifically and distinctively 'religious', religious positively in that it is somehow especially privileged to be expressive of the divine, and 'religious' also by contrast with other secular, discourses, such as those, perhaps, of politics, or science, or sex. Now the pseudo-Denys will have none of this. It is doubtful if he could have made sense of the idea of a 'religious' language as distinct from any other.[33]

This, in effect, answers to the attempt of the earlier Nancy (and many others) to dismiss the religious because it has no specific domain of discourse proper to itself. The religious is to be understood rather as a dimension inherent to language per se. By the same token, negative theology is not so much a theology or a philosophy as a dimension inherent to thought—precisely what escapes it in all its forms, hence its formless, unformulatable ground.

Turner demonstrates the thoroughgoing interpenetration of the kataphatic and the apophatic from Dionysius the Areopagite onward. He notes that "all our language fails of God, infinitely and in principle. But it is also true that, should we arbitrarily restrict the names with which we name God, we will fall short of that point of verbal profusion at which we encounter the collapse of language as such."[34] The radicality of negation of names of God presupposes their attribution in (dis)proportionate profusion.

A brief excursion into the scholarship on Neoplatonism will help give some historical perspective on the emergence to clear realization of this intimate interconnection of speech and apophasis or silence. Hilary Armstrong, even in his erudite, historical studies of ancient Hellenic Neoplatonism, was acutely conscious of the relevance of apophasis to contemporary thought in times that he characterized as shaken by the collapse of theological "absolutism," that is, by the demise of all doctrines claiming absolute foundations for belief. However, to specify the nature of this relevance we need to observe an important turning in the trajectory of Armstrong's own thinking. Armstrong's thought evolves from an early emphasis on Neoplatonism's sharp accentuation of the radically negative movement that denies any positive vocabulary for speaking about the ultimate principle to a later emphasis on the conjoining of the negative or apophatic way with positive or kataphatic ways. J. P. Kenney discerns in this turn toward the recognition that apophatic theology must work in tandem with kataphatic theology a "revised thesis," that is, a modification or "qualification" of Armstrong's view concerning the critical value of Neoplatonism.[35]

Armstrong's chief point in his earlier work was to stress how the negative theology of the Neoplatonists distinguishes itself from that of Middle Platonism, which unfolds between Plato and Plotinus. What is new about Neoplatonism is that it rigorously denies all positive representations concerning the supreme principle. Middle Platonic sources such as the *Corpus Hermeticum,* the *Chaldean Oracles,* Numenius of Apamea, and Philo of Alexandria, by contrast, are full of positive, dogmatic statements concerning God. Later Armstrong shifts this focus and sees more clearly the indispensability—even for the Neoplatonists—of combining negative theology with some form of positive theology. The radical negative emphasis is still there, but it is qualified by a coupling of negative with more positive forms of discourse.

Armstrong gives two reasons for this necessary conjunction, for why Neoplatonism's "emphasis on the positive power of the experience which generates and is strengthened by the negative way" leads necessarily to consideration of kataphatic theology. First, "negative theology needs a positive theology to wrestle with and transcend," and second, "The great negative theologians, from Plotinus onwards, are always aware as they follow the negative that in the end they must negate their own negations."[36] The first of these reasons points up the fact that negative theology does not propose to think without all relation to foundations but rather to think any articulation of foundations as transcended. In transcending any *articulable* foundation, one can nevertheless be oriented toward, and live and think from, what in fact sustains all that is, along with thinking itself. The second reason stresses how negation is not the end of inquiry and experience but rather an opening to an endless quest for the ineffable. Negation of one's own finite conceptual forms, far from being a dead end, is an opening toward the infinity of otherness. As a recursive negation of itself, the negation of the negation opens up from within and falls infinitely toward what is other than it as the source of all that is possible and positive.

Speaking in the voice of negative theologians collectively, Armstrong explains in his essay "Negative Theology, Myth and Incarnation" that "we are not content simply to say that God is not anything, but must say and be aware that he is not not anything either."[37] In this manner, apophatic thinkers learn to use ways of thinking and languages "freely and critically, always with a certain distance and detachment" (p. 51). Such is the spirit of Plotinus's *hoion*, "as if." There is much virtue in this *if*. It enables negative theologies to be open to and even to require the employment of myths and "icons." Unlike idols, which tend to substitute themselves for God, icons are transparently vehicles of communication, signs that openly disclaim any exact likeness to divinity. Following his ancient sources, Armstrong attributes to the Good or the Unnameable a propensity to communicate *itself*. It goes out from itself in "ecstatic eros," he writes, borrowing a phrase from Dionysius the Areopagite's *On Divine Names* 4.13 (712A–B). This energy, which is productive of being, is an "inexhaustible starting point" (p. 59) that also produces myths, that is, narrations imaginatively elaborating on experience of ultimate existential conditions that cannot be properly comprehended and expounded in rational terms. Such erotic energy produces a general or natural revelation involving human participation.[38]

In Armstrong's conception, then, negative theology consists essentially "in a critical negation of all affirmations that one can make about God, followed by an equally critical negation of our negations" ("Negative Theology," p. 185). Both steps are indispensable, he explains, for

> We must not be content to say that God is not anything. We must not only say, but experience and be aware, that he is not not anything either. If we go the whole way like this, we may experience a great liberation of mind, a freedom from language and concepts which will enable us to use them properly, in the endlessly critical way which I have indicated. We become, however dimly, aware, beyond our distinctions and definitions, positive and negative, not of an abstract, contentless monadic simplicity—which the pagan Neoplatonists are often mistakenly thought to believe in—but of an unspeakably rich and vivifying reality.[39]

This suggests how, as generating the methodological principle of limitless criticism, the supra- or quasi-ontological principle, the ineffable One of Neoplatonic speculation, exercises a positive force and influence, engendering positive productions and articulations of content, even though nothing at all can be said of what it is in itself. Everything that can be said about it comes up short and calls to be critiqued and indeed discarded. But then, these negations, too, in turn demand to be negated. So it is not as if negation had the last word. The point is rather that the word is not last in the order of revelation. Rather, the negation of the negation returns wordlessly to the ineffable principle that words endeavored to gain access to and grasp—but *in vain*. The transformation of the mind that has stripped itself of discourse points in the direction of the transcendent, wild oneness to which it finds itself related. But this experience is then further productive of an endless variety of expressions. This is the basis for what religions generally are engaged in expressing in terms that are proper to each community and its history and are even relative to the personal experiences of individuals.

A powerful, although too little recognized, thinker who has moved from the study of Neoplatonism to engagement with contemporary philosophical thought and its relation to Eastern alternatives such as Buddhism, all in an explicitly negative theological perspective, is Stanislas Breton. As a Catholic Passionist priest, Breton was ensconced in orthodoxy and yet drew inspiration freely from heterodox thinkers such as Eckhart and from the Neoplatonic vision in general. In *La penser du rien* (*The Thinking of Nothing*), especially in its third chapter, "Néoplatonisme et Mystique," Breton takes apophaticism as the key to the entire edifice of Neoplatonism and takes its guiding "thought of nothing" as crucial to all authentic philosophical thinking since antiquity. He discovers in its apophatic discourse on the One, which *is none* among beings, negation pushed to the extreme and even beyond to a relationality without limits: "Relational expansion by its irrepressibility extends little by little the horizon to the confines of the world" ("De fil en aiguille, l'expansion relationnelle, par son irrépressibilité étend l'horizon jusqu'aux confins du monde").[40]

Philosophy and mysticism alike emerge from an "original Excess, of which modern forms of knowledge have no notion" ("Philosophie et mystique ressortissent plus particulièrement, de cet Excès originel, dont les savoirs, au sens moderne du terme, n'on pas à se soucier," p. 40). Philosophy and mysticism are two "ways of excess" that are constituted under "the impression of the Ineffable" (p. 40). No discourse is capable of being adequate, but all discourses can correct and complete one another in the endless search for the origin—the beginning and the end—of philosophy and mysticism alike in an apophaticism that is both ancient and contemporary, and of which Breton was a pioneering explorer.

Breton's apophaticism, nevertheless, is far from triumphant. His philosophical thinking of "nothing by excess" finally leads to a Christian theology of the Cross, which is "nothing by defect" and which issues, well beyond intellectual critique, in ethical and political practice.

> The practice specified by the Cross is not centered on a liberating illumination of the initiated. It aims, on the horizon of suffering humanity, at the realization of a justice that would make the Christ of kenosis exist, in the light of a face and by the gift of what is most necessary and quotidian, in the most deprived of his brothers. It is by this feature that the 'theology of the Cross' actualizes a thinking of the nothing that defines its originality. (p. 121)[41]

Breton underlines the necessity of rupture within the bosom of the pure thought of nothing in order that it open upon something other than itself. Yet he discerns in Christianity an "improbable junction" between speculative philosophy and mystic-ethical practice. Historically, living the Cross of Christ became married to Neoplatonic thinking: "The Cross of Christ . . . bound itself independently of all logical necessity to Neoplatonism, whether metaphysical or mystical, by the chance of an encounter which was at first the grace of a great friendship" ("La Croix du Christ . . . s'est liée, indépendamment de toute nécessité logique, au néoplatonisme, métaphysique et mystique, par le hasard d'une rencontre qui fut d'abord la grâce d'une grande amitié," p. 121).

In advocating this vision, Breton positions himself against a "cheery optimism" ("bel optimisme") based on universal relational harmony because exclusion and incompatibility are also constitutive of relationality. There is more than just harmony in the contradiction of the Cross: there is even a contradiction of philosophical discourse *tout court*. Nevertheless, Neoplatonic thinkers, and particularly Damascius, in Breton's estimation, brought this contradictoriness into the orbit of their discourse, and that was their extraordinary accomplishment—one might even say their vocation. The theology of the Cross realized in Christian ethical practice is, Breton affirms, completely different from philosophical thought. And yet philosophical thought that annihilates itself is already on the way of the Cross, which is finally revealed to be the way of Christ. Such philosophy shows itself capable of exiting from itself: the philosopher can open in an offering of self to other. Is it only in ceasing to think or in practicing philosophy to its radical limits that one does so? Breton's oeuvre poses acutely the undecidable question of rupture or continuity between philosophy and a mystic-ethic-political practice.[42]

iii

From an apophatic vantage point, Radical Orthodoxy can be recognized as the positive, postmodern theology that works in tandem (at least implicitly and covertly) with postmodern negative theology. In its assertive, positive voice, Radical Orthodoxy expresses itself dogmatically. However, this assertiveness, with its powerful expressivity, can also be heard poetically. Indeed, its sense depends entirely on the negative theology that renounces the pretention to knowing God in any adequate human discourse. Divine revelation, as God's self-disclosure, can and must, of course, transcend human limitations, but its human appropriation is always still conditioned by the limitations of the finite and thus is not commensurable to the divine as such. We cannot encompass this infinite dimension beyond all our discourses, and yet we can nevertheless open ourselves to it in desire and prayer.

Both secular theology and Radical Orthodoxy are often suspicious of negative theology, which they tend to construe reductively as a rationalist metaphysics. But this is a sign of the intrinsic limit of each, namely, each one's perduring adherence to a *discourse*. An apophatic metaphysics tenders the keys to a space beyond the discourse that each current at least implicitly adheres to, and this space lies beyond the field of their conflict with each other. Apophasis *believes* in a reality, an *I don't know what*, that is undefined and infinite: it is often called divine but cannot be called properly by any name at all because it is beyond discourse altogether. Such is the shape of a belief that can believe all things, hope all things, love all things. It can be engaged with in acting on behalf of ideals, such as justice or freedom, for which it may choose to be responsible.

Vis-à-vis this indefinable dimension, dichotomies collapse, including the exclusive split between the secular and the postsecular, which ostensibly is the source of the antagonism between radical secular theology and radically orthodox theology. But we have already seen that this distinction between the secular and the postsecular gives way in current debates in philosophical theology. Radical Orthodoxy makes a claim, which can be found already in Aquinas, to valorize the secular world and to let it emerge undistorted in its pristine dignity and integrity. Symmetrically, secular theology ends by being interested not so much in the autonomy of a secular universe as in its breaking open to the radically Other, thereby reversing the secular paradigm of an autonomous order of immanence. This means attending to the wounds that open the world from within, opening it to what is impossible on its own terms. At this stage, secular theology recognizes itself—astonishingly—as postsecular.

Gabriel Vahanian, among secular theologians, takes as his leading theme the breakdown of dichotomies between the secular and the religious. He consequently relocates the religious within the secular and vice versa. For Vahanian, the secular is to be seen as the *realization* of the religious: the world is where God becomes real, and it is denatured without this recognition of religious transcendence as inherent within it. Nevertheless, for Vahanian, such transcendence is not opposed to but rather in some sort coincides with immanence. "Using a Tillichean image, one is compelled to observe that the vertical already lies in the horizontal. Or that transcendence consists in making room for that which is immanent."[43]

Vahanian presents man as the "condition" of God, the condition in which God is realized in the world, and this is a condition that is linguistic in nature.

> The Christ does not abolish either nature or history. He desacralizes nature and 'defatalizes' history. This is to say that the event of Christ is situated on another plane from that of nature or history. Like the creation, he is situated in the field of the word, in this utopianism of language where time and space coincide with each other and where, to use a biblical expression, the glorification of man meets that of God.[44]

The Christ event desacralizes nature and defatalizes history, without abolishing either, because it is on another plane from that of the ordinary world—it transpires in the non-place or, literally, the "utopia" of language.

Language is the place of this realization, and for all its utopianism it is nevertheless inherently negative. Vahanian concludes his contribution to the collection *Secular Theology* with a neither/nor statement: "What remains is a theology of language, the cutting edge of discourse reduced neither to the religious nor to the secular" (p. 23). Vahanian develops these hints more fully in terms that move even more clearly in the direction of negative theology in his *Dieu anonyme ou la peur des mots* (God Anonymous or the Fear of Words). Here language is refractory to the idol ("le langage est réfractaire à l'idole," p. 29), and speech per se immediately exits idolatry: "I need only speak of him, and God escapes the idol of him that I make for myself" ("Il suffit que j'en parle, et Dieu échappe à l'idole que je m'en fais," p. 33).

Vahanian is very close to Levinas and his conception of *le Dire*, Saying, as revealing the radical alterity of the Other. "In language is revealed on the contrary the radical alterity of God. So radical that the word alone is revelatory of God—every word" ("Au langage se révèle au contraire l'altérité radicale de Dieu. Si radicale qu'est révélatrice de Dieu la parole seule. Toute parole," p. 29). All language reveals God. This is a sort of ontological argument that has taken a linguistic turn. Yet Vahanian rejects the idea of a divine origin for language. Language is rather essentially human, "le propre de l'homme." This curiously converges with the eighteenth-century theological thinking about language of Vico and Herder, which so impresses Milbank. Herder and Vico in their different ways were both concerned to deny the divine origin of language in order to explain how language registers a human relation to what transcends it. Humanity creates its own language, but in so doing acts in the image of its Creator, whom it cannot comprehend and yet can blindly relate to through this poetic activity reaching out beyond itself toward what does not positively exist.

The linguistic focus is indeed a crucial point in common with Radical Orthodoxy as articulated by Milbank. But more exactly and incisively, this convergence rests on an apophatic point concerned with the limits of language. It is at their limits, beyond their proper significances, that words for divinity become not simply idolatrous but rather signs opening toward the unsayable as to the only true transcendence. And this sort of truth or vision is for humanity as such, not only for a specific chosen people or for believers in a special revelation. To this extent, it claims a universality for reason that is still in the spirit of the eighteenth-century Enlightenment: it is far from content to propose merely sectarian dogmas. Milbank's project must be understood in this perspective, not as obscurantist or as a merely confessional preaching to the choir, but as a pressing challenge for contemporary thought and philosophy.

Milbank argues for a theology that is not just dogmatic but rather makes a claim to universal philosophical truth. But this part of his argument, I contend, can only be justified in terms of what I call negative theology. It is not the discourse of orthodox Christianity itself that is universal. Indeed, Milbank admits that Christianity is not a truth that can be objectively proved but rather a *narrative* that is, first, simply embraced by those who believe it and find therein the truth for themselves. He is indebted here to Alasdair MacIntyre's discovery of an irreducibly narrative component even in philosophical truth.[45] Narrative can be a way of getting at what cannot be said in any conceptually adequate manner, but can only be imagined. Although the truth envisioned by Christianity is proclaimed as absolute, the discourse proffered by any determinate faith can approach this truth only by analogical means such as narrative affords.

Hans Frei's work, too, is crucial in bringing out the inherent narrativity of the biblical revelation as conveying a reality inaccessible to literal language and history. Revelation was reduced to mere pretended factuality by modern developments of deism, historical criticism, and empirical philosophy, with their idea of a "language-neutral historical veracity."[46] Frei delineates how eighteenth- and nineteenth-century hermeneutics narrowed the literal sense of Scripture to history in the sense investigated and established by the social sciences and so lost the pregnant sense of an inexhaustible mysterious reality beyond what could be said and objectively realized. Empirically manifest, demonstrable reality became the inescapable referent against which biblical narrative was measured and evaluated in its truth claims. All unspeakable, numinous meaning was banished from the scene. The Christian counter-Enlightenment figures championed by Milbank see narrative as encoding a truth that cannot be presented otherwise and cannot be verified independently of its own language and so cannot be reduced to "history" as an objective reality outside narrative. Such a unifying meaning that is real, yet irreducible to empirical history, and that manifests rather an inexhaustible source of truth, needs to be retrieved, Frei argues, in order to counter the pervasive "eclipse of biblical narrative."

Paul Ricoeur explains this imperative in more explicitly apophatic terms as aimed directly at the ineffable. He proposes a type of narrative theology that highlights the untellable at the heart of biblical narrative theology:

> There are stories of the exodus, of the passion, and even more fragmentary stories such as the story of Joseph or that of Peter's betrayal. But the story of the partnership between God and Israel, is, as such,

not only open and ongoing but unfathomable and unspeakable. At that point the character of the metastory as that which cannot be told joins the theological theme of God's ineffability. Or rather the ineffability of the Name is the same thing as the inexhaustibility of the metastory. This close connection is clearly asserted in the episode of the burning bush, which at the same time proclaims the retreat of Yahweh in the incognito 'I am who I am' and Yahweh's partnership with Israel's journey.[47]

Ricoeur links this idea of a metanarrative that cannot be told with Frank Kermode's analysis of narrative particularly in the Gospel of Mark as generating the so-called "Messianic secret" concerning the identity of Jesus.[48]

Building on Ricoeur, Richard Kearney pursues a form of dialogue among religions and especially between theism and atheism in the apophatic space of "anatheism."[49] He is concerned with extending hospitality to what is radically Other—what is strange and even monstrous.[50] However, Kearney, influenced here by Derrida, refuses to associate this approach with "subtle apologetics for apophatic theology" (*Anatheism*, p. 63), rejecting what sounds like a confessional genre employed by Christian proselytism. My purpose is to bring out how all these strains of contemporary thought are indeed based subtly on negation and specifically on negation of themselves—on feeling out their own limits and thereby gesturing toward their own beyond. I suggest, furthermore, that apophatic tradition has been developing just this type of insight all along in parallel with the affirmative traditions that have accompanied and qualified it.

The pervasiveness and ineluctability of the apophatic gesture seems to make it virtually imperceptible, so that it is typically denied, even in ambiguously "a/theological" thinking, which is actually nearest to and most inextricable from it. Among the most interesting and independent of secularly oriented religious thinkers, Mark C. Taylor has been deeply influenced all along by the apophatic (or negative theological) aspects of deconstruction. Yet he, too, is strongly tempted to turn away from theology altogether, and so a fortiori from negative theology, as a viable discourse in the contemporary world. In his essay for the collection honoring the work of Thomas J. J. Altizer, in crucial ways the outstanding figure among American "Death of God" theologians, Taylor dubs Altizer "the last theologian."⁵¹ In fact, Taylor outright denies that theology is possible in the postmodern world. In designating Altizer the last theologian, Taylor interprets Altizer's stubborn fidelity to a theological vision as anachronistic and as a betrayal of his essential vision of total darkness and of the total absence of God from the purview of modernity:

> This longing for a rebirth of theology, however, betrays Altizer's theological vision. His work provides an eloquent testimony to the *impossibility* of theology in a postmodern world. Theology ends with the death of God. Appearances to the contrary notwithstanding, the continuing chatter across the theological spectrum is a symptom of the exhaustion of theology.⁵²

The task at hand, according to Taylor, turns out to be one of forgetting theology—not theologizing the death of God but rather once and for all finally ceasing to speak theologically. Only then will the death of God be accomplished, so that we can join in saying "it is finished" and sigh in relief. Even then, however, there is still an absolute negativity or *différance,* an awe-inspiring religious and sacrificial sense of the wholly Other that cannot simply be forgotten. Taylor has ingeniously baptized this numinous otherness "Altarity." And opening up to this uncanny dimension is what, for Taylor, distinguishes a radical from a complacent postmodernism. And yet this radical alterity cannot but be forgotten: it can be remembered only under the form of remembrance that it has been forgotten. It has a past and a possible future *only*: it is given in no moment of presence as such. Taylor even seems to recommend that we forget it. It will come back somehow, especially through the arts and their ruptures or "tears," but whatever we might try to do theologically to preserve or evoke it seems sure to be in vain. Negative theology is part of the core tradition from which Taylor wishes to shake free. In his essay "Postmodern Times," Taylor defines his a/theology expressly against negative theology:

> A/theology *is not* a latter-day version of negative theology. As the inverse of the *via positiva,* the *via negativa* creates a mirror image that changes nothing. In accordance therewith, negation is covert affirmation, emptiness implicit fullness, and absence covert presence.

> A/theology, by contrast, seeks to think the unthinkable margin of difference that is the condition of the possibility and impossibility of all affirmation and negation, emptiness and fullness, presence and absence.[53]

Here Taylor chooses to work with a very impoverished idea of the *via negativa* as simply negation and inversion of possible affirmation, whereas the tradition from Pseudo-Dionysius to Eckhart and beyond is intensely engaged in transcending such simple, oppositional logic. Moreover, Taylor's own "quasi-transcendental" account risks complicity in continuing the attempt to achieve mastery by thinking rather than giving that up in order to let oneself *be* thought by the Other. By telling a story about negative theology that consigns it to the rubbish heap of tradition, Taylor makes a quasi-transcendental move of the type that comes under concentrated critique from Radical Orthodoxy in some of its most penetrating insights into the self-deceptions of militant secularity (see the previous essay). There is an important challenge in this critique, even if we do not need to accept any blanket ascription of a lack of moral fiber and of ethical values to secular authors of a deeply skeptical bent.

Taylor has always had a keen sensibility for the power, not to say the omnipotence, of negation. It seems to be something of a Rimbaldian drive, after the motto "we must be absolutely modern" ("Il faut être absolument moderne," "Adieu," in *Une saison en enfer*), that makes him want to dissociate this negative thinking from the nonetheless incalculably powerful tradition of negative theology that has thought it through so subtly and profoundly. This impulse to "make it new" ironically is modernist in origin: it is the title of a 1934 collection of essays by Ezra Pound and was destined to become a modernist slogan and rallying cry. And yet traditions such as negative theology always return from beyond the ruptures of every new modernity. They are always "post" whatever the new trend is and in this case have proved to be quite in step with the postmodern.

In an essay entitled "Denegating God" (as elsewhere), Taylor displays a remarkable sense of the intangible yet penetrating presence-absence, or rather *neither* presence *nor* absence of the Nothing that marks the dimension of the religious.[54] His elusive yet incisive thesis is that "[t]he sacred, which, as we shall see, does not exist and yet is not nothing, is what the concept of God is (unknowingly) constructed *not* to think" (p. 31). He explains as "the sacred" what he elsewhere treats with his witty coinage "Altarity" as a non-name for Derridean "différance." He thereby accentuates the irreducibly religious basis and overtones of "différance":

> Eluding every oppositional structure, the sacred is the condition of the possibility of opposition as such. Thus, the sacred is that which allows God to be God by enabling God to be other than everything that is not God. God, in other words, is an after-effect or symptom of the sacred. In this way, the denegation of the sacred is not simply negation but is the un-negation without which God cannot exist. While negation without negation is undeniably negative, it is, more importantly, at the same time radically affirmative. (*About Religion,* p. 32)

Taylor thus formulates his program of a/theology in terms that relate to and integrate, after all, a nonnegative sort of negative theology:

> A/theology is not the opposite of theology and must not be identified with atheism. Neither exactly positive nor negative, a/theology draws on the resources of deconstruction to develop a nonnegative negative theology that seeks to think what Western ontotheology leaves unthought. By so doing, a/theology traces the limits of theology in a way that displaces classical concepts of God. (*About Religion,* p. 40)

Yet this precisely is what the tradition of negative theology does—it displaces every classical and even every positive concept of God.

Taylor speaks also of the sacred as a secret "that secretes discourse by withdrawing from language. Older than the Logos, the sacred is the condition of the possibility and impossibility of all saying and saying not" (p. 42). And, echoing Meister Eckhart's formulation concerning the need of *not* knowing God—insights that were to be developed more systematically by Cusanus in terms of "learned ignorance"—he adds: "To know not is to know nothing. This learned ignorance is not the opposite of knowledge but is the knowledge of ignorance that knows it does not know. Rather than announcing salvation, the non-knowledge of the sacred brings the awareness of the impossibility of cure" (p. 43).

This can be heard as perfectly Eckhartian: we know God only in knowing our own unknowing—but as an incomparably intense and shattering experience. Despair in the sense of "hope-less-ness" finds its correlates in Eckhart and apophatic tradition, where giving up all that one hopes for, all the representations one hangs on to, and all attachments opens the way to the cure for human fallenness and sin. This last note of pessimism—"the impossibility of cure"—however, is Taylor's own signature, his characteristically modern feeling of abandonment and his rejection of theological tradition. Eckhart and other apophatic thinkers, in contrast, remain open to being reached and redeemed by the God that they cannot reach or grasp by their own efforts. Even Altizer's incurable passion remains still a theological pathology and, as such, still in relation to God.

Taylor is surely entitled to his preferences, but he presents them as generally valid readings of the times, and this is not possible on the terms that he himself embraces and that someone like Richard Rorty makes philosophically explicit.[55] Like Rorty's claims about philosophical discourse in general, Taylor's insights can and do make an appeal to solidarity and will be embraced by those whose experience leads them to see things similarly, but these insights are not simply insights into the nature of things; they do not command the objectivity that Taylor's rhetoric tends to attribute to them. At this point, one can hear as apposite Hans Urs von Balthasar's remark that the relentless effort of those who have gone on tirelessly proclaiming, for decades and centuries and with ever mounting intensity, that Christianity is bankrupt and historically finished testifies to the power of its presence.[56]

Taylor, however, takes the position that classical negative theology is just a repetition of tired old theological moves: "Contrary to expectation, the *via negativa* traditionally turns out to be a reversal that changes nothing but merely repeats, by inverting, the ontological and epistemological principles that lie at the foundation of Western thought and culture."[57] And yet he admits that the relation of Derrida, for example, to negative theology cannot be merely negative: "Derrida's deconstructive analysis insinuates an alternative reading of negative theology that creates the possibility of thinking God otherwise than by not refusing to think not" (*Nots*, p. 3). Taylor acknowledges that even the most radical refusal of negative theology is still in some sense caught within it. Still, he is determined to reject negative theology, to the extent that this is possible. Not to identify with this tradition seems to be his fundamental motivation, even though negative theology is the tradition, before all others, illuminating the impossibility of such identification. To deny one's father, so as to father oneself, is the irrepressible impulse from which much self-styled liberationist thought since the Enlightenment has sprung. It builds a sort of Oedipal complex into the psychopathology of modernism.

Taylor, consistent with his convictions, has in any case given up on theology in most of his recent writings. *After God* is in some ways his magnum opus, his definitive testament, yet it drops the subject of God in order to brilliantly illuminate the history of religion. This is the direction in which Enlightenment thinking has traditionally moved, but its most provocative moment remains the one of hovering over the dark abyss that harbors the all in which it still recognizes at least a vestige of "God," and it is the discourse of theology in all its negativity that keeps this moment open and alive.

Like Caputo, Taylor distances himself from negative theology, evidently because he agrees with Derrida's assessment that it remains a way of shoring up onto-theological assertions about God, to which it remains nostalgically attached, and bringing them back through the back door of abstraction. Such a view, however, is given the lie by the refocusing on world and body through the lens of apophasis of which we previously took note. Apophatic onto-theology, if that is what it is, is *not* abstract. To leave it simply with the positive qualification of "abstract" would be another unjustifiable circumscription of the infinite and uncircumscribable at which apophasis aims. The apophatic cannot be thought as such, but is rather apprehended in the concrete phenomena (Jean-Luc Marion's "saturated phenomena") that overwhelm all our conceptual structures.

The rejection of negative theology by secular and now postsecular theologians has been shown, once again with Taylor, to derive perhaps more from the motive of asserting one's originality than from any real limitations of negative theology—which is itself the evasion of all delimitations. Nancy, in thinking through the relation between deconstruction and Christian theology in the way I have already explored in the fourth essay in this volume, seems to me to advance decisively beyond Derrida, whose influential rejection of negative theology has often been taken as Bible by his disciples in the deconstructionist sect and sometimes by other commentators, too—with notable exceptions, such as Hent de Vries and Kevin Hart. Derrida saw negative theology as always attempting to use negation in order to make a positive, or rather super-positive, claim about God. Apophatic negation, he suspected, was simply affirmation of a hyperbolic order, attributing to God a super-essence. Even the prayers that frame all predicative discourse in authors such as Dionysius and Anselm he considered to be predicated necessarily on some at least implicit, minimal descriptive characterization of the one addressed in prayer (necessary to identify who is being addressed), hence on at least indirect attribution of predicates to God.

A corrective to such a deconstructive understanding of negative theology is provided by Jean-Luc Marion. Marion has written a detailed refutation defending especially Dionysius against such attempted deconstruction.[58] Marion emphasizes the indeterminacy of negative theology and suggests that it anticipates deconstruction and thereby also challenges the latter's originality. He demonstrates that deconstruction is itself on the defensive against negative theology, which not only escapes deconstruction but already performs it. Christian theology in this guise turns out to be not only *not* a metaphysics of presence but itself already a sort of deconstructing of the metaphysics of presence—without deconstruction! ("on pourrait déconstruire la présence sans elle!" p. 342). Marion presents negative theology in the tradition of Christian theology from the church fathers, particularly Dionysius, as a third way beyond affirmation and negation. Its negation opens upon the infinite and incomprehensible. Derrida ignores this third way beyond binary opposites and beyond metaphysics, which Marion comprehends as "de-naming" ("dénommer"). It entails an anonymity beyond naming and not-naming.

Marion uses this refined understanding of negative theology to answer Derrida's objections to it. He shows that it does not fall back on or presuppose predication, as Derrida charges. Naming God marks an absence as much as a presence. The proper name does not name an essence but rather an excess of presence to essence. The experience of the proper name never essentially fixes the presence of an individual but rather marks the excess of presence to any possible essence and therewith the anonymity of this presence ("que sa présence excède son essence—bref, que sa présence reste anonyme," p. 350). This "third way" is purely pragmatic rather than predicative:[59] it only orients toward what it cannot say or name. Onto-theology, by contrast, would require not an inconceivable *esse* but rather a univocal Being such as Scotus supplies (see the previous essay, sections ii and iii).

Along the apophatic third way, according to Marion, God is rather "de-named" in the horizon of the Good. He remains unknown, as all the Fathers whom Marion cites attest—for only things in the world can be known. Concerning God, we can know only his unknowability. Heresies from Arianism to Spinozism are all based on pretensions to knowledge of the divine essence. But the theological pragmatics of the name inscribe us rather into God's horizon. "With the third way, not only is it no longer a matter of saying (or of denying) something of something, but also of no longer either saying or unsaying at all—it is a matter of referring to Him whom nomination no longer touches. It is a matter uniquely of de-naming" ["Avec la troisième voie, non seulement il ne s'agit plus de dire (ou de nier) quelque chose de quelque chose, mais de ne plus ni dire, ni dédire—il s'agit de se référer à Celui que la nomination ne touche plus. Il s'agit uniquement de dé-nommer," p. 349].

Rather than naming or attributing something to something, apophasis so understood is a matter "of looking in the direction of, relating to . . . comporting oneself towards . . . reckoning with or counting on—in sum, of *working* with . . ." ("Il ne s'agit plus de nommer ou d'attribuer quelque chose à quelque chose, mais de viser en direction de ..., se reporter à ..., de se comporter envers..., de compter avec...—brief de *faire* avec ...," p. 351). This is the new function of the name, Marion suggests, which it takes on precisely in baptism. We are named from God's essential anonymity.

This theological paradigm, moreover, informs Marion's general phenomenology.[60] Marion develops the idea of a phenomenon that is excessive in the modes of being invisible, insupportable, unforeseeable, incommensurable, and impossible.[61] Such a phenomenon exceeds intentionality by the intuition that saturates it. It thereby escapes relations and common terms a priori and shatters the unity of experience. It cannot be fitted into any existing framework but is rather an experience unto itself, an absolute given—the "unconditioned" (p. 118). Phenomenology is placed on what is, in effect, an apophatic footing, and the tradition of apophatic theology from Dionysius and Maximus the Confessor as historical matrices serves as a canonical point of reference. A new beginning of phenomenology can be discerned as a fundamental coordinate of Marion's entire project.[62]

However, although Marion rightly and effectively defends the apophatic against being dismissed as simply a reversal of affirmative propositions concerning God, he nevertheless has a rather austere understanding of negative theology, which does not accord it full expressivity in the poetic and aesthetic and even corporeal forms that it has taken on in contemporary culture. For not unrelated reasons, from Milbank's point of view, Marion lacks an appreciation for the positive role of the world and the flesh in mediating our relationship with the Infinite. Marion, for Milbank, is a kind of Gnostic who gives up the order of the finite as having no intrinsic value as created but only as invested with meaning by consciousness. This has been the predicament of modern thought since Kant and even Descartes. It develops into the paradigm of Idealism in Hegel.[63] Milbank defends a vision in which the finite is "a participation in the infinite donating source of love," whereas for Marion, "beauty does not mediate in its visibility the invisible, but rather forecloses a world of idols or of the merely visible and radically finite as reduced to our representing awareness" (p. 272).[64]

One might say that Marion accepts negative theology as part of the theological tradition and defends it against the charge that it is inextricable from onto-theology. But, on the one hand, this is to give up onto-theology or metaphysics and its tradition and to be blind to *its* apophatic sense, which is surely much more its authentic meaning throughout its long history as marked especially by the thought of poet-metaphysicians among Christian mystics, from Dionysius the Areopagite to John of the Cross and Silesius Angelus. And, on the other hand, Marion does not fully affirm the relevance of apophatic theology to thought today because he misses the full measure of its hyper-positivity, its being at work in all manner of concrete discourses on sacraments and erotics or anything else concerning the created order. His project has often been more one of purifying phenomenology of metaphysical residues and thus thinking through the predicament and the premises of modern philosophy than of affirming, in concert with ancient and medieval theological tradition, an apophatic dimension as the disappearing mediator of all things that opens them to the infinite in their midst. This includes openness without restrictions or exclusions to an infinity of others and their different positionings and viewpoints. Marion's zeal to avoid the taint of metaphysics runs the risk of making an idol of pure givenness itself.[65] There is a residual positivity of Givenness here that captivates him and perhaps preempts complete abandon to the apophatic, particularly in its infinite, incarnate forms.

iv

From these select examples, it appears that some of the most influential thinkers in the philosophy of religion today typically find reasons for rejecting negative theology and for defining themselves against it. Of course, in a certain sense that is recognized sometimes more and sometimes less, this is not even possible. Like God, negative theology neither exists nor can be defined, except in ways that always turn out to be negated and erased or withdrawn. So it is useless or, more accurately, impossible to oppose it. Derrida shows his awareness of this situation in his complex engagement with negative theology in his essay "Comment ne pas parler: dénégations." He questions its very existence and coherence ("Is there a negative theology? Only one?") and hints that it cannot be asserted so much as apprehended only in being denied, when he suggests that there can never be anything other than a negative theology of negative theology.[66]

Yet there is something in the total surrender of propositional logic as assuring knowledge of truth, a surrender required by negative theology, from which other theologies or anti-theologies find it important to distance themselves. We have to remember that the withdrawals and negations are themselves not final, never the last word, and are always in a position themselves to be rescinded. Propositional discourse is indeed broken, but that does not mean that it cannot come back and be understood in a different way in a context that has been broken open by the operation of apophasis. Negative theology always involves also the *negation of negation.* Such negation does not contradict or refute what positive theology offers but rather translates it into another dimension, where it is not asserted in its finite content as true and demonstrated or even well-founded, but is opened toward the infinitely open. One of my personal touchstones for apophatic discourse, Dante's *Paradiso,* is a tight-knit weave of propositions ranging from Scholastic theology and experimental optics to popular astrology and providential historiography. But the ineffability topos, which spans the entire poem, projects all this into another relation—with what is other to all representations.

We must not treat "negative theology" as if it were a definite something, like a box into which one can fit Derrida's thinking or any other radical thinking. Derrida himself clairvoyantly realizes that negative theology, if it is anything, *is not.* The point of insisting on this deep affinity and even structural homology is that the moves made by Derrida and other radical thinkers are misunderstood if they are viewed as simply new and unprecedented; they repeat the conceptual moves made particularly by negative theological thinking in a tradition going back to Plato and even Heraclitus (to mention only Greek precedents). This enables us to see and also to think beyond the deconstructive paradigm—or any other paradigm—to the openness from which thinking originally springs. At this level, the shared ground between even apparently antagonistic theologies or philosophies, when they too are thought radically, becomes visible. And this opens a path for genuine dialogue.

What, then, is negative theology? It seems to be practically nothing—and potentially everything. It is desire reaching beyond the conceivable. Is there not necessarily a metaphysical residue in this form—or rather formlessness—of faith? It is a believing in what we cannot conceive by nevertheless desiring it with a desire directed beyond all that can be presently ascertained as either real or possible. This is the driving motive of thinking that opens itself without limit and becomes to that extent "religious," though this opening is also the realization of the vocation to thinking or the love of wisdom that is the founding charter of philosophy. Both thought-forms, philosophy and theology, discover this vocation especially in taking a turn to poetry—to recognizing human making at work in reaching out toward what is beyond itself.

It is perfectly understandable and indeed symptomatic that both of the theological or philosophical trends that have been examined here recognize the need at some point to differentiate themselves from and even to oppose negative theology, which is taken as having nothing positive to offer. It is even true, in a way, that negative theology has nothing positive to offer, since for negative theology nothing positive in an absolute sense can come from anywhere except from God. Negations of our own finite abstractions are necessary in order to allow the infinite concreteness of the absolutely real to be seen or at least glimpsed—thanks to the contrast created by the shadows cast against its pure light. Negations are necessary in order for the absolutely positive to be discerned at all.

In highlighting what they positively have to contribute, contemporary styles of religious philosophy routinely declare that they are *not* negative, are not like the traditional old negative theology that presumably everyone can agree is no longer needed. Do not mistake the *new* position being offered—they hasten to assert—for *that* outmoded style of onto-theology! They hasten to do so because this hoary tradition has anticipated without fail the emphases on otherness, fragmentation, indirection, pluralism, and all the proliferating possibilities of failure, as well as the possibilities for harmonization and concretization, arising in the wake of whatever else is being put forward as radically new.

There is something in these reactions of the attitude registered by Phillip Blond in accusing the "violence of denial" directed at any preceding world or order "present alongside and before them" (*Post-Secular Philosophy,* p. 3). But Blond himself also denounces the inadequacy of negative theology. He stresses the need for a "positive discourse about God" against these "theological sceptics" (p. 5). This may be granted, and in fact ever since Pseudo-Dionysius the Areopagite the inseparability of the negative and the positive ways has been paramount for negative theology and indeed normative. However, the inverse is in need of at least as much emphasis: no positive theology or orthodoxy can gain acceptance or be true to its own calling without the acknowledgment of its limits as prescribed, or pointed up, by negative theology.

The most general and widespread suspicion against negative theology is that it is merely negative and even nihilistic, but this is to misunderstand it completely, especially in light of its necessary linking with positive theology. Negative theology insists that human concepts and language are negative only in relation to the infinity of *Theos*. Another prevalent and related (mis)apprehension is that negative theology confuses our distinctions and blurs the clear lines of our thought. But is it not necessary to acknowledge the limits of all our own clear distinctions? If not, we make infinite the elucidations of our own devising and treat certain positive articulations as if they were all-enlightening and definitive rather than only our heuristic constructs. And it is hardly possible or responsible today, in our pluralistic culture and context, to promulgate any philosophy in this hegemonic way. We need negative theology as the language of limits to keep open our negotiations between various positive formulations. Only so can we keep them within boundaries, so that they can meaningfully divide up the territory into regions where different theories function best.

The indispensable service of the philosophy of the unsayable is one of checking the tendency toward idolatry to which almost any philosophy, as producing some image of truth, is subject. It requires us to leave truth open, and it also orients us toward some sort of blind vision of the unconditional, though this can never be the basis of any positive claims to know. This regulatory function for the philosophy of the unsayable is not exclusive of its being itself some sort of vehicle to truth, provided that it does not exclude other possible vehicles.

What this suggests is that, just as negative theology needs positive theology in order to have any content to negate or release, so also positive theology (inasmuch as it is a *logos*) is never purely positive, but requires negation in order to be able to articulate anything of the divine or even anything that is not just one more *thing*. No positive theological truth can be apprehended as true—rather than simply as dogmatic assertion—except via some path of negation (*via negativa*), although this passage may be completely submerged. Divinity and infinity are grasped always only in and through negations of human finitude.

Power of Negation—Vehicle to the Infinite

Throughout this book, I have attempted to accord apophatic philosophy a key place in and between the principal currents of thought today, as well as those of the past, in addressing the questions of the origin and destiny, or simply the status and structure, of the world and the sense of things, not to mention the meaning of our life as a projectable whole. Now the question arises: How far are we going to go with negation? Are there any limits here?

The simple but powerful insight that negative theology has to offer and constantly to recall apropos all discourses in the philosophy of religion is that whatever we can see and think and understand in this area must be qualified by negation because it can be thought and said only by means of the negations that are built into the very structure of thinking and saying. Ideas and propositions, as we apprehend them, cannot be adequate to the Other—other than all that can be thought and said—with which or with whom they are concerned. This Other is not even really "other"—nor *is* it in the usual sense of "is" of which we perhaps have some understanding. Our cognitions under the conditions of finitude are always inadequate, always already a negation of what they would be in the dimension of the infinite that is intended by statements taken as religious discourse.

This apparently simple avowal, however, contains many complexities. First of all, it might be considered a confusion to imagine an Infinite and to project it from finite thinking as some transcendent Other, whereas this very idea is itself only a convolution of finite thinking turned in upon itself.[67] Here we do have to recognize different perspectives that are not reconcilable by any ready method. There is here something like a choice of faith that the limitedness and negativity of human cognition is not all that there is. But this faith can be totally nonassertive. The idea that "there is" can be negated, so that rather than believing positively that there is something beyond my finite thoughts and perceptions, I admit that I do not even understand what "there is" means. It is nothng but this mystery toward which I open myself, without being able to define it, but simply by releasing my own ideas of what "to be" is and means. I allow that these are but shadowy ways in which I have apprehended what escapes my apprehension as incommensurable with it. They might be nothing besides the fabrications of my thought and language and, exposed as such, dissolve.[68] But do I comprehend what *that* is, or where it is, or where it comes from, or what it is based on? All my expectations and assumptions might turn out to be erroneous, but to be open to what I do not grasp is still an orientation that I can elect to adopt. This attitude will lead to distinctive types of comportment and possibly to discoveries that otherwise might never be made. At a minimum, it enables me to communicate with and participate in ways of thinking and believing that have been practiced throughout human history and especially prehistory, notably in forms of thought turned toward possibilities of religious experience and practice.

It is in relinquishing all my conceptions of what it is to be that I simply am—without qualification. This is to allow the bare *act* of discourse to precede all determination of its sense, at least enough so as to open the questions concerning God's nature and transcendence. Why have many people—from Taoists to Hindus in the advaitic Vedanta tradition of Sankaracharya, and Buddhists from Nagarjuna to Zen masters in the following of Dogen up to Nishitani, not to mention mystics in Western monotheisms and a host of paganisms—had recourse to similarly negative ideas and values? Reductive accounts such as those of Freud and Feuerbach project all religious reality simply from the human being. But other accounts admit that any such finite determinations of sense have something arbitrary about them. There is, after all, an absolute freedom and contingency in what is said about the unsayable. This emptiness and vagueness has in fact been filled in with the most astonishing and phantasmagoric contents by world religions—which read as testimonies to how human beings interpret their relation to an unsayable dimension of experience.

Of this variety across traditions, negative theology is the custodian. As such, it is one of the most valuable resources for our deepest and most necessary insight into human limits and dependency. Human thought depends on recognition of limits, although these limits seem not to be simply given but rather always in process of being determined. Human being remains in this respect open to infinity, never able to complete its interpretation of itself or to circumscribe itself definitively. Human being is characterized historically and essentially by its infinite openness to the infinite. It is the knowledge of what we do not know, or can only conjecture as the divine, that alone makes us human in this fullest and widest sense. This is the sort of insight that Schelling's "positive" philosophy, as well as Franz von Baader's theosophical neo-Gnostic philosophy, championed against the pretensions of a certain Hegelian idealism to have comprehended everything. Hegel rejected the notion of anything unthinkable or unknowable. Absolute knowing for him brings everything finally within the compass of knowledge. Yet he, too, thinks this absolute knowing as an infinite relatedness. The infinite self-relation of reality, as thought thinking itself, is God. For Hegel, everything is thinkable, though not necessarily by me as a finite, individual, and at least partly opaque mind. I will always participate only very partially and incompletely in the process that engenders absolute knowing by Spirit in its infinity. Indeed, as discussed in my second essay, Hegel's thinking too can turn on itself to become a form of negative theology.

Such, in effect, is the knowledge that animates theological currents that are divergent and apparently deeply opposed, although typically even they repudiate negative theology. Something different is understood under the name of negative theology from case to case, yet inasmuch as "something," some definable thing at all, is understood, a chance for finding a common ground of shared insight is thereby missed. It is not a particular content or idea that is missing, but rather a more open embrace and acceptance of the constitutive negativity of all our conceptualizations, of their originating and deriving their power of insight from a certain surrender to this unsayability in their midst and at their core. Similar insights have been developed in contemporary thought under the aegis of "deconstruction." The philosophy of unsayability, I submit, is at work at some level in almost any kind of philosophical thinking. It is that strain in thinking that dissolves philosophy into the impulse that precedes and motivates it—and which is typically expressed most powerfully in religion and literature.

The power of negation resides in two dimensions that Radical Orthodoxy and radical secular theology, respectively, bring to the forefront. On the one hand, negation is the space in which a transcendent God can be discursively evoked. Nothing can be said of this God except by way of negation. All the exquisitely determined and detailed aspects of the character and acts of the theistic God must come out of the womb of negation, if we are to avoid the profanation of equating our images of divinity with God himself. On the other hand, all the dynamism of the world is also latent in the gesture of negation. Change and dynamism and spontaneity and freedom are per se forms of negation, and they cannot be apprehended by language, except in forms that imitate and enact this negativity (as is shown, for example, by the poetry of Paul Celan). The negative is open to and receives all the presumed "attributes" of God and at the same time all the untrackable complexities of worldly existence.

As these formulations suggest, apophasis makes a basic choice to consider real not what we can empirically experience in objective terms, but an unconditioned reality of which our articulated thought and worldview are always only a negation. This world of negations points to the other reality, beyond our negations, which we do not grasp. This "other" reality might seem terribly alienated and estranged from our concrete experience. However, I maintain, on the contrary, that it is closer to the historical and especially to the prehistorical experience of humankind—the anthropological prehistory of religious rites, mysteries, and shamanism as all turned toward and animated by something beyond saying—from which modern culture has become so estranged. But now in our postmodern and even posthistorical times, there exist new and greater opportunities for reconnection than ever before. Humanity's knowing of itself in the course of history has entailed a loss of its unknown and unknowable "being" and has issued in a narrowing of focus on exterior and superficial, positive and factual, manifestations of this deeper reality. Apophasis uncovers the way of reopening to the hidden dimension at the origin and ground of all our experience, which is invariably lost in a penumbra, once articulation of that experience begins. Theological metaphor is a type of language characteristic of this *dis*articulation. It is "theological" inasmuch as it aims at reflecting what is never graspable as a positive presence as such and yet manifests itself in all experiences and can even be supposed to be their sustaining and ordering principle.

v

Radical Orthodoxy characteristically assumes a confrontational posture vis-à-vis secular culture. It accuses contemporary thought and culture of degrading the human and becoming nihilistic for lack of a theological perspective. It sometimes refuses or denies the possibility of dialogue with other, non-Christian religions and philosophies.[69] It wills to be tenaciously faithful to what it receives as revelation from God rather than listening to the sirens produced by prolific human thought and imagination that beckon in all directions. The challenge to secularism and its promotion of itself to the status of a self-evident, necessary framework is indeed highly necessary. Radical Orthodoxy shows how secularisms, with their transcendental claims, are also religions in disguise. Still, it should not merely reverse their claims. Indeed, *radical* secularism, too, finally assumes a critical perspective underscoring the *self-negating* character of secularism and thereby ironically proclaims itself *prophetic* of a postsecular age.

By elevating itself above universal human culture, either one of the types of religious philosophy compared here would become the purveyor simply of a certain set of images and theologoumena. Paradoxically, this would make Radical Orthodoxy or radical theology *like* the other cultural options vying for attention and competing for adherence in the contemporary marketplace of religions and cults and methods or techniques of salvation. It is rather in finally relinquishing all images, all idols, that we open to the openness in which truly transcendent divinity may be encountered. This unrepresentable dimension that is common to all cultures as underlying them has to be accorded priority over any positive credo, whether orthodox or heterodox.

This is why I maintain that deconstructive, apophatic approaches to Christianity need to be accepted first, at least as partners in dialogue, in order that we not remain confined within any framework of merely human making, including one that understands itself as "theological." What comes from this dimension beyond definable creeds in Radical Orthodoxy and the tradition it builds on, as well as in secular ideologies and their traditions, has to be embraced. Yet neither current should be accepted simply as a true discourse in and for itself. Rather, both are indicative of the "beyond" of discourse, where truth is at work revealing itself in the self-subversion of any and every discourse. In this momentous indicating resides the authentic kenotic vocation of Christian theology and also the invaluable and practically sacred achievement of critical and especially self-critical consciousness in the secular tradition.

Taken in this spirit, Radical Orthodoxy can be an excellent discourse from which to open a dialogue with other discourses of religion or secular philosophies. Revelation must not be identified with any one tradition nor be confined to this or any other religion's initial premises. It occurs most irresistibly at the point where all its articulated convictions are relinquished—at least as claiming exclusive and adequate knowledge of the divine. Revelation in a radical sense takes place in releasing our human logos. Even a polemical attitude could still be productive in generating debate, although not if it means that Radical Orthodoxy takes its own creed to be definitive. That would be the fatal mistake of identifying truth and revelation with one's own human discourse rather than with the beyond of all such discourses. And Milbank is well aware of this danger: that is why he proposes finally to engage in philosophical debate. In the previous essay, I brought out the dialectic of negative theology *within* Radical Orthodox theology, whereas here I have wished to overcome the impasse to dialogue between the two forms of philosophical theology that have been evoked ever since the title of this essay by refocusing them, beyond their competing claims and discourses, on what neither can say as what is most important in each. In each case, philosophy and religion become inseparable as the intellectual form and the lived, relational content of thought that is by its nature and vocation open and unqualified.

Schematically, then, we have seen that the terrain of the philosophy of religion today has become something of a battleground between, first, secularists and postsecularists and then, in more recent redefinitions, between radical theology and radical orthodoxy. Both camps at some point typically wish to mark their differences from negative theology, which is perhaps already a significant hint that precisely negative theology is their common ground and the root from which both theologies are nourished, at least to the extent that they really *are* radical. Rather than storming off further into alienation from one another, which is counter to the universalistic hopes and ambitions nursed by both, it would behoove each approach to understand more of the reasons (and beneath them the *un*reason, or beyond them the excess of reason) of the other, and so also more about what deeply drives the apophatic thinking that animates them both, however antithetical their articulated understandings and verbalizations of it become.

Both factions aim in the end, or ideally, to furnish the hermeneutic *instrumentarium* necessary for forming an inclusive, cosmopolitan culture adequate to postmodern times. Both share the vision of a universal, or at least unrestricted, nonexclusionary, nondiscriminatory, egalitarian, socially responsible, democratic society, and both are intent on transmitting the revelation of life in its fullness that Christianity in its own historical self-understanding affords. Thus they envision life without the typical constrictions that have characterized virtually all historical realizations of human and social existence. This ambition is perhaps shared in principle by any discourse that attempts to persuade and move others, potentially all others susceptible to the Logos, all individuals reasoning by the mediation of words—toward what lies beyond them.

INCONCLUSION

Elected Silence, sing to me . . .
Shape nothing, lips; be lovely-dumb: . . .
Which only makes you eloquent.
      —Gerard Manley Hopkins, from "The Habit of Perfection"

Hent De Vries's *Minimal Theologies* charts its course between two statements, taken as his book's epigraphs, of an anti-credo—of the refusal to believe and profess. The first is from Theodor W. Adorno's *Negative Dialectics:*

> One who believes in God therefore cannot believe in Him. The possibility for which the divine name stands is held secure by whoever does not believe. [Wer an Gott glaubt, kann deshalb an ihn nicht glauben. Die Möglichkeit, für welche der göttliche Name steht, wird festgehalten von dem, der nicht glaubt.]

The second is from Emmanuel Levinas's *Otherwise than Being or Beyond Essence:*

> To bear witness to God is precisely not to enunciate this extra-ordinary word. [Témoigner de Dieu, ce n'est précisément pas énoncer ce mot extra-ordinaire.]

Having dealt with what can and especially with what *cannot* be said according to apophatic thought, there is, then, for us finally the question of what, if anything, the apophatic thinker as such needs or is allowed consistently to *believe.*

326

On the one hand, apophatic thinkers appear to be those among all types of adherents to belief in religion or ideas of philosophy or commitments in ethics who least believe, those who really do not believe in anything. They alone have the matchless audacity to make profession of believing in nothing. Atheism itself is not unbelieving enough for them. They object to (or at least eschew) the atheist's stance in holding a definite conviction and defining a norm of (un)belief rather than evading or evacuating any fixed form of belief whatsoever. Not surprisingly, then, certain proponents of apophaticism have often been taxed with nihilism and other associated taints. But here again, it is necessary to insist on distinguishing between belief simply in nothing and actively *believing* nothing—where the latter does not consolidate its belief into the form of an object but maintains the openness of belief as a believing—even a tenacious and unshakeable believing—yet a believing, nonetheless, in nothing that can be defined or said. Such believing remains infinite and indeterminate, and yet infinitely determinable.

On the other hand, apophaticism is often suspected of being a way of smuggling religious belief back into forms of thought and culture that had ostensibly advanced beyond it: long after its banishment by logos, myth returns as a potential vehicle of truth. This move is patent among certain Neoplatonic thinkers, such as Porphyry in his exegeses of Homer. Apophatic thinkers, furthermore, beyond all their uncompromising negations, are prone to be secretly knights of faith, believing, after all, in a Dionysian night of luminous darkness. Contemporary philosophers of an apophatic bent sometimes seem to confound philosophy and theology and to propose a sort of hyperbole of belief. Free from determinate, limiting, articulated belief, the engaged apophatic can emerge as free to believe in all things in a nonlimiting or nonexclusionary manner. Such is the mode of belief suggested by the Pauline hymn to love: "love bears all things, believes all things, hopes all things, endures all things" (1 Corinthians 13:7). It can and must express itself in a variety of active engagements, which nevertheless remain always open to revision as to the determination of their ends.

Gianni Vattimo explains his position as a form of *believing* that he believes. This acknowledges that one is already inevitably within a position of belief, even in first positioning oneself vis-à-vis belief. Rendering explicit this predicament, which precedes our affirmation and its negations, and then embracing it without qualifications (or at least delimiting and relativizing all qualified forms of it), is characteristic of the strategy of apophatic thought. Apophaticism must be ambiguously philosophical and theological, to the extent that it refuses to definitively reject all beliefs that it nevertheless questions. It retains the beliefs that it questions and even affirms them as opening to questions pointing beyond its own powers of conception. We have seen it doing so throughout this book, exemplarily by means of poetic imagination.

The amphiboly of believing and unbelieving moments of apophasis belongs simply to the nature of this way of thought and relation to life. It first disbelieves whatever it believes and then believes in this disbelief itself as the path leading to what is beyond the very cleavage between belief and disbelief. Apophaticism is the soul of philosophy inasmuch as it critically questions everything that can be believed. But this very activity of questioning is a committed way of relating to all that is or of letting it be all that it can be, and, as such, this way of thinking and being proves to be profoundly religious. In this sense, for Heidegger, questioning was the *piety—die Frömmigkeit*—of thinking. So apophaticism turns out to be practically the opposite of a cold, distanced, analytical skepticism. It is an ardent questioning for the sake of opening all beliefs to their furthest reach of possibility. Among such beliefs, traditional religious teachings often prove to be the richest and the most laden with symbolic meaning and implications for ethics and for life in general. All beliefs are opened by apophasis to the infinity of sense beyond any determinate sense that they convey—such infinity beyond determinate sense comes into its truth only by being betrayed. Any formulation of the infinite is inevitably its *de*formation. Yet this does not mean that such deformation could or should be avoided: on the contrary, we need to retain the awareness of the infinite as conditioning all our formulations and as the horizon of their sense. The vocation of poetic literature in this projection beyond sense has proved to be particularly crucial.

Is this infinite, then, God (as in classical theism) or some Great Spirit or Great Mystery (*Wakan Tanka,* in Native American, specifically Lakotan parlance), or is it just the impulsions that are embedded in our psyche (according to Freud) as coming from we know not where? That is a question on which apophatic thinkers differ. It is a matter of personal belief and reaches beyond the apophatic form of thought that such thinkers nevertheless share in common. It remains perhaps *the* question that all are exercised by and struggle with and often become combative over. It is the question of the nature of reality and of our place and purpose within it. Everything we do and are as humans flows in some sense from our convictions concerning this issue. It is not answered by the philosophy of the unsayable. For Wittgenstein, it is beyond philosophy altogether. Whatever belief is finally embraced in this predicament remains the responsibility of each questioning and questing individual. The philosophy of the unsayable is committed rather to raising the question and to keeping it open. Such is the openness in which transpires conscious human reflection that refuses to be cut off from the mystery of its ground—or its relatedness without limits—and from the infinity of its possibilities.

NOTES

Pre-face

1. I use the term "trans-philosophical" in the sense of overflowing philosophy's disciplinary boundaries, notably in the directions of poetry and religion.

Chapter 1. Invitatory

1. Herman Melville, *Moby-Dick,* ed. Harrison Hayford and Hershel Parker (New York: Norton, 1967), p. 163.

2. Joseph Conrad, *Heart of Darkness,* ed. Ross C. Murfin (New York: St. Martin's Press, 1989), p. 42.

3. Bruce F. Kawain, *The Mind of the Novel: Reflexive Fiction and the Ineffable* (Princeton: Princeton University Press, 1982), pp. 61–62. In addition to treating *Moby-Dick* and *Heart of Darkness* as prime examples of narrating the ineffable, Kawain also dedicates detailed discussion to Proust, Faulkner, Jabès, Beckett, Borges, Gertrude Stein, and others.

4. See Patricia Odek Laurence, *The Reading of Silence: Virginia Woolf in the English Tradition* (Stanford: Stanford University Press, 1991), for Woolf's transformation in apophatic directions of the narration of interiority in the English novel.

5. On Des Forêts in comparison with Melville and Maurice Blanchot, see Ann Smock, *What Is There to Say?* (Lincoln: University of Nebraska Press, 2003).

6. John Auchard's *Silence in Henry James: The Heritage of Symbolism and Decadence* (University Park: Penn State University Press, 1986) documents James's "retreat from the word" and his embrace of "the gospel of silence" during the last twenty years of his life. See also Christopher J. Knight, *Omissions Are Not Acci-*

dents: Modern Apophaticism from Henry James to Jacques Derrida (Toronto: University of Toronto Press, 2010).

7. Henry James, *The Sacred Fount* (New York: Charles Scribner's Sons, 1923), pp. 241 and 223. For a reading of the novel informed by apophatic traditions, see Ann-Marie Piest, "In the Mystic Circle: The Space of the Unspeakable in Henry James's *The Sacred Fount,*" *Style* 34, no. 3 (Fall 2000): 421–43, special issue entitled "Go Figure: Troping the Unspeakable."

8. Peter Michelson, *Speaking the Unspeakable: A Poetics of Obscenity* (Albany: State University of New York Press, 1993), and Claude Olievenstein, *Le non-dit des emotions* (Paris: Odile Jacob, 1988), pursue some of these motives.

9. "Jetzt verstand ich, was der Gott verfügte: Du sprichst die Wahrheit, aber niemand wird dir glauben." Christa Wolf, *Kassandra* (Munich: Deutsche Taschenbuch Verlag, 1993), p. 157.

10. "Ich lernte, in dem ich die Arten zu schweigen beobachtete. Viel später erst lernte ich selbst das Schweigen, welch nützliche Waffe." Ibid., p. 56.

11. A good survey of high points of this apophatic literature in German tradition is Oskar Seidlin, "The Shroud of Silence," *Germanic Review* 28, no. 4 (1953): 254–61. More comprehensive is Christiaan L. Hart Nibbrig, *Rhetorik des Schweigens: Versuch über den Schatten literarischer Rede* (Frankfurt a.M.: Suhrkamp, 1981). For insightful discussion of examples from modern drama (Maeterlinck, Chekhov, Bernard, Beckett, Pinter, Albee), see Leslie Kane, *The Language of Silence: On the Unspoken and the Unspeakable in Modern Drama* (London and Toronto: Associated University Presses, 1984).

12. *The Riverside Shakespeare* (Boston: Houghton Mifflin, 1974). The motif is traced through Shakespeare's oeuvre by Alwin Thaler, *Shakespeare's Silences* (Cambridge, MA: Harvard University Press, 1929), and Harvey Rovine, *Silence in Shakespeare: Drama, Power, and Gender* (Ann Arbor: UMI Research Press, 1987).

13. Ludwig Wittgenstein, *Tractatus Logico-Philosophicus,* trans. C. K. Ogden, with introduction by Bertrand Russell (London: Routledge, 1992), originally 1921.

Chapter 2. In the Hollow of Pan's Pipe

1. Thomas Carlson, *Indiscretion: Finitude and the Naming of God* (Chicago: University of Chicago Press, 1999), pursues precisely this parallel between theology and thanatology in Western tradition from Pseudo-Dionysius to Hegel and Heidegger. Crucial junctures in its history are explored also by Alois Haas, *"Mors mystica:* Thanatologie der Mystik, inbesondere der Deutschen Mystik," *Freiburger*

Zeitschrift für Philosophie und Theologie 23, no. 3 (1976): 304–92, and Giorgio Agamben, *Il linguaggio e la morte* (Turin: Einaudi, 1982). Georges Bataille, Emmanuel Levinas, and Maurice Blanchot, following a suggestion of Heidegger's, dwell obsessively on the problem of the namelessness and "impossibility" of death, as well as of God.

2. Cf. Georg Wilhelm Friedrich Hegel, *Phänomenologie des Geistes* (Frankfurt a.M.: Suhrkamp, 1970 [1807]), "Einleitung," p. 70.

3. "[W]as das Unaussprechliche genannt wird, nichts anderes is als das Unwahre." Hegel, *Phänomenologie,* p. 92 (end of section on Sense-Certainty).

4. Hegel, *Grundlinien der Philosophie des Rechts* (Berlin: Nicolaischen Buchhandlung, 1821), Vorwort (preface), p. xix: "Was vernünftig ist, das ist wirklich; und was wirklich ist, das ist vernünftig." This thesis is developed more extensively by Hegel, especially in his rejection of Jacobi's philosophy of the unknown and ineffable, in *Glauben und Wissen* (1802). As Hegel lucidly shows, admission of such an ineffable principle can lead only to faith rather than to absolute knowing.

5. Jacques Derrida remarked that "Hegel is *also* the thinker of irreducible difference . . . last philosopher of the book and the first thinker of writing" ("Hegel est *aussi* le penseur de la différence irréductible. . . . dernier philosophe du livre et premier penseur de l'écriture," *De la grammatologie* [Paris: Minuit, 1967], p. 41). This suggests why Derrida also said in an interview that "we will never be finished with the reading or rereading of the Hegelian text and, in a certain sense, I do nothing other than attempt to explain myself on this point . . . . the movement by means of which the text exceeds what it intends to say, permits itself to be turned away from, to return to, and to repeat itself outside its self-identity" (*Positions* [Paris: Minuit, 1972], pp. 103–4). Derrida's *Glas* (1974) is just such an unendable rereading of Hegel. So is Werner Hamacher's reading of writing (and reading) in Hegel: see "Pleroma: zu Genesis und Struktur einer dialektischen Hermeneutik bei Hegel," in his edition of Georg Wilhelm Friedrich Hegel, *Der Geist des Christentums* (Frankfurt a.M.: Ullstein, 1978).

6. Alexandre Kojève, *Introduction à la lecture de Hegel* (Paris: Gallimard, 1947).

7. "Das Gefühl der Welt als begrenztes Ganzes ist das Mystische," *Tractatus* 6.45.

8. Walter Benjamin, "Über die Sprache überhaupt und über die Sprache des Menschen" (1916), in *Gesammelte Schriften* (Frankfurt a.M.: Suhrkamp, 1977), vol. 2, part 1, pp. 140–57, trans. Edmund Jephcott as "On Language as Such and on the Language of Man," in *Reflections: Essays, Aphorisms, Autobiographical Writings* (New York: Harcourt Brace Jovanovich, 1978), pp. 314–32.

9. Karl Barth, *Fides quaerens intellectum: Anselms Beweis der Existenz Gottes im Zusammenhang seines theologischen Programms* (Zurich: Theologischer Verlag, 1981 [1931]).

10. Michel de Certeau also treats Anselm's reflection as approaching the extreme limit, iconoclastic and apophatic, of language ("l'extrême bord, iconoclaste et apophatique, du langage"), where the name "God" becomes an index pointing to the inevitable failure of all signs. *La fable mystique,* vol. 1, *XVIe et XVIIe siècle* (Paris: Gallimard, 1982), p. 221.

11. Emmanuel Levinas, *Autrement qu'être et au-delà de l'essence* (Dordrecht: Kluwer, 1990 [1974]), p. 13.

12. Michel de Certeau, *Heterologies: Discourse on the Other,* trans. Brian Massumi (Minneapolis: University of Minnesota Press, 1986).

13. See Franz Rosenzweig, *Der Stern der Erlösung* (Frankfurt a.M.: Suhrkamp, 1988 [1921]), trans. William W. Hallo as *The Star of Redemption* (Notre Dame: University of Notre Dame Press, 1985). I defend this apophatic interpretation of Rosenzweig in "Franz Rosenzweig and the Emergence of a Post-Secular Philosophy of the Unsayable," *International Journal for Philosophy of Religion* 58, no. 3 (2005): 161–80. An apophatic reading of Rosenzweig, highlighting particularly his affinities with the Kabbalah, is proposed by Elliot R. Wolfson, "Light Does Not Talk But Shines: Apophasis and Vision in Rosenzweig's Theopoetic Temporality," in *New Directions in Jewish Philosophy,* ed. Aaron Hughes and Elliot Wolfson (Bloomington: Indiana University Press, 2009), chapter 3. At the conclusion of his introduction to this essay, Wolfson writes that "Rosenzweig's indebtedness to kabbalah, or at the very least the affinity of his path to the Jewish esoteric tradition, can be seen in his embrace of an apophatic discourse at the end, and this in spite of his explicit rejection of negative theology at the beginning."

14. Maurice Blanchot, "La littérature et le droit à la mort," in *Part du feu* (Paris: Gallimard, 1949), pp. 305–45, makes a powerful, precisely *Hegelian* argument for conceiving the imaginary as the whole.

15. See *On What Cannot Be Said: Apophatic Discourses in Philosophy, Religion, Literature, and the Arts,* edited with theoretical and critical essays by William Franke (Notre Dame: University of Notre Dame Press, 2007), vol. 1, *Classical Formulations,* vol. 2, *Modern and Contemporary Transformations.*

16. This is probed by Gerald L. Bruns's suggestive section, "The Moment Before Speech," in *Modern Poetry and the Idea of Language* (New Haven: Yale University Press, 1974).

17. An interesting span of such "philosophies of revelation," ranging from ancient Gnosticism to modern Romantic thought in reaction to Hegel, is treated

by Peter Koslowski, *Philosophien der Offenbarung: Antiker Gnostizismus, Franz Baader, Schelling* (Paderborn: Schöningh, 2001).

18. Cyril O'Regan, *Gnostic Return in Modernity* (New York: State University of New York Press, 2001), p. 227.

19. "Gnosis ist dynamisierte und erzählende Theorie der Totalität." Koslowski, *Philosophien der Offenbarung*, p. 246.

20. "Das erzählende Urteil ist daher die allgemeinste Urteilsform, und alle Urteile beziehen sich auf Erzählungen als ihre letzten Fundierungen." Ibid., p. 253.

21. Ibid., p. 253. In "Über Totalismus: Metaphysik und Gnosis," in *Oikeiosis: Festschrift für Robert Spaemann*, ed. R. Löw (Qeinheim: Acta humaniora, 1987), pp. 101–11, Koslowski further exposes the crypto-Gnostic narrative of alienation (*Entfremdung*) and reconciliation (*Versöhnung*) that undergirds Hegel's System from beginning to end.

22. *Allogenes* 61:14–22, trans. John D. Turner and Orval S. Wintermute, in James M. Robinson, *The Nag Hammadi Library*, rev. ed. (San Francisco: HarperCollins, 1960), p. 225.

23. Jacob Taubes, "Der dogmatische Mythos der Gnosis," in *Terror und Spiel: Probleme der Mythenrezeption*, ed. Manfred Fuhrmann (Munich: W. Fink, 1971), p. 151. Taubes extends this reflection in *Vom Kult zur Kultur: Bausteine zu einer Kritik der historischen Vernunft*, ed. Aleida and Jan Assmann et al. (Munich: Fink, 1996).

24. They may also be said to be "deconstructed," following Jacques Derrida, "La mythologie blanche: La métaphore dans le texte philosophique," in *Marges de la philosophie* (Paris: Minuit, 1972).

25. Such is the general condition of theological inquiry as explained by David Burrell, "Argument in Theology: Analogy and Narrative," in *New Dimensions in Philosophical Theology*, ed. Carl A. Raschke (Missoula: American Academy of Religion, 1982), pp. 37–52.

26. Essays by Martin Heidegger, translated in *Early Greek Thinking*, ed. David Farrell Krell and Frank A. Capuzzi (New York: Harper and Row, 1975), endeavor to recover this vision. In a feminist vein, so does Catherine Keller, *The Face of the Deep: A Theology of Becoming* (New York: Routledge, 2003).

27. Maurice Merleau-Ponty, "L'existentialisme chez Hegel (1)," in *Sens et Non-sens* (Paris: Les Éditions Nagel, 1948), p. 125.

28. See Kojève, *Introduction à la lecture de Hegel*, particularly Appendix II, "L'idée de la mort dans la philosophie de Hegel."

29. See Georges Bataille, "Hegel, la mort et le sacrifice," *Deucalion* 5 (1955): 22–43.

30. Jean Hyppolite, *Logique et existence: Essai sur la logique de Hegel* (Paris: Presses Universitaires de France, 1953), Part I, chapter 1, "L'ineffable." Part III, chapter 1, shows Hegel's speculative proposition to be designed to eliminate the ineffable as anything that could remain exterior to discourse.

31. Hegel's "theory of religious knowledge" is masterfully encapsulated by Merold Westphal, *Hegel, Freedom, and Modernity* (New York: State University of New York Press, 1992), pp. 183–295.

32. Slavoj Žižek, Clayton Crockett, and Creston Davis, eds., *Hegel and the Infinite: Religion, Politics, and Dialectic* (New York: Columbia University Press, 2011), p. 7. See also Andrew W. Hass, *Hegel and the Art of Negation: Negativity, Creativity, and Contemporary Thought* (London: I. B. Tauris, 2013).

33. David Walsh, *The Modern Philosophical Revolution: The Luminosity of Existence* (Cambridge: Cambridge University Press, 2008), p. 89.

34. One such reading of Hegel is Werner Beierwaltes, "Das seiende Eine: Neuplatonische Interpretationen der zweiten Hypothesis des platonischen 'Parmenides' und deren Fortbestimmung in der christlichen Theologie und in Hegels Logik," in *Denken des Einen: Studien zur Neuplatonischen Philosophie und ihrer Wirkungsgeschichte* (Frankfurt a.M.: Klostermann, 1985).

35. "Die spekulative Idee ist ein μυστήριον sowohl für die sinnliche Betrachtung wie für den Verstand. Μυστήριον nämlich ist das, was das Vernünftige ist; bei den Neuplatonikern heißt dieser Ausdruck auch schon nur spekulative Philosophie." Hegel, *Vorlesungen über die Philosophie der Religion,* ed. Georg Lasson (Hamburg: Meiner, 1966), vol. 2, part 2, p. 77.

36. Cyril O'Regan, *The Heterodox Hegel* (Albany: State University of New York Press, 1994), pp. 31–44.

37. As O'Regan, in "Jean-Luc Marion: Crossing Hegel," in *Counter-Experiences: Reading Jean-Luc Marion,* ed. Kevin Hart (Notre Dame: University of Notre Dame Press, 2007), pp. 95–150, puts it: "negative theology represents the death of Hegel's discourse, specifically of its semantic triumphalism and its self-satisfaction in and as the pleroma of self-consciousness" (p. 120).

38. Søren Kierkegaard, "The Absolute Paradox: A Metaphysical Crotchet," chapter 3 of *Philosophical Fragments,* trans. Howard V. Hong and David F. Swenson (Princeton: Princeton University Press, 1936–74), p. 46.

39. Kierkegaard, *The Concept of Irony,* trans. Lee M. Capel (London: Collins, 1966), p. 340.

40. "Was ich nur *meine,* ist *mein,* gehört mir als diesem besonderen Individuum an; wenn aber die Sprache nur Allgemeines ausdrückt, so kann ich nicht sagen, was ich nur *meine.* Und das *Unsagbare,* Gefühl, Empfindung, ist nicht das Vortrefflichste, Wahrste, sondern das Unbedeutendste, Unwahrste." Georg Wilhelm Friedrich Hegel, *Enzyklopädie der philosophischen Wissenschaften im Grundrisse. Erster Teil. Die Wissenschaft der Logik* (Frankfurt a.M.: Suhrkamp, 1986), §20.

41. Massimo Baldini and Silvano Zucal, eds., *Il silenzio e la parola da Eckhart à Jabès* (Brescia: Morcelliana, 1989), p. 11.

42. Quentin Lauer, S.J., "Hegel's Negative Theology," *Journal of Dharma: The International Quarterly of World Religions* 6 (1981): 46–58, and *Hegel's Concept of God* (New York: State University of New York Press, 1982); Jean-Louis Vieillard-Baron, "Le négatif en Dieu et la douleur infinie dans la pensée de Hegel à Iéna," in *Théologie négative,* ed. Marco M. Olivetti (Milan: CEDAM, 2002), pp. 645–59; Rowan Williams, "The Mystery of God in Hegel's Philosophy," in *The via negativa: Papers on the History and Significance of Negative Theology,* ed. Raoul Mortley and David Dockrill, *Prudentia* Supplementary number 1981 (Auckland, NZ: Prudentia, 1981).

43. Slavoj Žižek, "The Fear of Four Words: A Modest Plea for the Hegelian Reading of Christianity," in *The Monstrosity of Christ,* ed. Creston Davis (Cambridge, MA: MIT Press, 2009), pp. 24–109.

44. See also Slavoj Žižek, *The Puppet and the Dwarf: The Perverse Core of Christianity* (Cambridge, MA: MIT Press, 2003).

45. See chapter 9 on Rosenzweig in Franke, *On What Cannot Be Said,* vol. 2, pp. 139–44, together with section 2 of the general introduction, which makes a case for viewing him as a seminal apophatic thinker. Schelling's *Philosophie der Offenbarung* is excerpted and discussed in the same volume, pp. 62–73.

46. Hegel, *Vorlesungen über die Philosophie der Religion,* in G. W. F. Hegel, *Werke in 20 Bänden* (Frankfurt a.M.: Suhrkamp, 1978), vol. 16, p. 106.

47. Rowan Williams, "The Logic of Spirit in Hegel," in *Post-Secular Philosophy,* ed. Phillip Blond (London: Routledge, 1998), pp. 123–25.

48. O'Regan, *The Heterodox Hegel,* following Ferdinand Christian Bauer, *Die Christliche Gnosis* (1835), treats Hegel from precisely this point of view.

49. See Peter Koslowski, "Der Übergang von der negativen zur positiven Philosophie in der Spätphilosophie Schellings," in *Théologie négative,* ed. Marco Olivetti (Milan: CEDAM, 2002), pp. 645–60. The second draft of Schelling's fragment "Die Weltalter" (1813), translated by Judith Norman and published together with a Lacanian interpretation and commentary by Slavoj Žižek in F. W. J. von Schelling, *The Abyss of Freedom/Ages of the World* (Ann Arbor: University of Michigan Press, 1997), illuminates his appeal for poststructuralist thinkers. The contemporary rediscovery of Schelling as an (apophatic) alternative to Hegel is indebted to Jean-François Courtine, *Extase de la raison: Essais sur Schelling* (Paris: Galilée, 1990), and to *Le dernier Schelling: Raison et positivité,* ed. Jean-François Courtine and Jean-François Marquet (Paris: Vrin, 1994).

50. Christopher Lauer, *The Suspension of Reason in Hegel and Schelling* (London: Continuum, 2010), underscores the suspension (*Aufhebung*) of reason that both thinkers share in common.

51. John D. Caputo, "God Is Wholly Other—Almost: *Différance* and the Hyperbolic Alterity of God," in *The Otherness of God,* ed. Orrin F. Summerell (Charlottesville: University Press of Virginia, 1998).

52. Cusanus, *De li non aliud* (1462), trans. Jasper Hopkins, in *Nicholas of Cusa on God as Not-Other,* 3rd ed. (Minneapolis: Arthur Banning Press, 1987).

53. William Desmond, *Hegel's God: A Counterfeit Double* (London: Ashgate, 2003), p. ix.

54. William Desmond, *God and the Between* (Oxford: Blackwell, 2008), pp. 199–204.

55. Jean-Luc Marion, *De surcroît: Études sur les phénomènes saturés* (Paris: Presses Universitaires de France, 2001), and *Le visible et le relevé* (Paris: Cerf, 2005), pp. 35–74.

56. Dominique Janicaud, *Le tournant théologique de la phénoménologie française* (Combas: L'Éclat, 1991). In English, see Janicaud et al., *Phenomenology and the 'Theological Turn': The French Debate* (New York: Fordham University Press, 2000).

57. Jean-Louis Chrétien, *L'antiphonaire de la nuit* (Paris: L'Herne, 1989). For Michel Henry, see his *C'est moi la vérité: Pour une philosophie du christianisme* (Paris: Seuil, 1998), trans. Susan Emanuel as *I Am the Truth: Toward a Philosophy of Christianity* (Stanford: Stanford University Press, 2003); and Henry, *L'essence de la manifestation* (Paris: Presses Universitaires de France, 1990 [1963]).

58. Henri Meschonnic, "Dieu absent, Dieu présent dans le langage," in *Qu'est-ce que Dieu? Philosophie, théologie: Hommage à l'abbé Daniel Coppieters de Gibson (1929–1983)* (Bruxelles: Facultés Universitaires Saint-Louis, 1985), p. 358.

59. Ibn Arabi, *Fusus al-Hikam [Bezels of Wisdom],* ed. Abu'l Ala 'Affi (Beirut: Dar al-Kitah al-'Arabi, 1946), p. 70. See, further, Henri Corbin, *L'imagination créatrice dans le soufisme d'Ibn 'Arabî* (Paris: Flammarion, 1958), and William C. Chittick, *The Sufi Path of Knowledge: Ibn al-'Arabi's Metaphysics of Imagination* (Albany: State University of New York Press, 1989).

60. Thomas A. Carlson extends his work on "indiscretion" in a mystical anthropological direction in *The Indiscrete Image: Infinitude and Creation of the Human* (Chicago: University of Chicago Press, 2008).

61. Benjamin, "Über die Sprache überhaupt und über die Sprache des Menschen."

62. The phenomenon of witness is explored specifically vis-à-vis the unspeakable of the Holocaust by Claude Lanzmann's film *Shoah.* Text and commentary are available in Shoshona Felman and Dori Laub, M.D., *Testimony: Crises of Witnessing in Literature, Psychoanalysis, and History* (New York: Routledge, 1992), chapter 7, "The Return of the Voice: Claude Lanzmann's *Shoah,*" pp. 204–83.

63. Michel Henry, *Incarnation: Une philosophie de la chair* (Paris: Seuil, 2000). This Christian phenomenology of the divine mystery of the flesh is pursued through exegesis of ancient fathers and medieval doctors of the church by Emmanuel Falque, *Dieu, la chair et l'autre: D'Irénée à Duns Scot* (Paris: Presses Universitaires de France, 2008).

64. See *Apophatic Bodies: Negative Theology, Incarnation, and Relationality,* ed. Chris Boesel and Catherine Keller (New York: Fordham University Press, 2009).

65. A subtle and, I believe, supportive discussion of these issues can be found in Kevin Hart, "The Economy of Mysticism," in *The Trespass of the Sign: Deconstruction, Theology and Philosophy* (Cambridge: Cambridge University Press, 1989), chapter 6, pp. 173–206. Hart shows that apophatic mysticism and deconstruction are akin and bound up with one another.

66. Gorgias's "On Nature," preserved in fragments by Sextus Empiricus, cited according to Kathleen Freeman, *Ancilla to the Pre-Socratic Philosophers* (Cambridge, MA: Harvard University Press, 1957), p. 129.

67. The Sophists' noninstrumental use of language for pleasure and free invention is treated as poetically and ontologically revealing by Stanislas Breton, *La philosophie du rien* (Kampen, Netherlands: Kok Pharos, 1992), pp. 100–104. For Breton, the minimalist ontology of the Sophists is a mirror image of the maximalist ontology of the Neoplatonists: both aim to reveal the Nothing, but from opposite directions.

68. Jean-Luc Nancy makes this movement beyond sense the fulcrum for his thinking, as is brought out by Francis Guibal and Jean-Clet Martin, eds., *Sens en tous sens: Autour des travaux de Jean-Luc Nancy* (Paris: Galilée, 2004).

69. Meschonnic, "Dieu absent, Dieu présent dans le langage," p. 389, writes of such an invasion and the consequent "disappearance of language" as a goal for Hebrew and Arab mystics ("Un aboutissement, chez les mystiques, de cet envahissement de langage par Dieu, est donc une disparition du langage").

70. Hugo von Hofmannsthal, "Ein Brief," in *Gesammelte Werke in Einzelausgaben,* ed. Herbert Steiner (Frankfurt a.M.: Fischer, 1945), p. 467.

71. Jean-Luc Marion, *L'idole et la distance: Cinq études* (Paris: Grasset, 1977), dwells acutely on this imperative. He is followed up by Bruce Ellis Benson, *Graven Ideologies: Nietzsche, Derrida and Marion on Modern Idolatry* (Downers Grove, IL: InterVarsity Press, 2002).

72. For Stanislas Breton, *Le Verbe et la croix* (Paris: Desclée, 1981), the surpassing of Logos, traditionally understood as words of Wisdom, by the Word of the Cross ("le dépassement du Logos par le Verbe de la Croix," p. 9) leads to a negative, kenotic theology and an apophatic mysticism.

73. Such an apophatic theology of the Eucharist is developed by Jean-Luc Marion, *Dieu sans l'être* (Paris: Fayard, 1982), trans. Thomas A. Carlson as *God Without Being* (Chicago: University of Chicago Press, 1991), especially chapter 5, "The Eucharistic Site of Theology."

74. Henri de Lubac, *Corpus mysticum: L'eucharistie et l'église au moyen âge* (Paris: Aubier, 1944), trans. Gemma Simmonds as *Corpus Mysticum: The Eucharist and the Church in the Middle Ages* (Notre Dame: University of Notre Dame Press, 2007), and Regina Mara Schwartz, *Sacramental Poetics at the Dawn of Secularism: When God Left the World* (Stanford: Stanford University Press, 2008) illuminate this mystery with respect to specific historical contexts, the medieval and the early modern respectively.

75. John Milbank, *The Word Made Strange: Theology, Language, Culture* (Oxford: Blackwell, 1997), traces in their theological ramifications the apophatic insights opened by language theory from Vico to poststructuralism. He, however, at least at this stage, ultimately rejects the apophatic, as Luke Townsend convincingly demonstrates in an unpublished paper. I pursue this issue in the fifth essay of the present volume.

76. If we consider, furthermore, following Jean Baudrillard, *La précession des simulacres* (Paris: Minuit, 1978), the way that our social and cultural reality is produced by images, a projected world is no more phantasmatic than the supposedly real world.

77. This is convincingly demonstrated by Benjamin Pollock, *Franz Rosenzweig and the Systematic Task of Philosophy* (Cambridge: Cambridge University Press, 2009).

78. Maurice Blanchot, *L'écriture du désastre* (Paris: Gallimard, 1980), makes great play with this traditional etymological motif of the "un-starring" ("désastre") or coming undone of the cosmos.

79. Recent philosophy of science has uncovered the chaos underlying natural order and the order underlying chaos as mutually inextricable. See M. Mitchell Waldrop, *Complexity: The Emerging Science at the Edge of Order and Chaos* (New York: Simon & Schuster, 1992), and Edward N. Lorenz, *The Essence of Chaos* (Seattle: University of Washington Press, 1993).

80. Samuel Beckett, *Endgame* (New York: Grove, 1958), p. 50.

81. Leslie Kane, *The Language of Silence: On the Unspoken and the Unspeakable in Modern Drama* (London and Toronto: Associated University Presses, 1984), p. 106.

82. Harold Pinter, "Between the Lines," Speech to the Seventh National Student Drama Festival in Bristol, *Sunday Times* (London), March 4, 1962, p. 25. Quoted in Kane, *The Language of Silence*, p. 19. The demonstration is Pinter's lyrical piece *Silence* (London: Eyre Methuen, 1978).

83. For numerous examples, see both volumes of Franke, *On What Cannot Be Said.*

84. Kasimir Malevich, "God Is Not Cast Down," in Franke, *On What Cannot Be Said,* vol. 2, pp. 211–45.

Chapter 3. The Writing of Silence in the Post-Holocaust Poetry of Edmond Jabès and Paul Celan

1. For example, by Michel Rinn, *Les récits du génocide: Sémiotique de l'indicible* (Paris: Delachaux et Niestle, 1998); Saul Friedländer, ed., *Probing the Limits of Representation: Nazism and the Final Solution* (Cambridge, MA: Harvard University Press, 1992); and Thomas Trezise, "Unspeakable," *Yale Journal of Criticism* 14, no. 1 (2001): 39–66.

2. For this notion of Jewishness, cf. Maurice Blanchot, "Être Juif," in *L'Entretien infini* (Paris: Gallimard, 1969).

3. See Hans Jonas, *The Gnostic Religion: The Message of the Alien God and the Beginnings of Christianity* (Boston: Beacon Press, 1958).

4. Several of Hent de Vries's writings, particularly *Theologie im Pianissimo & Zwischen Rationalität und Dekonstruktion: Die Aktualität der Denkfiguren Adornos und Levinas'* (Kampen: J. H. Kok, 1989), and *Philosophy and the Turn to Religion* (Baltimore: Johns Hopkins University Press, 1999), revolve around this question as it arises from the work of Derrida, Levinas, and Adorno. See, further, Beth Hawkins, *Reluctant Theologians: Franz Kafka, Paul Celan, Edmond Jabès* (New York: Fordham University Press, 2003).

5. "Tu nies Dieu, car ton amour pour lui l'a ôté de ta vue—comme la lumière nous cache la lumière." Edmond Jabès, *Le livre des questions* (Paris: Gallimard, 1976), p. 140.

6. Jacques Derrida, *De la grammatologie* (Paris: Seuil, 1967): "Le signe et la divinité ont le même lieu et le même temps de naissance. L'époque du signe est essentiellement théologique" (p. 25).

7. One index is the role of these motifs in the Frankfurt school, starting from Horkheimer and Adorno.

8. Emmanuel Levinas, *Autrement qu'être ou au-delà de l'essence* (The Hague: Nijhoff, 1974).

9. See Levinas's essay on Celan: "Tout Autrement," in *Noms propres* (Paris: Fata Morgana, 1976), pp. 65–72.

10. German texts are quoted from Paul Celan, *Gesammelte Werke in fünf Bände,* ed. Beda Allemann and Stefan Reichert (Frankfurt a.M.: Suhrkamp,

1972), referred to hereafter as *GW*. The phrase "gab keine Worte her für das, was geschah" occurs in vol. 3, p. 185.

11. *The Poems of Paul Celan,* trans. Michael Hamburger (New York: Persea Books, 1995).

12. Cf. Peter Horst Neumann, *Zur Lyrik Paul Celans: Eine Einführung* (Göttingen: Vandenhoeck & Ruprecht, 1990 [1968]), p. 25.

13. Paul Celan, *Collected Prose,* trans. Rosemarie Waldrop (Manchester: Carcanet, 1986), p. 34. Further translations of the prose works of Celan are cited from this edition. The quotations in German are from Celan's poetological addresses at Bremen and Darmstadt ("Der Meridian"), in *GW,* vol. 3.

14. Celan, *Collected Prose,* p. 49. "Aber das Gedicht will zu einem Anderen, es braucht dieses Andere, es braucht ein Gegenüber. Es sucht es auf, es spricht sich ihm zu" (*GW,* vol. 3, p. 198).

15. "hindurchgehen durch furchtbares Verstummen, hindurchgehen durch die tausend Finsternisse todbringender Rede" (*GW,* vol. 3, p. 186).

16. Celan, *Collected Prose,* p. 34. "Sie ging hindurch und gab keine Worte her für das, was geschah; aber sie ging durch dieses Geschehen. Ging hindurch und durfte wieder zutage treten, angereichert von all dem" (*GW,* vol. 3, p. 186).

17. Edmond Jabès, *El, ou le dernier livre* (Paris: Gallimard, 1973), p. 93.

18. Edmond Jabès, *Le soupçon le desert* (Paris: Gallimard, 1978), p. 96.

19. Jabès, *Livre des questions,* p. 70: "Yukel, parle-nous du silence qui est le terme et le commencement, étant l'âme des mots comme le chantre et le martyre sont, au moment désigné, l'âme du monde."

20. In Edmond Jabès, *Du désert au livre: Entretiens avec Marcel Cohen* (Paris: Belfond, 1991 [1980]), Jabès admits that there are characters and a story in his books, but maintains that they belong to and finally disappear into the Book, becoming indistinct from it ("Oui, certes; mais ces personages se confondent avec le livre," p. 143).

21. My translation. Unlike Hamburger's, it does not attempt to imitate Celan's rhyme scheme.

22. Edmond Jabès, *Le petit livre de la subversion hors de soupçon* (Paris: Gallimard, 1982), p. 50.

23. I situate Rosenzweig in these contexts in Franke, *On What Cannot Be Said,* vol. 2, pp. 15–25.

24. Jabès, *El,* p. 93.

25. Cf. Gershom Scholem, "Der Name Gottes und die Sprachtheorie der Kabbala," in *Man and Speech/Mensch und Wort/L'homme et le verbe,* ed. Adolf Portmann and Rodolf Ritsema, Eranos-Jahrbuch 39/1970 (Leiden: Brill, 1973), p. 270.

26. Jabès, "The Question of Displacement into the Lawfulness of the Book," in *The Sin of the Book,* ed. Eric Gould (Lincoln: University of Nebraska Press, 1985), p. 230.

27. "La parole divine est tue aussitôt prononcée. C'est à ses anneaux sonores, qui sont nos paroles inspirées, que nous nous accrochons." Jabès, *Livre des questions,* pp. 92–93.

28. *"L'âme peut être comparée à une montagne de silence que la parole soulève. Une faiblesse des muscles et elle s'écroule."* Ibid., p. 96.

29. Jabès, *Le soupçon le désert,* p. 42.

30. Jacques Derrida, "Edmond Jabès et la question du livre," in *L'écriture et la différence* (Paris: Seuil, 1968), p. 108.

31. Here Jabès converges with Levinas, as well as with Blanchot. Cf. Christian Saint-Germain, *Écrire sur la nuit blanche: L'éthique du livre chez Emmanuel Lévinas et Edmond Jabès* (Québec: Presses de l'Université de Québec, 1992).

32. Helena Shillony, *Edmond Jabès: Une rhétorique de la subversion* (Paris: Archives de lettres modernes, 1991), p. 67.

33. "Le rapport du Juif—talmudiste, kabbalist—au livre est, dans sa ferveur, identique à celui que l'écrivain entretient avec son texte. Tous deux ont même soif d'apprendre, de connaître, de décrypter leur destin gravé dans chaque lettre où Dieu s'est retiré." Edmond Jabès, *Le livre des marges* (Paris: Le Livre de poche, 1987), p. 181. Susan A. Handelman, *The Slayers of Moses: The Emergence of Rabbinic Interpretation in Modern Literary Theory* (Albany: State University of New York Press, 1982), likewise situates Jabès in this Jewish hermeneutical context.

34. François Laruelle, "Le point sur l'Un," in *Écrire le Livre: Autour d'Edmond Jabès,* ed. Richard Stamelman and Mary Ann Caws (Seyssel: Champ Vallon, 1989), pp. 121–32.

35. Jabès, *Le petit livre de la subversion hors de soupçon,* p. 77.

36. Edmond Jabès, *Un étranger avec, sous le bras, un livre de petit format* (Paris: Gallimard, 1989), p. 13.

37. Gershom Scholem, *Die jüdische Mystik in ihren Hauptströmungen* (Frankfurt a.M.: Suhrkamp, 1980 [1957]): "Steht also in der Allegorie ein Ausdrückbares für ein anderes Ausdrückbares, so steht im mystischen Symbol ein Ausdrückbares für etwas, was der Welt des Ausdrucks und der Mitteilung entrückt ist" (p. 29).

38. Benjamin, *Ursprung des deutschen Trauerspiels* in *Gesammelte Schriften,* ed. Rolf Tiedemann and Hermann Schweppenhäuser (Frankfurt a.M.: Suhrkamp, 1991), vol. 1, pt. 1, p. 341. Benjamin is himself quoting Friedrich Creuzer.

39. Jabès, *Livre des questions,* pp. 134–35.

40. Edmond Jabès, *Aely* (Paris: Gallimard, 1972), p. 157.

41. Michel Deguy, *La raison poétique* (Paris: Galilée, 2000), comments, "Many theorists, many thinkers who are friends of poetry, like to speak today, and precisely in *citing* Celan, of poetry 'without image' and 'without metaphor' and 'outside representation'" (p. 94).

42. Edmond Jabès, *La mémoire des mots: Comment je lis Paul Celan* (Châtillon-sous-Bagneux: Fourbis, 1990), p. 9.

43. Aris Fioretos, ed., *Word Traces: Readings of Paul Celan* (Baltimore: Johns Hopkins University Press, 1994), p. xvii.

44. Theodor W. Adorno, *Ästhetische Theorie*, ed. Gretel Adorno and Rolf Tiedemann (Frankfurt a.M.: Suhrkamp, 1972), *Gesammelte Schriften*, vol. 7, p. 477.

45. Maurice Blanchot, *Le dernier à parler* (Saint Clément: Fata morgana, 1984): "Et ce qui nous parle, dans ces poèmes le plus souvent très courts où termes, phrases semblent, par le rhythme de leur brièveté indéfini, environnés de blanc, c'est que ce blanc, les arrêts, ces silences ne sont pas des pauses intervalles permettant la respiration de la lecture, mais appartiennent à la même rigueur, celle qui n'autorise que peu de relâchement, une rigueur non verbale qui ne serait pas destinée à porter sens, comme si le vide était moins un manque qu'une saturation, un vide saturé de vide."

46. Hermann Burger, *Paul Celan: Auf der Suche nach der verlorenen Sprache* (Zürich and Munich: Artemis Verlag, 1974), p. 9, echoing phrases from Celan's "Büchner-Preis-Rede."

47. Winfried Menninghaus, *Paul Celan: Magie der Form* (Frankfurt a.M.: Suhrkamp, 1980), reads Celan's poetry for its "Intention auf die Sprache," a phrase borrowed from Benjamin's "Die Aufgabe des Übersetzers."

48. Otto Lorenz, *Schweigen in der Dichtung: Hölderlin – Rilke – Celan. Studien zur Poetik deiktisch-elliptischer Schreibweisen* (Göttingen: Vandenhoeck & Ruprecht, 1989).

49. Marlies Janz, *Vom Engagement absoluter Poesie: Zur Lyrik und Ästhetik Paul Celans* (Frankfurt a.M.: Suhrkamp, 1976).

50. Seminal for interpretations focused on ways that Celan's language operates apparently to suspend normal referentiality is Gerhard Neumann, "Die absolute Metapher: Ein Abgrenzungsversuch am Beispiel Stéphane Mallarmés und Paul Celans," *Poetica* 3 (1970): 188–225. The same premise governs interpretations of the poems by Peter Horst Neumann, *Zur Lyrik Paul Celans: Eine Einführung* (Göttingen: Vandenhoeck & Ruprecht, 1990 [1968]). This approach is sharply contested by Marlies Janz, who underlines Celan's political engagement with history. Nuanced approaches pointing to the aporiae in any reference to reality have been ventured by Georg Michael Schulz, *Negativität in der Dichtung*

Paul Celans (Tübingen: Niemeyer, 1977), and, on the basis of deconstructive rhetoric, by Astrid Poppenhusen, *Durchkreuzung der Tropen: Paul Celans Die Niemandsrose im Lichte der traditionellen Metaphorologie und ihrer Dekonstruktion* (Heidelberg: C. Winter, 2001).

51. See Dietlind Meinecke, *Wort und Name bei Paul Celan: Zur Widerruflichkeit des Gedichts* (Bad Homburg: Gehlen, 1970); Joachim Schulze, *Celan und die Mystiker: Motivtypologisches und quellenkundliche Kommentare*, 2nd ed. (Bonn: Bouvier Verlag, 1983).

52. Shira Wolosky, "Mystical Language and Mystical Silence in Paul Celan's 'Dein Hinübersein,'" in *Argumentum e Silentio: International Paul Celan Symposium*, ed. Amy D. Colin (Berlin: Walter de Gruyter, 1987), p. 368. Albrecht Schöne, *Dichtung als verborgene Theologie: Versuch einer Exegese von Paul Celans 'Einem, der vor der Tür stand'* (Göttingen: Wallstein Verlag, 2000), excavates the poetry's covert theology.

53. Amy D. Colin, "Paul Celan's Poetics of Destruction," in *Argumentum e Silentio: International Paul Celan Symposium*, p. 178.

54. Some parts of these deconstructive readings translated into English may be found in Fioretos, *Word Traces*. Cf. Martin Jörg Schäfer, *Schmerz zum Mitsein: Zur Relektüre Celans und Heideggers durch Philippe Lacoue-Labarthe und Jean-Luc Nancy* (Würzburg: Königshausen & Neumann, 2003).

55. Jacques Derrida, "La langue n'appartient pas. Entretien avec Evelyn Grassman," *Europe: Revue littéraire mensuelle* (January–February 2001): 81–91.

56. Rochelle Tobias, *The Discourse of Nature in the Poetry of Paul Celan: The Unnatural World* (Baltimore: Johns Hopkins University Press, 2006), deftly conjoins the earthly, mortal, material, dismembered body with the religious obsession concerning homecoming to the stars as to an Unknown God: cosmogony intertwines with theogony, following the medieval Kabbalah (pp. 56–78).

57. Celan, *Collected Prose*, p. 55.

58. Leonard Olschner, "Poetic Mutations of Silence: At the Nexus of Paul Celan and Osip Mandelstam," in Fioretos, *Word Traces*, p. 369.

59. *GW*, vol. 1, p. 138. I have translated the first stanza; the rest of the translation is Olschner's, in "Poetic Mutations of Silence."

60. See, further, Leonard Moore Olschner, *Der feste Buchstab: Erläuterungen zu Paul Celans Gedichtübertragungen* (Göttingen: Vandenhoeck & Ruprecht, 1985), pp. 226–74 and 133–36.

61. This pairing, unlike that with Jabès, has received intensive critical attention. See especially Michael Eskin, "Mandel'shtam and Paul Celan: The Poetics of Dialogue," in *Ethics and Dialogue in the Works of Levinas, Bakhtin, Mandel'shtam, and Celan* (New York: Oxford University Press, 2000), pp. 113–60.

62. Celan, *Collected Prose*, p. 34.

63. The pervasive importance of wounding imagery in Celan's poetry is thoroughly researched by Ralf Willms, *Das Motiv der Wunde im lyrischen Werk von Paul Celan: Historisch-systematische Untersuchungen zur Poetik des Opfers* (Munich: AVM Verlag, 2011).

64. Subsequent quotations of Celan generally follow Hamburger's translations in *The Poems of Paul Celan.*

65. Celan also uses this same device in several other compositions of *Atemwende* (*GW*, vol. 1, pp. 222, 242–43, 245, 247), thereby figuring the turning point as a "turn of the breath."

66. Hans-Jost Frey, "Zwischentextlichkeit von Celans Gedichte: *Zwölf Jahre* und *Auf Reisen*," in *Paul Celan,* ed. Werner Hamacher and Winfried Menninghaus (Frankfurt a.M.: Suhrkamp, 1988).

67. Cf. Frey, ibid., for the anagrams of word and love and for his generally apophatic approach to the poem.

68. "Ich stehe auf einer anderen Raum—und Zeitebene als mein Leser; er kann mich nur 'entfernt' verstehen, er kann mich nicht in den Griff bekommen, immer greift er nur die Gitterstäbe zwischen uns." Hugo Huppert, "'Spirituell': Ein Gespräche mit Paul Celan," in *Paul Celan,* ed. Hamacher and Menninghaus, p. 319.

69. "Sa poésie ne fut que recherche d'une réalité. Réalité d'une langue. Le réel, c'est l'absolu." Edmond Jabès, *La mémoire des mots: Comment je lis Paul Celan* (Paris: Fourbis, 1990), p. 18.

70. "Mais la question se pose toujours: la langue du silence serait-elle celle du refus de la langue ou, au contraire, celle de la mémoire du premier mot?" (ibid., p. 14).

Chapter 4. Apophasis and the Predicament of Philosophy of Religion Today

For the traditional motto used as the epigraph, see Achim Wurm, "Mystisches Sprechen," in *Philosophie der UnVerbindlichkeit: Einführungen in ein ausstehendes Denken,* ed. Paul Janssen (Würzburg: Königshausen und Neumann, 1995), p. 225.

1. Arthur Bradley, *Negative Theology and Modern French Philosophy* (New York: Routledge, 2004), develops this parallel, and Stephen Gersh, *Neoplatonism after Derrida: Parallelograms* (Leiden: Brill, 2006), especially chapter 4, section 2, treats Heidegger's and Derrida's disruptions of logic and syntax hermeneutically as a "subtext of Neoplatonic discussions of Being" (p. xiv).

2. The Tübingen school is building upon work by earlier generations of scholars, including Werner Jaeger, John Burnett, and J. N. Findlay, as Cornelia Johanna de Vogel brings out in "Plato's Written and Unwritten Doctrines: Fifty Years of Plato Studies, 1930–1980," in *Rethinking Plato and Platonism* (Leiden: Brill, 1986), pp. 3–56.

3. "[D]ie Erkenntnis der Seinsprinzipien *an sich* ist dem Logos entzogen und einer intuitive-'mystischen' Erfahrung vorbehalten." Konrad Gaiser, *Platons ungeschriebene Lehre: Studien zur systematischen und geschichtlichen Begründung der Wissenschaften in der Platonischen Schule,* 2nd ed. (Stuttgart: Klett, 1968), p. 5.

4. Hans Joachim Krämer, "Platons ungeschriebene Lehre," in *Platon: Seine Dialoge in der Sicht neuer Forschungen,* ed. Theo Kobusch and Burkhard Mojsisch (Darmstadt: Wissenschaftliche Buchgesellschaft, 1996), pp. 249–75. Translated by Mario Wenning as "Plato's Unwritten Doctrine," this essay can now be found, along with other seminal contributions of the school, in *The Other Plato: The Tübingen Interpretation of Plato's Inner-Academic Teachings,* ed. Dmitri Nikulin (New York: State University of New York Press, 2012), pp. 65–82.

5. Jürgen Wippern, ed., *Das Problem der ungeschiebenen Lehre Platons: Beiträge zum Verständnis der Platonischen Prinzipienphilosphie* (Darmstadt: Wissenschaftliche Buchgesellschaft, 1972), p. xxviii. See also Gaiser, *Platons ungeschriebene Lehre,* p. 10.

6. Plotinus, *Enneads* V.v.6, attributes this etymology to "the Pythagoreans."

7. Christina Schefer, *Platons unsagbare Erfahrung: Ein anderer Zugang zu Platon* (Basel: Schwabe Verlag, 2001), pp. 176–79. This argument is extended by Schefer in *Platon und Apollon: Vom Logos zurück zum Mythos* (Sankt Augustin: Academia Verlag, 2002). Pursuing a similar line of argument is Karl Albert, *Philosophie als Religion* (Sankt Augustin: Gardez! Verlag, 2002). Anticipating it in original ways is Giorgio Colli, *La nascita della filosofia* (Milan: Adelphi, 2009 [1975]).

8. Cf. Pierre Aubenque, "Plotin et le dépassement de l'ontologie grecque classique," in *Le Néoplatonisme,* ed. Pierre Maxime Schuhl and Pierre Hadot (Paris: Éditions du Centre National de la Recherche Scientifique, 1971).

9. Dionysius's Neoplatonic treatise *The Mystical Theology,* near the source of Christian negative theology, turns on a knowledgeless knowing, a "knowing by knowing nothing" and by being rather "unknowingly elevated" (chapter 1, sections 1 and 3).

10. Damascius, *Traité des premiers principes,* vol. 1, *De L'Ineffable et de l'Un,* ed. Leendert Gerrit Westerink, trans. Joseph Combès (Paris: Les Belles Lettres, 1966), part I, ch. 21, lines 8–10. See, further, Joseph Combès, "La théologie aporétique de Damascius," in *Études néoplatoniciennes,* 2nd rev. ed. (Grenoble: Jérome

Millon, 1996), and John M. Dillon, "Damascius on the Ineffable," in *The Great Tradition: Further Studies in the Development of Platonism and Early Christianity* (London: Variorum Editions, 1997).

11. H.-Ch. Peuch, "Plotin et les Gnostiques," in E. R. Dodds, *Les Sources de Plotin: Entretiens* (Vandoeuvres-Genève: Fondation Hardt, 1960), pp. 161–90.

12. Thomas Böhm, "Unsagbarkeit und Ubegreiflichkeit des Prinzips in Gnosis und Neuplatonismus: Zur prinzipientheoretischen Auslegung der ersten Hypothesis des platonischen Parmenides bei Allogenes und Plotin," in *Gnosis oder die Frage nach Herkunft und Ziel des Menschen,* ed. Albert Franz and Thomas Rentsch (Paderborn: Schöningh, 2002), pp. 81–95.

13. I present texts supporting this argument in my introduction to and translation of Damascius, *Doubts and Solutions Concerning First Principles,* Part I, cc. 3–8, in *Arion: A Journal of Humanities and the Classics* 12, no. 1 (2004): 111–31.

14. Cf. John H. Heiser, "Plotinus and the *Apeiron* of Plato's *Parmenides,*" *Thomist* 55 (1991): 80, as well as A. Hilary Armstrong, "Plotinus's Doctrine of the Infinite and Its Significance for Christian Thought," in *Plotinian and Christian Studies* (London: Variorum Reprints, 1979), chapter 5, p. 47. More broadly, see Leo Sweeny, S.J., *Divine Infinity in Greek and Medieval Thought* (New York: Peter Lang, 1992), and Markus Enders, *Zum Begriff der Unendlichkeit im abendländischen Denken: Unendlichkeit Gottes und Unendlichkeit der Welt* (Hamburg: Boethiana, 2006).

15. A. Hilary Armstrong, "Negative Theology," in *Plotinian and Christian Studies,* chapter 24, p. 178. See, further, J. P. Kenney, "The Critical Value of Negative Theology," *Harvard Theological Review* 86 (1993): 439–53.

16. Jean Trouillard, "Valeur critique de la mystique Plotinienne," *Revue philosophique de Louvain* 59 (1961): 440.

17. A. Hilary Armstrong, "The Escape of the One: An Investigation of Some Possibilities of Apophatic Theology Imperfectly Realised in the West," in *Plotinian and Christian Studies,* chapter 23, p. 87.

18. The formula *omnis determinatio est negatio,* as attributed to Spinoza by Hegel in his *Lectures on the Philosophy of History,* gave this principle widespread currency.

19. This confluence of traditions is envisaged by David Burrell, *Knowing the Unknowable God: Ibn-Sina, Maimonides, Aquinas* (Notre Dame: University of Notre Dame Press, 1986).

20. The struggle against conceptual idolatry in contemporary philosophical thinking is analyzed by Benson, *Graven Ideologies.* Conceptual idolatry is traced in

its continuity with various types of traditional religious idolatry by Moshe Halbertal and Avishai Margalit, *Idolatry,* trans. Naomi Goldblum (Cambridge, MA: Harvard University Press, 1992).

21. J. P. Williams, *Denying Divinity: Apophasis in the Patristic Christian and Soto Zen Buddhist Traditions* (Oxford: Oxford University Press, 2000), p. 8; see also J. P. Kenney, *Mystical Monotheism* (Hannover, NH: University Press of New England, 1991).

22. See Williams, *Denying Divinity,* introduction and p. 18.

23. Good examples can be found in the readings of selected classic authors in *Silence and the Word: Negative Theology and Incarnation,* ed. Oliver Davies and Denys Turner (Cambridge: Cambridge University Press, 2002).

24. The traditional appeal to "finesse" or discernment in intuitive judgment as opposed to the "spirit of geometry" (l'ésprit de géométrie"), which proceeds by definition and proof, goes back to Blaise Pascal and is echoed insistently by William Desmond in *God and the Between.*

25. Denys Turner, *The Darkness of God: Negativity in Christian Mysticism* (Cambridge: Cambridge University Press, 1995), p. 34.

26. Sara Rappe, *Reading Neoplatonism: Non-Discursive Thinking in the Texts of Plotinus, Proclus, and Damascius* (Cambridge: Cambridge University Press, 2000).

27. Gabriel Marcel, *Position et approches concrètes du mystère ontologique,* 2nd ed. (Louvain: Éditions Nauwelaerts, 1967), and Luigi Pareyson, *L'esistenza e il logos: Filosofia, esperienza religiosa, rivelazione,* ed. Paolo Diego Bubbio and Peiro Coda (Rome: Città nuova, 2007).

28. This distinction can be traced back in Neoplatonic tradition through Gregory of Nyssa and Philo all the way to Plotinus. See *On What Cannot Be Said: Apophatic Discourses in Philosophy, Religion, Literature, and the Arts,* vol. 1.

29. Walter Benjamin, "Über die Sprache überhaupt und über die Sprache des Menschen" (1916), in *Gesammelte Schriften* (Frankfurt a.M.: Suhrkamp, 1977), vol. 2, part 1, pp. 140–57, trans. Edmund Jephcott as "On Language as Such and on the Language of Man," in *Reflections: Essays, Aphorisms, Autobiographical Writings* (New York: Harcourt Brace Jovanovich, 1978), pp. 314–32; Maurice Blanchot, "Comment découvrir l'obscur?" in *L'Entretien infini* (Paris: Gallimard, 1969), pp. 57–69, trans. Susan Hanson as "How to Discover the Obscure?" in *The Infinite Conversation* (Minneapolis: University of Minnesota Press, 1993), pp. 40–48.

30. Emmanuel Levinas, *De Dieu qui vient à l'idée* (Paris: Vrin, 1986); Michel Henry, *L'essence de la manifestation* (Paris: Presses Universitaires de France, 1990 [1963]); Jean-Louis Chrétien, *L'inoubliable et l'inespéré* (Paris: Desclée de Brouwer, 2000); Jean-Luc Marion, *Etant donné: Essai d'une phénoménologie de la donation*

(Paris: Presses Universitaires de France, 1997) and *Le visible et le révélé* (Paris: Cerf, 2005). For a critical appraisal, see Dominique Janicaud, *Le tournant théologique de la phénoménologie française* (Combas: L'Éclat, 1991) and its sequel, *La phénoménologie éclatée* (Paris: L'Éclat, 1998). For selected translations from these and other relevant authors, see Janicaud et al., *Phenomenology and the 'Theological Turn': The French Debate* (New York: Fordham University Press, 2000). For further commentary and Anglophone spin-offs, see Bruce Ellis Benson and Norman Wirzba, eds., *Words of Life: New Theological Turns in French Phenomenology* (New York: Fordham University Press, 2009).

31. For the theory of the trace, see especially Emmanuel Levinas, "La Trace de l'Autre," trans. as "The Trace of the Other," in *Deconstruction in Context: Literature and Philosophy,* ed. Mark C. Taylor (Chicago: University of Chicago Press, 1986), pp. 345–59, and "Énigme et phénomène," in *En découvrant l'existence avec Husserl et Heidegger* (Paris: Vrin, 1967). My descriptions are obviously indebted also to Jacques Derrida's numerous discussions of the trace.

32. Steven T. Katz, "Mystical Speech and Mystical Meaning," in *Mysticism and Language,* ed. Steven T. Katz (New York: Oxford University Press, 1992), p. 33.

33. Michael Sells, *Mystical Languages of Unsaying* (Chicago: University of Chicago Press, 1994), p. 8. See also his conclusion.

34. Jean-Luc Nancy, "Des lieux divins," in *Qu'est-ce que Dieu? Philosophie / Théologie. Hommage à l'Abbé Daniel Coppieters de Gibson* (Bruxelles: Facultés Universitaires Saint-Louis, 1985), pp. 541–53. The essay has also appeared more than once in book form as *Des lieux divins* (Toulouse: Mauvezin, 1987). It is translated into English by Peter Connor as "Of Divine Places" in *The Inoperative Community* (Minneapolis: University of Minnesota Press, 1991), pp. 110–50, though I translate citations directly from the French myself.

35. I restrict myself, for the moment, to discussing Nancy's position in this essay only. Nancy has more recently published the two volumes of his *Deconstruction of Christianity,* in which the argument is new and in crucial ways reverses his thinking about theology. Here Christianity turns out to be eminently a negative theology that carries out its own deconstruction of itself and of Western tradition as a whole. It is the agent rather than only the object of deconstruction. I completely agree with Nancy's outlook here and will treat it separately in the next two sections (iii and iv) as a crucial turning, a *Kehre,* in his thought, which becomes in effect what I would call a religious philosophy. He paradoxically becomes a model apostle (complete with evangelical forenames!) of what I mean by a "philosophy of the unsayable." But first we need to follow his refusal of theology as advanced in "Des lieux divins."

36. Among the most pertinent construals of this tradition is Jan Miernowski, *Le Dieu néant: Théologies négatives à l'aube des temps modernes* (Leiden: Brill, 1998).

37. See Jean-Luc Nancy, *Être singulier pluriel* (Paris: Galilée, 1996). In fact, for Nancy every "I" already presupposes a "we," but that fact must not be used to suppress contrasting "I"s.

38. Nancy reverts persistently to this Roman Catholic matrix, for example, in his *Corpus* (Paris: Métailié, 2000) and *Noli me tangere: Essai sur la levée du corps* (Paris: Bayard, 2003).

39. Thomas A. Carlson, *Indiscretion: Finitude and the Naming of God* (Chicago: University of Chicago Press, 1999), pp. 4–5.

40. See especially Jacques Derrida, *Sauf le nom* (Paris: Galilée, 1993), pp. 15–21, 38–65, translated as "Sauf le nom (Post-Scriptum)" in Jacques Derrida, ed. Thomas Dutoit, *On the Name* (Stanford: Stanford University Press, 1995).

41. Mark C. Taylor, *Tears* (Albany: State University of New York Press, 1990), p. 106. See also Taylor's *Altarity* (Chicago: University of Chicago Press, 1987).

42. Rudolf Otto, *Das Heilige: Über das Irrationale in der Idee des Göttlichen und sein Verhältnis zum Rationalen* (Munich: Beck, 2004 [1917]).

43. Jacques Derrida and Antoine Spire, *Au-delà des apparences* (Latresne, Bordeaux: Le Bord de l'eau, 2002), p. 53.

44. See Graham Ward, ed., *The Postmodern God: A Theological Reader* (Boston: Blackwell, 1997), and *The Blackwell Companion to Postmodern Theology* (Oxford: Blackwell, 2001); Orrin F. Summerell, ed., *The Otherness of God* (Charlottesville: University Press of Virginia, 1998); Robert P. Scharlemann, ed., *Negation and Theology* (Charlottesville: University Press of Virginia, 1992).

45. John D. Caputo and Michael J. Scanlon, eds., *God, the Gift, and Postmodernism* (Bloomington: Indiana University Press, 1999), p. 12. See, further, John Caputo, Mark Dooley, and Michael J. Scanlon, eds., *Questioning God* (Bloomington: Indiana University Press, 2001).

46. See, for example, *MicroMega* and the journal *Filosofia*, edited by Gianni Vattimo, from the 1990s through 2001, as well as Vattimo's *Dopo la cristianità: Per un cristianesimo non religioso* (Milan: Garzanti, 2002), trans. Luca D'Isanto as *After Christianity* (New York: Columbia University Press, 2002), which has been followed by a stream of further publications.

47. Giorgio Agamben, *Idea della prosa* (Macerata: Quodlibet, 2002), pp. 9–12. See also Giorgio Agamben and Monica Ferrando, *La ragazza indicibile: Mito e mistero di Kore* (Milan: Electa, 2010).

48. See Isle N. Bulhof and Laurens ten Kate, eds., *Flight of the Gods: Philosophical Perspectives on Negative Theology* (New York: Fordham University Press, 2000).

49. De Vries, *Philosophy and the Turn to Religion*, p. 27.

50. De Vries, *Theologie im Pianissimo: Zur Aktualität der Denkfiguren Adornos und Levinas*, trans. Geoffrey Hale as *Minimal Theologies: Critiques of Secular Reason in Adorno and Levinas* (Baltimore: Johns Hopkins University Press, 2006). A further monumental resource is Hent de Vries's edited volume *Religion: Beyond a Concept* (New York: Fordham University Press, 2007).

51. Alois Halbmayr and Gregor Maria Hoff, eds., *Negative Theologie heute? Zum aktuellen Stellenwert einer umstrittenen Tradition* (Freiburg: Herder, 2008); Gregor Maria Hoff, *Aporetische Theologie: Skizze eines Stils fundamentaler Theologie* (Paderborn: Schöningh, 1997).

52. Especial worthy of notice are Marco Olivetti, ed., *Théologie Négative* (Milan: C.E.D.A.M., 2002); Massimo Baldini and Silvano Zucal, eds., *Le forme del silenzio e della parola* (Brescia: Morcellina, 1989); and Massimo Baldini and Silvano Zucal, eds., *Il silenzio e la parola da Eckhart a Jabès* (Brescia: Morcellina, 1989).

53. See "Negative Theology *redivivus*," the final pages of Kevin Hart's *Trespass of the Sign*, pp. 265–69. Richard Kearney's *Anatheism: Returning to God after God* (New York: Columbia University Press, 2009) is written especially in the spirit of dialogue between postmodern religious belief and atheism (represented by the unholy trinity of Daniel Dennett, Richard Dawkins, and Christopher Hitchens). Kearney does not subscribe to negative theology, and he repeats a common caricature of it as simply negative, but he is nevertheless very much aligned with broadly apophatic currents both here and also in his *The God Who May Be: A Hermeneutics of Religion* (Bloomington: Indiana University Press, 2001).

54. Readers in philosophy of religion cannot help but take stock of the new dialogical genre of multi-author books in theology in which different, often divergent religious thinkers—such as Slavoj Žižek and John Milbank (*The Monstrosity of Christ*), John D. Caputo and Gianni Vattimo (*After the Death of God*), and Gianni Vattimo and René Girard (*Christianity, Truth, and Weakening Faith*)—speak alongside and with and against each other. Such split speech can be revealing in ways that exceed the reach of monographical discourse. An instance especially relevant to the return of religion in secular culture is Richard Rorty and Gianni Vattimo, *The Future of Religion*, ed. Santiago Zabala (New York: Columbia University Press, 2005).

55. Jean-Luc Nancy, *Déconstruction du christianisme*, vol. 1, *La Déclosion* (Paris: Galilée, 2005).

56. Jean-Luc Nancy, "La déconstruction du christianisme," *Les Études philosophiques* 4 (1998): 503–19; quotations p. 517. This essay is also reprinted in *La Déclosion* as its penultimate piece. However, my citations are from the original article.

57. "l'idée de la révélation chrétienne est qu'au bout du compte *rien n'est révélé*, rien sinon la fin de la révélation elle-même, sinon ceci que la révélation veut dire que le sens se dévoile purement comme sens, en personne, mais en une personne telle que tout le sens de cette personne consiste à se révéler. Le sens se révèle et ne révèle rien, ou révèle sa propre infinité."

58. Michel Henry, *C'est moi la vérité: Pour une philosophie du christianisme* (Paris: Seuil, 1998), develops a confessedly Christian version of this enunciation taken as a philosophical and specifically phenomenological insight.

59. See Jean-Luc Nancy, "L'athéisme, essence des monothéismes," Entretien avec Jérôme-Alexandre Nielsberg, *Les Lettres françaises*, n.s. 15, 24 May 2005, on the appearance of *La Déclosion*.

60. Nancy, "Le nom de Dieu chez Blanchot," *Magazine littéraire* 424 (October 2003), pp. 66–68, reprinted in *La Déclosion*, pp. 129–34. I cite the original article.

61. "C'est pourquoi le don le plus précieux de la philosophie consiste pour Blanchot non pas même dans une opération de négation de l'existence de Dieu, mais dans un simple évanouissement, dans une dissipation de cette existence. La pensée ne pense qu'à partir de là."

62. "Mais un 'sens absent' fait sens dans et par son absentement même, en sorte que pour finir . . . il n'en finit pas de ne pas 'faire sens.'"

63. Jean-Luc Nancy, *Déconstruction du christianisme*, vol. 2, *L'Adoration* (Paris: Galilée, 2010).

64. See Nancy, *Une pensée finie* (Paris: Galilée, 1990), translated as *A Finite Thinking*, ed. Simon Sparks (Stanford: Stanford University Press, 2003).

65. "la Raison ne se satisfait pas de raisons rendues mais se pousse elle-même vers un incommensurable et un innommable du sens—ou vers une vérité sans concept ni figure : si elle manque à faire droit à cette pulsion, la raison s'étiole et sombre dans la commensurabilité générale et dans la nomination interminable dont tous les noms sont interchangeables."

66. "L'infini dans le fini. La finitude en tant qu'ouverture à l'infini : rien d'autre n'est en jeu. Il n'y aurait pas ce que nous nommons 'finitude'—mortalité, natalité, 'fortuité—si, du fait même que nous le nommons, nous ne laissions pas

transparaître que nous existons et que le monde existe ouvert sur l'infini, par l'infini."

67. "C'est-à-dire que le fait même de l'existence nie qu'elle soit 'finie' au sens où elle manquerait d'une extension au-delà d'elle-même. Ce fait atteste au contraire que l'existence porte, qu'elle apporte avec elle son extension entière et son expansion pleine. Ici et maintenant, entre naissance et mort, sans rien dénier ni refouler de cette 'finitude', puisque c'est elle qui *est* infini : entre naissance et mort, chaque fois, un absolu s'accomplit."

68. Cf. François Nault, "'Le secret du commun': Jean-Luc Nancy et la déconstruction du christianisme," *Science et esprit* 60, no. 1 (2008): 39–53.

69. "L'élément de ce renvoi est le langage. Celui-ci nous adresse tous ensemble à ce qu'il fait essentiellement surgir : l'infini d'un sens que nulle signification ne remplit, et qui, cette fois disons-le, enveloppe avec les hommes la totalité du monde avec tous ses existences."

70. "Elle n'est pas à joindre : elle forme la jointure et la junction de nos paroles, la possibilitié infinie de sens."

71. "une adresse tournée vers un dehors qui n'est pas extérieur au monde mais qui l'ouvre en lui-même."

72. Nancy, *Hegel: L'inquiétude du négatif* (Paris: Hachette, 1997). Also crucial to Nancy's struggle with Hegel is his *La Remarque spéculative: Un bon mot de Hegel* (Paris: Galilée, 1973). For Žižek, see "The Fear of Four Words: A Modest Plea for the Hegelian Reading of Christianity," in John Milbank and Slavoj Žižek, *The Monstrosity of Christ* (Cambridge, MA: MIT Press, 2009).

73. Slavoj Žižek, *The Puppet and the Dwarf: The Perverse Core of Christianity* (Cambridge, MA: MIT Press, 2003), p. 138.

74. "l'esprit . . . est l'inégalité à soi de l'éveil qui ouvre à l'incommensurable."

75. As advertised by Derrida's *Le toucher, Jean-Luc Nancy* (Paris: Galilée, 2000), trans. Christube Irizarry as *On Touching: Jean-Luc Nancy* (Stanford: Stanford University Press, 2005).

76. See Vattimo, *Dopo la cristianità* (*After Christianity*).

77. Gianni Vattimo, *Nichilismo ed emancipazione: Etica, politica, diritto* (Milano: Garzanti, 2004), trans. William McCuaig as *Nihilism and Emancipation: Ethics, Politics and Law*, ed. Santiago Zabala (New York: Columbia, 2004).

78. "recuperare la propria funzione universalistica senza implicazioni coloniali, imperialistiche, eurocentriche. . . . accentuando la sua vocazione missionaria come ospitalità e come fondazione religiosa (paradossale quanto si vuole) della laicità (delle istituzioni, della società civile, della stessa vita religiosa individuale)" (Vattimo, *Dopo la cristianità*, p. 107).

79. See Talal Asad, *Formations of the Secular: Christianity, Islam, Modernity* (Stanford: Stanford University Press, 2003).

80. On the controversial role of religion in public space and debate, see especially José Casanova, *Public Religions in the Modern World* (Chicago: University of Chicago Press, 1994), and Judith Butler, Jürgen Habermas, Charles Taylor, and Cornel West, *The Power of Religion in the Public Sphere*, ed. Eduardo Mendieta and Jonathan Van Antwepen (New York: Columbia University Press, 2011).

81. These questions are explored in *Christian Uniqueness Reconsidered: The Myth of a Pluralistic Theology of Religions*, ed. Gavin D'Costa (Maryknoll, NY: Orbis, 1990).

82. "le langage s'adresse et nous adresse à ce dehors de la communication et de la signification homogènes. . . . Il n'est là que pour ça, il ne fait que ça: il adresse, il appelle, il interpelle l'innommable, le strict revers de toute la nomination possible. Ce revers n'est pas une face cachée du monde, ni une 'chose en soi' ni un être ou un étant. Il n'existe pas: c'est de lui et vers lui que s'ouvre toute existence. 'Lui' ou 'ça' ou 'rien' : la *chose même* qui n'est aucune chose mais ceci *qu'il y a quelques choses, et un monde, ou des mondes, et nous, nous tous, tous les existants.*"

83. Parallel reflections, bringing out in biblical terms the apophatic implications and underside of bodily operations and organs, can be found in Jean-Louis Chrétien, *Symbolique du corps: La tradition chrétienne du Cantique des Cantiques* (Paris: Presses Universitaires de France, 2005).

84. Vattimo, *Dopo la cristianità*, p. 9, has also argued this persuasively. Even self-described "religiously unmusical" Richard Rorty agrees with Vattimo about this (Rorty and Vattimo, *The Future of Religion*, p. 33). Nancy's Christian atheism is shared, on the other hand, by Žižek, who sees "Christianity as the religion of atheism" (*Puppet and the Dwarf*, p. 171).

85. Jacques Lacan could be added to this list for his late recognition of and regret over what seems to him to be Christianity's "invincibility." See Lacan, *Le triomphe de la religion: Discours aux Catholiques* (Paris: Seuil, 2005). Merold Westphal, *Suspicion and Faith: The Religious Uses of Modern Atheism* (New York: Fordham University Press, 1998), provides arresting perspectives on Freud and other great modern atheists' ambiguous indebtedness to religion.

86. Theodor W. Adorno, *Negative Dialektik* (Frankfurt a.M.: Suhrkamp, 1990), 6th ed., p. 371.

87. The logic of other or possible worlds, including fictional worlds, has been developed with great sophistication in philosophy drawing especially from modal logic. An orientation can be obtained from Daniel P. Nolan, *Topics in the Philosophy of Possible Worlds* (New York: Routledge, 2002).

88. "il n'y a de nomination que sur fond d'innommable et ce dernier n'est rien d'autre que ce qui se dit dans toute nomination. . . . Nommer ouvre à l'inatteignable, à l'irréductible de la chose, du réel, de l'existant. Seul le langage donne cette ouverture, mais seul aussi il la désigne comme béant sur l'infini, hors langage et pourtant toujours à nouveau répétée, redemandée dans la parole."

89. "Pour finir, ce que je nomme ici 'adorer' veut dire : décider d'exister, se décider pour l'existence, se détourner de l'inexistence, de la fermeture du monde sur soi."

90. "une catégorie qui n'en est même pas une et qui pourtant est un mode réel et consistent du sentir."

91. "mais je crois, je veux croire, je laisse se former l'esquisse d'un possible ou plutôt d'un non-impossible, d'une façon inouïe de faire sens, ou même pas sens mais simplement de se tenir et de tenir à—rien, rien que ce désir ou rien *comme* ce désir même de croire."

92. See Werner Jaeger, *Die Theologie der frühen griechischen Denker* (Stuttgart: Kohlhammer, 1953), trans. Edward S. Robinson as *The Theology of the Early Greek Thinkers* (Oxford: Clarendon, 1960).

93. See Pierre Hadot, *Exercices spirituels et philosophie antique* (Paris: Albin Michel, 2002 [1981]), trans. Arnold Davidson and Michael Chase as *Philosophy as a Way of Life: Spiritual Exercises from Socrates to Foucault* (Malden, MA: Blackwell, 1995); André-Jean Voelke, *La philosophie comme thérapie de l'âme: Études de philosophie hellénistique* (Paris: Cerf, 1994); and Martha C. Nussbaum, *The Therapy of Desire: Theory and Practice in Hellenistic Ethics* (Princeton: Princeton University Press, 1994).

Chapter 5. Radical Orthodoxy's Critique of Transcendental Philosophy and Its Mistaken Mistrust of Negative Theology

1. Programmatic essays are found in *Radical Orthodoxy: A New Theology,* ed. John Milbank, Graham Ward, and Catherine Pickstock (London: Routledge, 1998).

2. Phillip Blond, ed., *Post-Secular Philosophy: Between Philosophy and Theology* (London: Routledge, 1998), p. 2.

3. A radically orthodox approach, pivoting on kenosis, is sketched by Graham Ward, "Kenosis and Naming: Beyond Analogy and towards *allegoria amoris,*" in *Religion, Modernity and Postmodernity,* ed. Paul Heelas (Oxford: Blackwell, 1998).

4. John Caputo, *The Weakness of God: A Theology of the Event* (Bloomington: Indiana University Press, 2006), p. 310n.

5. John Milbank, "A Critique of the Theology of Right," in *Word Made Strange*, p. 7.

6. Milbank's move, in effect, theologizes Heidegger's critique of modern philosophy in its search for epistemological foundations and its concomitant forgetting of Being—the indispensable presupposition of thinking itself and so of any possible ascertainment of truth.

7. The Thomistic bases of this thinking are developed in John Milbank's and Catherine Pickstock's *Truth in Aquinas* (London: Routledge, 2001).

8. John Milbank, *The Future of Love: Essays in Political Theology* (Eugene, OR: Cascade, 2009), p. 146.

9. Milbank, "Only Theology Overcomes Metaphysics," in *Word Made Strange*, p. 50.

10. Notably Franz Rosenzweig's, for which, see Leora Faye Batnitzky, *Idolatry and Representation: The Philosophy of Franz Rosenzweig Reconsidered* (Princeton: Princeton University Press, 2000). Milbank's magnum opus in this genre is *Theology and Social Theory: Beyond Secular Reason* (Oxford: Blackwell, 1993).

11. Benson, *Graven Ideologies*, p. 29.

12. John Milbank, *The Religious Dimension in the Thought of Giambattista Vico, 1668–1744*, 2 vols. (Lewiston, NY: Edwin Mellen Press, 1992).

13. Robert Sokolowski, *The God of Faith and Reason: Foundations of Christian Theology* (Washington, DC: The Catholic University of America, 1995 [1982]). See also David Burrell, "The Christian Distinction Celebrated and Expanded," in *The Truthful and the Good: Essays in Honor of Robert Sokolowski*, ed. John R. Drummond and James G. Hart (Dordrecht: Kluwer, 1996), pp. 207–14.

14. Moshe Halbertal and Avishai Margalit, *Idolatry*, trans. Naomi Goldblum (Cambridge, MA: Harvard University Press, 1992), reconstruct in these terms the prehistory of critical thinking.

15. Catherine Pickstock, "Duns Scotus: His Historical and Contemporary Significance," *Modern Theology* 21, no. 4 (2005): 543–74. Rpt. in *The Radical Orthodoxy Reader*, ed. Simon Oliver and John Milbank (London: Routledge, 2009).

16. Rolf Schönberger, "Negationes non summe amamus: Duns Scotus' Auseinandersetzung mit der negative Theologie," in *John Duns Scotus: Metaphysics and Ethics*, ed. Ludger Honnefelder, Rega Wood, and Mechthild Dreyer (Leiden: Brill, 1996), pp. 475–96.

17. Against the common misconstrual of Aquinas's doctrines as validating an autonomous rational metaphysical knowledge of being (and also its converse,

namely, heteronomous "revealed" knowledge), see Milbank and Pickstock, *Truth in Aquinas*, p. 30. Cf. pp. 24–39 against dividing faith and reason into distinct "phases."

18. Milbank, "Faith, Reason, and Imagination: The Study of Philosophy and Theology in the 21st Century," in *The Future of Love*, p. 316.

19. There is, however, another, countervailing aspect of Descartes as a thinker of the Infinite and the ontological argument. It is ignored by this indictment but is picked up and developed by Levinas in *De Dieu qui vient à l'idée* (Paris: Vrin, 1982) and by Jean-Luc Marion, *Sur la théologie blanche de Descartes: Analogie, création des vérités éternelles et fondement* (Paris: Presses Universitaires de France, 1981).

20. Gabriel Marcel's *Le mystère ontologique*, for example, can be read as an existentialist version of negative theology. I pursue this in "Existentialism: An Atheistic or a Christian Philosophy?" in *Phenomenology and Existentialism in the Twentieth Century*, ed. Anna-Teresa Tymieniecka, Analecta Husserliana 103 (London: Springer, 2009), 371–94.

21. Halbertal and Margalit, *Idolatry*, pp. 112 and passim.

22. John Milbank, *The Suspended Middle: Henri de Lubac and the Debate Concerning the Supernatural* (Grand Rapids: Eerdmans, 2005).

23. Milbank responds specifically to essays, including Hicks's, in *The Myth of Christian Uniqueness: Toward a Pluralistic Theology of Religions*, ed. John Hicks and Paul F. Knitter (Maryknoll, NY: Orbis, 1987), with his essay "The End of Dialogue," in *Christian Uniqueness Reconsidered*, ed. D'Costa.

24. This, finally, is the lesson also of Adorno's *Negative Dialectics* as formulated in its concluding section, III.iii.12, on "Self-Reflection of Dialectics," in *Negative Dialektik* (Frankfurt a.M.: Suhrkamp, 1966), pp. 395–98. This parallel suggests how a similar critique of secular reason arises from a different religious and cultural matrix for thinking, one that, however, is likewise trained on the pervasive idolatry of reason in the modern world.

25. For example, in Milbank's "The Conflict of the Faculties," in *Future of Love*, p. 314.

26. Milbank, "On Theological Transgression," in *Future of Love*, p. 159.

27. Stanislas Breton proffers suggestive explorations along these lines in his *La philosophie du rien*, as does Reiner Schürman, *Des hégémonies brisées* (Mauvezin: Trans Europ Repress, 1996), trans. Reginald Lilly as *Broken Hegemonies* (Bloomington: Indiana University Press, 2003).

28. John Milbank, "The Double Glory, or Paradox versus Dialectics: On Not Quite Agreeing with Slavoj Žižek," in Milbank and Žižek, *The Monstrosity of Christ*, pp. 110–234.

29. Hent de Vries emphasizes this in the epilogue to his *Minimal Theologies*.

30. De Vries develops such hints in *Minimal Theologies*, chapter 12, "'The Other Theology': Conceptual, Historical, and Political Idolatry."

31. Again, Milbank's critique of modernity doubles Heidegger's, this time echoing the latter's "Die Zeitalter des Weltbildes" ("The Age of the World Picture"), in *Holzwege* (Frankfurt a.M.: Klostermann, 1950).

32. Milbank, "Sublimity: The Modern Transcendent," in *Transcendence: Philosophy, Literature, and Theology Approach the Beyond*, ed. Regina Schwartz (New York: Routledge, 2004), and Ward, "Kenosis and Naming."

33. Catherine Pickstock, "Liturgy and the Senses," in John Milbank, Slavoj Žižek, and Creston Davies, *Paul's New Moment: Continental Philosophy and the Future of Christian Theology* (Grand Rapids: Brazos, 2010).

34. Derrida and Marion have again been at the center of voluminous discussions on this point, some of which are contained in *God, the Gift, and Postmodernism*, ed. John D. Caputo and Michael J. Scanlon (Bloomington: Indiana University Press, 1999).

35. Hart, *Trespass of the Sign*, pp. 183ff.

36. See particularly "La logica poetica" and paragraph 402 of *La scienza nuova* (1744), trans. Thomas Goddard Bergin and Max Harold Fisch as *The New Science of Giambattista Vico* (Ithaca: Cornell University Press, 1968).

37. Olivier-Thomas Venard, *Thomas d'Aquin poète-théologien*, 3 vols. (Geneva: Ad Solem, 2002–9), elicits largely from modern linguistic and poetic theory a "theology of language" parallel to medieval metaphysics in vol. 1, *Littérature et théologie: Une saison en enfer*. Milbank enthusiastically reviews this "trilogy" in "On Thomistic Kabbalah," *Modern Theology* 27, no. 1 (2011): 147–84.

38. I develop this argument in "The Deaths of God in Hegel and Nietzsche and the Crisis of Values in Secular Modernity and Post-Secular Postmodernity," *Religion and the Arts* 11, no. 2 (2007): 214–41, particularly the second section, "Secularism's Implosion: Graham Ward."

39. See, for example, Robert John Russell et al., *Chaos and Complexity: Scientific Perspectives on Divine Action* (Notre Dame: University of Notre Dame Press, 1996).

40. This theme is taken up with Vahanian and others in the next essay.

41. See De Vries, *Minimal Theologies*.

42. The vast literature on this subject reaches from John Rajchman, ed., *The Identity in Question* (New York: Routledge, 1995), to reconsiderations by Seyla Benhabib, *The Claims of Culture: Equality and Diversity in the Global Era* (Princeton: Princeton University Press, 2002), and to Linda Martín Alcoff, Michael Hames-

García, Satya P. Mohanty, and Paula M. L. Moya, eds., *Identity Politics Reconsidered: Future of Minority Studies* (New York: Palgrave Macmillan, 2006).

43. Graham Ward, ed., *The Postmodern God: A Theological Reader* (Oxford: Blackwell, 1997), bears significant witness in this regard, as does Ward's treatment of all of these French thinkers in his *Theology and Contemporary Critical Theory*, 2nd ed. (New York: Macmillan, 2000).

44. Reflections by Hans-Georg Gadamer, *Wahrheit und Methode* (Tübingen: J. C. B. Mohr, 1960), Part III, bring out the fundamental importance of the incarnate, Christian Logos and the interior Word in underwriting the linguistic turn in modern philosophy.

45. Milbank, "The Linguistic Turn as a Theological Turn," in *Word Made Strange*, p. 97. John R. Betz, *After Enlightenment: The Post-Secular Vision of J. G. Hamann* (Oxford: Wiley-Blackwell, 2009), pursues this line of interpretation, following especially Pickstock's *After Writing* (cited below) from its very title.

46. John D. Caputo, *The Prayers and Tears of Jacques Derrida* (Bloomington: Indiana University Press, 1997).

47. Milbank, "A Christological Poetics," in *Word Made Strange*, p. 137.

48. Michel de Certeau has also developed this line of thinking, particularly in *La faiblesse de croire* (Paris: Seuil, 1987).

49. This essay appears in *Word Made Strange*. Milbank's critique of Marion is pursued in his "The Gift and the Mirror: On the Philosophy of Love," in *Counter-Experiences*, ed. Hart, pp. 253–317.

50. Milbank, "Only Theology Overcomes Metaphysics," in *Word Made Strange*, p. 50.

51. Kevin Hart, *The Dark Gaze: Maurice Blanchot and the Sacred* (Chicago: University of Chicago Press, 2004), and his introduction to *Counter-Experiences*, pp. 1–56.

52. On "bad metaphysics," see Graham Ward, "The Metaphysics of the Body," in *Apophatic Bodies: Negative Theology, Incarnation, and Relationality*, ed. Chris Boesel and Catherine Keller (New York: Fordham University Press, 2010).

53. Jean-Luc Marion, "Le phénomène saturé," in *Phénoménologie et théologie*, ed. Jean-Louis Chrétien (Paris: Criterion, 1992), pp. 79–128. This essay is translated by Robyn Horner in *In Excess: Studies of Saturated Phenomena* (New York: Fordham University Press, 2002).

54. In "St. Thomas d'Aquin et L'Onto-théo-logie," *Revue thomist* 95, no. 1 (1995): 31–66, Marion signals certain "retractions" from his strict rejection of an analogical language of being in *Dieu sans l'être: Hors texte* (Paris: Presses Universitaires de France, 1991 [1982]).

55. Derrida's oeuvre is read in this sense by De Vries, *Philosophy and the Turn to Religion*.

56. Cf. Žižek and Milbank, *The Monstrosity of Christ*.

57. I argue this in "Franz Rosenzweig and the Emergence of a Post-Secular Philosophy of the Unsayable," *International Journal for Philosophy of Religion* 58, no. 3 (2005): 161–80, and in *On What Cannot Be Said*, vol. 2. A powerfully apophatic reading of Rosenzweig is proposed also by Elliot R. Wolfson, "Light Does Not Talk But Shines: Apophasis and Vision in Rosenzweig's Theopoetic Temporality," in *New Directions in Jewish Philosophy*, ed. Aaron Hughes and Elliot Wolfson (Bloomington: Indiana University Press, 2009), chapter 3.

58. Milbank converges here significantly with Agamben, *La chiesa e il regno* (Rome: Nottetempo, 2010), trans. Leland de la Durantaye as *The Church and the Kingdom* (Chicago: University of Chicago Press, 2012).

59. François Cassingena-Trévedy, *Poétique de la théologie* (Paris: Ad Solem, 2011), alongside Venard, *Thomas d'Aquin poète-théologien*, demonstrates this exemplarily.

60. Jan Assmann, *The Search for God in Ancient Egypt* (Ithaca: Cornell University Press, 2001).

61. Miriam Lichtheim, *Ancient Egyptian Literature*, vol. 2 (Berkeley: University of California Press, 1976), p. 96.

62. See, for example, Denys Turner, "Apophaticism, Idolatry and the Claims of Reason," in *Silence and the Word*, ed. Davies and Turner.

63. Thomas-Olivier Venard's second volume of his trilogy, *La langue de l'ineffable: Essai sur le fondement théologique de la métaphysique* (Paris: Ad Solem, 2004), is an explicitly Catholic confessional version of this argument.

64. See Karl Albert, *Philosophie als Religion* (Sankt Augustin: Gardez! Verlag, 2002), and Giorgio Colli, *La nascita della filosofia* (Milan: Adelphi, 2009 [1975]).

65. Greek text from Proclus, *Hymnes et prières*, ed. Henri D. Saffrey (Paris: Arfuyen, 1994), p. 78. I have preserved the punctuation of the hymn as it appears in *Patrologia Graeca*, vol. 37, p. 507, ed. J.-P. Migne (Turnholti: Brepols, 1862), where it is attributed to Gregory Nazianzus.

66. A somewhat different translation of the first several verses of the hymn is offered by Deirdre Carabine, *The Unknown God: Negative Theology in the Platonic Tradition, Plato to Eriugena*, Louvain Theological and Pastoral Monographs, vol. 19 (Louvain: Peeters Press, 1995), p. 162.

67. *Commentarium in Parmenidem*, ed. Victor Cousin, 2nd ed., Paris, 1864. Reprinted in *Procli Philosophi Platonici*, Opera inedita, pars Tertia, Continens Procli Commentarium in Platoni Parmenidem (Hildesheim: Georg Olms Verlagsbuchhandlung, 1961).

68. Proclus, *Théologie platonicienne*, 6 vols., ed. H. D. Saffrey and L. G. Westerlink (Paris: Les Belles Lettres, 1968–97). See, further, H. D. Saffrey, "Accorder entre elles les traditions théologiques: Une caractéristique du Néoplatonisme Athénien," in *On Proclus and His Influence in Medieval Philosophy*, ed. E. P. Bos and P. A. Meijer (New York: Brill, 1992), p. 44.

69. Cited from R. M. van den Berg, *Proclus' Hymns: Essays, Translations, Commentary* (Leiden: Brill, 2001), pp. 14, 16, 22.

70. Anselm of Canterbury, *Proslogion* (Notre Dame: University of Notre Dame Press, 1979). Among innumerable reflections emphasizing the centrality of this liturgical setting for philosophy in Anselm are Jean-Luc Marion, "L'argument relève-t-il de l'ontologie?" and Mark C. Taylor, "How Not to Think God," in *L'argomento ontologico*, ed. Marco Olivetti (Padua: CEDAM, 1990).

71. Marjorie O'Rourke Boyle, "Chaff: Thomas Aquinas's Repudiation of His *Opera omnia*," *New Literary History* 28 (1997): 383–99.

72. "Omnia, quae scripsi, videntur mihi paleae respectu eorum, quae vidi et revelata sunt mihi." *S. Thomae Aquinatis Vitae Fontes Praecipuae*, ed. A. Ferrua (Alba: Edizioni dominicane, 1968). See, further, Josef Pieper, *The Silence of St. Thomas*, trans. John Murray, S.J., and Daniel O'Connor (New York: Pantheon, 1957).

73. John Milbank, "On Thomistic Kabbalah," *Modern Theology* 27, no. 1 (2011): 147–84, citation p. 154.

74. Samuel Vollenweider, *Neoplatonische und christliche Theologie bei Synesios von Kyrene* (Göttingen: Vandenhoeck & Ruprecht, 1985).

75. *Synesii Cyrenensis Hymni et Opuscula*, ed. Nicolaus Terzaghi (Rome: Typis R. Officinae polygraphicae, 1939–).

76. Synesius, *Dion* 8.48a.

77. Catherine Pickstock, *After Writing: On the Liturgical Consummation of Philosophy* (Oxford: Blackwell, 1998), p. xii.

78. The thesis that liturgical language makes the predicative language of philosophy possible can also be found in Jean-Luc Marion, *Dieu sans l'être*, chapter 7, where it likewise aims to clear a space for a positive theology.

79. See especially Jacques Derrida, "Comment ne pas parler: Dénégations," in *Psyché: Inventions de l'autre* (Paris: Galilée, 1987), pp. 435–95.

80. Catherine Pickstock, "Asyndeton: Syntax and Insanity. A Study of the Revision of The Nicene Creed," in Ward, *The Postmodern God*.

81. John D. Caputo's *The Prayers and Tears of Jacques Derrida* fleshes out this side of Derrida.

82. Jacques Derrida, "La pharmacie de Platon," in *La dissémination* (Paris: Seuil, 1972), originally published in *Tel Quel* 32 and 33 (1968).

83. De Vries, *Philosophy and the Turn to Religion*, does this, although De Vries places *Kehre* or turning to religion as early as 1972 with *La dissémination*.

84. Jacques Derrida, "Foi et savoir: Les deux sources de la 'religion' aux limites de la simple raison," in *La Religion*, ed. Thierry Marchaisse (Paris: Seuil, 1996), p. 28.

85. See Herbert Marks, "On Prophetic Stammering," in *The Book and the Text*, ed. Regina Schwartz (Oxford: Blackwell, 1990), pp. 60–80.

Chapter 6. Apophatic Thought as the Missing Mean between Radically Secular and Radically Orthodox Theology

1. The violent potential of religion in a postmodern world has been highlighted notably by Hent De Vries, *Religion and Violence: Philosophical Perspectives from Kant to Derrida* (Baltimore: Johns Hopkins University Press, 2002), and Clayton Crockett, ed., *Religion and Violence in a Secular World: Toward a New Political Theology* (Charlottesville: University of Virginia Press, 2006).

2. Clayton Crockett, "Introduction," in *Secular Theology: American Radical Theological Thought*, ed. Clayton Crockett (New York: Routledge, 2001), p. 3.

3. Graham Ward, "Introduction, or, A Guide to Theological Thinking in Cyberspace," in *The Postmodern God*, ed. Ward, pp. xlii–xliii. Ward develops this idea further in his *Cities of God* (New York: Routledge, 2000).

4. "Introduction," in *Radical Orthodoxy*, ed. Milbank, Pickstock, and Ward, p. 1.

5. Proclus, *Commentarium in Parmenidum*, especially book VII. Dionysius lays out this mutual dependence in *On Divine Names* and in *Mystical Theology*. The interdependence is emphasized by Marion, Turner, and Hart, as discussed later in this essay.

6. Conor Cunningham, *Genealogy of Nihilism: Philosophies of Nothing and the Difference of Theology* (London: Routledge, 2002), monumentalizes Radical Orthodoxy's allergy to "nihilism," even while emphasizing the mutual implication of affirmation and negation, presence and absence.

7. Benson, *Graven Ideologies*, effectively focuses on this aspect of deconstruction.

8. Henry Corbin, "De la théologie apophatique comme antidote du nihilisme," in *Le paradoxe du monothéisme* (Paris: L'Herne, 2003 [1981]).

9. Kevin Hart's *Trespass of the Sign* is a careful argument against such misconstruals of deconstruction and its supposed undermining of theology.

10. Key Derrida texts from this phase include *Sauf le nom* (Paris: Galilée, 1993), *Donner la mort* (Paris: Galilée, 1999), and *Foi et savoir* (Paris: Seuil, 2000).

11. François Nault, "Déconstruction et apophatisme: À propos d'une dénégation de Jacques Derrida," *Laval Théologique et Philosophique* 55, no. 3 (1999): 393–411. The denial begins from Derrida, "Discussion autour de *La différance*," *Bulletin de la Société française de philosophie* 62 (1968): 82, and is confirmed notably in "Comment ne pas parler: dénégations" (1986), in *Psyché: Inventions de l'autre* (Paris: Galilée, 1987), pp. 535–95, trans. in *Derrida and Negative Theology*, ed. H. Coward and T. Foshay (Albany: State University of New York Press, 1992).

12. Nicholas of Cusa, *De pace fidei*, ed. Klaus Berger and Christiane Nord (Frankfurt: Insel Verlag, 2002).

13. Steven Shakespeare, *Derrida and Theology* (London: T&T Clark, 2009), chapter 7, inventories such theological responses to Derrida.

14. Caputo, *Weakness of God*, p. 11.

15. Caputo, *Prayers and Tears*, pp. 7–8, 11, rejects negative theology as "an onto-theology *eminentiore modo*" that only intensifies metaphysical claims to pure presence. Merold Westphal, *Transcendence and Self-Transcendence: On God and the Soul* (Bloomington: Indiana University Press, 2004), pp. 107–9, adroitly defends negative theology against Caputo's dismissal as too narrow a construal of negative theology.

16. René Girard, *La route antique des hommes pervers* (Paris: Bernard Grasset, 1985).

17. Long before he "came out" as a theologian, Caputo was developing this essentially apophatic style of deconstructive thinking in writings included in his *Against Ethics: Contributions to a Poetics of Obligation with Constant Reference to Deconstruction* (Bloomington: Indiana University Press, 1993) and *More Radical Hermeneutics: On Not Knowing Who We Are* (Bloomington: Indiana University Press, 2000).

18. From Predigt 9 in Meister Eckhart, *Die deutschen Werke*, ed. Josef Quint (Stuttgart: Kohlhammer, 1958).

19. John D. Caputo, *On Religion* (New York: Routledge, 2001), pp. 115, 128.

20. Cf. Carl Schmitt's dictum in the opening sentence of his chapter "Politische Theologie": "All significant concepts [Alle prägnanten Begriffe] of the modern theory of the state are secularized theological concepts." *Politische Theologie: Vier Kapitel zur Lehre von der Souveränität* (Berlin: Duncker & Humblott, 1922), chapter 3.

21. Gilles Deleuze, *Logique du sens* (Paris: Minuit, 1969), pp. 326–27.

22. Samples of this literature can be found in Chris Boesel and Catherine Keller, eds., *Apophatic Bodies: Negative Theology, Incarnation, and Relationality* (New York: Fordham University Press, 2009); and Amador Vega, *Arte y santidad: Cuatro lecciones de estética apofática* (Pamplona: Universidad Pública de Navarra, 2005), or, in summary form, "Estética apofática y hermenéutica del misterio: Elementos para una crítica de la visibilidad," *Diánoia* 54, no. 62 (2009): 1–25.

23. Clayton Crockett, *Radical Political Theology: Religion and Politics after Liberalism* (New York: Columbia University Press, 2011), p. 170.

24. "Un mysticisme immédiat mais sans intuition, une sorte de kénose abstraite le libère de toute autorité, de tout récit, de tout dogme, de toute croyance, et à la limite de toute foi *déterminable* . . . d'où ce parfum d'hérésie, ces procès, cette marginalité subversive du courant apophatique dans l'histoire de la théologie et de l'Église" (Derrida, *Sauf le nom,* pp. 85–86).

25. Richly indicative is Graham Ward's *Barth, Derrida and the Language of Theology* (Cambridge: Cambridge University Press, 1995) and, in a similar vein, Walter Lowe, *Theology and Difference: The Wound of Reason* (Bloomington: Indiana University Press, 1993).

26. Catherine Pickstock, "Liturgical Twilight—A Footnote to Andrew Louth," in *Encounter Between Eastern Orthodoxy and Radical Orthodoxy: Transfiguring the World through the Word,* ed. Adrian Papst and Christian Schneider (London: Ashgate, 2009), pp. 232–38.

27. See Milbank, "The Linguistic Turn as a Theological Turn," in *Word Made Strange,* p. 85. Redeploying Derridean deconstructive insights, Milbank accords primacy to relation and metaphor and the recognition of differences rather than to univocal signification of substance by signs.

28. See Milbank and Pickstock, *Truth in Aquinas.*

29. Paradoxically, this again makes it *like* deconstruction as described by J. Hillis Miller, "The Critic as Host," *Critical Inquiry* 3, no. 3 (Spring 1977): 439–47.

30. For Plotinus's and Aristotle's roles in this development, see Patrick Madigan, S.J., *Christian Revelation and the Completion of the Aristotelian Revolution* (Lanham, MD: University Press of America, 1988).

31. Eriugena, *De divisione naturae* I, 509C–512D, and *Expositiones super Ierarch. cael.* 136C. See, further, Werner Beierwaltes, ed., *Begriff und metapher: Sprachform des Denkens bei Eriugena* (Heidelberg: Universtitätsverlag, 1990).

32. Miernowski, *Le Dieu néant,* p. 14.

33. Denys Turner, "Apophaticism, Idolatry and the Claims of Reason," in *Silence and the Word,* ed. Davies and Turner, p. 17.

34. Turner, *The Darkness of God*, p. 25. See also Hart, *Trespass of the Sign*, pp. 190–91.

35. J. P. Kenney usefully charts Armstrong's intellectual trajectory in "The Critical Value of Negative Theology," *Harvard Theological Review* 86 (1993): 439–53.

36. A. H. Armstrong, "On Not Knowing Too Much About God" (1989), in *Hellenic and Christian Studies* (London: Variorum Reprints, 1990), chapter 15, p. 137.

37. A. H. Armstrong, "Negative Theology, Myth and Incarnation" (1981), in *Hellenic and Christian Studies,* chapter 7, p. 51.

38. The erotic expressions are particularly prominent in certain Gnostic and Kabbalistic spin-offs of apophaticism, as is effectively emphasized by Elliot R. Wolfson, *Language, Eros, Being: Kabbalistic Hermeneutics and Poetic Imagination* (New York: Fordham University Press, 2005).

39. Armstrong, "Negative Theology," chapter 24, p. 188.

40. Stanislas Breton, *La penser du rien* (Kampen, Netherlands: Kok Pharos, 1992), p. 34.

41. "La pratique, que la Croix spécifie, n'est pas centrée sur l'illumination libératrice de l'initié. Elle vise, sur l'horizon d'humanité souffrante, la réalisation d'une justice qui ferait exister, dans la lumière d'un visage, et par le don du nécessaire le plus quotidien, le Christ de la kénose en ses frères les plus démunis. C'est par ce trait que la 'théologie de la Croix' actualise une pensée du rien qui définit son originalité."

42. See, further, the forthcoming volume of essays from the 2011 CERISY colloquium "Philosophie et Mystique: Autour de Stanislas Breton."

43. Gabriel Vahanian, "Theology and the Secular," in *Secular Theology,* ed. Crockett, p. 21.

44. "Le Christ n'abolit ni la nature ni l'histoire. Il désacralise la nature, il 'défatalise' l'histoire. C'est-à-dire l'avènement du Christ se situe sur un autre plan que celui de la nature ou de l'histoire. De même que la création, il se situe dans le champ de la parole, dans cet utopisme du langage où le temps et l'espace coïncident l'un avec l'autre et où, pour employer une expression biblique, la glorification de l'homme rejoint celle de Dieu." Gabriel Vahanian, *Dieu anonyme ou la peur des mots* (Paris: Desclée de Brouwer, 1989), pp. 90–91.

45. A good, condensed exposition is Alasdair MacIntyre, "The Virtues, the Unity of a Human Life and the Concept of a Tradition," chapter 15 of *After Virtue: A Study in Moral Theory,* 2nd ed. (Notre Dame: University of Notre Dame Press, 1984).

46. Hans W. Frei, *The Eclipse of Biblical Narrative: A Study in Eighteenth and Nineteenth Century Hermeneutics* (New Haven: Yale University Press, 1974), p. 11.

47. Paul Ricoeur, "Toward a Narrative Theology: Its Necessity, Its Resources, Its Difficulty," in *Figuring the Sacred: Religion, Narrative, and Imagination*, trans. David Pellauer (Minneapolis: Fortress Press, 1995), pp. 242–43.

48. Frank Kermode, *The Genesis of Secrecy: On the Interpretation of Narrative* (Cambridge, MA: Harvard University Press, 1979).

49. Richard Kearney, *Anatheism: Returning to God after God* (New York: Columbia University Press, 2009). See, further, John Panteleimon Manoussakis, ed., *After God: Richard Kearney and the Religious Turn in Phenomenology* (New York: Fordham University Press, 2006).

50. Richard Kearney, *Strangers, Gods, and Monsters: Interpreting Otherness* (New York: Routledge, 2003).

51. Mark Taylor, "Betraying Altizer," in *Thinking through the Death of God: A Critical Companion to Thomas J. J. Altizer*, ed. Lissa McCullough and Brian Schroeder (Albany: State University of New York Press, 2004).

52. Mark C. Taylor, Foreword to Thomas J. J. Altizer, *Living the Death of God: A Theological Memoir* (Albany: State University of New York Press, 2006), p. xviii.

53. Mark C. Taylor, "Postmodern Times," in *The Otherness of God*, ed. Ollin F. Summerall (Charlottesville: University Press of Virginia, 1998), p. 189.

54. In Mark C. Taylor, *About Religion: Economies of Faith in Virtual Culture* (Chicago: University of Chicago Press, 1999).

55. Richard Rorty, "Solidarity or Objectivity?" in *Post-Analytic Philosophy*, ed. John Rajchman and Cornel West (New York: Columbia University Press, 1985), pp. 3–19.

56. Hans Urs von Balthasar, *Herrlichkeit: Eine theologische Ästhetik*, Band 3/2: Theologie, Teil 2: Neuer Bund (Einsiedeln: Johannes Verlag, 1988 [1969]), p. 500.

57. Mark C. Taylor, *Nots* (Chicago: University of Chicago Press, 1993), p. 3. Of course, Taylor's use of "traditionally" suggests that there might be another way of making the negative way turn out differently. In fact, Taylor pursues innovative forms of negative theological thinking in his *Tears* (Albany: State University of New York Press, 1990).

58. Jean-Luc Marion, "Au nom: Comment ne pas parler de 'théologie négative,'" *Laval Théologique et Philosophique* 55, no. 3 (1999): 339–63.

59. Marion takes up and develops specifically this point, in terms of the speech act theory of Austin and Searle, in "L'apophase du discours amoureux," in *Le visible et le révélé* (Paris: Cerf, 2005), especially pp. 121–23, trans. Christina

Gschwandtner as *The Visible and the Revealed* (New York: Fordham University Press, 2008).

60. Epitomizing this widening of scope, the 1999 essay of Marion from which I have been quoting ("Au nom: Comment ne pas parler de 'théologie négative,'" in *Laval Théologique et Philosophique*) reappears as "Au nom ou comment le taire," in *De surcroît: Études sur les phénomènes saturés* (Paris: Presses Universitaires de France, 2001), trans. Robyn Horner as *In Excess: Studies of Saturated Phenomena* (New York: Fordham University Press, 2002).

61. Marion, "Le phénomène saturé," in *Phénomènologie et théologie,* ed. Chrétien, pp. 79–128. This essay, as noted earlier, together with Marion's most relevant essays, has been republished in *De surcroît (In Excess).*

62. As pointed out by Kevin Hart, ed., *Counter-Experiences,* p. 1, in introducing this indispensable volume.

63. Milbank's essay "The Gift and the Mirror: On the Philosophy of Love," in *Counter-Experiences,* ed. Hart, diagnoses Marion's decisions as "recognizably Hegelian decisions" (p. 255) in line with a consummation of modern metaphysics. Cyril O'Regan's "Jean-Luc Marion: Crossing Hegel" in the same volume, pp. 95–154, relates Marion specifically to the Hegelian problematic explored in my first essay, section ii.

64. Extending Orthodox thinking in the direction that Milbank indicates is David Bentley Hart's *The Beauty of the Infinite: The Aesthetics of Christian Truth* (Grand Rapids: Eerdmans, 2003).

65. Benson, *Graven Ideologies,* provocatively concludes that "Marion denies the true iconic nature of Christ and so succumbs to the idolatry of transcendence" (p. 223).

66. Derrida, *Psyché,* p. 546.

67. The idea that the nonconceptual is but a projection of concepts has a considerable history: in different ways, it is argued relentlessly from Hegel to Donald Davidson. "Against ineffability" has been a slogan, furthermore, in recent analytical philosophy and cognitive theory, following the controversy sparked off by the influential article of Daniel C. Dennett, "Quining Qualia," in *Consciousness in Contemporary Science,* ed. Anthony J. Marcel and Edoardo Bisiach (Oxford: Oxford University Press, 1988).

68. In this sense, negative theology might metamorphose into a Wittgensteinian therapeutics *pace* Kevin W. Hector's polarization of the two in *Theology without Metaphysics: God, Language, and the Spirit of Recognition* (Cambridge: Cambridge University Press, 2011).

69. Milbank, "The End of Dialogue," in *Christian Uniqueness Reconsidered,* ed. D'Costa.

INDEX

WILLIAM FRANKE

is professor of philosophy and religions at the University of Macao and professor
of comparative literature and religious studies at Vanderbilt University.

Lightning Source UK Ltd.
Milton Keynes UK
UKHW02f1058271117
313424UK00006B/738/P